# HURRYING
# TOWARD
# ZION

# HURRYING TOWARD ZION

■

*Universities,*
*Divinity Schools, and American*
*Protestantism*

CONRAD CHERRY

Indiana University Press
*Bloomington and Indianapolis*

The paper used in this publication
meets the minimum requirements of
American National Standard
for Information Sciences—Permanence of Paper
for Printed Library Materials, ANSI Z39.48-1984.

Manufactured in the United States of America

**Library of Congress Cataloging-in-Publication Data**

Cherry, Conrad, 1937–
Hurrying toward Zion : universities, divinity schools,
and American Protestantism / Conrad Cherry.
p.    cm.
Includes bibliographical references and index.
ISBN 0-253-32928-0 (alk. paper)
1. Protestant theological seminaries—United
States—History—19th century.
2. Protestant theological seminaries—United
States—History—20th century.   I. Title.
BV4030.C46   1995
207'.73—dc20      95-3526

1  2  3  4  5  00  99  98  97  96  95

TO THE MEMORY OF
LUTHER H. HARSHBARGER
1914–1986

# CONTENTS

∎

# PREFACE

∎

In the late nineteenth and early twentieth centuries, leaders of American Protestantism envisioned the university divinity school as the vanguard of a Christian movement destined to shape the culture of the nation. To join the mission of the church with the educational venture of the emerging modern American university was, in this vision, to move the cause of Protestant Christianity to the very core of the commanding values, ideas, and aspirations of the American people. Sweeping in its perspective and resolute in its institution-building, the effort to create a learned ministry through alignments with the American university constituted one of this country's most notable educational endeavors. It also produced a history that has been largely neglected.

This book aims to correct that neglect by offering a historical analysis of American Protestant university-related divinity schools for the period from the 1880s to the 1980s, or roughly from the time of the rise of the modern American research university to the present. The history of the schools is recounted within the categories of four powerful social and cultural forces that decisively influenced American higher education in general and Protestant theological education in particular: specialization, professionalization, social reform, and pluralism. The story told here is that of the transformation of the divinity schools by these forces, which the leaders of the schools willingly embraced and perpetuated as they joined the purposes of their institutions with those of the American university.

The book draws most of its data from the records of eleven institutions: the five non- or interdenominational divinity schools at Chicago, Harvard, Vanderbilt (at one time a Methodist school), and Yale universities, and Union Theological Seminary in New York City; and six Methodist schools—Boston University School of Theology, Candler School of Theology at Emory University, Claremont School of Theology (whose faculty were previously affiliated with the University of Southern California), Drew Theological School, Duke Divinity School, and Perkins School of Theology at Southern Methodist University. Two of those schools have been only loosely affiliated with universities. Union and Claremont were separately incorporated institutions and have been governed by their own boards of trustees and administered by their own presidents. Yet, as this book demonstrates, historically Union and Claremont were caught up in the same Protestant vision of America and defined their missions in the same terms as did the other schools. Although other denominational theological schools have affiliated with universities, the Methodists, by virtue of the large number of their university-related divinity schools, furnish the most impressive case for denominational interest in the university education of ministers. Roman Catholic and African American institutions of theological education have struck significant alliances with American universities, but their stories merit a separate telling; their histories cannot be explained by the Anglo-American Protestant vision that inspired the founding of the schools examined in this book.

For the most part, this study examines the divinity schools as a group. The histories of the individual schools are sketched in the introduction to the book, attention is called occasionally to the schools that constitute exceptions to generalizations about the group, and paradigmatic events within the lives of particular schools are analyzed for their inherent meaning as well as for the implications they hold for the other schools. Still, the overall interest of the book is what the divinity schools have held in common. As a result, much of the tenor of distinctive stories and much of the ambience of particular places do not emerge in the book. Only histories of the individual schools could begin to capture the uniqueness of time and place for those institutions. Yet I am persuaded that whatever is lost in sensitivity to particular climate is redressed by awareness of how the individual schools participated in an educational and religious movement animated by a common vision, implemented with similar strategies, and shaped by the same pervasive social and cultural forces.

In an effort to gain an intelligible perspective on such a complex religious and educational phenomenon, I have transgressed some methodological and theoretical boundaries sometimes viewed as impassable in the contemporary academy. The historical movement I have analyzed does not divide neatly into intellectual, social, institutional, or cultural history. It is all of those and more than their sum. A movement awakened and impelled by ideas and visions, incarnated in institutions and people, and influenced by social patterns and cultural values demands a perspective that gathers together several interpretative approaches and refuses to reduce the significance of the movement to any one of them. It is for others to say whether I have adequately met the demand; meeting it, in any case, has been my effort.

The university-related schools on which this study focuses have used many designations (and sometimes have changed their designations several times): "divinity school," "theological school," "seminary," "school of religion," "department of theology." This book refers to them as a group as "divinity schools" or "university divinity schools" and employs "theological school" and "seminary" as the generic terms to denote free-standing as well as university-related institutions.

The religious perspective represented by the group of schools is variously referenced as "Pan-Protestantism," "Anglo-Saxon Protestantism," "mainline Protestantism," and (most frequently) "ecumenical Protestantism," terms meant to embrace the denominations of the Northern Baptists, the Congregationalists, the Disciples of Christ, the Episcopalians, the Methodists, the Presbyterians, and the Unitarians. I am aware of the limitations inherent in the use of all of the terms. It is questionable, for example, that these Protestants ever managed to attain the status of "mainline," and the very use of the term already is to relegate other religious groups to an inferior cultural status. And eventually these Protestant groups were not the only ones to join in "ecumenical" alliances. Nonetheless, each term when placed in historical context is serviceable in calling attention to the motives, ideas, and social policies that could unite Protestant groups behind the university divinity school movement. And each term when seen in historical context is useful for calling attention to the self-understanding that American Protestant leaders possessed when they envisioned the interrelationship of religion, school, and nation.

The divinity schools adopted several goals in addition to the education of Protestant ministers, and they offered several degree programs to meet those goals. At the outset, however, and during most of their history, all of the schools pursued as their chief purpose the training of ministers and placed at the center of their educational programs the professional ministerial degree (the Bachelor of Divinity, eventually changed to the Master of Divinity). Although I deal somewhat with other degree programs offered by the schools—especially with the Ph.D. in chapter 3—I concentrate on the schools' founding and chief purpose of training ministers and on the B.D. or M.Div. degree program.

Support for my work has come from many sources. This history is part of a larger project that was based at Emory University and was funded by the Lilly Endowment, Inc. on "Theology and the University." I am grateful to Jim Waits, director of the project, and the officers in the religion division at the Endowment for their confidence in my ability to undertake this historical study and for the financial support that freed me from some teaching responsibilities and enabled me to meet the expenses of my research. The members of the advisory committee of the larger project, composed mostly of divinity school deans and faculty, responded with interest and thoughtful suggestions to the progress reports I made on my part of the project.

The deans and presidents of the schools on which I focused my study graciously opened the records of their institutions to me as an outsider, and they were most helpful in interpreting the current ethos of their schools and steering me to other spokespersons for their schools. I interviewed many faculty during my research trips. Although I refer to those interviews only occasionally in the pages of this book, and then only for confirming evidence, the faculty were indispensable in helping me understand the current situation and the recent changes at their schools.

I am immensely indebted to the librarians who guided me through the mazes of their archives and provided my research assistants and me with places to work. The following librarians went well beyond their normal duties as they tracked down obscure items, anticipated many of my needs, and joined me as collaborators in the historical research: Michael Boddy of the library of the School of Theology at Claremont, Donn Michael Farris of the Duke Divinity School Library and William King of the Perkins Library at Duke University, Channing Jeschke of the Pitts Theology Library at Emory University, Barent Johnson of the Special Collections at the Rose Memorial Library of Drew University and Kenneth Rowe of the Methodist Archives at Drew, Seth Kasten of the library at Union Theological Seminary in New York City, Roger Lloyd of the Bridwell Library at the Perkins School of Theology at Southern Methodist University, Stephen Pentek of the library at Boston University School of Theology, Alan Seaburg of the library at the Harvard Divinity School, and Martha Smalley of the library at the Yale Divinity School. The staff members of the Center for Research Libraries in Chicago were also extremely helpful to my research assistant Kenneth Sawyer.

Anne Fraker, Kimberly Long, and Kenneth Sawyer served as research assistants at different stages of the study. To all of them I am grateful for the intelligent and imaginative, as well as the industrious, performance of their tasks.

The manuscript for this book in its several stages has improved because of the critical responses of a number of readers. I am especially grateful to Brooks Holifield, Robert Lynn, Glenn Miller, Winton Solberg, and Barbara Wheeler for finding time within their busy schedules to read and comment on all of the chapters of the book. And I am thankful to Craig Dykstra, Amanda Porterfield, and James Wind for their comments on several of the chapters. I was particularly fortunate in being invited to join the Department of Religious Studies at Indiana University–Purdue University at Indianapolis (IUPUI) shortly after beginning the research for this book. For over twenty years the department has regularly convened in colloquy so that each faculty member annually may present and defend a piece of his or her own scholarly writing, and several chapters in this book profited from the responses of my departmental colleagues: namely, Thomas Davis, William Jackson, Jeffrey Kenney, Theodore Mullen, Tony Sherrill, Jan Shipps, and James Smurl.

It has been a pleasure to work with very able people at Indiana University Press. Nancy Ann Miller was a careful and at the same time a flexible editor, and the director of the Press, John Gallman, and acquiring editor Robert Sloan took almost as much interest in the book as I did.

For many reasons my wife, Ellie, may take credit for the completion of this book. In addition to assuming responsibilities that were justly mine so that I could perform my research and writing, she helped me sort through my jumbled ideas about divinity schools during our long walks at the end of each day. Above all, Ellie has continued to prove to me during our thirty-five years of marriage that there is so much more to life than the furies of the scholar.

The book is dedicated to the memory of a former friend, colleague, and mentor at the Pennsylvania State University who actively participated in many phases of the history analyzed in this study. I thought of Luther Harshbarger often when I wrote these pages. It is thus fitting that I dedicate the book to his memory.

Would that I could hold all of these helpful people responsible for the failings of the book, but of course I cannot. The failings are mine alone.

Indianapolis, Indiana
Summer 1994

# HURRYING
# TOWARD
# ZION

*Photo courtesy of the Department of Special Collections,*
*the University of Chicago Library.*

# INTRODUCTION

■

## *Visions and Strategies of Influence*

A photograph displayed in the Regenstein Library at the University of Chicago depicts two figures leading an academic procession toward the decennial celebration of the University in 1901. One is John D. Rockefeller, the principal benefactor of the institution. The other is William Rainey Harper, the man made president of the new university at the tender age of thirty-four. Both men are moving along briskly, but Harper outstrides Rockefeller by one good step.

The old photograph calls up a multitude of images of these two prominent Americans and their relationship. Both were devout Baptists, Rockefeller the billionaire businessman and Harper the scholar of Hebrew language and literature, whose shared conviction about the need to Christianize the nation through educational institutions locked them together in common cause. Rockefeller, however, was content to let others provide the leadership for the university he financed. He refused membership on the university's board of trustees, required only that the administration of the institution be led by persons with managerial skills proven successful in the business world, and did not even bother to visit the new university until five years after its founding. Rockefeller was willing to let Harper take the lead. But Rockefeller also had reason to draw back apprehensively from Harper. Harper kept seeking money from Rockefeller for the expansion of the University of Chicago. It all started with a Rockefeller matching pledge of $600,000 and was followed quickly by an outright pledge of $1,000,000; by 1910 the University had received $35,000,000 from its wealthy patron. After fifteen years of such largesse, Rockefeller's personal auditor advised his client that the University's fund-raising schemes amounted to a well-organized conspiracy to plunder Rockefeller wealth.[1]

Plundered or not, Rockefeller capital enabled Harper to hurry toward the creation of an American Zion, an exemplary city formed of the materials of religion and education. That vision of the future, more than any other image, is what is captured by the picture of the decennial procession. Harper was a young man in a hurry, a person of immense energy often overcome by fatigue and depression who was able to spring back into action, an architectonic thinker capable of assembling a vast array of ideas and schemes (to the puzzlement of his contemporaries, some of whom referred to his university as "Harper's Three-Ring Circus"), a popular teacher turned busy administrator who continued to teach the Hebrew language with a compelling passion. These personal traits were matched by a comprehensive religious vision.

Harper's vision was openly evangelical, even messianic. The task of the American university, of the University of Chicago especially, was to fashion the American nation, and eventually the world, in the light of a religious understanding of democracy. In Harper's own words, "Democracy has been given a mission to the world, and it is of no uncertain character." The mission of democracy is to spread a form of government dedicated to the principles of human equality and the authority of the public will. The university is to be "the prophet of this democracy and, as well, its priest and its philosopher; . . . in other words, the university is the Messiah of the democracy, its to-be-expected deliverer." As prophet, the university proclaims the principles of democracy, notes the failure of the realization of those principles, and calls for their full implementation in the future. As priest, the university mediates between the individual and the democratic ideal, safeguards the mysteries of the sacred democratic traditions, and devotes itself to serving sacrificially the whole of humankind. As sage, the university critically inquires into the historical origins and social problems of democracy and formulates the laws of the democratic order. Lest one assume that this vision of the university is religious only by analogy with biblical motifs, Harper adds, "Is democracy a religion? No. Has democracy a religion? Yes; a religion with its god, its altar, and its temple, with its code of ethics and its creed." The god of the religion is the whole of humanity; its altar is the home; its temple is the nation; its creed is human equality; and its system of ethics is the righteous defense of individualism.[2]

Harper's civil religion of democracy did not exhaust the religious nature of his educational vision. The superior form of religion was for him Christianity, particularly Protestant Christianity, and even more particularly Protestantism in the West. He believed that Protestant Christianity was commissioned by God to transform the world through democratic institutions and veneration of the individual. Harper's view of history, like that of many other religious Americans of his day, embraced the conviction that Christianity through the centuries was the story of the increase of the religious spirit in each person and the advancement of the rights and integrity of the individual, a story that reached its climax in American Protestantism. And like many another American and European of the time, Harper thought that the course of civilization was westward and that America represented the culmination of the westward march of history. In the words of the singer of the American self, Walt Whitman,

> thou born America
> For purpose vast, man's long probation fill'd,
> Thou rondure of the world at last accomplish'd.[3]

In Harper's prosaic rendition, the fulfillment of history in the West was simultaneously civil and Christian:

> ... we know, and the world knows, that what Babylonia was in the first period, what Syria was in the second, what England was in the third, all this and more America will be in the fourth.
> This westward movement has been synchronous with the history of the progress of civilization. And the history of civilization has been synchronous with the development of a pure and true conception of God [in Christianity], and of his relation to man.[4]

Harper believed that what America had been to lands across the Atlantic, the western states were now to America: the fulfillment of the westward course of history.[5]

Educational institutions were destined to lead the way in that spectacular historical march. The chief obstacles to the Christian civilizing influence—the sources of crime, skepticism, and the burdens of undemocratic institutions—were ignorance, prejudice, and intellectual dishonesty. Thus "in the future, education will constitute a larger part of the work of evangelization than in the past, both at home and abroad."[6] The educational evangel was to be directed to every class and every race in society, and its aim was social improvement, especially in addressing the problems of the city, as well as the elimination of ignorance. Educational institutions in the western United States were the prototypes of Harper's populist aims. Though nurtured by eastern institutions (Harper held a Yale doctorate), schools in the west were less defined by wealth and privilege than were those in the east. They were thus better able to respond to the people's demands for an education that was useful for their daily professional lives. Harper thought that this broad educational charge could be met only by an equally comprehensive system of institutions collaborating for the education of Americans of every age and circumstance. The system included public schools, academies, Sunday schools, correspondence courses, Bible study groups, summer schools, vocational schools, magazines, and chautauquas.[7] It included, as well, universities and their divinity schools.

## BUILDING ZION

Harper's overall plan for the University of Chicago was as diverse in its parts and as comprehensive in its scope as his system for the evangelization of the West. The general organization consisted of five divisions: the University proper, composed of colleges, schools, and pre-college academies; an extension division, with its evening and correspondence courses; the university press, which issued books, journals, reports, and special papers; university libraries, laboratories, and museums; and affiliations or colleges informally linked with the University. In Harper's own synthesizing mind, what unified this university sprawl was the service of humanity driven by the religious motive of sacrificial efforts of the educated on behalf of the uneducated. Religiously motivated philanthropy was, for Harper, the great integrator of corporate, as well as individual, life.[8] As Leonard Sweet has written, in this great university scheme religious education, which was to supply the philanthropic motives in the corporate university, was not "an *addendum* or *corrigendum* to the university, but a constitutive quality, a synthesizing force, a unifying process that gave completeness, unity, and consequently, strength to the whole."[9]

In the light of his understanding of what held the whole educational system together, it is hardly surprising that Harper made the Divinity School an integral part of the University of Chicago. (In fact, he insisted on that status for the Divinity School as a condition of his acceptance of the University presidency.)[10] The School was to serve the University internally by bringing religion into connection with the various branches of learning, and it was to aid the society at large by dispatching a legion of well-educated ministers to Christianize and civilize the globe. The two complementary missions of the Divinity School harmonized with

Harper's refrain that education should now constitute the larger part of the evangelical task.

The foundation for the Divinity School was laid by the transfer of the Baptist Union Theological Seminary at Morgan Park, Illinois to the new university in 1890, thus making the Divinity School the first professional program at the University of Chicago. (Harper had taught at the seminary between 1879 and 1886 before joining the Yale faculty.) Harper and fellow-Baptist Rockefeller resolved to use the resources of the Seminary to assist in the creation of a divinity school that was an organic part of a new, modern university. Although the Baptist Union would continue as a separate corporation, the tapping of Baptist resources was not to result in the establishment of a narrowly denominational seminary.[11]

In those early years, President Harper, who exercised tight control over the Divinity School, was intent on making the professional divinity program as ecumenical in its erudition as in its religion. He devised ways to prevent the alienation of the School from the life of the larger University. During their first three years, Divinity School students were permitted to take a third of their elective courses in other departments of the University. Fourth-year students could take up to one-half of their work in such fields as philosophy, political economy, history, social science, anthropology, comparative religion, Semitic languages and literature, Greek, and English. A "Divinity Conference" was formed, consisting of select faculty from the Divinity School and from cognate disciplines in the University, which oversaw curricular development and guided the students' programs of study. Harper decided to make his own field of Old Testament a department within the University Graduate School, rather than a department within the Divinity School, and thus called the attention of the learned community to his conviction that the scientific study of the Bible deserved respect as an enterprise with its own scholarly integrity.[12]

Harper's strategies for making the professional study of religion integral to the larger university arose from his belief that only a university environment could prepare a minister suitable for the modern age. A theological curriculum intimately connected with a university would offer the resources for the thorough development of the individualism of the student so treasured by Harper as the supreme value of Protestant Christianity and westward-marching democracy. And such a curriculum would offer breadth of social vision, "secured by mingling with men who have other points of view" in the university, and thus would satisfactorily launch students into pluralistic modern America.[13]

In a matter of a few years, that curriculum came to mean for the University of Chicago Divinity School an equal emphasis upon professional training and specialized graduate education. At first the academic program of the School appeared to be little more than what today would be called a "preacher factory." Early catalogues proclaimed straightforwardly that "the purpose of the Divinity School is primarily and chiefly to fit men to become preachers of the Gospel." The School assigned the highest priority to the parish ministry, and the largely required course of study for the Bachelor of Divinity degree was heavily weighted toward biblical exegesis and the managerial and homiletical skills required of the parish preacher. By 1912, however, the curriculum had been designed to train ministerial candidates in graduate specialties and to accommodate eighteen different ministerial vocations.[14]

Harper wanted it both ways: he wanted a professional school, and he wanted a graduate school of theology, within the same walls. The two in conjunction were necessary to prepare ministers to carry the gospel of education to the modern world. In an argument that was to be repeated by others throughout the twentieth century, Harper insisted that the training of ministers should be every bit as practical as the training of attorneys and physicians. In a culture that increasingly measured work by the effective application of specialized expertise, the divinity schools were well advised to prepare ministers in the diversity of skills they would need in that culture: skills in psychology, social analysis, money management, educational methods, general administration. The schools should devote no more than 10 percent of their time to training ministers how to preach, since no higher percentage of a minister's time would be consumed by that task. And in a society characterized by the haphazard proliferation of professions, the divinity schools should take a lesson from schools of law and medicine which were beginning to tighten their professional standards and raise their admission requirements. Harper was convinced that raising standards could rectify the problems afflicting ministers in comparison with those pursuing other professions— low pay, low status, and low intelligence—and that raised standards just might improve enrollments at the schools.[15]

At the same time, Harper believed that divinity schools should be more than professional mills. They should educate. And education in the modern world meant the acquisition of specialized academic knowledge. Like other university presidents of the day, Harper sought to prevent what he saw occurring at his own institution: specialization creating a balkanized universe of learning.[16] In an effort to stem the forces of frag-

mentation, Harper even proposed that his own beloved subject of Hebrew language be abandoned as a Divinity School requirement in favor of a more comprehensive view of the biblical world attained through
the study of the English Bible. Nonetheless, specialized, graduate-level
education was an essential ingredient in the education of the modern
minister. Intensive work in the disciplines of Bible, church history, and
theology—within the framework of an elective system and through the
methods of the seminar—would teach prospective ministers to think for
themselves and would avoid the superficial knowledge so detested by the
world of specialization they would be serving. And through education
in a university built of units of specialized knowledge, the ministerial
candidate would learn to converse in a pluralistic society composed of
people of diverse tastes, temperaments, and types of education.[17]

But would it work? Could professional training and graduate education, both with their own sets of specializations, be held together? Could
the students acquire efficient professional skills and intensive education
in three or four years? Were the two aims capable of realization by the
same student? Would the faculty be willing, and able, to devote equal
attention to the two missions? Harper himself came to have his doubts.
In his Presidential Report of 1903, he cited some problems besetting the
Divinity School. One of those problems revealed serious trouble in the
institutionalization of Zion:

> The interest of the University is distinctly in a School of Theology
> which shall partake exclusively of a scientific character, while it is also
> within the scope of the University to develop a School of Theology
> which shall emphasize the practical side of this same work. It is a ques-
> tion whether both of these things can be accomplished in the same
> school. . . .
> The line between scientific Divinity, if such a phrase may be used, and
> practical Divinity must be more sharply drawn, and such reorganization
> of the work should be brought about as will adapt it more closely to the
> needs of different classes of students.[18]

Thirty-three years later, Shailer Mathews, reminiscing about his long
and eventful years as dean of the Divinity School (1908–1933), remarked
that the School was constantly under pressure to decide between the
promotion of detached scholarship and the provision of professional
training, but it decided over and over again to do both. "It would have
been much simpler to have chosen one or the other of these alternatives,"
Mathews concluded. "There have been times during the forty years of my

association with the School in which the temptation to do so has been great."[19] There would be times when not only Harper and Mathews, but numerous leaders of university divinity schools, would be similarly tempted. The tension, at times the outright conflict, between the aims of professional training and those of graduate education would bedevil the history of the divinity schools for a century.

Whatever trouble brewed for the linked goals of graduate and professional education, Harper and his kind could take great hope from the support they received from allied religious movements. Divinity schools constituted the spearhead of a massive religious endeavor to influence the culture, but they were only a part of that larger effort. Harper's own tireless activity on behalf of numerous interrelated causes testified to a Protestant conviction of the time that the nation could be shaped by an integrated system of religious education. Harper was the founding spirit and convener of the Religious Education Association, an organization designed in part to reform the educational programs of churches according to the insights of critical biblical scholarship. He served as Sunday school superintendent of the Hyde Park Baptist Church, the functional equivalent of a "university church" for over three decades and a laboratory for modernist Protestant projects in biblical scholarship, the social gospel, graded curriculum, and ecumenical Protestantism. He was an active member of Chicago's public school board, working to free the office of superintendent from political party control and advocating (unsuccessfully) the restoration of the teaching of the Bible in the common schools. Even while serving as a university president, Harper's own frenzied educational activities included summer lectures at Chautauqua, editing and writing for several popular biblical journals, participation in a widespread national program of continuing religious education, and conducting countless Bible study groups.[20]

Harper's promotion of popular religious education outside the formal classroom betokened his confidence that "we live in an environment largely dominated by the spirit of democracy," that the times were right for addressing the desire of the general populace for the best that education had to offer concerning religion.[21] That confidence was shared by Shailer Mathews as he implemented a program at the Divinity School devised to "democratize scholarship." The sociohistorical method which for several generations pervaded scholarship in biblical studies, church history, theology, and practical training at the Divinity School was not intended as a means simply of fostering conversation among professional scholars. The empiricism, pragmatism, and historicism informing the method were thought to spring from a uniquely American democratic spirit. It surely followed that it was a method suitable for circulation to the masses.

Like the larger university of which it was a part, the Divinity School was organized to reach its tentacles into every crevice of the democratic social order. The School's extension division, the American Institute of Sacred Literature, in one year (1927–28) circulated 1,000 popular books, mailed 300,000 pamphlets, and responded to 6,000 inquiries respecting religious subjects. Highly regarded scholars in the School wrote handbooks for laity on such topics as "Science and Religion," "The Story of the Bible," and "Religions of the World."[22] Harper's and Mathews's Divinity School assumed its role in a popular *paideia* that marshaled the nineteenth-century revivalist strategies of tract societies, Sunday schools, colleges, and public schools—all for the purpose of Protestantizing America.[23]

Deep fissures appeared in this educational system, however. The state universities, which were to attract an increasing proportion of the nation's students, offered few opportunities for the advanced study of religion. Many denominational seminaries, competing against university divinity schools for student enrollments, proved to be more committed to conserving their distinctive doctrines and traditions than to building a Pan-Protestant Zion. Divinity school professors began to think it more important to achieve recognition as scholars from their professional societies than to reach the masses through popular publications. Religious laypeople, it turned out, were not at all interested in having their Sunday schools wrested from their control by highly educated professionals. Breaks in the system that would soon lead to the disintegration of the whole were epitomized by the fate of the American Institute of Sacred Literature. That correspondence school which had flooded the country from Chicago with a torrent of publications in the 1920s was down to a trickle in the mid-1930s, and by the mid-1940s its functions had been merged with the Divinity School Library or were discontinued.[24] Like the centering of the university on religion and the joining of professional training and graduate education, the creation of an interconnected system of religious educational ventures would prove easier to envision than to institutionalize.

Yet Harper's vision entailed still another strategy. Divinity education was to be aimed at a populace transformed by the twin forces of industrialization and urbanization. The modern world, which only the intellectual diversity of the university could prepare a minister to serve, the democratic society, which cried out for widespread popular education in religion and citizenship, teemed with problems generated by the concentration of wealth into the hands of a few families and corporations, bloody conflicts between labor and management, cities crowded with uprooted immigrants, and poverty and crime growing at an unprecedented rate. Chicago itself, which had increased in population tenfold between 1870 and 1890, was a case study of many of these problems. As in his prescriptions for the university education of ministers, Harper proposed a dual religious strategy for coping with the industrial and urban transformations.

On the one hand, ministers should be encouraged to move easily within the world of the powerful and the wealthy. Only thereby could they hope to represent the interests of labor and the poor by gaining access to the decision makers of society and infuse a social class with the motives of religious philanthropy. The leisure created by wealth must not be left untouched by a Christianity destined to shape the whole of culture. In Harper's judgment, "The various forms of recreation afford as legitimate a field for the minister's work as the deathbed." The Christian religion, while not the "mother" of art, music, poetry, and other modes of the "higher life" made possible by wealth and leisure, is their "older sister" who works sympathetically alongside them to elevate the human spirit. On the other hand, the minister bears a direct responsibility for the wretched of the earth, for those classes of people unable to receive the benefits of leisured high culture. Those in training for the ministry should "live in the midst of the misery and wretchedness of the poor," and their education should open their hearts to "the deep and murderous cry of a dejected and desperate humanity." The minister, in short, is required to be all things to all people in a society torn by deep class divisions.[25]

The curriculum and the faculty appointments of the Chicago Divinity School exhibited that inclusive aim. By requiring all Bachelor of Divinity candidates to take courses in Bible, church history, theology, music, public speaking, and administration, the School ensured that the minister would be an adequate representative of religion as the "older sister" of the other things of the "higher life." And elective work in the University's divisions of political economy and social science offered future ministers the opportunity to explore the role of wealth and power in the shaping of the social order. Preparation for dealing with the desperate cries of the underclass was also available, especially for those students concentrating in the area of social service. Under the direction of

Albion W. Small, whom Harper brought to the University as the head of the Department of Sociology, Charles R. Henderson, chair of Practical Sociology in the Divinity School, and Shailer Mathews, dean of the Divinity School and a professor of New Testament, students took work in the history of philanthropy, the administration of settlement houses and reformatories, and the social principles of the New Testament.[26]

Such study constituted training in what Henry May has called the conservative and progressive, rather than the radical, social gospel.[27] The Divinity School educated its prospective ministers in the need for relief missions to the poor, instructed them in the social meanings of sin and salvation, and instilled in them the conviction that through education and the Christian spirit corporate America could be reformed. This was a social gospel allied with the political and social reforms of the Progressive Era—reforms affecting such matters as child labor, trust regulation, prison conditions, voting rights, and workmen's compensation. It was a gospel of improvement rather than of sweeping reconstruction, a challenge to the conditions of the social order rather than a criticism of the social and economic sources of class discrepancy. As such, it could be joined with William Rainey Harper's view of religion as the spiritualizer of the leisured life and with Shailer Mathews's interpretation of the teachings of Jesus as a defense of the equality of religious privilege and duty regardless of class.[28] There were no pleas here for political socialism, nor any calls for the revolt of the masses against a cruel capitalist system. The minister was to be all things to all people.

There is no reason to doubt the probity of Harper when he advised ministers to correlate respect for wealth with concern for the underprivileged. Linking the two was part of his far-reaching religious and social vision, his architectonic way of thinking, and his office as university president, which called for cultivation of the wealthy and improvement of the disadvantaged. There is every reason to doubt that the linkage could avoid conflict, however. As the twentieth century wore on, the progressivist optimism of Harper's vision would be seriously challenged by a severe economic depression, the modernist theological underpinnings of the social gospel would be repudiated by conservative religious forces, and the interests of the wealthy and the powerful would prove resistant to the supplications of the evangelists of democratic education.

But difficulties also appeared to be inherent within the very religious synthesis of wealth and reform. Shailer Mathews, teacher of scores of theological students in the principles of the social gospel, admitted that it was "hard to induce the average church person to do much more than vote the prohibition ticket" and that the "financial interests of laymen make them hesitant to take action which might subject them to the retaliation of those who directly profit from the so-called 'open town.' "[29] The fragility of the synthesis also became evident to Harper when, in 1894, an associate professor in the University's extension program, Edward Bemis, criticized the railroads during the Pullman Strike, thus compromising the University's plans to solicit the railroads for support of the College of Business. Professor Bemis lost his faculty position.[30]

Mathews and Harper had encountered the conflict of values created by the incorporation of America during the last half of the nineteenth century. In their structure, post–Civil War corporations were characterized by the authority of their managers to act in the interests of unrelated stockholders, thus allowing companies to operate in a competitive economic marketplace with quickness and flexibility. In their aims, corporations were no longer defined as institutions serving the public interest (a chief ground for corporate charters prior to the Civil War); they were now instruments strictly of private enterprise. These shifts of structure and aim exacerbated the conflicts between management and labor during the Industrial Revolution.

Yet as Alan Trachtenberg has pointed out, the new corporate world also produced two antagonistic views of America. On the one hand, America was celebrated as the creator of a democratic "high culture," offering to the aspiring middle class all those non-utilitarian activities of art, science, music, literature, and liberal religion previously accessible only to the wealthy. On the other, America was censured for its unfeeling exploitation of farmers and industrial laborers and for its smothering of American ethnic and racial differences under a cloak of Anglo-Saxon sameness. Trachtenberg finds this conflict running through much American imaginative literature.[31] It runs, as well, through much of the history of the American university divinity schools. Harper's vision of the schools as places for training ministers to deal with all classes of people inadvertently institutionalized conflicting views of America.

To start with Harper is by no means to start at the beginning. Theological seminaries had been sprinkled widely over the American landscape long before Harper's Chicago experiment. Throughout the nineteenth century, Protestant competition for the allegiance of the American people, the desires of immigrants to preserve their religious traditions, and doctrinal factions within the denominations led every Protestant denomination to found its own seminaries, even if that sometimes meant creating a school with two faculty and ten students. Between 1820 and

1831 eleven new denominational seminaries materialized, and between 1839 and 1869 thirty-seven new seminaries were born.[32] Also before Harper came sweeping onto the scene with his grand educational vision, other American universities had made non- or interdenominational divinity schools organic members of their educational programs. That had been the policy of presidents Timothy Dwight of Yale and Charles Eliot at Harvard in the 1880s. Harper cannot even be viewed as a recapitulation of the history of theological and university education that preceded him. After all, he had given up three simultaneous professorships at Yale (in the College, the Graduate School, and the Divinity School) to do something different: to preside over a fully democratic university destined to lead in the westward march of history.

Harper is best understood neither as originator nor as imitator, but, rather, as eponym.[33] In his commanding messianic vision and his ambitious educational scheme, Harper was a figurative embodiment of an era when modernist, ecumenical Protestantism sought to determine the values of the whole of American culture through education. Others preceded Harper in the ideas and plans of his educational mission, but none quite brought together in such a singular and energetic way the dreams and designs of an educational Zion continuously enlivened by the Protestant religion.

## MODEL SCHOOLS

In 1924, Robert L. Kelly published the first comprehensive study of American theological education. Commissioned by the Institute of Social and Religious Research, Kelly's study found that in general American seminary education was in a shambles. The plight of the schools owed to a long list of problems that included inadequate numbers of faculty, a paucity of research libraries, scanty finances, students with deficient college training, and faculty reliance on outmoded teaching methods. Kelly did not mince words. In commenting on seminary students, for example, he said, "The occasional or frequent presence in any school of students of unwonted maturity is a common experience. . . . They are often mediocre men. In many cases they are men who have failed at other kinds of work."[34]

Although Kelly did not undertake to grade the 161 individual schools examined in his study, he did hold up certain schools as models of excellence in an educational field he believed to be overcrowded by the mediocre and the paltry. Those models were the schools with significant university alliances that enabled them to undertake respectable graduate education. Kelly's model institutions included the nondenominational divinity schools of Chicago, Harvard, Yale, and Union of New York City. Kelly had identified the Big Four that would serve throughout the twentieth century as the paradigms for Protestant education in divinity and would provide other Protestant theological schools with most of their faculty.

These model institutions made their own distinctive contributions to university theological education. Each in its own way, however, exemplified the components of Harper's educational proposal. Each understood its task to be sustained by an interconnected system of religious education, sought to combine professional training with graduate education, embraced the aims of both high culture and social reform, and built upon the conviction that religion belongs to the core of the university task.

In 1880, when Harvard president Charles Eliot turned a Unitarian seminary on the margins of Harvard University into a nondenominational divinity school organically connected with the larger University, he did so with none of Harper's Baptist piety, democratic messianism, or western-frontier populism. His action, however, was filled with its own kind of evangelical fervor. A Unitarian and a chemist and mathematician with no training in theology, Eliot was a passionate champion of the scientific method in all regions of learning, including divinity.

In Eliot's judgment, the emergence of the scientific method constituted "the chief addition made by the nineteenth century to the idea of culture." It had transformed not only the natural sciences but also the nature of knowledge itself, including liberal learning. Harvard University was to adopt this culture-transforming method in all of its branches. For the Divinity School this meant development "from a local School, undenominational in principle but in fact supported and used only by Unitarians, into a broad School of Scientific Theology and independent research." The Divinity School would continue to draw upon its Unitarian heritage in its rejection of all forms of dogmatism and sectarianism and in its dedication to rational, unbiased inquiry. The School, however, would be built upon no sect, not even the nonsectarian sect of Unitarianism. In contrast to the denominational dogmatism of Princeton Theological Seminary, controlled by the Presbyterian General Assembly and in the main unrelated to Princeton University, Harvard Divinity School was destined to take its place in the larger university program of free, unbiased research and nondenominational professional training.

The Divinity School thus would contribute to the advancement of the "cultivated man" and promote a national "system of popular education" dedicated to spreading a civilization formed by the scientific method.[35]

Under the leadership of President Eliot and Deans Charles Everett and Francis Peabody, development of the curriculum at the newly constituted Harvard Divinity School encompassed the same fundamental aims found at Harper's university. Yet there were differences. Study of foreign missions never became an integral part of the course of study at Harvard, and during most of the Divinity School's history systematic or constructive theology occupied a minor place in a curriculum dominated by the critical-historical study of Bible, church history, and world religions.[36] Yet Harvard was just as committed as Chicago to combining graduate education with professional training for the ministry.

Using the elective system of course work, for which Eliot became the national spokesman, Harvard Bachelor of Divinity candidates were required to elect courses in each of the departments of Old Testament, New Testament, church history, theology, and homiletics. The connection between religion and other dimensions of university life was fostered by a system of widely used crossover registration between the Divinity School and other departments of the University and by the appointment of Divinity School professors to the Faculty of Arts and Sciences. Through the instruction of Professors John Winthrop Platner, Ephraim Emerton, and George Foot Moore, students were encouraged to understand nondenominational Protestantism in terms of its setting within the network of worldwide Christianity and other major religious traditions. Francis Peabody, the creator of the first department of social ethics in an American university and a social gospeler cast in the same mold as Shailer Mathews, offered a popular course in "The Ethics of the Social Question" in which both college and divinity students examined the issues of temperance, management and labor, and changes in family structure engendered by the urban and industrial revolutions.[37] Through its Divinity School, Harvard staked out its own claim to leadership in the effort to shape America through Protestant higher education.

That became the aspiration of the Divinity School at Yale, as well. Founded in 1822 to train New England ministers to meet the increasing demands of the growth of Congregational and Presbyterian churches stimulated by the revivals of the Second Great Awakening, the School by the end of the nineteenth century enrolled students from diverse denominations, with only 12 percent of those students hailing from New England.[38] Yale Divinity's evangelical milieu was to continue into the twentieth century, but it was a milieu increasingly suffused with the aims of the modern research university as the Divinity School became a professional school alongside others at Yale. Under the presidency of clergyman Timothy Dwight (1886–99), the academic credentials of Divinity School faculty were increased, especially in the critical-historical study of the Bible, and the professional schools were brought up to a level of faculty talent almost on a par with that of the College. However, it was under the direction of Yale's first nonclerical president, Arthur Twining Hadley (1899–1921), that professional education prospered at Yale and the University was systematically arranged to dispense "scientific investigation, general culture, and professional training" in order to meet diverse student needs and provide broad public service.[39] Yale Divinity School adopted those sundry university tasks as a graduate professional institution.

After recovering from declining enrollments, a high number of faculty retirements, and financial difficulties in the early years of the twentieth century, the Divinity School at Yale began to exhibit those same features of Protestant professional education apparent at Chicago and Harvard. By 1910, the elective curriculum combined study in Bible, church history, and theology with a choice of training in pastoral education, missions, religious education, and social service. Under the instruction of Professor E. Hershey Sneath, and then Professor and Dean Luther A. Weigle, Yale students were educated in the conviction that religious education constitutes a network of learning from family training to higher education. For decades Yale Divinity School was to be the leader in training students preparing for careers in religion in higher education. Education in world missions was also given a strong emphasis at Yale under the instruction of Harlan Beach, John Archer, and Kenneth Scott Latourette.

In the 1920s, the Yale Divinity School's connections with the remainder of the University were augmented by a system of cross-registration between the School and the College. Dean Charles Reynolds Brown of the Divinity School especially encouraged divinity students with no exposure to the theory of evolution to take a college course in organic evolution. And Dean Brown himself was a social gospeler who taught courses in "practical philanthropy" and the "labor problem." (The Yale Corporation was reluctant to appoint him as dean until he convinced them that men of great wealth in the country should be persuaded rather than coerced into sensitivity to the plight of the poor.)[40] Brown aptly characterized the ethos of Yale Divinity School during the first three decades of the twentieth century when he insisted that the two prime requisites for a vital Protestant ministry were "love and knowledge, character and efficiency"—or, if you will, piety and understanding.[41]

The combination of piety and understanding also characterized the environment of Union Seminary in New York. Unlike the divinity schools at Chicago, Harvard, and Yale, however, Union Seminary has never been an organic part of a university. Henry Sloane Coffin, president of Union from 1926 to 1945, was fond of saying that "Union must live by its wits" since it enjoyed no official ecclesiastical or university sponsorship.[42] A great part of its witful living, however, has entailed aligning itself with both ecumenical Protestantism and the modern American university.

Founded in 1836 by New School Presbyterians (who in contrast to the Old School valued experience more than doctrine, supported revivalism, and inclined to antislavery sentiments), Union was from the beginning open to "students of every denomination of evangelical Christians" and served a multidenominational student body. Faculty and board members were required to subscribe to the Westminster Confession of Faith, however, and in 1870 when Union became a seminary of the reunited Presbyterian Church in the U.S.A., the Presbyterian General Assembly was given veto power over faculty appointments. Following the Assembly's rejection of Charles Briggs as professor of biblical theology and a series of heresy trials for Briggs in the early 1890s, Union declared its independence from Presbyterian control and by 1904 was clearly a nondenominational school.[43]

The shape of Union's curriculum and the faculty appointments during the first three decades of its independence indicated that the school, quite as much as Chicago, Harvard, and Yale, would assume a crucial role in spreading the Pan-Protestant educational gospel. Courses in Bible, church history, and theology were taught by specialized faculty and fused teaching with the latest research. Yet Union also understood itself, in Coffin's words, as a "vocational school," preparing ministers in missions, sacred music, religious education, preaching, administration, and social ethics. Under the direction of George Coe, a follower of the educational philosophy of John Dewey and president of the Religious Education Association, Union's Department of Religious Education and Psychology taught students to think of religious education as a process of human development and self-realization achieved through the diverse institutions of society.

Union supplemented a conservative and moderate social gospel, available through work in inner-city parishes and settlement houses, with a more radical form of that gospel. Ethics professor Harry F. Ward in the

1930s published a pointed attack on capitalism and became a defender of Soviet Communism. Ethics professor Reinhold Niebuhr, though in radical disagreement with his colleague Ward on the issue of communism, during his early years at Union engaged in Marxist social analysis, endorsed for U.S. President the Socialist Party candidate Norman Thomas, and himself ran for the state senate on the Socialist ticket. The political postures of Ward and Niebuhr endeared neither of them to the Union administration or the board of directors, both of which were concerned about the reactions of wealthy donors and the reputation that Union was earning as "the Red Seminary."[44]

Although Union Seminary has always been governed by its own independent board, it has struck frequent alliances with Columbia University. In 1917, a long list of university courses was carried in the Union catalogue as meeting Bachelor of Divinity requirements. In 1928, an arrangement was formed that was to continue: Union faculty were recognized as a constituent body of Columbia, and M.A. degrees—and eventually the Ed.D. and some Ph.D. degrees—were awarded by the University on the recommendation of the Union faculty.[45] The place of Union in the scheme of religion and higher education, however, is not to be found simply in these structural arrangements with Columbia. It is to be located as well in Union's understanding of itself as a place of learning offering many of the advantages and few of the limitations of advanced university education.

In the early twentieth century, Charles Briggs described this understanding of Union in his argument for a "theological university," an argument picked up by his students (who were later presidents of Union) Francis Brown and Arthur Cushman McGiffert. According to Briggs, Union was positioned to pursue technical critical scholarship and yet overcome the fragmentation of the disciplines apparent in the German universities and in the modern American universities so enamored of the German model. Union could unify the disparate disciplines with piety and theological learning. The task of Union as a theological university was to "theologize knowledge" by fostering a devout practice of Christian piety and by viewing all branches of learning as aspects of the knowledge of God (what at the time was known as "theological encyclopedia"). For Briggs and many others who would succeed him at Union, Protestantism had a higher calling than establishing a Protestant professional school of religion among others in the university. It was to become the vital center, the unifying core, of human learning as such.[46]

The concept of the divinity school as a theological university was by no means peculiar to Union. It was very much in the air in late nineteenth and early twentieth century theological seminaries, put there by instructors like Briggs who through their courses in theological encyclopedia stipulated that theological reflection could unify human knowledge. A version of the idea appeared as late as the 1970s at Fuller Theological Seminary, the evangelical theological counterpart to Union's liberalism, as Fuller undertook to expand into programs of graduate study normally reserved to secular universities.[47] It was an idea that also pervaded the Methodist divinity schools, most of which struggled, rather than hurried, toward Zion.

## THE CASE OF THE METHODISTS

The story of the Methodist schools involves one of the most curious ironies of American religious history. The monumental growth of that denomination in the early nineteenth century resulted from conversions wrought by a largely unschooled clergy. In 1784, at the "Christmas Conference" in Baltimore which formed the American version of the denomination, a simple course of self-directed study was recommended to ministers, but with this caveat: "Gaining knowledge is a good Thing, but saving Souls is a better. . . . If you can do but one, let your Studies alone."[48] Less than a century and a half later, American Methodism alone among the denominations could boast of the formation of seven divinity schools organically related to universities. The story of the movement from this denomination's deliberate neglect of advanced ministerial study to its broad promotion of graduate ministerial training illuminates factors in American society that prompted Methodists, as well as Baptists like Harper, to seek a blend of religious ideals and educational strategies.

By 1830 the Methodists had become the largest Protestant denomination in America, and by 1870 one out of every twenty-eight Americans was a Methodist. Methodists had won most of their converts on the southern and western frontiers with a minimally educated ministry. Even the program of reading for ministers, known as the Conference Course of Study, was widely neglected throughout the nineteenth century. Methodism had effectively employed two strategies to boost its membership: the arousal of experiential religion through evangelical preaching, and, in Charles Ferguson's apt double entendre, the ability to "organize to beat the devil." Methodism had become the largest Protestant denomination by speaking the language of the people, winning those people to a heart-felt religion, and creating a system of circuit riders and local lay leaders and exhorters to establish societies of Methodists across the frontier.[49]

Why disturb such a successful approach with plans to equip Methodist ministers with a graduate theological education? That was precisely the question raised repeatedly throughout the nineteenth century by Methodists adamantly opposed to seminaries. In 1834, when a young Methodist minister proposed in the *Methodist Magazine and Quarterly Review* that the New England Conference establish a theological school, his proposal was greeted by a storm of protest which included the claim that a plan for such a seminary was "a dangerous and ruinous innovation" calculated "to sap the foundations of the ecclesiastical structure." In 1854, in the pages of the *Christian Advocate*, James Sewell of Philadelphia responded to a proposal for a Central Theological Seminary for Methodism with the remark, "The great body of our people prefer heat to light, and strong spiritual common sense to all the literary refinements that were ever concocted in all the theological seminaries in the universe." At a debate over theological education at the 1870 Conference of the Methodist Episcopal Church, South, one vocal delegate insisted that Methodists should compare their traditions with those of other denominations and reach the only sound conclusion: "Our Church has produced some of the greatest men of this or any other age, without theological training, or any other college besides God's great Word." In a particularly heated controversy published in the pages of the *Nashville Christian Advocate* in 1872, two southern bishops lined up against each other. Bishop Holland McTyeire, a proponent of Methodist theological education who would become president of the board at the newly established Methodist university of Vanderbilt, drew the fire of Bishop George Pierce. Pierce's opposition was premised on his understanding of the distinctiveness of the American Methodist heritage: "Methodism was born when the world was piled full of other churches, filled to the rafters with dead forms and shadows of religious experience. Methodism came and brought to the world a live experience."[50]

There seemed to be no reason to disrupt a successful evangelical heritage with the requirement that ministers be highly educated. In fact, however, that heritage already had been disrupted by the emergence of a new America, and the Methodist advocates of theological education sensed that newness. They noticed that the circuit rider had dismounted, forced from his saddle by a disappearing frontier.[51] By the middle of the nineteenth century, increasing numbers of Methodist ministers were settled pastors of frontier outposts and small towns rather than itinerant preachers. And like ministers in other denominations, by the time of the Civil War they were called to serve in a variety of professional posts such as teachers in academies, administrators of benevolence societies, and editors of religious publications. Furthermore, the American laypeople— the white ones—were changing. They were going to college, frequently at one of Methodism's many small institutions of higher education, were advancing in social status because of their education, and were settling into comfortable professions in small-town America. With the emergence of industrial, urban America after the Civil War, Methodists also took their places in the cities and in the corporate world. Before the end of the nineteenth century, the people called Methodists were immersed in the currents of an upwardly mobile, urban, middle-class America.

These changes were not lost on the exponents of theological education for Methodist ministers. Although they often appealed to John Wesley's Oxford University education and personal habits of disciplined study, they aimed the force of their argument at the new American situation. Quite simply they insisted that Methodism would lose touch with a changing America if it did not direct an educated, professional ministry to an educated, professional American laity. It was a question of status: the words of an uneducated preacher would not be taken seriously by an educated laity. And it was an issue of competition: Methodism would lose members to Presbyterians, Congregationalists, and Episcopalians if its clergy were not equally well-educated professionals. As James Strong of Flushing, New York, observed in the 1850s, Methodists had moved "from the lower to higher stratums of society," and uneducated ministers were bound to lose those people who were "the flower of the flock."[52] According to Landon C. Garland, president of the University of Mississippi and later the first chancellor of Vanderbilt University, "The social position [of the highly educated] minister would be greatly elevated. He would find ready access into every circle of society, instructing and entertaining all with whom he might come in contact. His company would be sought universally, and his influence would be felt throughout the community."[53]

None of these champions of theological education even remotely suggested a departure from what they took to be the undeniable strengths of the American Methodist heritage, namely, evangelical preaching, heartfelt religiosity, and a well-organized system of church supervision. Yet all of them held that new social conditions called for enhancing those strengths with an educated clergy that would move Methodism into the American mainstream and keep it there.

Despite the opposition, the reformers had their way. John Dempster, the Father of Methodist theological education, founded the Newbury Biblical Institute in New Hampshire in 1839, which moved in 1847 to Concord, and then to Boston where in 1871 it was incorporated into Boston University as a graduate school of theology. Dempster also persuaded Eliza Garrett, the widow of a wealthy businessman and Chicago mayor, to donate the bulk of her fortune in 1855 to the establishment of Garrett Biblical Institute in Evanston, Illinois. Garrett Institute was to become a graduate-level institution at Northwestern, but not as an organic part of the University. In 1866, Daniel Drew, who made his fortune by investing in transportation, dumping dummy stocks on Wall Street, and watering his cattle before sale, was induced by his Methodist minister, John McClintock, to establish a theological school in Madison, New Jersey. Although the original charter of the institution authorized it to become a university, Drew remained a theological school until 1928, when a college of liberal arts was added.

Southern Methodist proponents of theological education saw their dreams come true in 1875 when Cornelius Vanderbilt endowed a Methodist university in Nashville, Tennessee, complete with a Biblical Department for the training of Methodist ministers. In 1914, Vanderbilt University won a court case that denied governing control of the institution to the Methodist Church, and the University's Biblical Department became an interdenominational School of Religion. Their hopes dashed and their ire provoked by the Vanderbilt decision, Southern Methodists acted quickly to establish two other institutions of higher education. Bishop Warren Candler, who had argued unsuccessfully for Methodist control of Vanderbilt, secured from his Atlanta businessman brother, Asa, a gift of one million dollars to found Emory University in 1915; one-half of that gift was allocated to the new Candler School of Theology. Also in 1915, Southern Methodist University opened in Dallas, Texas and included a School of Theology as the Methodist Church's official ministerial training school for the region west of the Mississippi. In 1924, the education of Southern Methodist ministers received a significant boost when James B. Duke, who had accumulated his wealth from the tobacco and water mechanics industries, turned Trinity College in Durham, North Carolina, into Duke University. The Duke School of Religion emerged two years later for the professional training of Methodist ministers.

In the Far West at the end of the nineteenth century, the Maclay College of Theology moved from the San Fernando Valley to Los Angeles to join the Methodist-sponsored University of Southern California, and in 1922 the Maclay College became a School of Religion integrally related to USC. In 1956, following the severance of ties between USC and the Methodist Church, a new corporation was formed, the Southern California School of Theology, which moved the USC School of Religion faculty to the Claremont College complex.

The theological schools at Boston, Drew, Vanderbilt, Emory, Southern Methodist, USC-Claremont, and Duke adopted the same basic aims and strategies articulated so forcefully by William Rainey Harper at the University of Chicago. To be sure, most of these Methodist schools lacked the finances and the faculty and library resources of Chicago, many were outside the range of urban sprawl, most in their early days accepted theological students who lacked college degrees, and some were joined with institutions that were universities in name only. Yet they were committed to creating a Protestant Zion with the same strategies employed by the Big Four divinity schools.

All of the Methodist divinity schools, though serving chiefly as instruments for training Methodist ministers, were open to students of every Christian denomination and insisted in their mission statements that Wesleyan Methodism was by nature ecumenical. Each and every one of them was founded on the conviction that the minister, in order to function effectively in modern America, needed to master a graduate-level specialty, acquire skills as a professional, and learn to move easily within the high culture available to middle-class Methodists. And all of the institutions at some point in their histories were fortified by the infusion of capital from wealthy individuals or families who were persuaded that theological education served a large public good. The schools also offered courses in social analysis of urban and rural problems and sent their ministers-in-training into fieldwork in urban ghettos and poor farming communities. And all of them sprang to their tasks from the belief that American society needed the benefactions of a broad-based system of religious education and that the modern American university, for the fulfillment of its task, required the presence of the advanced study of religion.

In 1924, when Mr. Duke set up a $40,000,000 trust fund for charitable institutions in North Carolina, he explained why the university that took his name would be a chief beneficiary:

> I have selected Duke University as one of the principal objects of this trust because I recognize that education, when conducted along sane and practical, as opposed to dogmatic and theoretical, lines, is, next to religion, the greatest civilizing influence. . . . And I advise that the courses at this institution be arranged, first, with special reference to the training of preachers, teachers, lawyers, and physicians, because these are most in the public eye, and by precept and example can do most to uplift mankind. . . . [54]

Neither Harper nor Rockefeller could have said it better. American Methodism clearly had abandoned its early frontier attitude toward education. Methodists had created colleges, universities, and divinity schools—and divinity schools were especially called to shape American civilization.

## DIVINITY SCHOOLS AS SYSTEMS
## OF INFLUENCE: TRANSFORMATIONS

The years 1880 to 1925, the period of the rise of modern American universities and the development of Protestant university divinity schools, stand out as a robust, visionary phase in the history of higher education. The times were marked by the blending of Protestant hopes and democratic expectations, of liberal Protestantism and educational evangelism. They were times when universities were thought to be the chief instruments of both cultural progress and social reform, and their divinity schools the religious pacesetters for those educational tasks. The strategies for turning the visions into institutional realities were equally bold. Universities and divinity schools were brought together so that the resources and missions of the two could strengthen each other. Divinity schools, though tied to the goals and structures of the university, would simultaneously draw upon and serve a large religious educational system composed of Sunday schools, academies, colleges, study groups, and the media of the masses. And even while they strove to offer future ministers a graduate specialization, a professional training, and an exposure to high culture as respectable as any in the university, they would also teach students to fasten their attention on the problems that would meet them in the modern social order.

These strategies were devised to make the divinity schools agencies for decisively shaping the values, ideals, and aspirations of the American people. They were, in other words, means of creating institutions to promote a Protestant establishment. By aligning divinity schools with the American university, itself an institution of immeasurable cultural influence, the churches sought to extend their own influence. To speak here of an "establishment" is by no means to suggest that the divinity schools and the Pan-Protestant visions that gave birth to them ever really managed to capture the power that drives modern America. Rather, it is to propose that the visions and strategies of university divinity schools sought a religious hegemony in modern America, that their hundred-year history cannot be understood apart from that effort, and that their history exemplifies Protestantism's transformation in a radically pluralistic America in which no religious hegemony could prevail.[55]

The following chapters examine the transformation of an educational tradition. The substance of that now strange world symbolized by the picture of William Rainey Harper hurrying toward Zion did not disappear; it assumed different forms. And the transformation was not simply the consequence of the university divinity schools being overwhelmed by external influences, though such influences did share in the transformation. It resulted also from factors inherent within the visions and strategies of the schools themselves and from their endorsement of forces in the culture at large.

Although the divinity schools witnessed around them powerful pressures leading to the breakup of the religious educational system on which they had come to depend, they themselves contributed to the disintegration of the system with their emphasis on specialization. Though the ministers they educated were in many ways disfranchised by an expanding culture of professionalism based on technical expertise, the divinity schools were often leaders in their universities in promoting specialized competence and professional standards. Although most of the divinity schools were traditional, even conservative, in their postures on social change and the advantages of high culture, they were often at the forefront of reform movements and protests that sanctioned the rapidly changing lifestyles and values so characteristic of an unsettled modern America. And for all of their efforts to place religion at the center of the university, the schools fostered an appreciation for a pluralism that would render the university one of society's most decentered institutions. No helpless victims of blind historical forces, the university divinity schools were, rather, active contributors to the transformation of their own heritage.

# PART I

■

# SPECIALIZATION

# CHAPTER I

■

## *Strategies for a System of Education*

In the 1950s, Christian ethicist Reinhold Niebuhr looked back on his time spent at the Yale Divinity School forty years earlier. Although he recalled the thrill of studying at an eastern university, he also remembered an atmosphere in which his midwestern accent and his denominational college preparation embarrassed him on a campus of cultured "Yale men." In the 1970s, feminist ethicist Beverly W. Harrison reflected on her student days at Union Theological Seminary in the 1950s. She also remembered feeling out of place as a midwesterner in a school dominated by students from Ivy League colleges.[1] Ironically, Harrison's sense of alienation arose at precisely the time in Union's history when Niebuhr was a commanding presence on that school's faculty.

Niebuhr's and Harrison's discomfort certainly was not created by the majority of the student body at the Yale and Union seminaries. A mere 6 percent of Niebuhr's Yale class of 1914 came from elite eastern schools, with 40 percent arriving from denominational schools west of the Ohio River. Seventeen percent of the class in which he received the M.A. degree graduated from prestige eastern institutions. Only 16 percent of Harrison's class of 1956 were graduates of select eastern colleges and universities; more than twice that number, 33 percent, hailed from denominational colleges in other sections of the country. The remainder of her class derived from large American public and private universities, colleges and universities in Asia and Europe, and Bible institutes and music training schools.[2]

Niebuhr's Yale Divinity School and Harrison's Union Seminary reflected the student body profile that would prevail in theological schools in the United States until the late 1960s. Students were typically white males in their twenties, liberal arts graduates of church-related colleges and universities, who left behind rural and small-town backgrounds to attend seminary in the city. Most of their fathers were farmers, ministers, tradesmen, or owners of small businesses. These students were reared in the churches, participated in religious activities in college, maintained their denominational connections while divinity school students, and returned to their denominations as ministers or as other religious professionals. None of the theological schools they attended was dominated by Ivy League products in the early or mid-1900s. In fact, a trend was already evident in the early part of the century that would grow with time: there was an inverse relation between those areas of the country with the highest educational ratings and those producing candidates for the ministry. Most graduates of the elite eastern colleges would choose then, as now, professions other than the ministry.[3]

If Niebuhr and Harrison overestimated the presence of Ivy League students within their seminary communities, what was the source of their discomfort? Each indicated the real source. Niebuhr remarked that though he valued the religious devotions at Yale Divinity School, he often found the scholarship of the place cold, desiccating, and lacking in inspiration. And though he discovered in some of his professors a nice blend of devotion and critical scholarship, Yale ultimately did not satisfy his deep desire for "relevance rather than scholarship." Harrison complained that at Union she "got a 'book orientation' to too many questions without an accompanying commitment to praxis" and that her previous work in a campus ministry program, rather than her studies at Union, gave her a sense of the connection between Christian faith and the practical issues facing ministers in society.[4]

Niebuhr and Harrison had found themselves in the strange, new world of the divinity school modeled after the modern research university. The aura of that world, defined much more by the faculty and the curriculum than by students from the Ivy League, was alien to their denominational college backgrounds and their practical piety. It was a world of specialized scholarship that made their fellow students from the better eastern schools seem to be a favored lot and made their own experiences shaped by a system of religious education appear to be out of accord with the demands of critical scholarship.

Founders of university divinity schools were convinced that specialization could be bent to the service of Protestantism's wide influence on American culture. And they believed that such a goal could be accomplished as the specialized scholarship of divinity education was connected with other parts of a broad, interconnected system of religious education. Effective cultural influence thus would be achieved as scholarship was correlated with piety, specialized professional training with the religious needs of the churches, and theological learning with the diverse life of the modern university. As the observations of Niebuhr and Harrison suggest, however, those correlations would be difficult to sustain.

## UNIVERSITY SPECIALIZATION

When William Rainey Harper, Charles Eliot, and other advocates of university divinity schools insisted on the importance of specialized graduate work for prospective ministers, they were championing a central role of the modern university in American society. The university offered to its graduates a learning in depth, one appropriate to an American society rapidly expanding in its uses of knowledge in the various professions. If the minister were to avoid superficiality in such a world, he (eventually she) also must master a specialty. University specialization, despite its danger of balkanizing the universe of learning, was the avenue for the educated minister's entry into the modern world. Furthermore, divinity schools in their practice of piety and their holistic religious perspective just might possess the means for avoiding the fragmentation characteristic of university life.

The rise of the modern American university is usually dated from the founding of the Johns Hopkins in 1876, a university that began as a graduate school devoted to specialized research. Earlier in the nineteenth century, however, educational reformers in the United States had contended for the necessity of specialization. In defending an elective system for college undergraduates, Harvard president Charles Eliot had argued in the 1860s that the university must give specialized attention to "the individual traits of different minds," a possibility foreclosed by a uniform curriculum. And in making his case for advanced scientific education, Eliot proposed that "no subject of human inquiry can be out of place in the programme of a real university. It is only necessary that every subject should be taught at the university on a higher plane than elsewhere." In the 1850s, Henry Tappan, president of the University of Michigan, held that the principle governing the true university is a simple one: "That each member as a thinker, investigator, and teacher shall be a law unto himself, in his own department." Such autonomy meant that the university should become a "cyclopedia" of education, "where in libraries, cabinets, apparatus, and professors, provision is made for studying every branch of knowledge in full . . . ; where study may be extended without limit."[5]

The proponents of university specialization were determined to overcome what they took to be the severe limitations of the college system of education. They believed that the colleges founded before the Civil War were controlled by the sectarian outlook of the Protestant denominations, were centered on a curriculum of classical languages irrelevant to life in the modern world, were preoccupied with the training of ministers, and were so superficial in their course offerings that they neglected new fields of knowledge. There is considerable evidence that leaders of the new universities badly caricatured the American colleges, which as a whole were not as sectarian, classical, superficial, or clerical as the leaders claimed.[6] Nevertheless, the American university that emerged in the late nineteenth century was devoted to the proliferation of specialized fields of knowledge in a way unequaled by any college. Specialization was the propelling spirit of the modern American university.

That spirit derived in large measure from a German model of education. Throughout the last half of the nineteenth century, American educators issued calls for the pursuit of *Wissenschaft* in all branches of learning. Many of those educators had made their pilgrimages to German universities and had returned eager to reform their home institutions. In the German system, *Wissenschaft*, "systematic scholarship," was to serve the purposes of *Bildung*, "education for cultivation" or the development of the unique individualism of the scholar. And *Wissenschaft*, if it were to avoid positivism and radical relativism—the very antitheses of "cultivation"—should be informed by *Weltanschauung*, or the synthesis of observations and values. Thus the highest form of *Wissenschaft* for the German educator was not the natural sciences but *Geisteswissenschaften* or the humanistic disciplines. And the arts faculty, with their non-utilitarian emphasis on cultivation and values, represented the heart of university education.[7]

American educators did not adopt this German view of education without modification. "Science," the translation of *Wissenschaft*, often came to mean in the American university empiricism and, eventually, positivism, the very ideas opposed by the German concept. The ideal of "cultivation" was limited to American humanities departments and did not represent a central goal of the American university as a whole. In making the Ph.D. the highest degree for certifying specialization, Americans overlooked the fact that the degree was not the highest on a scale of several degrees in Germany and that the German doctorate required a demonstration of broad learning.[8] However much nineteenth-century Americans may have misunderstood or substantially modified the ideals of German higher education, they found in those ideals inspiration for their own version of specialization. *Wissenschaft* meant the freedom to pursue any subject with open-minded curiosity and painstaking discipline. In their own fashion, American educators appropriated the dictum of the German philosopher and educational reformer Immanuel Kant: "*Sapere aude*! 'Have courage to use your own reason!'—that is the motto of the Enlightenment."[9] The spirit of the Enlightenment in American universities would mean the unshackled pursuit of knowledge in its wide diversity through work in specialized fields of learning.

Specialization of knowledge characterized the American scene on a wide front in the late nineteenth and early twentieth centuries. Libraries were transformed from "storehouses" into "workshops" for scholars, with the Dewey decimal classification system and the card catalogue providing a map of specialized fields. The American publishing industry began to diversify and expand the number of its titles (with a sixfold increase in new titles between 1880 and 1910), and university presses were founded to disseminate scholarly works with limited readerships. The social sciences appeared as separate fields of study, and all academic disciplines, including most of those in the humanities and the arts, aspired to be scientific in their inductive method and their focus on limited subject matter. The organization of universities into departments, which began in earnest in the late nineteenth century, was both a recognition of the value of specialization and an acceptance of the need for specialist scholars to engage in self-governance.[10]

From the outset, the American university was launched in the direction of what Clark Kerr would call the "multiversity," a collection of several communities rather than one community, a series of social processes aimed at a series of different results, rather than a unified intellectual assembly.[11] The structure of the multiversity was begotten by an industrial, capitalist, bureaucratic social order which it was founded to serve, and its spirit was derived from the Enlightenment principle of the unshackled pursuit of knowledge. Each area of such a social order required technical knowledge for the achievement of specific goals, and the efficient operation of its complex organizations necessitated bureaucrats with limited, assigned tasks and areas of competence. The American university, as a complex modern organization, would adopt a bureaucratic administration for its operation. As a seat of higher learning, it would direct its educational programs to the acquisition of technical knowledge appropriate to the achievement of specific results.

In short, the specialization of the American university was the product of a social system that valued intellectual multiplicity and structural harmony. As Douglas Sloan has observed, "The late nineteenth-century university not only reflected, but in a paradoxical way was born out of and shaped by [a] growing lack of social and intellectual cohesion. . . . The emergence of the university and its successful functioning have been possible because its members achieved and maintained a consensus not around eternal verities, but rather around certain structural arrangements and working procedures."[12]

Divinity schools, however, would not so easily abandon a desire for intellectual unity based on eternal verities. They would seek to hold together the multifarious disciplines bred of specialization with something more than working procedures.

## THE PRACTICE OF PIETY AND THE STUDY OF SPECIALTIES

Reinhold Niebuhr's sense of the dissonance between the devotional life and the attitude of critical scholarship at Yale Divinity School in the early twentieth century attests to a synthesis sought, partially found, and eventually lost by the university divinity schools. Although the mission of the schools called for them to offer graduate study of the highest order in the specialties of divinity, it also summoned them to serve as extensions of the religious institutions that sent them their students. They were required to be university-like in their teaching and scholarship, and church-like in their promotion of piety.

Throughout their history, the divinity schools provided opportunities for their students to pursue and expand their religious life. In the latter years of the nineteenth century and the early years of the twentieth, some of the schools were so rife with such opportunities that they appeared to be as much places of worship as institutions of higher learning. At Union every class was opened with prayer down through the 1930s, and daily chapel services were well attended by faculty and students until the mid-1960s. In the late nineteenth and early twentieth centuries, Drew students attended daily public prayers, evening prayer meetings four times a week, preaching every Wednesday morning, periodic all-day spiritual retreats, and an annual love feast on the Wednesday of commencement week. At Yale and Emory during the same period, theological faculty and students organized revivals that swept through their universities and led to conversions of students from diverse academic departments. At Harvard from 1922 to 1953, Willard L. Sperry functioned in the dual capacity of dean of the Divinity School and minister to the Harvard University Memorial Church, the latter serving as a voluntary chapel for the entire University community and drawing in the 1930s an average of fifteen hundred worshipers to its weekly services. Charles Gilkey performed a similar function at Chicago, where from 1910 to 1928 he served as a popular minister for many faculty and students at the Hyde Park Baptist Church, and then as a professor of preaching at the Chicago Divinity School and as first dean of the University Chapel in 1928. At universities across the country, divinity school students joined college students in religious work by participating in the activities of YMCAs, denominational campus ministries, and the Student Volunteer Movement. An aura of practical piety pervaded the divinity schools and most of their larger university communities until the Second World War—and for some of the schools for decades after the War.[13]

The scholarship at the schools was meant to build upon, not destroy, this active religious practice. To be sure, the scholarship was designed to be free of dogma, based only on evidence unearthed from the sources by the careful scholar, and in keeping with scientific methods of the age. Yet none of the faculty, either at Reinhold Niebuhr's Yale in the early part of this century or at Beverly Harrison's Union at mid-century, thought that the life of the mind cultivated by a "book education" constituted a serious threat to the life of religious belief and practice. Charles Briggs of Union, tried for heresy by the Presbyterian Church because of his source criticism of the Old Testament, made clear that he understood the higher criticism of the Bible as the means for cutting through ecclesiastical dogma and fundamentalist assumptions about "inerrancy" in order to discover the Word of God within the words of the Bible. "The Bible, as a book, is paper, print, and binding,—nothing more," Briggs said in his defense of an approach to the Bible intended to be as critical as the examination of any book. He added, however, that the Bible "is entitled to reverent handling for the sake of its holy contents, because it contains the divine word of redemption for man."[14]

Douglas Clyde Macintosh, Niebuhr's academic advisor at Yale, sought to make systematic Christian theology as scientific in approach as physics. "As the task of physical science is to generalize on the basis of experience of the physical, to formulate laws of nature and ultimately a reasonable theory as to the character of the natural world," Macintosh said, "so it is the task of a scientific theology to generalize on the basis of experience of the revealed divine Reality, to formulate laws of the divine activity and ultimately a reasonable theory as to the nature of the divine Reality." Macintosh insisted, however, that his own scientific theology was developed to preserve the truth of Christian religious experience that in a scientific age "languishes because of intellectual doubts and skepticism."[15]

Shirley Jackson Case, who in the 1920s and 1930s built at Chicago a distinguished and influential Department of Church History, was the chief spokesman for that school's "socio-historical method." Eschewing metaphysical speculation and theological presuppositions for empirically verifiable data, Case sought to drive behind the Christian canon of texts to the social experiences of the Christian people, thus making church history as scientific as secular history, sociology, and anthropology. Case believed, however, that such scientific study would reveal that history is evolutionary, entailing the progressive growth of religions and cultures from the simple to the complex, from the ethnic and the tribal to the general and the inclusive. Case could thus counsel his Protestant American students that the practical result of historical study is the realization that for their own religion "the best is yet to be."[16]

During the 1940s and 1950s, the heyday of neoorthodoxy in many of the divinity schools, faculty challenged the rationalism, progressivism, and scientism of their liberal theological predecessors, but not their commitment to technical scholarship. Reinhold Niebuhr, for example, scorned the dogmas of human perfectibility and historical progress entailed in theological liberalism, and he complained of the tyranny of the scientific method in America's attempt to grapple with human dilemmas. He did not, however, reject the approaches and findings of the natural and social sciences themselves or the technical disciplines of the divinity schools.[17] Faculty in the university divinity schools have consistently maintained that rigorous, technical scholarship can build upon Christian faith and bring it into the modern world; it need not wreck it nor discredit it.

The divinity schools have differed in their ways of correlating piety and intellect. Harvard Divinity School, for example, throughout most of its history emphasized the historical approach in all areas of its curriculum, and its relative neglect of doctrinal theology attracted large numbers of conservative Protestant students who were able to separate their study of history from their doctrinal viewpoints.[18] In its early years, the Candler School of Theology at Emory University determined faculty appointments with the criteria of standing in the church and preaching ability rather than with the standards of scholarly accomplishment, and Candler's first dean possessed no college or seminary degree.[19] At the Boston School of Theology in the 1950s, faculty in the New Testament department decided to tighten the alliance between faith and scholarship for its Bachelor of Divinity students by "relegating critical and technical issues to a secondary place, in order to bring out the historical meaning and the contemporary relevance of the great themes and experiences [of the New Testament]."[20]

Despite these differences, most faculty at the schools would have had little difficulty endorsing the claim of a former dean at Duke in the 1970s. During its entire history, Robert Cushman insisted, Duke Divinity had resisted the fall into "a merely scientific and phenomenological study of religion." The curriculum of the divinity school, unlike the "merely scientific study of religion" in university departments of religion, had assumed a posture of "faith seeking understanding" on the part of a believing and worshiping church.[21]

If the divinity schools have avoided becoming "merely scientific," if most of them have kept before them the vision of scholarship in the service of the church, they have not maintained an even balance between the practice of piety and the pursuits of the intellect. During the past four decades, deans of many of the schools have found it necessary to urge upon faculty and students the importance of worship within a community of scholars devoted to the ongoing life of the church.[22] Even as early as the 1930s, a comprehensive study of theological schools in North America observed that the institutions made "little provision for the systematic oversight and discipline of the individual religious life" and that professors who led worship services in the schools "have too often contented themselves with brief talks of a more or less perfunctory character." The study concluded that this state of affairs doubtless had many causes but that no minor cause was "the multiplication of departments, the spread of specialized theological learning, and the increased academic responsibility within a restricted field imposed upon members of a modern faculty."[23] A study of theological schools in the 1950s reached a similar conclusion. In addition to being diverted by family responsibilities, fieldwork in the churches, and the diverse pastimes available in multiple forms of entertainment, theological students working in schools modeled after the modern university found most of their attention occupied by their studies rather than by the practice of their religion.[24]

In the 1970s and 1980s, the student bodies of most of the divinity schools became so diverse that there was no apparent shared religious experience that could issue in common religious devotion. Long before that time, however, the model of the university had worked its effects. It was, in part, a question of time. Faculty and students were preoccupied with the scholarly pursuit of specialties. Faculty had their classes to prepare, their books and articles to write, their presentations before professional societies to deliver in order to enhance and maintain their standing as university educators. Students had their research papers to compose, their reading to do, their seminar reports to frame in order to meet the requirements of a specialized education. But it was also a matter of appropriateness. What did source criticism of the Old Testament have to do with worship? epistemological theory with the life of the church? the sociological reconstruction of the early church with the everyday tasks of the minister?

Answers to those questions were not immediately apparent to divinity school students. Reinhold Niebuhr's impatience with uninspired scholarship and Beverly Harrison's disquiet over impractical book-education attested to an environment in the divinity schools that failed to make manifest the connections between the practice of religion and the study of specialties. Neither the opportunities for worship nor the insistence that theological education was a form of faith seeking understanding could quite stem the fragmenting and time-consuming forces of university specialization.

Divinity school specialization was dictated not only by the ethos of the modern university, however, and the divinity schools' attempt to overcome fragmentation was not vested merely in the practice of religious devotion. The schools looked outward to the institutions they were designed to serve as they took the measure of their specialized curricula, and they sought within their mission to the outside world a cohesion beyond the efficiency of working procedures. When William Rainey Harper and other early leaders of university divinity schools argued for the necessity of specialized graduate education for ministers, they had their eyes fixed on the needs of the churches and other institutions of American culture, as well as on the trends in higher education. When they instituted courses to meet those needs, they were convinced that the purpose of the courses, quite as much as the religious practice of students and faculty, would carry within it a unifying force.

## DIVINITY SCHOOLS AND "LOWER" RELIGIOUS EDUCATION

From their founding, university divinity schools were conceived as vital components in a system of national religious education, and their mission included service of those institutions linked below them in the educational chain. Harper's activities on behalf of study groups, Sunday schools, adult education courses, and the lecture circuit, as well as the University of Chicago Divinity School's publication of popular books on religion and its massive correspondence course of study, were simply the most dazzling expressions of this wide sense of educational mission. University-style specialization in divinity education was to be aimed at the lives of the people outside the walls of the divinity school.

That sense of mission was mandated as much by the changed nature of the American Protestant churches as by the new shape of the modern American university. By the late nineteenth century, many churches had ceased to be simple congregations devoted to the twin purposes of worship and the regulation of the morality of their members. They had become "social congregations" or institutions with diverse goals and manifold activities. When Henry Ward Beecher, a popular nineteenth-century preacher, advised Yale seminarians to "multiply picnics as much as possible" in their congregations, he was suggesting a means of holding together socially a collection of people who joined church congregations for a variety of reasons.[25] Particularly in urban churches, congregational activities included Sunday schools, concerts, church socials, sewing circles, and youth groups, as well as worship. And in what came to be known as the "institutional churches"—those congregations that sought to meet the diverse social needs of their neighborhoods—the activities encompassed soup kitchens, clinics, employment bureaus, circulating libraries, gymnasiums, and countless other relief programs. By 1906, New York City boasted over one hundred institutional churches, and Chicago twenty-five. Even many small urban and rural churches that lacked full-time ministers and the financial resources for large-scale relief programs had, by the second quarter of the twentieth century, multiplied their programs beyond those of worship and discipline and administered them with lay volunteers.[26]

Like other institutions in industrial America, churches became internally differentiated, embracing diverse, special activities directed to distinct audiences. The old voluntary associations of the late eighteenth and early nineteenth centuries had been clearly defined by singleness of purpose and simplicity of function. They had become by the end of the nineteenth century complex organizations marked by segmentation of aim and diversity of task. As forms of the new voluntary associations, Protestant churches provided increased opportunities for lay participation across a wide spectrum of activities. In the view of divinity school leaders, the multipurpose churches demanded the specialized educational skills of religious professionals. Specialized training offered to divinity students in such areas as preaching, administration, music, and social work was a response to the internally diversified congregation. And training in the course of study known as "religious education" held the promise that the specialties directed to the congregation could be held together as a whole educational system.

The formation in 1903 of the Religious Education Association by William Rainey Harper and other educational leaders signaled a bold, visionary effort to reform Protestantism's diverse educational activities. It also was the first national effort to enlist specialization on behalf of the educational programs of the multipurpose American churches. The REA was, in the words of historian Dorothy Bass, "a base for advocacy, fashioned by liberal Protestants to bring the findings of modern scholarship to bear on the educational activities of the churches, while at the same time strengthening what they saw as the waning educational influence of religion in the larger society."[27] The REA could, in Harper's words, "make new contributions to the cause of religious and moral education, and this will be done through the light of scientific investigations."[28]

With their university-style curricula, the divinity schools were designed to prepare specialists for this large cultural task. Among the eighteen ministerial vocations available to Chicago Divinity School students in the early twentieth century, the school offered a major in religious education that included graduate-level courses as well as "practice work in Sunday schools and other agencies of religious education." The Divinity School at Chicago housed one of the nation's most comprehensive programs in religious education through the first three decades of the twentieth century. With the city of Chicago serving as the headquarters for the

REA and the International Council of Religious Education, the Divinity School could provide its students with documents, studies, and practical advice pertinent to their preparation as religious educators. Through forty-five advanced courses, the Divinity School trained the parish minister, the educational minister, the lay supervisor, the missionary, the college teacher, and the editor in the tasks of religious education.[29]

If less comprehensive in their efforts than Chicago, all of the divinity schools took up the challenge of Harper and the REA to train both the generalist minister and the religious education director in a specialization pertinent to the modern congregation. By 1924, religious education courses offered in American seminaries had outstripped courses in evangelism, leading Robert Kelly to observe at the time, "If this is an index of the interest the seminary product will manifest in these lines of church promotion during the coming decades, it will be apparent that the future church is to be advanced on an educational rather than on an evangelistic program *per se*."[30] Along with other seminaries, the divinity schools had caught the vision of Harper. They had adopted education as the principal means of winning Americans to the truth of the Protestant religion and enlarging the sphere of Protestant influence. And they had undertaken that task through the instruction of ministers in the discipline of religious education.

The emphases of that discipline have changed frequently over the course of a century, and the changes have reflected modifications in educational philosophy and altered assessments of the nature of religion's influence on the culture. Much divinity school training in religious education before the Second World War was dominated by the educational philosophy of John Dewey. Religious education was then founded on the liberal theological and philosophical confidence that people and institutions are capable of progress toward self-realization. Divinity school faculty understood religious education as a complement to public school education: both were supposed to promote the realization of self and society through stages of growth. During this phase, divinity school students learned to use graded materials in their church schools and to discover the needs and motives of people as they moved toward fulfillment in their lives.

In the 1930s and 1940s, with the waning of liberal confidence in progressive education, many faculty in the field of religious education began to adopt the position that their discipline should be guided by the different areas of the seminary curriculum. Divinity school students came to think of religious education as Christian education—that is, as education into a perspective on the world appropriate to a specific religious tradition—and they were taught to impart to people in the churches their own discoveries in Bible, church history, theology, and ethics. By the mid-1960s, the field of religious education appeared to be in considerable disarray, and like other leaders of a declining mainstream Protestantism, religious educators admitted that their distinctive religious contributions were unclear. By the 1970s, it seemed that the only thing holding together specialists in religious education was agreement that programs for educating congregations should be directed to a radically pluralistic constituency.[31]

A common thread of perspective has run through much of the changing history of religious education: "lower" religious education is to be conducted under the supervision of the "higher"; the people in the Protestant congregations are to be the recipients of the specialized expertise of those with advanced theological training. That thread explains both the enormous industriousness and the waning strength of the divinity schools' effort to shape the religion of the churches. Both the strength and the weakness of the effort are illustrated in the history of the American Sunday school.

Ministers and directors of religious education have been taught in divinity schools that the Sunday school, or the "church school" as religious educators have been wont to call it, can be reformed through the expertise of the specialist. For the most part, however, the Sunday school has manifested a stubborn resistance to the influence of the specialist. It has remained lay-led and largely unshaped by the biblical criticism, modern theology, and church historical studies of the divinity school. Specially trained religious educators have encountered in the Sunday school a folk religion that, despite significant changes over its two-hundred-year history, has consistently retained its folk character and its suspicion of the specialists.

Arising in the late eighteenth century from British influences, American Sunday schools were originally instruments for evangelizing and civilizing the continent. They functioned as agencies of conversion, as systems for instructing children and youth in biblical doctrines, and as devices for erasing the lawlessness and the "Catholic threat" from the American frontier. In post–Civil War America, as the Sunday school movement was organized into interdenominational conventions, leaders of the movement shifted their focus from evangelism and doctrine to educational methods. At a national convention in 1872, these leaders introduced the uniform lesson plan, which provided for the study of brief biblical passages by Sunday school pupils of all ages in all parts of the world on the same day. According to the plan, the entire Christian Bible would be studied over a seven-year period, each denomination could set the content of each Sunday's lesson, and the lessons could be presented by minimally trained lay instructors. This standardized plan proved to be enormously appealing to the denominations. In 1900, three million American students were instructed through the plan, and forms of it survive in the denominations today. The standardized plan of religious education gave to Protestant laypeople a sense of connection with comrades in other parts of the nation and the world on any given Sunday, unified age groups within the same church by providing them the same Bible lesson to study, and permitted busy laypeople to teach their classes with minimal preparation.[32]

The change of the Sunday school from a voluntary agency aimed at the evangelization of the nation to an institution guided by interdenominational conventions was a fundamental shift from simplicity to complexity, from localism and denominationalism to nationalism and interdenominational cooperation, from a precorporate to a corporate American institution. What survived the change was the Sunday school as an institution of the folk relatively untouched by university specialization. Women, who for a century were excluded from the upper echelons of the Sunday school conventions and from the supervisory tasks at the local church level, throughout the long history of the school have supplied the majority of Sunday school teachers. As Anne Boylan has remarked, "in founding and teaching Sunday schools, evangelical women helped both to enlarge women's sphere and to entrench and perpetuate the whole notion of separate gender spheres."[33]

Over the years, however, laypeople of both sexes have determined the ethos of the Sunday school. They have seen to it that the Sunday morning experience is marked by free discussion of the doctrinal and moral implications of biblical passages, the singing of familiar hymns, the study of maps of the Holy Land by children, memorization of Bible verses, and awards for attendance. A defender of this Sunday experience in the early twentieth century spoke the mind of some later generations as well. The Sunday school, he said, is sustained by "plain yeomanry who come from factory and office and farm, and take boys and girls an hour a week with no other compulsion than that of love, and with little other preparation than the love of God's Book and the hope to make it an instrument of salvation to those whom they teach."[34] If this defender of the Sunday school romanticized the institution, he certainly did not overstate its control by laypersons.

When reformers in the Religious Education Association and the divinity schools called for the reshaping of religious education in the churches with "scientific investigations," one of their targets was the old-time Sunday school. They found the uniform lesson plan insensitive to the levels of understanding appropriate to different age groups, and so they instituted graded lessons. They bristled at the lack of focus in the hustle and bustle of the typical Sunday school class, and so they trained ministers and educational directors in the importance of class decorum and room environment. They worried about the teachers' lack of sophistication in the Bible, and so they planned to train Sunday school teachers in the implications of biblical criticism. In short, the reformers were concerned about the amateurism of the Sunday school movement. In the words of Robert W. Lynn and Elliott Wright, "*Professional* leadership must take over. And why not? Experts were evident in public schools, social work and municipal life. Should Protestant education be different? Volunteer leaders, in the reformers' scheme, should be aided by a full-time 'director of religious education' if a congregation could afford one. If not, the minister was expected to assume the mantle of the professional."[35]

That summary of the professionalism of the reformers of the Sunday school movement points to the enormous commitment required for the task of transforming the educational program of the churches. The task required nothing less than the careful training of specialists in the divinity schools, as well as the careful training of Sunday school teachers themselves in the professional approach to their classes. Yet the summary points also to a contradiction inherent within the attempt to reform the Sunday school. The professionals would try to transform a folk religion with the ways of university specialization.

For the most part, the attempt to refurbish the Sunday school with theological specialties failed. Except for an interval in the 1950s, when an upswing in the acceptance of experiments in the mainline denominational Sunday schools paralleled a surge of widespread national interest in "mainline" religion as such, church educational curricula developed by specialists have not won wide appeal among church members. A number of factors have hindered the appeal. Educational programs under the direction of specialists are expensive, and during economic crises directors of religious education have been the first to be dropped from church staffs. Busy ministers who do not enjoy the assistance of associate ministers have been willing to let the church's educational program move right along under the control of nonspecialists. With the increasing divorce of the aims and methods of the public schools from the religious viewpoint of mainline Protestantism in the twentieth century, ministers of religious education have been unable to make connections between their tasks and those of the teachers who monopolize the time and attention of children during the week.

Clearly, however, specialization in religious education also has accounted for the lack of appeal of church school reform. Movement beyond Bible stories to critical biblical scholarship, infusion of the long history of the Christian church into the awareness of the contemporary Christian, and reflection upon contemporary social and personal dilemmas within the framework of theology and ethics have required a level of sophistication the rank-and-file volunteer church school teachers and their pupils have had neither the time nor the motivation to develop. The failed attempt to transform the people's religion with the methods of specialized scholarship has led one scholar of religious education to take hope only from what has become a phoenix-like situation: religious education has moved "from excitement and euphoria to depression and confusion, from certainty about its self-understanding and mission to uncertainty and a fresh search."[36]

## DIVINITY SCHOOLS AND "HIGHER" RELIGIOUS EDUCATION

University divinity schools sought to influence "higher" as well as "lower" education. The efforts in both directions were conceived as closely related components of the educational system involved in the university training of a broad-based ministry.

Ph.D.'s and M.A.'s in divinity school specialties have long been awarded by the graduate divisions of the universities, but most of the education has been carried out by divinity school faculty, the same faculty who oversee the education of professional ministers. Furthermore, until recently, the Ph.D. in any of the divinity school specialties was viewed as preparation for the "teaching ministry." In the early 1940s, the dean of Harvard Divinity School, Willard L. Sperry, offered a justification for basing a newly established Ph.D. in the area of the history and philosophy of religion in the Divinity School rather than in a separately constituted department of religion. His position on the issue was typical of divinity school educators until the 1970s. Sperry said of the new graduate program: "Hereafter, we can allow a man who has taken his S.T.B. [the three-year professional ministerial degree] with us to continue residence in the Divinity School as a candidate for the Ph.D. . . . The new arrangement will enable us to prepare here at Harvard a few men for the type of work represented by a college chaplaincy linked to a teaching position in a department of religion. Such men must be ordained ministers, but for academic purposes need the Ph.D."[37] Clearly for Sperry and other divinity school educators of the time, college and university teaching was a form of Christian ministry.

Graduate work in the theological disciplines represented only a part of the divinity schools' attempt to influence the college and university world. Until the 1970s, many of the schools included within their departments of religious education a curriculum for those who would not go on for the Ph.D. but who aspired to be teachers, chaplains, campus ministers, and YMCA workers at American colleges and universities. Other schools instituted separate departments or programs in "religion in higher education" for students bound for one of those roles in colleges and universities. In the late 1940s and early 1950s, Yale Divinity School assumed national leadership in this area, offering courses to ministers in the "problems of religion in higher education and their significance for the university religious worker and teacher of religion." Areas of study included "the church-related college, the teaching of religion, the Student Christian Associations, the schools of religion, the newer plans for the official leadership of religious programs, and the World Student Christian Federation."[38] All of the divinity schools, if with less ambition and with the allocation of fewer resources than Yale, provided for such functions of religion in higher education as various forms of the Protestant ministry.

Beginning in the late 1960s, the growth of religious studies programs in state universities would force a clear separation between teaching about religion and the ministry. Until then, however, the divinity schools offered within the area of religious education a united set of strategies aimed as much at the college campus as at the local congregation. The history of the development of those strategies is disclosed in the career of an organization closely aligned with the divinity schools for a half-century, the National Council on Religion in Higher Education.

The founder of the Council, Charles Foster Kent, the Woolsey Professor of Biblical Literature at Yale, was distressed at the general condition of the study of religion in American colleges and universities. His motive for improving that condition was not altogether altruistic. In a speech at a meeting of the Eastern Region of the Association of College Teachers of the Bible in 1911, Kent revealed that his concern for the sorry state of religious studies in colleges and universities was at base a concern for theological seminaries, and particularly for his own field of biblical studies in the seminaries:

> ... it is the right and duty of the theological seminaries to demand with increasing insistence that the students who come to them shall have had, while in college, certain fundamental biblical courses. The recent expansion of the curriculum of the theological seminary makes this step necessary, but American colleges can meet, or can be made to meet, this demand. Unless the theological seminaries take this step they will certainly lose a great opportunity.[39]

Kent was perturbed by the neglect of primary texts and foreign languages on the part of colleges, a neglect that forced seminaries like Yale to engage in remedial education instead of getting on with their education of students in advanced specialties. Nonetheless, Kent cautioned that in providing better training to prospective seminarians, colleges should also pay attention to the practical religious experience of those students. He proposed the requirement of a college course in the "Educational Values of the Bible" in which the Bible would be studied for its implications for the development of the religious lives of students.[40] In his speech, Kent captured the fundamental aims of the Council which he would help found in 1922. For over fifty years the organization would devote itself simultaneously to the improvement of the academic study of religion in colleges and universities and to the promotion of the religious lives of faculty and students at those institutions. The pursuit of both aims entailed the attempted interweaving of the educational purposes of the divinity school with the larger purposes of higher education.

Following visits to several large midwestern state universities in 1921, Kent returned to New Haven and discussed with prominent persons in business, religion, and education his strategies for fostering the growth of independent schools of religion in the vicinity of state universities and for educating more faculty in the academic field of religion. In 1922, the National Council of Schools of Religion was incorporated to pursue these strategies; in 1924, the name of the organization was changed to the National Council of Religion in Higher Education in order to emphasize the second strategy, the graduate training of faculty. The Council's activities eventually included the competitive selection and funding of graduate Fellows; an annual "week of work," which was a hybrid of a learned society meeting and a family reunion; a publication program of books, bulletins, and research reports; a consulting and placement service designed to expand the study of religion in colleges and universities and to secure

jobs for Fellows in those institutions; a series of conferences to enhance
the religious and psychological counseling of students by faculty, deans,
and campus ministers; and consultations on how best to expose undergraduates to the study of religion. This extensive program of activities
was supported financially by gifts from John D. Rockefeller, Jr., as well
as from the Hazen, Dodge, Lilly, and Danforth foundations. In 1962, the
Council found new, much-needed funding as the Danforth Foundation
took over the operation of the Kent Fellowships, opened membership in
the Council to Danforth Teaching Fellows (who represented several academic fields), and changed the name of the organization to the Society
for Religion in Higher Education.[41]

The history of the programs and publications of the Council (and Society) illustrates the manner in which the organization responded to
the changing environment of higher education in America. In the first
twenty years of its existence, it sought through research to determine the
extent of the study of religion on American campuses, and through conferences and fellowships to develop strategies to magnify religion's presence in higher education. Those efforts reflected Kent's conviction that
religion courses were "pitiably disproportionate to the total undergraduate student body."[42] In the 1940s and 1950s, without totally abandoning
the emphasis of the first period, the conferences, research, and books un-
derwritten by the organization stressed the role of religion as an academically and experientially unifying force for a Western civilization torn
apart by a tragic world war and facing the threat of nuclear extinction.
Also during that phase, the Council developed textbooks for an expanding college curriculum in New Testament, Old Testament, and Eastern
religions. During the 1960s and 1970s, the Society commissioned examinations of the role of religious studies in the tax-supported universities
that were rapidly expanding in the field, provided fellowships for cross-
disciplinary work and for women scholars, and stepped up its support
of the study of Asian religions, an area which was gaining popularity
among undergraduates.[43] The changing emphases of the organization
founded by Charles Foster Kent reflected the trends of religion in higher
education in the twentieth century.

The organization has served as more than a mirror of changing trends,
however. Throughout most of its history it has provided a set of tactics by
which Protestant university divinity schools sought to influence American higher education. From the outset, the Council was deliberately elitist in its selection of Fellows. The best and the brightest students were
sought out to receive financial aid for their graduate training in religion

as a way of building a pool of well-prepared teachers.[44] Although the Council was open to members of diverse religions and to "seekers," the Fellows and officers were overwhelmingly Protestant, and most of them obtained their graduate specialization in Protestant university-related divinity schools such as Kent's Yale.[45] Members of the Council developed through their conferences and their annual "weeks of work" an intimate professional and personal network, and the Council's placement service proved to be an effective means of assisting divinity-school-educated Fellows to gain positions of influence in colleges and universities. An officer of the Council reported in 1951 on an increasing "number of requests for help of many sorts, particularly in the matter of teaching personnel, which come to our office from educational institutions." He also pointed with some pride to "the important positions which the Fellows increasingly hold. Frank Aydelotte, formerly president of Swarthmore and later director of the Institute for Advanced Studies, and American Secretary to the Rhodes Trustees, has said that our selection of Fellows has panned out better than any comparable process he knows about."[46]

The Council's emphasis on the placement of well-educated Fellows in positions of influence in higher education did not eclipse its commitment to Charles Foster Kent's aim of increasing the practice of religion in higher education. Fellows and officers of the Council were dedicated to the spread of the "Judeo-Christian" religious tradition throughout the lives of students and faculty, especially in the large public and private universities that were attracting so many of the nation's college students. In the words of Clarence Prouty Shedd, director of Yale Divinity School's model program in Religion in Higher Education and author of one of the Council's Hazen Foundation pamphlets on religion and education, "If we really believe that there is an inescapable university function in the field of religion, then we will set ourselves to the task of putting religion at the heart of the educational process, as a guiding, motivating, and integrating force."[47] According to Merrimon Cuninggim—Shedd's student, a Kent Fellow, and the Danforth executive who fused the Danforth and Kent programs in the 1960s—religion could perform an integrating function on campus only if provision is made for "all the various ways in which religion lends itself to human expression and ministers to human need," in worship, counseling, social action, and the examination of religious issues in the several university disciplines, as well as in the study of religion in separate departments or schools.[48]

Thus the Council endorsed, supported, and perpetuated the university divinity schools' creation of a profession of religion in higher education that would join specialized theological education with the several campus religious activities in order to shape and unify the modern American university. In the judgment of one Council leader in the 1950s, campus religious leaders increasingly "have viewed the ministry to student religion as a totality, and have seen the division of labor between the classroom teacher, the college chaplain, the church foundation, and the Christian Associations as of secondary importance."[49] The relegation of such divisions to secondary importance very much conformed to the Council's attempt to combine practical, experiential religion with scholarship among its Fellows. It accorded, as well, with the divinity schools' dedication to that combination as they prepared the Fellows for their integrated ministry on American campuses.

In 1976, following considerable debate, the Society for Religion in Higher Education changed its name to the Society for Values in Higher Education. The name change reflected a new situation both within the Society and within the area of religion in higher education. That year, 1976, the Society had received the last of its regular funding from the Danforth Foundation as the Danforth board decided to concentrate its grants elsewhere. Broadening the work of the Society into the area of values was in part an attempt to meet an impending financial crisis by enlarging membership appeal to those outside the field of religious studies and by expanding the grounds for support from other funding agencies. The name change was a response, as well, to developments in the academic study of religion in American colleges and universities. The American Academy of Religion, created in 1964 out of the older National Association of Biblical Instructors, had become the professional society appropriate to the work of academic specialists in the field of religion. In order to avoid duplication of the mission of the AAR and to perform a function neglected by societies defined by academic specialization, the Society chose to promote the study and spread of moral values in higher education. In making that choice, the Society emphasized a heritage implicit in its original charge to make religion pervasive among faculty and students. And in expanding its membership beyond scholars in religious studies, it built upon its recent history of support for multidisciplinary and interdisciplinary scholarship.[50]

The history of the National Council and its successors is an index of the changing mission of university divinity schools to American higher education. Conceived, like the deliberately elitist Council, as a way of elevating the scholarly expertise of teachers of religion in colleges and universities (as well as a means of training seminary teachers), divinity school graduate programs gave birth to advanced, specialized disciplines and a professionalized field that would overflow the boundaries of a close personal network of Fellows and the Pan-Protestant commitment to the values of the "Judeo-Christian tradition." Most divinity schools, in keeping with the aims of the Council, originally understood the purpose of graduate programs as preparation for a form of a widespread and integrated "campus ministry." By the 1970s, however, graduate programs in university divinity schools no longer required as a basis for doctoral work the Master of Divinity degree, the degree designed for ordained ministers. And special, extensive curricula in "religion and higher education" had been dropped from divinity school catalogues, replaced by a campus ministry "field experience" or "vocational track" as one of several ministerial options available to divinity school students.

In the 1960s and 1970s, a field known as "religious studies" would emerge on university campuses and would challenge the links binding ministry to scholarship, and theological studies to the study of religion. Before those decades, however, the Council on Religion and Higher Education had illustrated the effort of divinity schools to shape the American university with a unified system of "higher religious education."

## OBSTACLES TO THE FORMATION OF A SYSTEM

Protestantism's considered adoption of university specialization as a strategy for ministerial education and cultural influence was joined with the conviction that religious learning could be preserved in its wholeness. Education of ministers in university divinity schools was to be a part intimately connected with other parts in an interconnected system of education. Those who envisioned the purposes of the divinity schools believed that American Protestantism contained a tradition of practical piety and a pattern of religious devotion that could unite even where specialization might try to divide. And the espousal of specialized academic expertise in the different areas of divinity had a singularity of purpose: it was meant to meet an educational need of the American people inside and outside the walls of the university. Protestantism's divinity schools thus were thought of as places of practical piety, as extensions of the church at worship, as well as locations for the pursuit of discrete academic disciplines. And their mission was to be coextensive with a unified system of religious education aimed at the culture as a whole.

Given the shattering effects of specialization, it is remarkable that the divinity schools managed to attain even a measure of a unified educational system. Until the 1960s, most of the schools were able to provide their students with serviceable opportunities for worship, devotion, and work in the churches. If clearly subordinate to the exigencies of scholarship, these opportunities allowed for the continued practice of religion and served as reminders that the scholarship was intended to facilitate the work of the church's ministry. The divinity schools also were able to export some specialized knowledge to the educational programs of the churches. Though usually greeted with skepticism by the laity and sometimes by neglect on the part of the clergy, divinity school inspired religious education did place professionals in the church schools, did open to some laypersons a world of learning beyond Bible stories and map study, and did introduce graded lessons into the denominational curricula. The divinity schools also were successful for a while in fostering an interconnected religious system in higher education. The persons educated by the schools for that task never managed to make religion a fully pervasive or unifying force in the university. With the assistance of such agencies as the National Council on Religion in Higher Education, however, they did manage to forge some connections among the functions of teaching, counseling, and the various campus ministries.

Ultimately the strategies for creating an integrated system of education were defeated by the responses to, and the effects of, specialization. Divinity school educators underestimated or misunderstood some powerful forces circulating through modern America. The folk religion of the church schools proved to be more staunchly lay-led than specialty-educated professionals had bargained for. The university proved to be too diverse in its functions, and its social foundations too pluralistic in their composition, to be encompassed by a unified strategy of "religion in higher education." Yet problems also inhered in the very adoption of specialization as the manner of educating ministers. The demands and standards of specialized scholarship were so heavy that they could be balanced with the practice of piety by few faculty and students. Ministerial candidates' advanced work in the disciplines of church history, theology, and biblical studies inevitably meant that their educational levels in religion would far outstrip those of the people they were preparing to lead in the churches. And university-level specialization offered to divinity school faculty and their graduate students its own professional rewards—national recognition through published research, tenured faculty posts, and association with colleagues in cognate university disciplines—none of which were coupled with the daily lives of people in the pews.

The divinity schools' strategies of cultural influence, based upon visions of an interconnected system of educational parts, met the obstacles of the fragmenting consequences of specialized study and specialized professional function. That outcome would by no means prevent the divinity schools from continuing to appropriate both the aura and the approaches of university specialization. In fact, adoption of specialization would lead to notable achievements in scholarship and professional standing among divinity school faculty. Yet the schools would continue to struggle with the question of what, if anything, united their fields of study and gave overall purpose to their educational tasks.

# CHAPTER II

■

## *Educating to Understand the Other*

In many respects, the visions of the university divinity schools at their founding sprang from the heritage of nineteenth-century evangelical Protestantism. Even Harvard Divinity School, which did not grow out of that tradition and which continued for decades to represent a kind of Unitarianism in principle, did embrace a perspective on education identical in its essential parts to that of the schools which owed their origins to the evangelical denominations of the Methodists, Baptists, Congregationalists, and Presbyterians. It was a perspective that envisioned the merging of Protestantism with the life of the nation and called for a system of educational strategies appropriate to that amalgamation. The strategy of specialized scholarship was originally bent toward that visionary purpose.

The attempt to win America to Protestantism through education required the cooperation of Protestants across the denominational divisions that had multiplied on the American scene. There were obstacles to that cooperation. As Martin Marty has observed about the difficulties that would face the twentieth-century ecumenical movement, "the Protestant churches in the past had made greater gains through their divisions than they could have made as a united church. These diverse churches reached different sections of the country and appealed to different temperaments."[1] Nevertheless, many of the Anglo-Saxon Protestant churches in the nineteenth century had recognized the need for cooperation. If the West were to be won for their brand of Protestantism, if lawlessness in the new nation were to be eliminated, if the Protestant religion were to govern the morals, education, and practices of the American people, then the denominations must find ways to overcome their differences. They found those ways in their Bible societies, missionary societies, Sunday school associations, tract societies, and a host of other voluntary associations. Although hardly united into one Protestant church, many nineteenth-century Protestant denominations acknowledged in practice the power of collaboration in common causes.

One of those causes was the "Other"—other religious (including other Christian) viewpoints, other cultures, and other national origins. Cooperation across denominational lines was spurred by the intermingling of the desire to address the Other with the hope of shaping the nation. Congregationalists and Presbyterians joined forces in the American Home Missionary Society, and most of the evangelical denominations joined together in the American Evangelical Alliance, to preserve the country from the non-Protestant and "undemocratic" forces of "Romanism," "Mormonism," "rationalism," and European "sectarianism."

Josiah Strong, leader in the Home Missionary Society and then the general secretary of the Evangelical Alliance, published in 1886 a book that synthesized for thousands of evangelical Protestants hopes for a Protestant America and fears of forces that threatened those hopes. Strong's *Our Country*, which had sold 175,000 copies by 1916 and was excerpted in newspapers and magazines across the country, was a vigorous call for evangelicals to adopt a social gospel directed to the modern social problems of urbanization, monopolization of wealth, illiteracy, alcoholism, and poverty. Strong's social gospel flowed from his conviction that America's future depended upon the triumph of Anglo-Saxon Protestantism, preserver both of the civil liberties of Western civilization and of "pure spiritual Christianity." Strong thought that such a future could be assured only by an aggressive Protestant evangelism dedicated to erasing the perils presented by European immigrants untutored in democratic principles, Catholics allegedly obedient to the authority of Rome rather than to the laws of the land, and Mormons united by an "ecclesiastical despotism."[2] These others were believed to constitute threats to the very future of the nation. By symbolizing what Anglo-Saxon Protestants were not, they also became germane to the self-definition of many nineteenth-century evangelicals.[3]

For all of the harmony and sense of identity that the perils of the Other could arouse among American Protestants, the perils alone could not ensure a unified strategy for dealing with them. What exactly did it mean to eliminate the threats? What means were at the disposal of Protestants for maintaining control over the religion, morals, and behavior of the American people in the face of religious groups that would not assimilate into Anglo-Saxon Protestantism? In the Evangelical Alliance in the 1870s, Protestant leaders were beginning to disagree over the answers to these questions as well as over such frequently noted issues as Darwinism, the social gospel, and the meaning of biblical authority.[4] Philip Schaff, a German-educated Swiss immigrant who taught church history at Union Seminary, invited his fellow evangelicals to look beyond the nineteenth-century "popish" forms of Roman Catholicism to a longer Catholic history which was part of their own story as Christians. And Roswell Hitchcock, Schaff's colleague in church history at Union, although fearful of papal influences on the lives of the American people, advised other evangelicals to look into any Christian face and find in it "something of the old family likeness."[5] Schaff's and Hitchcock's means of dealing with the perils inherent in the differences of other religious people, in this case Catholic Christians, contrasted sharply with other evangelicals like Strong who called for efforts to convert, civilize, and educate the differences away.[6]

In short, nineteenth-century evangelicals divided over whether the non-Protestant Other should first of all be understood or be converted. And, as the century drew to a close, the issue was complicated by consideration of the aims of understanding. For what purpose should those who are different be understood? For the sake of evangelization? for collaboration? for the sake of self-recognition? for the purpose of understanding as an end in itself? Questions such as these gained vivid embodiment at the World Parliament of Religions in Chicago, where, during the World's Fair in 1893, many Americans, including educators at university divinity schools, were exposed for the first time to religious and cultural differences quite beyond the domestic "perils" of Romanism, Mormonism, rationalism, and sectarianism. And some of the emergent aims of the specialized study of other religions and cultures clustered together at the Parliament.

## MUSEUMS AND TEACHERS

When William F. Warren, president of Boston University and professor of the comparative study of religion in Boston's School of Theology, learned of plans to include a Parliament of the world's religions at the Chicago World's Fair, he sent a letter of endorsement to the organizers of the Parliament:

> I am glad to know that the World's Religions are to be represented at the World's Fair. Were they to be omitted, the sense of incompleteness would be painful. Even a museum of idols and objects used in ceremonial wor-

ship would attract beyond any other museum. Models and illustrations of the great temples of the world and of the world's history would be in a high degree instructive. Add to these things the living word of living teachers, and the whole world may well pause to listen.[7]

Warren's hopes for the Parliament were realized in many ways. Of the twenty congresses at the Fair held on such topics as art, women's progress, government, literature, and medicine, the gathering of representatives of the religions of the world attracted the largest crowds and evoked the most commentary in print.[8] The response was not uniformly appreciative. The Archbishop of Canterbury sent word that he could not approve the Parliament because Christianity is the one true religion and "I do not understand how that religion can be regarded as a member of a Parliament of Religions without assuming the equality of the other intended members and the parity of their position and claims."[9] The General Assembly of the Presbyterian Church in the U.S.A. passed a resolution disapproving the Parliament for the same reasons. Letters and articles by conservative evangelical Christians called the event a "masterpiece of Satan" and an occasion when "God's elect flirted with the daughters of Moab."[10] For most of the thousands of people who crowded into the sessions extending over seventeen days, however, the Parliament was a chance to behold a spectacle of religious diversity and to listen in on exotic and scholarly teachings about the religions of the world. It would prove to be, as Warren had predicted, a mix of museum and teaching.

On the opening day, September 11, 1893, four thousand spectators witnessed a procession of representatives of the world's faiths file to a platform under the waving flags of many nations. The Roman Catholic cardinal James Gibbons of the United States assumed center stage, clad in scarlet robes and surrounded by the red, yellow, orange, and white attire of Buddhists, Hindus, and Muslims.[11]

The sessions were not all spectacle, however. Those in attendance heard proponents and scholars of religion from around the world reflect upon the modern import of the world's living faiths. Swami Vivekananda of India recounted a fable to illustrate the human propensity to magnify a particular religious perspective. P. C. Mozoomdar's outline of Brahmo-Somaj, a synthesis of Hinduism and Christianity, brought the audience to its feet in applause. Mohammed Alexander Russell Webb's description of the "Spirit of Islam" evoked from the auditors hisses and cries of "Shame!" American Protestant leaders and scholars were well represented among the speakers. A gravely ill Philip Schaff, ignoring his physician's advice, made some brief remarks on "the cause of Christian Union" and prepared a paper on Christian unity read at a session by a stand-in. Spokesmen for the social gospel—Washington Gladden, Francis Peabody, Richard Ely, and Albion Small—dealt with the need for religion's response to the social and economic problems created by industrialization and urbanization. Scholarly papers by George S. Goodspeed of the University of Chicago, George Park Fisher of the Yale Divinity School, and Thomas Dwight of Harvard University addressed, respectively, the themes of "What the Dead Religions Have Bequeathed to the Living," "Christianity an Historical Religion," and "Man in the Light of Science and Religion."[12]

The Parliament was not as pluralistic as the range of viewpoints might suggest. A Protestant, modern American perspective pervaded the sessions of the congress. The initial act of worship following the pageantry of the procession was the singing of the Watts-Wesley version of the Old One Hundredth, with organ accompaniment. Each day the sessions were opened with the recitation of the Lord's Prayer. The chairman of the organizing committee, John Henry Barrows, minister of the First Presbyterian Church in Chicago, used the concluding session of the Parliament to express the driving religious conviction behind his months of hard work: "I desire that the last words which I speak to this Parliament shall be the name of Him to whom I owe life and truth and hope and all things, who reconciles all contradictions, pacifies all antagonisms, and who from the throne of His heavenly kingdom directs the serene and unwearied omnipotence of redeeming love—Jesus Christ, the Saviour of the world." A similar religious outlook had informed the planning for the Parliament. The expressed aims of the event included the manifestation of "important truths the various Religions hold and teach in common"; the display of "the impregnable foundations of Theism, and the reasons for man's faith in Immortality," which could provide for the strengthening of "the forces which are adverse to a materialistic philosophy of the universe"; and the discovery of the light that all the religions of the world could throw on the social problems of the day.[13]

The assumptions by the organizers of the Parliament about the tacit theism, fundamental harmony, and social relevance of the world's religions conformed to the controlling postulates of the World's Fair, or Columbian Exposition, as a whole. Clearly the Fair was designed to celebrate (one year late) the four hundredth anniversary of the discovery of America with material demonstrations of the American success story.

The overall theme was progress, attested in numerous exhibits of mechanical power, technical achievements, and scientific advancements. At the same time, the Fair aimed to spiritualize the material progress of America. The construction of a giant Fair City on a Chicago swampland portrayed an America aspiring to be known for more than its material progress. The all-white buildings, the symmetrical order of the entire fairgrounds, the neoclassic architecture of the Fair were attempts to drape the storms and stresses of the Industrial Revolution with an aura of the sublime.

The numerous congresses, including the Parliament on Religion, were intended to achieve the same end. The congresses took as their motto "Not Matter, But Mind; Not Things, But Men," and they announced as their philosophy that the crowning glory of the World's Fair "should not be the exhibit . . . of the material triumphs, industrial achievements, and mechanical victories of man, however magnificent that display may be. Something still higher and nobler is demanded by the enlightened and progressive spirit of the present age."[14] The World Parliament of Religions stood ready to supply the higher and nobler things. John Henry Barrows's testimony to an all-embracing redeemer, the use of the Lord's Prayer (what was called the "Universal Prayer") at the sessions, the organizers' aim of exhibiting truths common to all religions and productive of social peace—all these things signified an American Protestantism bent on infusing a tolerant religious harmony into the progressive spirit of the age.

The pervasive Protestant presence at the Parliament confirmed what Reid Badger has judged to be the significance of the entire Fair: "the Victorian era's attempt both to acknowledge the reality of rapid change and to understand and control its direction." The Fair illustrated "the age's faith that man could have his revolution and control it too."[15] That faith would deteriorate, beginning almost immediately with the Great Railway Strike of 1894 and terminating with the Great War and the Great Depression. The religious dimension of the Victorian faith would also fall apart. A tolerant, if domineering, Christian theism tied to a confidence in human progress and a belief in the universality of religious truth would give way before the shattering events of the early twentieth century and before a global pluralism that would not abide Christian hegemony.

Still, Protestantism had committed itself at the Parliament of Religions to a new posture toward the Other. The Protestants in attendance, unlike their conservative counterparts who dismissed the entire undertaking out of hand, indicated their conviction of the appropriateness of exposure to and understanding of other religions. As William F. Warren of Boston had said in his letter of endorsement, there was value to be gained in observing the objects and listening to the teachers of other religions. If such liberal Protestants were not altogether delivered from their fears of what the "perils of the others" meant for their attempt to control the destiny of Western civilization, they at least indicated their belief that the attempt to understand the religions of the world was the right way to go about dealing with their fears. So Warren and other divinity school professors set about to bring the realm of university specialization to bear upon diverse religions, including non-Protestant Christianity, and thereby educate Protestant ministers into the strange world of the Other.

## OTHER CHRISTIANS

Education of ministers into a Christian universe grander than that of the Protestant denomination was prompted by the disposition of scholars such as Union Seminary professors Philip Schaff and Roswell Hitchcock. The ability, in Hitchcock's words, to behold another Christian and find there "something of the old family likeness" required more than an act of charitable tolerance. It demanded an appreciation of the historically extensive and culturally diverse traditions that had made up the Christian story. Schaff caught the spirit of that requirement when, as founder and first president of the American Society of Church History in 1888, he insisted that the study of the history of the church could "prepare the way for the healing of the divisions of Christendom and unite all the worshippers of Christ." Rigorous study of the divisions of the church through the ages would reveal that "no one of them was perfect, but that they were mutually necessary to the other."[16] From the outset, the university divinity schools were motivated by a vision like that of Schaff. And as that vision increasingly attained institutional embodiment in ecumenical organizations, it would provide the principal intellectual setting for divinity education. As Yale Divinity School professor H. Richard Niebuhr would say in his assessment of theological education in the 1950s, "the primary context of Protestant theological education in the United States and Canada is the Christian community in its wholeness."[17]

One could expect the nondenominational and interdenominational schools to embrace the Christian community in its wholeness as the primary context of their educational ventures. Their alliance with the broad cultural tasks and professional programs of the modern university had entailed a repudiation of religious "sectarianism." "Sectarianism," the word used to connote the restriction of religious truth to the domain of a single church or denomination, would, in the language of Harvard President Charles Eliot, "impair the public confidence in the impartiality and freedom of the university."[18] In defiance of sectarianism, the divinity schools at Harvard, Chicago, Yale, and Union prepared ministers for diverse Protestant denominations, taught Protestant students to understand their denominational traditions within the larger context of the entire Christian community, and secured faculty from different Protestant churches—and eventually from the Roman Catholic church.

The same approaches to ministerial education were adopted by the Methodist schools. Although they would always understand their chief role to be the education of ministers within their own denomination and would continue to draw the large majority of their students and faculty from the Methodist church, the Methodist divinity schools were as ecumenical in their bearing as their nondenominational counterparts. At the Boston School of Theology in 1871, where the university charter allowed the School to insist on adherence to Methodist principles, the leadership of the School chose to subscribe to the law that applied to Boston University as a whole: "No instructor in said University shall ever be required by the Trustees to profess any particular religious opinions as a test of office, and no student shall be refused admission . . . on account of the religious opinions he may entertain."[19]

Some eighty years later, faculty of the divinity school at Boston would insist that it was precisely the ecumenical and university orientation of the Methodism created by John Wesley that prompted subscription to such a law and that gave tangibility to the ecumenical movement. With an eye doubtless cast toward their neighboring competitor, Harvard, the dean and the chairman of the curriculum committee at the Boston seminary claimed that "Ecumenicity in theological education is often wrongly, because superficially, identified with non-denominational schools. These non-denominational institutions have often made outstanding contributions through individual teachers and graduates. But they also tend to develop, in the soil of the Church, a superficial root system and to nourish the ecclesiastical docetism which accompanies so much ecumenical discussion."[20] Spokesmen for other Methodist divinity schools also proclaimed, if with less defensive edge to their voices, that Methodism boasted a heritage that could found an educational mission directed simultaneously to denominational specificity and Christian catholicity.[21]

A roll call of American luminaries actively involved in the different phases of the twentieth-century ecumenical movement would produce a long list of leaders from the university divinity schools. Chicago's Shailer Mathews served as president of the Federal Council of Churches. Union's William Adams Brown guided the work of the Conferences on Faith and Order and Life and Work which would issue in the World Council of Churches, and the same school's Henry P. Van Dusen helped steer the formation of the WCC. Boston's Walter G. Muelder was an active leader in the National Council of Churches and the World Council of Churches. SMU's Albert Outler, as a Protestant observer at Vatican II, was reputedly the most quoted person at the Council with the exception of the Pope.[22]

These were only a few of the numerous faculty, administrators, and alumni of university divinity schools who worked through the international, national, and local structures of the ecumenical movement to create understanding across the divisions of Christianity. They also labored to build a Christian coalition for meeting global social and economic problems, to promote the mergers of Protestant churches and denominations, and to foster cooperation among Christians and Jews. Their leadership was instrumental in the creation of the educational ethos of the schools. Their faculties became increasingly multidenominational, occasionally included Jewish scholars, and, particularly after the Catholic modernizations of Vatican II, incorporated Roman Catholics. Most of the schools increased their efforts to build religiously diverse student bodies, many found ways to share courses with non-Protestant schools through theological school unions and crossover registrations, and all developed their curricula within the context that H. Richard Niebuhr identified as "the Christian community in its wholeness."[23]

Understanding other Christians within that context was by no means construed as an end in itself. During most of the present century, education to understand other Christians was governed by the practical purpose of preserving Christianity's social influence in the world. To be sure, over the course of the century, the ecumenical spirit expanded the number of Christian communities it would embrace, and it changed its view of the nature of social influence. Before the Second World War, the Federal Council of Churches, for example, functioned as a kind of Protestant state church. It slighted denominational differences, provided mainstream Protestant denominations access to powerful decision makers in government and business, appointed carefully selected representatives from those denominations to key Council offices and projects, and opposed U.S. alignments with the Vatican.[24] During this same period, ecumenical education in the Protestant divinity schools was understood as the production of nonsectarian Protestant ministers capable of exercising a unified Protestant Christian influence upon an increasingly heterogenous American culture.[25] With the formation of the World Council of Churches during the Second World War and the National Council of Churches in 1950, and with the emergence of dialogue and cooperation between Protestants and Catholics following the Second Vatican Council in the 1960s, American Protestant leaders in the divinity schools emphasized an ecumenical education inclusive in its scope, cooperative in its attitude, and increasingly non-Western in its sanctions.

Nevertheless, until the 1960s the purpose of Christian unity remained that of influencing the world social order. In 1945, Henry P. Van Dusen, ecumenical leader and newly appointed president of Union Theological Seminary, stated a conviction widely shared by divinity school educators throughout the United States. The role of the ecumenical divinity school, Van Dusen said, is to educate Christian leaders into an awareness of their participation in a world Christian community. Such a sense of unity is the *sine qua non* of practical Christian influence:

> The halting of secularism, the reclamation of education, the confrontation of Government, the amelioration of social disease and disorder, the reaching of the unchurched—the most flagrant bypassed job of the churches—to each there is only one answer: the massed Christian strength of all churches directed unitedly upon common responsibilities. In a world crying for the healing of its divisions and breaking to pieces for lack of it, the Churches have no right to exert a significant influence—and they certainly will not in fact do so—so long as they perpetuate in their own beings the very infection of disorder and disunity which requires cure. Unity is, first of all, the clear counsel of expediency, of practical statesmanship.[26]

Van Dusen's pronouncement was no social gospel of the late nineteenth and early twentieth centuries, cast in terms of the progress of the Anglo-Saxon race or pinned to the power of an American empire. Yet it echoed a theme of that earlier gospel. Like the social gospelers present at the World's Fair in Chicago, Van Dusen insisted that only a unified faith is sufficient to heal the wounds inflicted by the modern world. And like the founders of the Federal Council of Churches in 1908, he pressed for the practical consequences of Christian unity. One of the chief purposes of the Federal Council was "to secure a larger combined influence for the churches of Christ in all matters affecting the moral and social conditions of the people, so as to promote the application of the law of Christ in every relation of human life."[27] For Van Dusen, as well, the purpose of ecumenism, and of ecumenical education, was the practical, even the expedient, influence of a unified Christianity on all regions of human life.

In 1969, former Union Seminary professor and active ecumenist Robert McAfee Brown could lament, "These are tough times for the ecumenical movement." Brown believed that a definite downturn had occurred for the movement. "Again and again one hears the estimate 'Ecumenism has had it,' with the implication that the movement peaked somewhere around the end of Vatican II and has been going downhill ever since."[28] Brown was observing a critical transition that had taken place in the ecumenical movement. Indeed, if defined by its institutional expressions in councils of churches, large-scale denominational mergers, and divinity school education, ecumenicity in America had peaked and begun its decline in the 1960s. Displays of Christian unity would continue to appear in the charismatic movement, in the mutual recognition of ministries, in local church mergers, in alliances among evangelicals, and in diverse divinity school student bodies. But the spirit of a far-flung, well-organized ecumenical movement influencing diverse domains of the social order with a unified Christianity had been broken.

An assortment of interconnected circumstances had arisen in the 1960s and 1970s to undermine the large-scale institutional ecumenism of mid-century. Students at institutions of higher education, including those attending university divinity schools, protested the authoritarianism and inflexibility of American institutions and their bureaucracies, challenged the Western imperialism implicit in visions of Christian influence, and rebelled against the sluggishness of the "establishment" in responding to conditions of social injustice. At the same time, many laypeople in American churches, already feeling estranged from the complex national and international ecumenical organizations dominated by the clergy, resisted the social activism of ministers beholden to such organizations rather than to local churches. Laypeople were also polarized by the positions that church councils took when condemning racial segregation, U.S. involvement in Vietnam, and Western capitalism's effects in the Third World. Furthermore, decline in membership between 1960 and 1980 among the Protestant denominations supporting ecumenical organizations led to a decrease in money available to ecumenical councils.[29]

Robert McAfee Brown was right: the ecumenical movement had entered "tough times," and it could no longer define the context of divinity education. In 1985, Joseph Hough and John Cobb, professors at the Claremont School of Theology, complained, "Unfortunately, little attention is paid to the World Council of Churches at any level of North American church life. This is true even of most seminaries."[30] ·

That complaint, however, sounded a call for a new form of divinity education and a new ecumenical awareness appropriate to the 1980s. Hough and Cobb recommended that the divinity schools provide for a straightforwardly "practical education," one premised on the need for church leaders and divinity faculty to develop a "global consciousness."

> Thinking in a global context cannot be taken for granted. Most North American whites have little understanding of what is occurring among blacks in the United States. They have even less knowledge of the world beyond their borders. A central task of the church, therefore, is to widen the horizons within which life is understood. If the church's future leaders are to do this, the seminary needs to help them widen their own horizons. Exposure to key elements of the global reality is essential to theological education.[31]

The sense of interconnectedness within the "global village," Hough and Cobb suggested, requires on the part of the educated minister an understanding of the diversity of the constitutive elements of that village. Visions of the social influence of a Christianity springing from unity of religious purpose and strategy have been replaced by views of a global relatedness engendered by knowledge of cultural and religious difference.

Throughout the 1980s, proponents of revision in theological education issued calls for the "globalization" of the educational task. During that decade, the Association of Theological Schools (ATS), the accrediting body for over two hundred seminaries in the United States and Canada, made "globalization" a recurrent theme at its biennial meetings and commissioned several studies of the theme by theological school leaders. The theme turned out to carry multiple meanings, some of them incompatible. Don Browning of the Divinity School at the University of Chicago discerned four distinct meanings of "globalization" among his associates in theological education: the church's mission to evangelize the globe; the call for ecumenical cooperation among Christians throughout the world; the need for dialogue between Christianity and other religions; and the requirement that Christianity improve the lives of the poor and the politically disadvantaged around the globe.[32] By crosscutting Browning's definitions with variables from social analysis, Mark Heim of Andover Newton Theological School came up with twenty minimal meanings of "globalization."[33]

ATS case studies of several theological schools also produced a variety of interpretations of the term. Joseph Hough described a wide-ranging program at Claremont that placed theological education in the context of international affairs. Jane Smith pointed to Harvard Divinity School's long-standing tradition of studying the Christian traditions in the light of the religions and value systems of the world. Kosuke Koyama emphasized Union Seminary's continuing heritage of examining Christianity in terms of worldwide ecumenism.[34]

By the end of the decade, the ATS Task Force on Globalization, while celebrating the fact that a majority of its institutions deemed globalization "more than important," had to admit that it "struggled with the need to lay a firm theological and intellectual basis for the Association's work in globalization without supporting a particular perspective or definition of globalization."[35] Globalization, it would appear, had become more buzzword than concept.

Amid the swirl of disparate definitions, however, the emphasis on globalization in the 1980s exemplified the growing importance of religious, cultural, ethnic, racial, and class *difference* in theological education. The "Christian community in its wholeness" that H. Richard Niebuhr had detected as the aura of Protestant theological education in the 1950s had been supplanted by an atmosphere of pluralism that nourished Christianity in its diverse contexts. The purpose of understanding other Christians was not the achievement of unity of social influence. The purpose, rather, was to preserve the integrity of otherness and to allow diverse Christians access to their own power and influence. As the ATS Task Force on Globalization stated in its vision for theological education, the curriculum should make explicit "the multicultural nature of Biblical sources" and the "cultural contexts of various theological approaches." It should examine "various forms of pastoral practice" in the light of "diverse cultural conditions." Faculty should be "multicultural in composition," and leadership in the schools should reflect "powersharing with groups within the theological community."[36]

The ATS report insisted that its multicultural vision stood as a condemnation of Western ethnocentrism that endured in most theological schools.[37] Yet the vision had grown out of movements in the Protestant divinity schools of the 1960s and 1970s. Those years were marked by student and faculty demands for cultural and ethnic diversity within their own ranks, the emergence of liberation theologies directed to the causes of blacks, women, and Latin Americans, and the turn of the attention of social ethicists to conditions within the Third World.[38] The theme of globalization in the 1980s was born in the pluralistic tumult of the 1960s and 1970s.

Both the tumult and the vision in the divinity schools were parts of the larger scene in American higher education. The schools were very much the partners of their universities in affirmative action hiring, the repudiation of a fixed canon of Western literary texts and philosophical perspectives, and expressions of concern for the distinctive positions of power and powerlessness defined by race, class, and gender.[39]

But the divinity schools also aligned themselves with new forces within the worldwide ecumenical movement, forces that reflected a changed political situation in the world. As neglected as the work of the World Council of Churches may have been in the seminary curriculum, as crippled as ecumenical councils had been by controversy and loss of finances, a new form of ecumenism occasioned the preoccupation with globalization. The World Council, in particular, had changed in the 1960s from an organization dominated by the cultural and churchly interests of North Americans and Europeans to one oriented to the cultural and churchly interests of decolonized nations in Asia, Africa, and Latin America. When the WCC Assembly met in Nairobi in 1975, it condemned Western instances of racism, sexism, and the military-industrial complex. It defended the rights of the people of the world "freely to determine their political status and freely to pursue their economic, cultural, and social development." And it insisted that the principal theological challenge facing the churches was a theology of liberation for the oppressed peoples of the world.[40] In a keynote address at Nairobi, Robert McAfee Brown condemned the exploitation of Third World peoples by American business and called for the churches' defense of the full spectrum of the world's underprivileged races and cultures.[41]

In one sense, therefore, the ecumenical movement was still alive and well in the 1970s and 1980s, but the spirit of the movement had changed. Konrad Raiser, recently appointed as the general secretary of the World Council of Churches, has described the change in terms of a shift away from an old theological paradigm toward a new paradigm not yet fully developed. The former theological model of the ecumenical movement stressed the visible unity of the Christian church predicated on the universal significance of the Christ. The quest for a new model is now underway that honors the variety within and between churches and that respects the distinctive differences of sex, class, and race.[42] Certainly for those American Protestant theologians who construe ecumenicity in terms of globalization, unity among Christians no longer is to be understood as a means toward the end of social and cultural influence. For them, the paradigm shift entails making unity the end itself, sought through the process of respecting social and cultural difference. As one liberation theologian has put it, "the order of knowing and doing" in this new ecumenical age "moves from the particular to the universal," and solidarity among peoples arises from "a constantly expanding human universe of particularity and of new experiences."[43]

An order of knowing that moves from the particular to the universal has laid an increased demand upon the divinity schools to expand their specialties. That demand had appeared in the older form of ecumenical education as well, as courses and faculty expertise were added in such areas as Roman Catholicism, Eastern Orthodoxy, denominational history, and the historical and geographical development of the ecumenical movement itself. With the rise of globalization and the study of Christians in their particularity, however, the need for specialties increased. In addition to understanding the theology, history, and ethics of other Christians, the Protestant divinity school student who would cultivate a global perspective should understand the social, cultural, and economic conditions that account for much of the otherness of those Christians. And an understanding of the particularities of race, class, and gender required the specialties of the social sciences and foreign languages. By the end of the 1980s, it was unclear what consequences would result from the new pressures for specialization. Most plans at the time called for the addition of a few new social science courses to the curricula but with an emphasis on imbuing the traditional areas of theology, history, Bible, and practical ministerial training with a global awareness of ethnic and cultural difference.[44]

Whatever the outcome of those plans, ecumenical education in the past adopted the principle of university specialization to educate Protestant ministers into the worlds of other Christians. And the schools adapted that specialized education to the changing aims of knowledge of the Other. There is no evidence that either the older ecumenical perspective or the newer outlook of globalization thoroughly unified the several parts of divinity education into a comprehensive whole, but the two viewpoints did create two distinctive educational environments that determined the ends of knowledge. Until the middle of the 1960s, the purpose of understanding other Christians through a study of their doctrines, history, and practices was the attainment of a sense of Christian unity. That unity, in turn, was thought to be a decisive force for Christianity's social influence around the world. With the shift in the 1960s toward contextual pluralism within the university and within the ecumenical movement, the purpose of understanding other Christians became the achievement of understanding itself. That understanding, it was hoped, could lead to a sense of relatedness among differences. Similar changes occurred in the divinity schools' aims in understanding the religions of the world.

## OTHER RELIGIONS

At the conclusion of the Third Assembly of the World Council of Churches in New Delhi in 1961, Methodist Bishop James K. Mathews summed up the development of much of the ecumenical movement: "The road to ecumenicity has been a missionary road."[45] Indeed, collaborative efforts in the foreign missions field had often led the way in ventures into Christian unity. The New Delhi Assembly recognized that fact when it integrated the International Missionary Council into the World Council on the grounds that "the purposes and functions of the two bodies are inseparable."[46] But it was also true that the road to the Protestant understanding of other religions had been a missionary road. In most university divinity schools, ecumenical education, training in world mission, and the study of world religions were closely entwined.

For all of the caricatures of missionaries abroad as imperialistic, uneducated, moralistic do-gooders, in the late nineteenth and early twentieth centuries they were among America's most highly educated in the dimensions of other cultures. As William Hutchison has remarked, "Missionaries on the whole belonged to the tiny cohort of the college-trained; and male missionaries generally had been educated beyond college. If deficient from a modern point of view in sensitivity to foreign cultures, they were measurably superior in that regard to most contemporaries at home or abroad." And their exposure to other cultures was not without long-range influence: missionary offspring accounted for roughly 50 percent of American foreign-affairs experts during the era of the Second World War.[47] University divinity schools occupied the center of the process of educating Americans into the strange world of other cultures through their courses on the history of the expansion of Christianity, their training schools for missionaries, their institutes on ecumenicity, and their curricula in world religions.

Representatives of the divinity schools took considerable pride in the effects of that process. Harlan Beach, first occupant of the chair of missions at Yale, could boast that as of 1901, one hundred sixty-two Yale graduates were serving as missionaries in twenty-eight different countries. Henry Sloane Coffin, president of Union Theological Seminary, estimated that during its first century one out of every twelve of Union's alumni had gone to a foreign missionary field. Bard Thompson, church history professor at Vanderbilt Divinity School, observed in 1958 that "at the International Missionary Council which met at Jerusalem at Eastertime of 1928, more representatives of Vanderbilt were present than of any other university in the world."[48] Similar glories could be claimed by the divinity schools at Boston, Drew, and Duke.[49]

The achievements so celebrated were not simply those of *sending* itself; they were the accomplishments of sending *educated* missionaries into other cultures. During the first half of the twentieth century, most of the schools established separate departments of missions, complete with a series of courses in the theology, history, and sociology of world missions. This move into specialization was prompted in large measure by the Student Volunteers for Foreign Missions and other "mission bands" of students eager to obtain training appropriate to the evangelization of the world. Until the mid-1960s, specialization in missions entailed the study of the world's diverse religions. In the divinity school at Southern Methodist University in the academic year 1954–55, for example, a newly installed curriculum required a course in "Christian Mission and Other Religions" that introduced all ministerial candidates to "the place of Christianity in the religious experience of mankind, the relations of the Christian community to the peoples of other cultures, and its unfinished missionary task in our own day."[50] And as late as 1961, at the divinity school of Boston University, which had shed its separate School of Religious Education aimed in great part at future missionaries, mission study was included in a Department of Ecumenics, Missions, and World Religions.[51]

The blending of the aims of ecumenicity, missions, and the study of world religions was not as simplemindedly apologetic as its critics have sometimes supposed. If the tendency of modern Americans has been to portray the missionary, *New Yorker* cartoon style, as an uneducated, bumbling innocent abroad, a similar inclination has appeared in the caricature of the missions-oriented study of world religions as a parochial defense of the Christian religion.[52] The apologetic approach to non-Christian religions was more diverse and more nuanced than this image suggests, and it represented only one position in a changing missionary philosophy of the world's religions.

Between the 1880s and the 1960s, the study of world religions aligned with the missionary enterprise adopted three distinct approaches at the divinity schools: the apologetic approach, which sought in more than one way to demonstrate the superiority of the Christian religion; the essentialist posture, which viewed all religions as different but equal expressions of one truth; and the mediating approach, which argued simultaneously for the superiority of Christianity and the continuities among all religions.[53]

The divinity school professors who pursued the apologetic approach were convinced that a comparison of the major religions of the world would reveal Christianity as the crowning glory of the human religious experience. Such a defense of the superiority of the Christian religion could assume any number of theological faces. Unitarian Transcendentalist James Freeman Clarke, lecturer in natural religion and Christian doctrine at Harvard from 1867 to 1877 and author of the widely used textbook *Ten Great Religions* (originally published in 1871 and reissued eighteen times), was fully abreast of British and German scholarship. He turned his scholarly apparatus to a description of the major beliefs and practices of ten "ethnic religions." Clarke, however, did not include Christianity among the ten. At the end of each chapter of his book he discussed Christianity as a faith that was catholic from its very inception, and in a concluding chapter he portrayed Christianity as a universal and progressive religious perspective designed eventually to enfold the other major religions of the world.[54]

Apologetic comparison sometimes could wear a stern countenance toward the Other. At the Candler School of Theology at Emory in 1915, professor of missions W. J. Young taught his students that religion is "a common possession of the race, found in some form everywhere, and indestructible." But he also taught them that the Christian religion is "the corrective of [other religions'] errors."[55] At Vanderbilt in the 1920s, professor of comparative religion and missions Oswald E. Brown elaborated on the "social and religious values" of Hinduism and on the "personal character, social ideals, and moral and religious teachings" of the Buddha in order to reveal their similarity, but also their comparative inferiority, to the "essential Christianity" of Jesus.[56] At Yale in the early twentieth century, Harlan Beach joined his teachings about missions with a conviction about Christianity's power progressively to civilize other religions.[57]

For the most part, the Christian apologists sought to combine scholarly inquiry into other religions with a defense of the doctrinal, moral, or civil superiority of Christianity. That combination was conspicuously illustrated in the career of William Warren, the president and professor of comparative religion at Boston University who expressed such excitement about the World Parliament of Religion. Warren studied oriental antiquities at Halle and archeology at Rome before going to Boston, and he kept current during his career with developments in the "science of religion" (*Religionswissenschaft*) in Germany and England. Warren's late nineteenth- and early twentieth-century courses at Boston approached the world's religions apologetically, as well as descriptively, comparatively, and philosophically. As professor of systematic theology and then the occupant of the first chair of comparative religion at an American divinity school, Warren required his students to attain competence in scholarly methods and apply to their study of religion the "auxiliary sciences" of sociology, history, and the philosophy of worldviews.[58]

Oxford don Louis Henry Jordan, outspoken critic of the confusion of Christian apologetics with the comparative study of religions, could say of Warren the apologist/comparativist in 1905, "The influence he has wielded on behalf of this new discipline [of the comparative study of religion], both directly and indirectly, and covering so long a period of time, has been of the very greatest value."[59] Warren was an exemplary case of the Christian apologist who, though scarcely judging all religions as equals, sought through the academic specialties to understand the religions of the world in their social, historical, cultural, and philosophical contexts. One purpose of that understanding was to demonstrate the preeminence of Christianity. But another purpose was to appreciate the value of religion as such in its diverse manifestations.

Undergirding the perspectives of most of the apologists was the premise that Christianity is a form of human religiosity. In adopting that premise, those university divinity school professors set themselves apart from the American Protestants—and the Archbishop of Canterbury— who insisted that Christianity as the one true, revealed religion is different *in kind* from other religions, and who therefore condemned the World Parliament for giving the diverse religions an equal hearing with Christianity. The apologists compared Christianity to other religions, and in making the comparisons they usually pointed to commonality of religiosity between Christianity and other religious forms.

Uniting most of the apologetic approaches, however, was still another conviction: the need for evangelism. If the proximate ends of the study of other religions were understanding, defense, and comparison, the long-range goal was evangelistic mission. The inclusion of the study of comparative religion within the divinity school foreign missions curriculum of the late nineteenth and early twentieth centuries was motivated by the watchword of the Student Volunteer Movement for Foreign Missions: "The Evangelization of the World in This Generation." As explained by John R. Mott, general secretary of the movement and later chairman of the International Missionary Council, "The evangelization of the world in this generation should not be regarded as an end in itself. The Church will not have fulfilled her task when the Gospel has been preached to all men. Such evangelization must be followed by the baptism of converts, by their organization into churches, by building them up in knowledge, faith and character, and by enlisting and training them for service."[60] And by the beginning of the twentieth century, evangelization included even more than baptism and the formation of new churches. Mott himself insisted that the founding of schools, the supplying of medical services, and the provision of social relief were vital parts of the foreign missionary task.[61] The "evangelization of the world in this generation" was tied to the ideal of "civilizing" foreign cultures with the devices of Western, especially American, institutions. And that ideal, in turn, was linked with America's efforts to expand its political, economic, and cultural influence in the non-Western world.[62]

A serious challenge to the evangelistic view of missions and its apologetic approach to the world's religions appeared in 1932 with the publication of the widely discussed *Re-Thinking Missions: A Laymen's Inquiry After One Hundred Years*. The study was commissioned and funded by John D. Rockefeller, Jr., was conducted by a large team of researchers under the auspices of the Institute for Social and Religious Research, and was overseen by a board of distinguished laypeople and clergy. As summarized by the eminent Harvard philosopher William E. Hocking, the published report burst like a bombshell in two directions, striking both the practice and the theory of foreign missions.

Although supportive of the inclusion of social, medical, and educational services within the missionary enterprise, the report was severely critical of the quality of those services. It drew a picture of most missionaries as well-intentioned but second-rate professionals who had been beaten down by the bureaucratic demands of denominational missionary boards, who were burdened by the requirement to deliver converts as well as social services, and who were badly trained in the helping profes-sions.[63] In the summary of its investigations of missionary social work, for example, the report concluded:

> It is disappointing that with great industrial problems in the Orient con-fronting the missions with their challenge and opportunity, there is hardly a social worker to be found in the whole roster of missionaries trained to deal scientifically and intelligently with human beings trying to adjust themselves to the new factory environment.[64]

The report also offered a stinging indictment of the evangelistic theory concerning non-Christian religions. The attempt to convert non-Chris-tians by pointing to their religious errors or inferiority had confused the Christian spirit with church membership and had compromised the helping intent of the missionary. In the judgment of the report,

> It ought to be the primary business of an interpreter of the Christian religion in the future to permeate the personal life of the individual and the fabric of human society with creative ideals and energies which will renew and revitalize both the single units and the group rather than to build a church as an institution to stand out as an entity in itself apart from the larger whole of society.[65]

The report's criticism of evangelistic missions was clearly the work of the chairman of the study commission, William E. Hocking, whose own phi-losophy of religion operated on the premise that religion is a universal ideal with partisan expressions. In Hocking's view, Christianity, because of its diverse particularities, had not attained the status of universality and so was not justified in making conversionist demands. The essence of all religions was for him a "passion for righteousness," and he believed that Christianity should collaborate with other religions to stem the cor-rosive, unrighteous tides of worldwide secularization.[66]

Most American leaders of the missionary movement greeted the so-called "Laymen's Report" with criticism, disappointment, or alarm. Its critique of the missionary bureaucracy and the quality of professional services embarrassed missionary boards that had approved the need for the study, and it seemed to leaders of world mission to play into the hands of an American press already hostile to the missionary enterprise. Its phi-losophy of religion struck conservative Protestants as a cowardly aban-donment of Jesus' "Great Commission" to go into the world and make disciples of the nations, and its view of religion appeared to moderate Protestants as a collaborationist repudiation of the uniqueness of the Christian revelation.[67]

Despite these reactions, the report reflected a changed world situation and the beginnings of a new missionary response to that situation. The First World War and its aftermath constituted a frontal assault on the alleged benevolence of muscular American imperialism, the termination of any easy confidence in the "civilizing" effects of Western institutions, a growing awareness of rising nationalisms in the East, and deepened worries over large-scale war, poverty, and racial injustice. A world that previously had seemed to American Protestants an eager recipient of Western religion and culture was now riddled by fear, diversity, and conflict. In Hocking's words, "the world was opened yesterday to the free impact of civilization on civilization, and therewith of religion on religion."[68]

The new situation of mutual cultural impact was by no means ignored by divinity school scholars. Union Seminary's Daniel Johnson Fleming, professor of missions and director of Union's Department of Foreign Service, took that situation most seriously in his approach to non-Christian religions following the First World War. Although Fleming was more Christocentric than Hocking in his approach to other religions, he was one with Hocking in drawing a distinction between Christianity's own essential truths and its particular social and historical embodiments. And like Hocking, he held that all religions share an essence that permits collaboration for common social ends. "The most effective popular apologetic on the mission field," Fleming insisted, "has passed from origins to consequences, from roots to fruits.... Not only the ethnic faiths, but Christianity itself, must stand or fall by their power to enlarge and enrich life."

Fleming believed that collaboration between Christianity and other religions, and between Western and non-Western cultures, should enrich the lives of people by opposing the common enemies of the modern world. Those enemies were new "continents" that demanded conquering by the Christian missionary program. The whole world was increasingly divided by the landmasses of "competitive nationalism, race prejudice and pride, the ready resort to war, ignorance, poverty." Conquering those new areas of the modern world required the assumption that "God has not been working exclusively through Christianity. No part of mankind has a monopoly of His gifts." Fleming's collaborative, anti-imperialist approach to non-Christian religions was premised on his view that "Every religion in its essence is ... a prolonged prayer for life from the unseen world," a religious essence that, when grasped by Protestant

Christians, enables them to enlarge their own religious faith, honor the integrity of other religions, and cooperate with other religions to cure the social ills of the modern world.[69]

Fleming anticipated the thinking and proposals of the mid-century ecumenical movement in his abandonment of talk of "foreign missions" and his insistence that "the whole world is the missions field."[70] He also anticipated a mid-century scholarly approach to comparative religions, one detached from all missionary aims, that would claim for the study of other religions the purpose of self-understanding on the part of the scholar.

Before mid-century, however, another position on missions and world religions had emerged in the divinity schools. Between the two extremes of evangelistic apologetics and collaborative essentialism advocates of a mediating position had appeared. The mediators joined the two claims that God most fully revealed himself in Jesus Christ and that other religions offer genuine knowledge of God. The aims of studying other religions, and the goals of undertaking missions, were to attest to the former claim and to acknowledge the latter. The mediators' witness to the full revelation of God in Jesus Christ shared the apologists' assumption that the Christian faith is superior, but they engaged in comparative study less to prove Christianity's superiority than to point to the continuities between Christianity and other religions. The mediators' acknowledgment of the awareness of God in other faiths conceded to the essentialists the postulate that all religions embrace a common core of truth, but they developed that theory less in terms of the need for collaboration among religions than in terms of the distinctive posture and contribution of each religion.

Edmund Davison Soper was an influential spokesman for the mediating position. Soper served as professor of missions and comparative religion at Drew Theological School from 1914 to 1919, as professor of the history of religion at Northwestern University from 1919 to 1925, as dean of the School of Religion at Duke from 1925 to 1928, and as professor of the history of religion at the Garrett School of Theology from 1938 until his retirement in 1948.

Soper took a middle position between Hocking and the conservative critics respecting the "Laymen's Report" on foreign missions. "We believe in the uniqueness of Christianity," he said, "and we also believe in its continuity with other religions."[71] Neither Christianity's uniqueness nor its continuity with other faiths, however, could serve as an excuse for the dilettante's attitude toward other cultures and religions. Missionaries and other students of the world's religions were obligated, first of all, to understand the distinctive features of those religions.[72] The primary task in the study of non-Christian religions was to learn the historical facts about their origins and development, and to grasp their roles in the lives of individuals and in the structures of society. Only after the methods of history, psychology, sociology, and anthropology had been employed could the philosophical task be undertaken of comparing the truth claims of other religions with those of Christianity. For Soper, the last step, philosophical comparison, always led to his affirmation that Christianity fulfills the potential of other religions. Christianity in India, for example, could bring to completion the democratic egalitarianism of high-minded Hindus, and Christianity around the world could serve as the fulfillment of Judaism's longing for a Messiah.[73]

After the Second World War, the interweaving of the study of non-Christian religions with the missionary task began to unravel in the university divinity schools, and by the middle of the 1960s the two were completely disentangled. Signs of the separation appeared in programmatic developments at many of the schools. By the late 1960s Union, Yale, Boston, Drew, Emory, Duke, and SMU had shifted the bulk of the study of world religions out of the seminary curriculum into graduate programs and undergraduate departments of religion.[74] Missions courses were no longer required of ministerial candidates in these schools, doctoral programs in missiology were abandoned, and key professorships in missions were not filled.[75]

The dissociation of the study of world religions from ministerial training, the waning of interest in world missions, and the changed course of the ecumenical movement were interconnected events. Rejection of all remnants of American colonialism in the missionary legacy by theological school students and faculty, as well as the new ecumenical emphasis on the integrity of distinct cultures, dislodged the study of other religions from its missionary moorings and set it free as a discrete academic specialty. But that freedom already had been promoted by the divinity schools at Chicago and Harvard long before the events of mid-century. The "science of religion," *Religionswissenschaft*, had been cultivated at those schools for over fifty years as a specialty altogether independent of the cause of Christian missions.

In 1904, George Foot Moore, a Presbyterian minister who formerly taught Hebrew and comparative religions at Andover Theological Seminary, became the first occupant of Harvard's Frothingham Chair of Religion. Named after the popular nineteenth-century Transcendentalist minister Octavius Brooks Frothingham, the professorship assumed by Moore was established to promote the unity of the religions of human-kind rather than the world missionary enterprise. Harvard's creation of the professorship marked a significant departure in the comparative study of religion at American divinity schools. As George H. Williams has observed, "Whereas elsewhere the comparative study of religion commonly grew out of the seminary interest either in world mission or in the Christian origins in the Greco-Roman world, in the New England university most affected by Transcendentalism the first chair *in religion* was a consequence of philosophical interest in the generic religious im-pulse of mankind."[76]

However, Moore chose to pursue a scholarly agenda that departed from the Transcendentalist quest for the generic origins of a universal religion. For all of his continuing interest in common factors among religions, Moore was most concerned with what separately distinguished the reli-gious traditions. He summed up his approach in the introduction to his two-volume *History of Religions*: "In religions as in civilizations it is not the generic features but the individual characteristics that give them their highest interest and, we may say, value." Moore adopted as his fun-damental aim as an author and teacher that of "bring[ing] into relief the individuality of the several religions as it expresses itself in their his-tory."[77]

As one of America's earliest proponents of the German discipline of a "science of religion," Moore discarded the aims of education born of the missionary movement. The primary purpose of understanding other re-ligions was not to defend the superiority of Christianity, nor to demon-strate the essential oneness of diverse religious faiths, nor to mediate be-tween those two theological goals. It was, rather, "to understand and appreciate ways of thinking and feeling remote from our own."[78] That purpose did not mean for Moore the abandonment of the comparative task, nor even the denial that some religions are superior to others. He claimed, for example, that the prime religious motive lay in the human impulse of self-preservation, that most of the great religions of the world evolved beyond that impulse to a desire for exaltation of what lay beyond human limitations, and that Judaism and Christianity excelled in offer-ing such exaltation. Such comparisons were of secondary importance, however. Moore turned most of his attention to how physical environ-ment, ethnic consciousness, and national life shaped the religions of the world.[79]

Moore's successor in the Frothingham Chair, Arthur Darby Nock, carried on the tradition of educating Harvard's divinity students in religions "remote from our own," but with more emphasis on the social and psychological comparisons of the backgrounds and origins of Christianity.[80] In the early 1930s, Nock was instrumental in establishing a collaborative doctoral program between the Harvard Department of History and the Divinity School in the area of the history of religions, thus assuring the academic integrity of the science of religion and its clear separation from the missionary impulse.[81] Then in 1958, on land adjacent to the Divinity School, Harvard founded a Center for the Study of World Religions as a residence for faculty, students, and visiting professors. Operating as a base for doctoral programs in the comparative study of religions in the University's Graduate School of the Arts and Sciences, the Center faculty also eventually came to serve as the Department of the History of Religion in the Divinity School. The founding of the Center marked still another stage in Harvard's approach to the study of world religions.

In its statement of purpose the Center moved beyond Moore's aim of understanding the "individuality of the several religions." The aim was expanded to include self-understanding. The Center sought "to encourage the sympathetic study of the religions of the world, from which each person may gain a clearer insight and firmer faith in the truth of his own religion, by communication between men of differing religious faiths."[82] In one sense, the Center had taken Harvard still another step beyond the missionary purposes of understanding the Other. The goal of understanding was understanding itself, achieved through the twofold mode of the enhancement of one's own faith and the sympathetic understanding of the Other. Nothing could have been farther from apologetics or any aggressive missionary scheme. Yet the Center's statement of purpose accorded with Daniel Johnson Fleming's new Christian missionary agenda of honoring the integrity of other religions and enlarging the Christian faith. The statement was also made very much in the spirit of the new ecumenism that had abandoned the task of converting foreign cultures. It was thus altogether fitting when Samuel H. Miller, dean of the Harvard Divinity School, celebrated the fifth year of the Center by claiming that it was at the forefront of the school's dedication to "Christian unity and ecumenical understanding."[83]

The ecumenical nature of Harvard Divinity School's approach to world religions was fostered by Wilfred Cantwell Smith, the Center's director from 1964 to 1973. Smith insisted that the discipline of comparative study should expand its purpose still further if it were to contribute significantly to ecumenicity. That expanded purpose would include what he called "personalization." Explicitly repudiating all Christian theologies and missionary ideologies that favored Western cultures or that assumed the completeness of the knowledge of God in Christianity, Smith called for an understanding of the faiths of others from a non-exclusivist position.[84] Such an understanding, however, overlooks the very life of religious faith if it concentrates simply on the political, social, and cultural expressions of the religions of the world—what had become the overwhelming tendency of the discipline of the history of religions as it had freed itself from the missionary motive and endeavored to become "scientific." For Smith, "the study of a religion is the study of persons," or, rather, it is the inference of human concerns from the diverse social, political, and cultural manifestations of a religion.[85]

Supporting Smith's commitment to the personalization of the study of religion was his conviction that people across the world share a fundamental religiousness, and that concern for the religions of persons would lead to the scholar's integration of understanding of what was different with self-understanding:

> We may look now for a history not so much of the disparate religions but of man's religiousness. Such a history should be persuasive to students of that total history, themselves from diverse faiths. It should be such and they should be such that they can recognize and acknowledge their own separate communities within it, and at the same time recognize and acknowledge the totality, of which also they are learning to be a part.[86]

Smith's personalistic, integrative approach to the study of religion expanded and continued the Harvard tradition of self-understanding achieved through an understanding of other religions, a tradition that extended into the 1980s. In the academic year 1981–82, at the instigation of Dean George Rupp, the Divinity School's restructured curriculum for ministerial students included the history and comparison of religions as one of three required areas of study. The religions of the world were construed as forming the critical context for ministerial education, one that could lead the student both to see the distinctive otherness of cultures around the globe and to cultivate self-understanding through comparison: "in the area of comparative religion, the overall curriculum supports ministerial education in which the careful study of other traditions provides the distanced perspective that illumines dynamics in one's own community that one is at first too close to see."[87] Harvard Divinity School in the 1980s still held out the hope that the science of religion could lead to the complementary goals of understanding the Other and understanding oneself.

The study of the history of religions at the University of Chicago has been distinguished less by the expansion of the aims of understanding than by a continuous quest for a method appropriate to such understanding.[88] In 1926, A. Eustace Haydon, professor of comparative religion at the University of Chicago from 1919 to 1945, remarked about developments in the field as a whole, "the history of religions has only slowly been groping its way toward a scientific method."[89] Haydon's remark would prove to be a particularly apt description of both his own work and that of the scholars who would follow him at the University of Chicago Divinity School.

From the outset, the comparative and historical study of religion at Chicago was clearly differentiated from any apologetic, missionary, or even largely theological purpose. For many years, the Department of Comparative Religion was housed in the Graduate School of Arts and Sciences. The graduate faculty in comparative religion did teach in the Divinity School, but not until the 1940s, with the creation of the Federated Theological Faculty, did comparative religion become a division within the Divinity School curriculum. The field would always be understood at Chicago as a university discipline with a preponderant orientation toward graduate work, and most of the Chicago faculty who taught in the field would view themselves as standing within the Enlightenment, European tradition of the unbiased study of religion, rather than within the traditions of Christian theology. The faculty also claimed as their chief professional allies, not seminary professors across the country who taught missions and world religions, but those archaeologists, sociologists, historians, and other scholars at Cornell, Brown, Yale, Johns Hopkins, Columbia, and Pennsylvania universities who engaged in the social scientific study of religion outside the divinity school environment.[90] Haydon had accurately characterized the study of world religions at Chicago: it groped its way toward a scientific method. And it would seek a method that harmonized with the American university's emphasis on specialized disciplines.

Haydon himself was willing to settle for a minimalist definition of religion in order to get on with the pursuit of method. The common thread uniting the religions of the world was "human life seeking satisfaction in a specific environment." Haydon's attention, however, was directed neither toward the commonality uniting religions nor toward their similarities and differences. He believed that his chief task as a historian of religions was "to deal not with religion but religions, each of them the product of the life of a human group and claiming to be interpreted in all the richness of its individuality."[91] Haydon's pluralistic view of religion was complemented by his multidisciplinary approach to the religions of the world. "The method of history of religions is no longer the simple historical method used by the founders of the science before the opening century; it is an aggregate of all the sciences whose domains cover data which the historian must use. The success of history therefore depends upon the adequacy of the methods and findings of the various sciences involved."[92]

Haydon had produced a method for the history of religions that would satisfy few of his successors at the University of Chicago Divinity School. In the 1960s, the eminent Chicago historian of religions Mircea Eliade expressed his dissatisfaction with the state of *Religionswissenschaft*. Eliade found that it was "progressively more difficult to become a historian of religions. A scholar regretfully finds himself becoming a specialist in *one* religion or even in a particular period or a single aspect of that religion." Eliade suspected that the situation had been created by the nature of specialization itself, by "the inhibitions provoked by the triumph of 'scientism' in certain humanistic disciplines."[93] By way of implication, Eliade suggested that Haydon and other proponents of *Religionswissenschaft*, in their affirmation of radical difference among the religions of the world and their endorsement of multiple university disciplines, had created conditions unacceptable to a field of learning: narrow specialization and the lack of a unifying approach.

Historians of religion who preceded Eliade at Chicago had attempted to overcome that state of affairs. Haydon's successor, Joachim Wach, pursued an approach of "relative objectivity," one designed to escape any "anarchical subjectivism" or any "normative exposition of one particular faith" characteristic of Christian theology. His predominantly historical and sociological approach, however, was aimed at uncovering more than the diverse cultural manifestations of the religions of the world; it sought, as well, to point to the "objective primacy of religious experience," to the experience of what the German philosopher Rudolph Otto had called *Das Heilige* or the awe-inspiring, fascinating, unapproachable Holy Reality.[94]

Wach's student, Joseph Kitagawa, carried on his teacher's simultaneous attention to the scientific classification of religious expressions and religious people's experience of Ultimate Reality. Kitagawa also proposed that the historian of religion should deal with the "universal human themes, such as birth, death, love, marriage, frustration, meaningless-ness, and beatific vision" that are bound up with the cultural manifesta-tions of religion. Eliade was less explicitly concerned with method than was Haydon, Wach, or Kitagawa, but in his study of the central phenom-ena of religion—religious symbols, myths, objects of devotion, and ritu-als—he suggested that the historian of religions must attempt to under-stand religious data for what they say about discrete religions, for what they reveal about patterns that cut across various religions, and for what they indicate about the human being as *homo religiosus*.[95] Like so many of his predecessors and colleagues at the University of Chicago Divinity School, Eliade sought a method for the history of religions that would both attain respectability as a university discipline and integrate a field of study—goals to be achieved through a *human* instead of a *theological* science of religion.

By the 1980s, there were indications that the quest for method at the University of Chicago may have been made to bear too much the bur-den for achieving integration of a field. Charles Long, who had earned his doctorate at Chicago in the 1950s and stayed on for more than two decades to teach in the division of the history of religions, later looked back on his Chicago years as an exciting attempt by lively minds to shape a university discipline. But he believed that finally the venture had been hampered by Western Enlightenment presuppositions regarding "scientific" reason that subjected the Other to the categories of the West-ern interpreter. According to Long, "there is confusion or conflation of what is Other in the culture and history of the interpreter with the reality of the Others who are the object of interpretation." Long proposed that instead of searching for a scientific model that reduces the religions of non-Western others to Western categories, the historian of religion should pursue a knowledge about the distinctive otherness of the interpreter and the distinctive otherness of the religion under interpretation. "Our goal would then not be a science, but a serious human discourse."[96]

At the same 1983 conference in Chicago in which Long delivered his remarks, Joseph Kitagawa, professor of the history of religion and former dean at the Chicago Divinity School, expressed different reservations about the success of the quest for a unifying method. He alleged that the discipline of the history of religions was in disarray, a consequence of scholars in the field taking their methodological cues from the diverse human sciences. Submissions to the journal *History of Religions* and hir-ing practices in colleges and universities signified for Kitagawa a widespread notion that any study of non-Western religions, regardless of the methods employed, constituted the history of religions. He concluded that the field "urgently needs to articulate its own identity and to define its own mode of relating to other fields of inquiry, instead of allowing other disciplines to define the relationship from their perspectives."[97] It would appear that the history of religions at Chicago was still groping its way toward an integrative method.

The search for a unifying purpose at Harvard and the quest for an integrative method at Chicago contributed to the transformation of the aims of educating to understand the Other. The two schools formed the nation's premier alternatives to those divinity schools that defined the field of study in terms of the missionary task. They also stood as the country's foremost attempts to render the field a university discipline. As such, they represented both the promises and the risks of the American divinity school's pursuit of its mission within the ambience of the modern university. With full access to the educational methods, aims, and resources of the university, they could undertake the exacting scholarly task of understanding other religions and other cultures in all their diversity. In assuming that responsibility, however, they sanctioned a pattern of specialization that narrowed intellectual focus and sent scholars in search of a unifying aim for their academic tasks.

## WORLDS OF THE OTHER, WORLDS OF THE UNIVERSITY

The spirit of a tolerant Protestantism that was so conspicuous at the World Parliament of Religions in 1893 permeated the Protestant university divinity schools for over a century. The spirit emerged from the belief of evangelicals, Unitarians, Transcendentalists, and social gospelers that non-Protestants should first of all be understood before any course of action respecting their otherness could be undertaken. Stirring only slightly beneath the surface of that conviction was the assumption that scholarly understanding would reveal how the religious beliefs of the world are essentially Christian. It was also assumed that scholarly understanding would establish American Protestantism and its cultural accoutrements as the measure of civilization and would prove the social significance of all religions in decidedly Western terms. An attitude of religious toleration, in short, often was cast within a mold of an assumed American Protestant hegemony. That mold would be broken by the birth of new nationalisms and the rise of anticolonialism, by constraints on and changing philosophies of world missions, and by radical revisions in ecumenical thinking.

Nevertheless, solid support had been gathered in the nineteenth century for merging the worlds of the Other with the worlds of the university. A modern American university dedicated to specialized knowledge provided the appropriate milieu for Protestants to struggle with the otherness of other religions and cultures, and leaders of university-related divinity schools were quick to utilize the resources of that environment. Advanced, specialized education in non-Protestant religions, driven by the aims of the ecumenical and missionary movements and by the agenda of *Religionswissenschaft*, was included as a component in the training of American Protestant ministers. Adopting the university outlook of "nonsectarian" education, the university divinity school employed specialization to expand the horizons of ministers, place Protestantism in the context of worldwide Christianity and world religions, and broaden the sense of the society and the church which the ministers would serve.

The changing aims of understanding what was different manifested other features of university specialization. With the disappearance of hopes for an American Protestant hegemony, brought about by Protestantism's and Western Christianity's changed status in the world, the ultimate purpose of understanding through specialization increasingly tilted toward individual self-understanding or the understanding of others in their integrity, or both. With the growing awareness of the radical diversity of peoples occupying the "global village," an awareness prompted by the insistent presence and voices of those peoples themselves, the final purpose of understanding other religions inclined toward the appreciation of their distinctive otherness. And with the persistent growth of specialties within the divinity schools, fostered by the environment of their universities, one of the chief goals of understanding would prove to be understanding itself.

The adoption of specialties by the divinity schools designed to understand the Other led to an expansion of ministerial education and of educational worlds, as well as to a narrowing of educational focus and the loss of a large, integrative purpose. Those consequences issued both from the transforming social forces which impinged upon the world of the university and from the aggressive contributions made to those forces by the leadership of the divinity schools. In a recent critique of American higher education, Dinesh D'Souza has accurately observed that the university is more than a mere reflection of its larger social sphere. "Universities are a microcosm of society. But they are more than a reflection or mirror; they are a leading indicator."[98] D'Souza could have added, they are a social indicator in large measure because university leadership has historically taken the initiative in promoting new social forces and cultural values. Certainly leaders of divinity schools affiliated with American universities did not shrink from that initiative as they incorporated the study of other religions into their curricula. In educating their students into the diverse worlds of other religions, they exalted the pluriform world of university specialization. That outcome, by no means always intended, would become even more apparent in the emergence of the field known as "religious studies."

# CHAPTER III

■

## *Theological and Religious Sciences*

In its October 18, 1971 issue, *Time* magazine carried a story about a study of graduate education in religion that had been sponsored by the American Council of Learned Societies. Appearing a week before the official publication of the study, the story focused on the section of the ACLS probe that rated graduate programs in religion. *Time* named some of the programs that the study had assigned a rating of "marginal"— those at Fordham, Temple, California at Santa Barbara, Saint Louis, Southern California, Catholic, and Drew universities. And it pointed to "giant Southwestern Baptist Seminary in Fort Worth" as a notable example of institutions offering doctoral programs in religion judged by the study to be "inadequate." "These days," the *Time* reporter concluded, "it seems even mediocrity is ecumenical." A few days later *The Chronicle of Higher Education* printed an article that included responses from several critics of the study, but the headline revealed the article's emphasis: "Cut Doctorates in Religion, Report Urges."[1]

The ACLS study, *Graduate Education in Religion*, came to be known popularly as the "Welch Report," named after the study's director and principal author Claude Welch, previously chairman of the Department of Religious Thought at the University of Pennsylvania and newly appointed dean of the Graduate Theological Union in Berkeley, California. The Welch Report stirred a storm of protest. Some scholars in religion, such as Robert Michaelsen of the University of California at Santa Barbara and Franklin Littell of Temple University, declared the report to be overwhelmingly "managerial," "administrative," "quantitative," and lacking in awareness of the changing dynamics characteristic of the study of religion and its setting in the modern university.[2] For the most part, however, the responses to the report centered on its ratings of the graduate programs. Picking up on the ratings controversy, the editors of the *Christian Century* decided to conduct a poll of the twenty-four schools downgraded by the Welch study. The poll revealed that eighteen of twenty responding schools said they had not been told there would be ratings, four said they had not been visited by Welch or his associate, none reported a formal interview structured so that a fair rating could be developed, twelve schools believed that the ratings were based on errors of fact as well as judgment, and all agreed that a one-man rating system was inappropriate in view of the role of official accrediting agencies.[3]

Associate editor of the *Century* Martin Marty observed that the wide publicity respecting the ratings placed graduate education in religion in a position of double jeopardy—from a general public that was a source of extramural financial support, and from educational administrators facing hard budgetary times who were looking for opportunities for retrenchment within their institutions. Indeed, such publicity during the entire inflationary 1970s exacerbated the precarious situation of the study of religion across the country, in some cases providing justification for the cutback or elimination of programs.[4] But Marty also was concerned about another risk. "It would be unfortunate," he said, "if . . . public controversy over the ratings chapter prevented higher education in religion from dealing with the pros and cons of the other chapters in the ACLS study."[5] His concern was legitimate. Most of the public attention was directed to the ratings—to a mere 9 pages in a 254-page book.

If the substance of the ACLS report was largely obscured by the ratings controversy, however, other observers of the study of religion in America in the 1970s would confirm many of Welch's judgments about the changing nature of a field of study. Welch had detected some diverse implications of an emergent area in the academic study of religion, one that was rapidly growing independent of its mother institution, the university divinity school. He had discerned the effects of a field to be known as "religious studies."

Welch's research had turned up some revealing data. Of the 30 percent of the public four-year institutions of higher education with undergraduate programs in religion, 90 percent had established their programs since 1940; of the 48 percent of private nonsectarian institutions with religious studies programs, 56 percent had established them in that same period. Enrollments in undergraduate courses in religion had grown three times faster than the student populations in public institutions between 1964 and 1969; they had grown at the same rate in private nonsectarian schools between 1954 and 1969. Registrations in religion courses at Protestant and Catholic schools, on the other hand, had declined relative to the student population as denominational colleges and universities eliminated or reduced requirements in the study of religion. Welch also produced evidence of a recent graduate education boom in religion. Of the fifty-two Ph.D. programs in religion existing in the United States and Canada in 1970, twenty had been established in the 1960s, and by the end of the decade those new programs enrolled more than a quarter of North American doctoral students in religion. Between 1964 and 1968, students in all graduate programs in religion grew from a total of 7,383 to 12,620—in percentages, that meant that graduate education in religion had expanded more rapidly than any other field during the period.[6]

The Welch Report revealed more than rapid growth in the study of religion; it also exposed some signs of the changing nature of the study. Increasing numbers of the students receiving their doctorates from Protestant university divinity schools were finding employment as undergraduate teachers of religion in colleges and universities. And graduate training was no longer conforming to the pre–World War II pattern of "preparation for the teaching ministry." In 1970, nineteen universities in North America were offering doctorates in religion without any reliance on theological school faculties, numerous students of religion were receiving their graduate education in university departments such as Semitic languages and literature and Asian studies, and fully one-half of the Ph.D. programs at theological schools were under the administrative control of university graduate schools of the arts and sciences. The profiles of the graduate student, the young professor, and the undergraduate major in religion were also changing. Most Ph.D. students (71 percent) were undertaking graduate work immediately after receiving an undergraduate degree in some area of the liberal arts, abandoning the earlier pattern of first earning a ministerial degree before entering a graduate program in religion. The undergraduate students whom many of the doctoral students would teach were enrolling in religion courses chiefly out of intellectual curiosity, or to engage issues of personal importance, or to fulfill a distribution requirement in liberal arts—rather than with any preprofessional plans in mind. And some professors who had concentrated their graduate work on traditional divinity school areas were shifting away from their specialties to accommodate their new university environment and the interests of undergraduate students. In a survey of undergraduate teachers who had specialized in theology, for example, the Welch study discovered that only a little more than half still claimed that area as their specialty.[7]

Welch was persuaded that his data signaled a late twentieth-century situation fraught with both problems and possibilities for the study of religion. The rapid expansion in the 1960s had created its own set of problems. The period of expansion in higher education was over, undergraduate enrollments and majors in religion and in other liberal arts programs had begun a precipitous slide, and too many Ph.D.s were being produced for a declining academic market. Concern over this assortment of problems lay behind Welch's controversial one-man rating of graduate programs in religion. He also believed that, given the patterns of undergraduate education in religion, the mixing of professional-ministerial and academic-graduate education in the divinity school was extremely problematic. It had confused two distinctive educational aims and taxed faculty time and energy. It also had focused on specialties appropriate to education in Christianity, to the neglect of widespread undergraduate interest in non-Western religions. Welch was convinced, however, that for all the problems, the study of religion in North America presented undergraduate and graduate teachers with some distinctive possibilities for the future. The times were replete with opportunities for religion scholars to connect more closely graduate training and the undergraduate study of religion, to learn from the methods of other university disciplines, and to enlarge the horizons of a field by attending to different manifestations of the religious experience. Welch also believed that the times were propitious for the field of the study of religion to attain a new sense of coherence.[8]

In historical perspective, the chief significance of Welch's study lay neither in his identification of problems nor in his specification of opportunities. It lay, instead, in his analysis of what bred both the problems and the opportunities. What led to both was the emergence of something new out of something old—the birth of a new university discipline out of the womb of theological studies.

On the one hand, by 1970 a new field had established itself as a legitimate academic enterprise within the liberal arts curriculum of the university. Aided by the Supreme Court decision in 1963 that teaching *about* religion, as distinct from instruction *in* religion, is an acceptable undertaking in public institutions, the study of religion had won its way into increasing numbers of colleges and universities as a nonconfessional examination of religious phenomena. On the other, this emergent academic field had not yet attained a coherent identity of its own, one interpreted in terms independent of the terms definitive of divinity school education. Welch believed that "the problem of this new sort of identity can be focused quite simply: what is to take the place of the theological degree as the base on which advanced studies in religion are built?" No clear answer had yet appeared to that question or to the larger theoretical question of what would constitute the new field as an independent domain of inquiry. The study of religion was thus enmeshed in a kind of identity crisis. It had passed beyond the stage of birth and nurture by theological education, and in some cases even beyond the stage of having to prove itself among its disciplinary peers in the university, but it had not yet struggled through to its own sense of integrity.[9]

Welch's study was sponsored by the American Council of Learned Societies and funded by the Henry Luce Foundation, but the proposal for the study had come initially from a task force of the Society for Religion in Higher Education, the successor organization to Charles Foster Kent's early twentieth-century National Council of Religion in Higher Education. In one sense, the situation in the study of religion reported by Welch had fulfilled Kent's highest hopes. Undergraduate courses in religion at American universities had moved well beyond the pathetic state that Kent had described in 1911. Students were now receiving a solid education in the specialties constitutive of a respected field of learning, and they were instructed by highly trained teachers, many of whom had acquired their doctorates at university divinity schools like Kent's own Yale.

In other respects, however, the late twentieth-century situation was a jarring rejection of Kent's dreams. The nonconfessional, nonministerial approach to the study of religion marked a clear departure from Kent's desire to blend the specialized study of religion with the enhancement of the religious and professional lives of faculty and students. And the growing independence of the study of religion from theological studies was a direct repudiation of Kent's vision of the university divinity school as a shaping influence upon the whole of university life. Some critical developments had occurred between Kent's dreams of 1911 and Welch's report of 1971. Alliances between divinity school education and the study of religion in America's universities had passed through three distinct phases, each with its own view of the purposes served by academic specialization.

## "SCIENCE"

When Charles Foster Kent and his fellow divinity school educators of the early twentieth century picked up the task of promoting the academic study of religion in American colleges and universities, they had in mind the spread of their own "scientific" approach.[10] In part, they meant by "scientific" what professors in nineteenth-century German universities had meant by *Wissenschaft*: the systematic nature of scholarship and learning. They further borrowed from developments in Germany by construing their disciplines of biblical, historical, theological, and practical studies as "theological sciences" or discrete areas of systematic scholarship.[11]

In making the case for a scientific study of religion, however, divinity school professors also claimed as their ideal the natural sciences and technologies that were transforming America and its universities. By 1876, the date of the founding of Johns Hopkins as America's first major research university, modern American science and technology already had evolved into many specialties, had begun to create professional societies, and had drawn the awestruck admiration of the American public for their practical contributions to the progress of an industrial age.[12] As Robert Bruce has remarked, when American scientists came to occupy professorships at Hopkins and other American universities, they were inclined to view "the German university through their own prism, ignoring its principles of *Bildung* and *Idealismus* in favor of its specialization and meticulously detailed research."[13] The natural sciences also became for other occupants of the American university, including professors in university divinity schools, a lens through which the whole of the scholarly life was beheld.

The divinity schools' adoption of the natural scientific paradigm contained a considerable irony, for it was based on little exposure of faculty to the increasingly complex, specialized work of their scientific colleagues in the university. In 1899, William Rainey Harper observed that ministerial candidates, educated almost exclusively in the humanities, were ill prepared to deal with an American culture shaped by modern science. He proposed, therefore, that the theological schools consider including natural scientists on their faculties. "A specific amount of laboratory work in science is in our day as necessary for the prospective theological student as a knowledge of Greek, and if the college does not furnish the student this equipment, the seminary must take the necessary steps to provide it"—even if that means trading off required courses in Greek and Hebrew for required work in science.[14]

Most theological school educators were unconvinced by Harper's argument. They responded that scientific education was the responsibility of colleges and universities, that adding the natural sciences to the divinity curriculum would burden the students with still another extraneous specialty, and that replacing the study of ancient languages with courses in science would prevent seminarians from fully appropriating their religious traditions.[15] Divinity schools would by no means ignore the natural and physical sciences in the twentieth century. They eventually would require of their matriculating students elementary work in science at the college level, they would sponsor visiting lecturers in the sciences, and they would offer courses on the theology of science. On occasion they would also urge their students to take elective courses in science in other parts of the university.[16] Yet such policies did not meet Harper's demand that ministers gain firsthand exposure to the work of modern scientists.

Like their students, divinity school faculty were products of education in the humanities and, eventually, the social sciences. When they attempted to relate their disciplines to the natural and physical sciences, therefore, they did so with little or no acquaintance with the changing and multiplying sciences that were winning such popular approval and attaining such high professional status in American society. Although university divinity school professors would defend the theory of evolution against its fundamentalist critics and, in some cases, would develop an evolutionary philosophy of the emergence and growth of the Christian religion, they did so with little familiarity with the biological and paleontological details of Darwin's *Origin of Species* and the studies that followed that groundbreaking study. And although some faculty—especially at the University of Chicago and at Claremont—would formulate by mid-century a "process theology" to accord with modern physics, biology, and paleontology, their theology was at least one step removed from the complicated models and formulas of those sciences since they made theological use of science filtered through the philosophy of Alfred North Whitehead. More commonly, divinity school theologians were content throughout the twentieth century to define science and religion as separate spheres of understanding, each with its distinctive, parallel, and legitimate approaches to reality.[17]

Divinity school faculty thus contributed to the formation of what C. P. Snow called the tradition of "two cultures," one literary and one scientific, each with its own set of values, modes of communication, and symbols of reality.[18] The separation of the two in higher education harked back at least as far as 1828 when Yale College determined that the purpose of undergraduate education was to "learn to learn," thus setting the dominant policy for the future that college should serve to provide a general classical education as the ground for advanced, specialized graduate education. Seminaries endorsed the Yale decision and opted to dispense advanced, graduate-level training in the literary traditions acquired in a general way in college.[19] It is by no means an exaggeration, therefore, when Glenn T. Miller concludes about the consequences of the paucity of science in the background of the theologically educated: "the American minister who graduated from a first-rate department of religion and a good seminary may be more able to converse with a Hindu sage than with a local computer club, a researcher in electronics, or a modern biologist."[20]

In the early part of the twentieth century, if divinity school faculty were unable to converse meaningfully with scientists, they were by no means diverted from adopting what they took to be a scientific model for their study. Their aim, in any case, was to be as scientific as the chemist in the laboratory. That aim was embodied in what they called their "scientific method," by which they meant an allegiance to the facts of an objective, empirical world, matched by an unbiased, inductive approach to those facts. If, as was certainly the case, epistemological questions regarding the possibility of a totally unbiased perspective, the status of an uninterpreted fact, and the nature of the correlation between objective knower and objective known went begging, that was because commitment to science was more than commitment to mere method. It was, above all else, faithfulness to an overarching worldview.

Peter Novick's explanation of the appeal of objective science to American historians prior to World War I applies equally to many divinity school faculty during the period: "Science had offered prewar historians not just a method—well or ill understood—but above all a vision of a comprehensible world: a model of certitude, of unambiguous truth; knowledge that was definite, and independent of the values or intentions of the investigator."[21] Scholars in university divinity schools, like their counterparts in other divisions of the university, were often caught up in a view of the world generated by the wonders and achievements of science and technology—a view consisting of the values of progress, certitude, and unambiguous truth. That worldview, more than firsthand familiarity with scientific theory or even the pursuit of method deemed scientific, comprised the meaning of their scientific approach.

Divinity school infatuation with the scientific approach was nowhere more apparent than in the field of church history, and it was nowhere more starkly stated than by Ephraim Emerton, professor of ecclesiastical history at the Harvard Divinity School from 1882 to 1918. Having completed his graduate work at the universities of Berlin and Leipzig, as a divinity school professor Emerton was firmly committed to the principles of German Enlightenment *Wissenschaft*. Church history was the systematic examination of manuscript sources to determine inductively the facts of the past independently of received opinion. The study of history as such was "the search for absolute truth, as far as our means of information supply it, upon the working of men in masses," and church history was the study of "the record of the life of men together, under the form of the Christian Church."[22] Church history so conceived could have no larger agenda than the discovery of the facts of the past—no political, no ecclesiastical, and certainly no theological agenda.

Although Emerton believed that theology had its place in the divinity school, it should never be allowed to govern the task of the church historian. The theologian operates with preconceptions about the supernatural purposes of history, while the church historian, when loyal to the historical task, must abandon all *a priori* hypotheses and all speculative constructs about the overall meaning of history. When the church historian is required to deal with sources that report supernatural interventions in the realm of empirical reality, severe constraints upon historical investigation should apply:

> I should consider myself trespassing beyond my own limits, if I should say that on a certain day the gift of tongues descended upon the disciples of Jesus, and gave that impulse from which the Church as an organization derives its origin. It belongs only to me [as a church historian] to say that there is a written record that on a certain day a company of men started out upon the mission of preaching to the world the doctrine they had received from Jesus. If you desire to know whether these men received on that day a gift from God, marking them out as men especially detailed on a divine mission, you must inquire of a professed theologian, not of me.[23]

Emerton's willingness to turn speculative issues over to the theologian depended as much upon his view of himself as a natural scientist as upon his perception of himself as a bona fide modern historian, for to his way of thinking the two were one:

> It is not a matter of chance that natural science has been called also natural *history*. The method of natural science is the method of history; namely, the observation of facts and inductions from them. The fundamental principle of all modern historical science is that every event in the life of man is the result and the cause of an endless series of other events, reaching backward and forward to both eternities. You perceive at once the analogy with the method which has carried the modern science of nature to its colossal triumph.[24]

Other church historians of the time, if less rigorously positivistic than Emerton, were no less concerned to join the colossal triumph of modern science. Williston Walker at Yale, Arthur Cushman McGiffert at Union, Shirley Jackson Case at Chicago, and Walter Rauschenbusch at Rochester Theological Seminary formed a chorus that called for the church historian to stick to the tried and true inductive methods of modern science. They did believe that theology and history could be more closely joined than Emerton was willing to allow, but they insisted that theological judgments should rest upon empirical assessments of the orderly world of nature and history.[25] The same assumptions shaped most of the historical and literary interpretations of the Bible and the "natural" approaches to pastoral care in the divinity schools.[26]

Some theologians, unwilling to have their subject assigned by the likes of Emerton to a "supernatural" sphere, also celebrated the cultural triumph of natural science by claiming that their reflections upon God agreed with the perspective of the sciences. Douglas Clyde Macintosh of Yale, for example, was convinced that his theological system conformed to the demands of the scientific age because it was a logical reflection upon the quite empirical reality of the human experience of the divine. And Boston personalist theologian Albert C. Knudson, though critical of any mechanistic science that would reduce all reality to the phenomenal world, insisted that his concern for the power of natural and divine persons complemented—it did not contradict—the discoveries of modern science about the world around us.[27]

In the later years of the nineteenth century and the early years of the twentieth, the discrete disciplines or "scientific" specialties in the divinity schools were thought to attain unity in the course in theological encyclopedia. Usually required of first-year theological students and always taught by the professor with the most encompassing intellect, the course examined the connections among the separate theological sciences. Like the encyclopedic system of the German theologian Friedrich Schleiermacher, from which the American teachers borrowed heavily, the courses in theological encyclopedia introduced students to the formal relations among the disciplines. In the words of John McClintock, president of Drew University and teacher of Drew's course on the subject, the purpose of theological encyclopedia was to "sketch the different branches of Theology" and their "connections with each other" as the course undertook "an arrangement of the sciences and knowledges of men in order."[28]

Such a formalist arrangement of the divinity school disciplines possessed neither the vigor nor the allure required to hold together the separate theological specialties that were advancing along their own empirical routes, and by the time of the First World War the required course in theological encyclopedia had disappeared from the divinity school curriculum. What did not disappear until long after the war, however, was natural science as the archetypical model for the diverse theological disciplines. Divinity school educators assumed that the same model was appropriate to the university's undergraduate study of religion.

In 1911, the same year that Charles Foster Kent made his demand that colleges provide prospective divinity school students with a sound education in biblical studies, a special commission of the Religious Education Association conducted a study of the status of the study of religion in colleges and universities across the United States. Included on the five-man commission was Harry Emerson Fosdick, renowned liberal Baptist preacher and professor of homiletics at Union Theological Seminary. Fosdick and his colleagues determined on the basis of a questionnaire sent to two hundred institutions of higher education that university presidents across the land were committed to the accomplishment of two complementary tasks: educating the future religious leaders of America, and advancing the specialized study of religion. Although the commissioners found that most universities, both public and private, had not yet established a fully developed curriculum suitable for the attainment of those two tasks, the commissioners were encouraged by the "prevailing sentiment" among university educators. Few of the educators were willing to confine the training of religious leaders and the specialized study in religion to the domain of the theological schools. And unlike colleges representing the "evangelical standpoint," university leaders seemed dedicated to the promotion of scholarly methods that abandoned the parochialism of "awakening an enthusiasm for religion" among undergraduates or that "taught every subject from a Christian viewpoint."[29]

In short, the members of the study commission were convinced that most universities and many colleges in America were on the brink of a breakthrough to a scientific study of religion, one modeled on the achievements of the natural sciences:

> The scientific study of religious phenomena, the psychological interpretation of religion, the historical and critical study of the Bible, have come already not infrequently to constitute a part of the college curriculum. . . . If this department of human interest is going to look toward the continued healthy development of humanity, it must have need of its Keplers, its Darwins, its Fechners, its Kelvins, its Bergsons, or at least a large number of master minds who will widen, deepen, and enrich our

insight into the meaning of religion and interpret its place and function in the scheme of things.[30]

The emergence of the Keplers and the Fechners for the scientific study of religion, however, would by no means preclude the practical task of training the lay and clerical leaders of tomorrow. Fosdick and his collaborators believed that academic science and practical piety went hand in glove. That was a lesson to be learned from the links connecting scientific theory and technological development:

> The furtherance of the scientific and philosophical interpretation of religion will in the highest sense in the long run contribute to the practical phases of life. It is the healthy development of the *science* of biology and botany that is perfecting our herds and increasing our harvests; it is the sciences of physiology and chemistry that are rapidly improving the practice of medicine until diseases are being eliminated and longevity and happiness increased. In the coming decades we shall not expect less of the science of religion.[31]

Science as a worldview springing from confidence in the cultural accomplishments of the natural sciences and technology was thus thought to be as appropriate for directing the undergraduate study of religion as in shaping theological education. Theological educators were determined to foster that view of things in the nation's universities by educating teachers in the theological sciences, supporting the founding of schools and departments in religion across the country, and encouraging teachers in the several university disciplines to treat religion scientifically in their classrooms.

Divinity school educators believed that large public or tax-supported universities offered especially fertile ground for the scientific study of religion. Founded to educate a wide constituency of the American public, designed to educate Americans in the vocations appropriate to science and technology, and set up to provide low- or no-tuition opportunities to American students, public universities attracted increasing numbers of the college-bound. Divinity school educators were impressed by the fact that by 1930 two-fifths of all American students in higher education were enrolled in public institutions.[32]

Early in the twentieth century, William Lowe Bryan, president of Indiana University, could read considerable religious significance into the student gravitation to state universities. "Today," he said, "the greatest missionary field in the world, and the field which is almost unoccupied by the churches, is the field which is offered in the great American state universities."[33] In deeming the university a great missionary field, Bryan expressed above all a concern for those students away from home for the first time and in need of the guidance of their churches. But he and others of the time also saw in the universities a field for the cultivation of the scientific study of religion. Unable to indoctrinate students in tax-supported universities without crossing the barrier separating church and state, the professor of religion at the state university could enjoy a favorable environment for the scientific study of religion. In the words of the author of a major study of religion in public universities in 1928, "The state universities by reason of their freedom and spirit of research are in a peculiarly favorable position to carry on research in religion, the results of which will be available for all religious beliefs and which will stand or fall on their inherent value, and not because they express the particular opinions of any one religious sect." Such nonsectarian study could be accomplished only through the scientific method, which consists of the "classification of facts, the recognition of their sequence and relative significance," and the "habit of forming a judgment upon these facts."[34]

American Protestant leaders employed several strategies to promote the scientific study of religion in public universities. Through consultations and conferences, they sought to stimulate awareness among university administrators and faculty of the need for the study of religion in separate undergraduate courses and in cognate courses in literature, philosophy, and history.[35] In addition, American Protestants founded at numerous universities "Bible chairs" (usually adjacent to campuses and taught by ministers without faculty status), denominationally incorporated religious foundations, and schools of religion. The churches' argument for the existence of all of these institutions was that the elective study of Bible and religion, devoid of the aims of proselytizing, was appropriate to a sound undergraduate education. A description of the ideal occupant of a Bible chair in 1910 by the National Council of the Congregational Church typified the desire of the denominations to blend the study of religion with its practice on public university campuses—the former sometimes coming as an afterthought:

> What is felt to be needed is a broad-minded, sympathetic leader who shall be constantly on hand, looking after the children of Congregational parents while they are away from their homes and who may be in need of moral and spiritual guidance and brotherly counsel, who in short shall be a University Congregational Pastor. Such a man might also conduct courses of instruction in ethics and Biblical literature.[36]

Schools of religion represented a more ambitious, and a much more scholarly, attempt to move the study of religion into tax-supported universities. Although in many cases the schools of religion were little more than administrative collections of Bible chairs, others like those at the universities of Indiana, Oklahoma, and Iowa offered a wide range of courses in religion, received financial support from several denominations, and enjoyed some success in making the study of religion an integral part of liberal studies. The School of Religion at the University of Iowa became a model for other experiments after its official opening in 1927. Thirty years later its faculty and courses had been fully integrated into the College of Liberal Arts, and the school was offering graduate degrees in religion.[37] Supported financially by Protestants, Catholics, and Jews, the Iowa school initially appointed professors to represent each of the three groups, formed a board of trustees made up of denominational and university officials, and offered courses in biblical studies, religious education, ethics, and comparative religion. The founders of the school stated that they "aspired to supplement state education with religious inspiration, instruction and practice" and to "complete a well-rounded education" with "religion taught scientifically by scholarly specialists."[38]

By the late 1920s, it was apparent that the blending of the aims of scientific study, the practice of piety, and training in religious leadership in American universities had not produced the results sought by Charles Foster Kent, Harry Emerson Fosdick, and other divinity school educators. In a complaint that echoed Kent's lamentation of 1911, Professor Luther Weigle of the Yale Divinity School commiserated with his fellow theological educators in 1926 over the miserable preparation in the study of religion that most ministerial students brought with them to divinity school.[39] Eight years later, in his comprehensive study of ministerial education in America, Professor William Adams Brown of Union Seminary in New York expressed the same grievance, noting that the student from a Harvard or a Yale college, quite as much as the student from a state university, a denominational college, or a vocational school, brought "no uniform preparation on which his theological course may be built."[40]

Surveys of the interwar period revealed that although most tax-supported universities included some form of the study of religion in their curricula, for a decade enrollments in religion courses had been falling relative to total enrollment in the universities. Similar enrollment declines in religion courses had occurred in independent and denominational institutions of higher education.[41] By the 1940s, it also seemed that the attempt to make the study of religion a pervasive force within the university had not measured up to the expectations of religious educators. Scholars from diverse fields in colleges and universities testified to hostility toward religion in college textbooks and widespread neglect of reading in the field of religion on the part of undergraduate students.[42] The effort to extend the scientific study of religion into the American university—a study linked with the practice of piety and governed by the disciplines of the divinity schools—had largely failed.

Reasons for the failure were abundant. Economic conditions culminating in the Great Depression had forced the curtailment and elimination of fledgling religion programs. A well-planned but short-lived School of Religion at the University of Michigan, for example, fell victim to the depressed economy.[43] Faculty and administrators at many universities, especially at the state schools, concluded that the joining of the study of religion with the exercise of religion violated the principle of the separation of church and state.[44] Still other schools, including private, nonsectarian universities, viewed with skepticism the ability of teachers educated in Protestant divinity schools to address a religiously pluralistic student body with anything resembling neutrality, and so they confined those teachers and their courses to the margins of university life.[45]

Above all, an American social order shaped by the natural sciences and technology contained little sympathy for an approach to the study of religion that was at best a pale imitation of scientific ideals in its claims to inductive method and practical importance. Observers of the role of the study of religion in higher education were forced to admit in the 1930s and 1940s that the large universities catering to the interests of diverse classes of American society were emphasizing "the technical or vocational as distinct from the cultural" aspects of higher learning, and that even the denominational colleges were succumbing to the pressures of technical vocationalism.[46]

Some analysts of the situation were unwilling to rest the matter there. While recognizing the difficulties created for the study of religion by the economic, educational, and social conditions of the interwar years, they believed that the faculty had to assume some responsibility for the weakness of the field. Reviewing the role of religion in higher education during the first half of the twentieth century, Merrimon Cuninggim concluded in 1947 that too many religion courses had become known among undergraduate students as "snaps" or "crips" and did not deserve the respect or support of the colleges and universities. Cuninggim did complain about the lack of opportunities for the development of the study of religion in institutions of higher education, but he insisted that finally those opportunities had to be earned: "it is not merely that religion be *given* comparable educational standing with other departments; it is also that religion *merit* such standing on the basis of the quality of the work it is now allowed to offer."[47]

Cuninggim's indictment fell as heavily upon the divinity schools that trained the college teachers of religion as upon the teachers themselves. In fact, his analysis of the state of the field entailed a repudiation of the so-called "scientific" perspective of his predecessors in both the theological and the religious sciences. Concerned about what he judged to be a pervasive atmosphere of secularism and relativism in postwar America, he believed that the study of religion should abandon the " 'objectivity' pose of the pseudo-scholar" and should meet the crisis of the times with programs of study that both reflect upon and promote religious values.[48] Only such a strategy could simultaneously infuse higher education with the values requisite for the survival of human civilization and earn the respect which religion deserved in the university. Cuninggim's position would be adopted widely by leaders in divinity schools and universities who had lost confidence in the promises of science and who would seek a scholarly approach to religion appropriate to an age of anxiety.

## DOMINANCE OF THE BIG ISSUES

"You better give me something. You better give me something fast." That indefinite, urgent demand made by Jim Stark (played by James Dean) to his father (Jim Backus) in the 1955 movie *Rebel Without a Cause* speaks volumes about an age. As one of the first Hollywood depictions of juvenile delinquency among the American middle class, the movie dramatized the lives of rebellious teenagers caught up in knife fights, games of "chicken" played with fast cars, and a moody state of alienation from suburban parents unsympathetic to their adolescent dilemmas. The subtext of the film, however, was a pervasive sense of anxiety about the future, compressed into fears of an impending threat of nuclear holocaust. Stark's desperate entreaty to his father came just before he left the house to accept a fateful challenge to a game of chicken and following a terrifying planetarium portrayal of the destruction of the solar system. Stark's friend, played by Sal Mineo, kept pressing throughout the movie the question of when the world would end.

Stark's expression of a free-floating *Angst* and the movie's theme of apocalyptic ending gave voice to a plaintive plea found elsewhere within a postwar America characterized structurally by economic prosperity, educational opportunity, and renewed hopes for American international influence. If, as *Rebel Without a Cause* signifies, the mood of white middle-class adolescents in the 1950s cannot quite be captured by the portrait of bobby-soxers slow-dancing to dreamy music, neither can the attitudes of their elders be summarized simply as a mindless rush to college fraternity parties, suburban houses and gadgets, and sentimental family togetherness. The times were marked by visions of peril as well as of promise, by dark fears about the future as well as by frivolous enjoyment of the present.

A sense of optimism sprang from the massive social expansion of the times. America had survived a deep economic recession, had won the war, and had assumed a new set of international responsibilities contingent upon the possession of nuclear power. Financed by mortgage money with low interest rates, millions of Americans moved to the newly developing suburbs, and they bought cars to carry them between home and work. The construction and automobile industries flourished. Spurred by low tuition costs, the promise of American businesses that a college degree assured one a good job in the corporate world, and the GI Bill of Rights that offered veterans the opportunity to go to college at government expense, increasing numbers of the middle class sought the bachelor's degree. In the 1950s, more than twice the number of Americans graduated from college than in the previous generation. But the postwar years also saw the urbanization of black people devoid of the same opportunities for higher education and economic abundance, conflicts created by demands for racial integration, and fears of the spread of "godless communism" nationally and internationally. Polls indicated that those Americans who could remember the days of the Great Depression continued to worry about their economic security. And as they built their bomb shelters against the day of the nuclear holocaust, it was as if they, quite as much as Jim Stark, were haunted by the grave warning of Albert Einstein in 1946: "The unleashed power of the atom has changed everything save our modes of thinking, and thus we drift toward unparalleled catastrophe."[49]

American religion was a beneficiary of both the national prosperity and the national anxieties of the time. The period from 1945 to 1960 witnessed a generalized turn to religion, what was then called a widespread "revival of religion." By the end of the period a large majority of the American population claimed to be affiliated with some religious institution, more than half said they attended church or synagogue regularly, new congregations had multiplied dramatically (in some years at a rate of one new congregation every three days for the Methodists), and expenditures on new church buildings had surpassed a billion dollars annually. Those were also times when publishers discovered that religious books sold well, preachers became national celebrities, and the phrase "under God" was added to the national Pledge of Allegiance. Fundamentalist and evangelical churches flourished quite as much as did the liberal churches associated with the ecumenical movement, and Billy Graham's revivalist admonitions competed with Norman Vincent Peale's peace-of-mind assuagements for the attention of the American people.

As Winthrop S. Hudson has remarked, "Unlike earlier religious revivals, the 'return to religion' of the 1950s was formless and unstructured, manifesting itself in many different ways and reinforcing all religious faiths quite indiscriminately." But lurking beneath the different manifestations of religious renewal, Hudson suggests, were the Cold War with the Soviet Union as a threat to the survival of Western values, continuing worries over the economy, and an anxiety fostered by the existence of The Bomb.[50] Religion appeared to be offering multiple ways of meeting Jim Stark's demand, "Give me something fast."

The university divinity schools prospered from the national turn to religion, and their faculties offered their own answers to the postwar anxiety. Many of the schools undertook expensive building programs, all hired new faculty, and most found themselves for the first time carefully selecting the most highly qualified students from a surplus of applicants.[51] Widespread interest in religious questions also created a receptive environment for divinity school theologians, especially for those who could translate their ideas into the compelling issues of the day. Paul Tillich and Reinhold Niebuhr became public theologians in a way unparalleled in America before or since their time. Tillich and Niebuhr were much in demand on the college lecture circuit, were often featured in the mass media, and were sometimes sought as advisers to political leaders on national and international affairs.[52]

Tillich's appeal lay in his expression of the existential concerns of a postwar America as he preached sermons on the "shaking of the foundations" of Western civilization, translated the meaning of Christian faith into the psychological categories of "the courage-to-be in the face of anxiety," and interpreted God as "the Ground of Being" supportive of a human existence fractured by an epidemic alienation.[53] Impatient with Tillich's preoccupation with the anxiety of the individual and his abstruse philosophical categories, Niebuhr preferred the language of history, the Bible, and politics. In his own way, however, Niebuhr sought to speak to the anxiety of the times as he probed the Christian tradition's portrayals of human hubris and divine solace. Attacking what he took to be the irrelevant, sentimental piety of much American Protestantism, he argued that a contemporary world riddled by awesome power conflicts requires a hardy biblical religion that is simultaneously forgiving of human foibles through love and active in the approximation of justice through the use of power.[54]

Tillich and Niebuhr were the most visible of a number of Protestant theologians who sought to address an American public made receptive to religious messages by the postwar environment. Operating at academic bases (both of them at Union Seminary, then Tillich at Harvard and Chicago), they also typified theologians of the day who had disavowed science and the scientific method as adequate descriptions of their tasks, as suitable avenues into the university world, or as appropriate ways of connecting with the times. Mindful of the culmination of science and technology in the horrors of atomic warfare and in the dangerous brinkmanship of the Cold War, they believed that the impassioned interpretation of the great themes of human nature and destiny, not the disinterested discovery of empirical facts, constituted their charge from the culture. And they experienced more intellectual kinship with their university colleagues in the humanities and the humanistic social sciences than they did with the scientist in the laboratory or the archeologist in the field. They felt summoned, by their times and by their environment, to deal with the Big Issues.

That sense of calling, more than anything else, is what united most theologians in the divinity schools between 1945 and 1960. Beyond that unifying sense, there was considerable variety of theological perspective in the schools. It was not unusual to find on the same faculty theologians who took their bearings from such diverse sources as the neoorthodoxy of Karl Barth, various philosophical schools of existentialism, the major Protestant reformers, contemporary literature, Old Testament themes regarding the "acts of God in history" (*Heilsgeschichte*), and Niebuhrian social analysis.[55] Furthermore, individual theologians had arrived at their reservations about the adequacy of the old scientific worldview for different reasons and with different consequences.

Some theologians, like H. Richard Niebuhr of Yale and Edwin Lewis of Drew, had been particularly attracted to Karl Barth's resounding *Nein!* to the confusion of the Christian message with any form of human culture in Europe. Others, like Henry Nelson Wieman, Bernard Loomer, and Bernard Meland at Chicago, turned their backs on the neoconservative winds blowing from across the Atlantic and continued to be guided by modern scientific theories in their theological constructions. Even many of those theologians who had been influenced by neoorthodox German thought were, in H. Richard Niebuhr's language, more concerned than their German counterparts with the opportunities for "Christ transforming culture." What characterized most theologies in America during and after World War II, however, was a conviction that any easy confidence in the beneficent powers of science and technology so characteristic of theology in the first quarter of the twentieth century had been a dangerous illusion.[56] The judgment was widespread among Protestant theologians of many different stripes that the grand themes of the Christian tradition, not the values constitutive of the worldview of science, should direct the course of theology.

That judgment extended beyond divinity school professors responsible for teaching in the curricular division of theology. It often pervaded the other divinity school disciplines as well. University of Chicago Divinity School professor of church history Jerald Brauer, who was to become the first dean of the Chicago Federated Theological Faculty in 1955, remembered the decade of the 1950s as a period when emphasis at the Divinity School was placed on theology as a ubiquitous project to be pursued from several disciplinary approaches. "It was stressed that this was a 'theological faculty' and that all members did theology from the perspective of their particular disciplines. One was a theologian first and an historian of Christianity second."[57]

The theological emphasis derived in large part from the insistence of the Divinity School's dean, theologian Bernard Loomer, that the purpose of divinity education should be the development of a theological intellect among students, rather than the provision of ministerial skills. Adopting the philosophy of Chicago president Robert M. Hutchins that higher education should cultivate minds, not vocational talents, Loomer gave that philosophy his own theological twist: "The aim of divinity education is the disciplined development of heart and mind toward the integrity of faith and intellectual inquiry for the sake of the cultivation of the human spirit's relation to and service to God." Such an aim presupposes the more specific educational goal of becoming "more perceptively aware of the ways and work of God in human life" through separate "historical, biblical, theological, and practical" studies.[58]

As Brauer pointed out, the mere statement of these aims did not unite the theological faculty at Chicago into a neatly complementary set of disciplinary approaches: "the fact that the faculty was far from unanimous in its acceptance of [Loomer's] point of view made for both interesting interchange and occasional tension."[59] But at Chicago and other divinity schools of the period, interchanges and disagreements among the faculty over the role of theology in the curriculum *did* occur, and the liveliest student and faculty colloquia centered on theological issues.[60] If all of the approaches of faculty in the various disciplines of the schools did not become simply variant ways of talking about the "ways and work of God in human life," the overriding trend in biblical studies, church history, and practical studies at most of the schools was toward consideration of the Christian theological motifs of sin, redemption, reconciliation, and the purposes of God in history.[61]

That same trend was apparent in the teaching of religion to undergraduates in American colleges and universities in the postwar period. A Christian theological perspective was allied with the goal of promoting the humanities in colleges and universities, and that alliance in turn was designed to restore to undergraduate learning an appreciation of human values through a process of "general education."

Divinity school educators were somewhat encouraged by two landmark studies, *General Education in a Free Society,* or the "Harvard Report" (1945), and *Higher Education for American Democracy,* or the "President's Report" (1948). Each report, representing the work of a team of educators, viewed the fragmentation of education through overspecialization as a neglect of the education of the whole person and of the historic traditions which shape whole persons. Each also called for an integrated curriculum that would deal with values that were constantly imperiled in the contemporary world. At the center of any integrative, general educational scheme should reside the humanities, which educate students to understand the cultural heritage of the past and to appropriate that heritage for their present lives. Although the reports lifted up the importance of undergraduate studies that would expose learners to cultures other than their own, they were clear that a broadened international understanding should not neglect the merits of the students' own Western heritage. And although the reports recognized the need for specialized education in a professionalized society, they insisted that the future of a democratic social order depended upon an education in the values of democratic citizenship. Each report also acknowledged the importance of the student's appreciation of religion's role in the development of national cultures and, most especially—in the words of the Harvard Report—in fostering belief "in the dignity and mutual obligation of man."[62]

In recognizing both the role of religion in human cultures and the need for the integration of higher education through the humanities, the two reports seemed to Protestant educators to open up new possibilities for the study of religion in American colleges and universities. In fact, it struck them that the study of religion, because of its forthright attention to human values and its commitment to dealing with the pressing human issues facing Western civilization, could occupy the very center of a higher education aimed at students struggling through their education to become whole persons and responsible citizens.

Merrimon Cuninggim submitted that both "democracy" and "humanistic studies" were too circumscribed to provide a unifying factor to general education. Religion, however, shaped by the "temper of theological thinking," was sufficiently broad, inclusive, and "representative of all the ideals and values which the college cherishes" to perform the unifying function. Yale Divinity School's Clarence Shedd proposed that undergraduate education in "the Hebrew-Christian faith" was a decisive way of providing "our American democracy with abiding foundations." And Will Herberg, who would later join the faculty of Drew, was convinced that the times called for nothing less than a "biblical theology of education": "I would suggest that the purpose of liberal education is to give us a more profound insight into the human situation, into man's creaturely existence in the world—in his alienation from God—and in this way enhance our understanding of, and sensitivity to, the condition and need of our neighbor as well as our own."[63]

The study of religion from the Christian theological perspective, or from the lumped perspective of the "Judeo-Christian heritage" (itself a Christian theological category), was widely recommended by divinity school educators in the postwar years as an effective humanizing and integrative factor in a general education designed to overcome the fragmenting effects of specialization. That recommendation was made very much in the spirit of an age which was troubled by national and international conflicts, which was distressed over the failure of the specialized sciences to deliver on their promises of peace, prosperity, and the unbiased pursuit of truth, and which was engaged in numerous searches for religious answers to the Big Issues.

Down to the mid-1960s, faculty responsible for academic religion programs in colleges and universities differed over the question of whether the large, integrative function of the study of religion was best accomplished through a departmental structure. Alexander Miller of Stanford University and Huston Smith of Washington University in St. Louis argued for the viability of the programs at their institutions that worked toward the diffusion of the study of religion throughout the liberal arts curriculum. Adhering to the neoorthodox premise that "biblical and Christian faith" cannot be subsumed under the generic category of "religion," Miller maintained that a study of that faith was best advanced through courses offered through Stanford's administrative unit of Special Programs in Humanities. Also fearful that a departmental structure would isolate the biblical/theological perspective from the rest of the university, Miller believed that religion professors based in a humanities division would enjoy the freedom to encourage faculty in the departments of philosophy, history, sociology, and psychology to study that perspective in their own programs.[64] Huston Smith defended a program in religion that would draw upon faculty in several disciplines, with a specialist in the study of religion serving as a link among the several cooperating departments. The overall aim of Smith's program was to disseminate the study of religion widely throughout the curriculum and provide a "vision of unity" for large sectors of a fragmented university.[65]

Many educators in the field were unconvinced by the diffusionists' positions, on both practical and theoretical grounds. Clyde Holbrook of Oberlin College, Luther Harshbarger of Pennsylvania State University, and Robert Michaelsen of the School of Religion at Iowa found Miller's neoorthodox presuppositions inappropriate to the pluralism of American institutions of higher education, and Smith's strictly interdisciplinary approach lacking in the power required to effect change in institutions organized departmentally. Furthermore, why assume that the study of religion is by nature any more interdisciplinary than is history or sociology? What assurances were there that administrators, faculty, and students would take professors outside departmental structures seriously, or that the faculty teaching religion in other departments would be adequately trained in the field? And what would serve to unite a diffuse faculty intellectually or promote their scholarship in the field of religion?[66]

Reservations about the diffusionists' position, coupled with opportunities provided by the growth in higher education in the 1950s and early 1960s, tilted the national pattern toward the formation of departments of religion. Yet those convinced of the need for the departmental structure often warned that the larger, integrative role of the study of religion should not be abandoned. As Holbrook put it, "Certainly the danger persists that if there is a department of religion, some instructors in other fields will feel that religion is taken care of 'over there' and will neglect their own academic responsibility in this area."[67] Holbrook's caveat suggests the way in which many faculty in charge of undergraduate programs in religion down to the mid-1960s refused to understand their field as just another specialty among a welter of specialties in the liberal arts. They continued to adhere to the notion that the study of religion in a liberal arts setting should serve as an integrative discipline, should ramify throughout the curriculum, and should engage the mammoth issues affecting human nature and destiny.

Educators who believed that the study of religion within a separate department should be clearly differentiated from the chapel and other forms of the practice of religion could still hold that the study of religion could—and should—avoid becoming a merely rational enterprise divorced from the religious lives of persons and institutions. That conviction was clearly stated by George F. Thomas, appointed a professor of religious thought to found a separate Department of Religion at Princeton University.

Princeton had taken the official position in 1935 that the study of religion in the university should be clearly differentiated from worship and that religion had a well-defined subject matter that could not be subsumed under the other disciplines in the liberal arts. In his inaugural lecture of 1940, Thomas stated his belief that both principles could be maintained without severing the study of religion from its vital connections with religious persons, religious institutions, and humanistic learning as a whole:

> . . . the rational analysis of religion, which we are undertaking should never be allowed to become a substitute for the *living experience* of religion. This means that the University Chapel, the churches, and other religious organizations are indispensable allies of any program of religious instruction which is to be effective. . . . There is no place for preaching in the class room; and there is no time when rigorous analysis should be softened because it conflicts with religious preconceptions. But historical description and philosophical reflection cannot take the place of the direct insight or stimulus which may come to the student from a psalm, parable, or poem in the Bible or in other classical literature.[68]

Thomas further held that the study of religion in the university should align itself with the insider perspective of student and professor:

... to demand of the student that, outside or even inside the class room, he exclude all desires, all feelings, all hopes, all fears, as if the whole meaning of life for him were not at stake and he could be completely indifferent to the result of the analysis, is to ask something impossible and inhuman. . . . In short, the analysis and evaluation of religion from the outside, from the point of view of the observer, must be supplemented by an attempt to penetrate to the heart of it by intuition and to identify oneself with it in feeling.[69]

Thomas's call for a symbiotic relation between the academic study of religion and the practice of religion, and for the teacher's and student's intuitive participation in religion's own inner world, echoed through the language of those responsible for the creation and justification of programs in the study of religion in America's universities.[70] It was a call born of the postwar *Zeitgeist* and nurtured by the dominance of the theological perspective in the divinity schools that supplied the faculty for the emerging programs.

The ethos of the divinity schools had done more than influence the thought and rhetoric of scholars of religion. It had also fashioned the undergraduate curriculum. Throughout the 1950s, those colleges and universities that offered a full panoply of courses in the field of religion had in the main duplicated the divinity school curriculum. The same was true of the university graduate programs in religion that had begun to emerge as alternatives to divinity school education. Although courses in such areas as introduction to religion and Eastern religions had found their way into the courses of instruction, most courses were offered in those areas, with the exception of the practical areas like preaching and pastoral counseling, that the divinity schools utilized for the education of ministers—courses in church history and the history of Christian thought, Bible (usually following the Christian division between the "old" and the "new" testaments), contemporary theology or Christian thought, and Christian ethics. As late as 1965, a collection of essays commissioned to survey the status of the field of religion devoted 90 percent of its attention to the areas of study that duplicated divinity school education.[71]

Some professors of religion contended that the parallels between the curriculum in the liberal arts and that of the divinity schools did not result from a direct borrowing. That was the judgment of Paul Ramsey respecting the very divinity-school-like curriculum in his own religion department at Princeton. Ramsey insisted that the area divisions "have their own integrity wherever they may be taught or studied" and that the "division of subject matter and the appropriate methods of research arise from the nature of religion as a scholarly discipline."[72]

It is more than a little likely, however, that other factors accounted for the parallels. Most of the teachers in the liberal arts programs had been educated in a Protestant theological curriculum. As Robert Michaelsen was to say in 1965, the duplication of areas of interest sprang at least in part from "the fact that most of the programs designed to produce qualified scholars in religion have been associated with theological faculties in seminaries and university divinity schools where there has been a primary interest in theological scholarship and related areas."[73] And as Van A. Harvey was later to observe about the 1950s and early 1960s, "Departments of religion were obviously making exceedingly fine distinctions within one religious tradition by offering courses in Christian ethics, the history of Christianity (early, medieval, and modern), theology, and Bible (the term is Christian) and then adding one or two catch-all survey courses into which Hinduism, Buddhism, Taoism and everything else must fit." Furthermore, according to Harvey, this Christian theological bearing led teachers of religion to understand their field as belonging primarily to the humanities, which sought to help students come to terms with their own "life posture," an understanding that resulted in the neglect of the social sciences.[74]

By the time of the Welch Report in 1971, the preoccupation of divinity school educators with theological issues and the preponderant orientation of the study of religion toward a theological interpretation of the humanities were disappearing. Scholars in the study of religion, oriented in the postwar period to theological trends in the divinity schools and to the general turn to religion in the culture at large, were now launched in search of an independent specialty and set of subspecialties. They were seeking to define their field by reference to other specialties in the universities, specialties which were not connected to theology and which exhibited no ambition of unifying a fragmented higher education.

## FROM THE STUDY OF RELIGION
## TO RELIGIOUS STUDIES

By the dawn of the 1970s, the postwar religious revival, at least that aspect of the revival from which the Protestant churches had profited, was finished. Deep divisions within the churches over civil rights agitation, the war in Southeast Asia, and the American "military-industrial complex" not only had ended the old ecumenical climate in the divinity schools and contributed to the decline of the mainline churches. The divisions also had created a different religious climate in institutions of higher education. For undergraduates who were religiously inclined, a religious quest was often joined with either a loud or a quiet countercultural protest against the "establishment," including the organized religion of their upbringing.

College youth were exemplary embodiments of what social psychologist Robert J. Lifton called the "Protean Man" of the time. Because of widespread social dislocations, it was not unusual for a single individual to pass through several ideological shifts in a lifetime. For undergraduates the shifts could entail experimentation with diverse religious personae—this year a Presbyterian, next year a Buddhist, and the next a practitioner of Transcendental Meditation. In one sense, the religious experimentation of youth was similar to the postwar religious revival: both were characterized by anxiety over the future. But the latter-day anxiety seemed to arise more from the dread of being drafted to serve in an unpopular war in Vietnam than from worries over nuclear holocaust, and more from feelings of the individual's powerlessness within American institutions than from apprehensions about economic uncertainty.[75]

In any case, the religious postures of America's youth were not so frequently tied to the impulse to prepare for the traditional Protestant ministry. Divinity schools found that increasing numbers of their students were uncertain about their vocational goals and entered theological study to "find themselves" or to find ways to change the structures of society.[76] And as the Welch study had discerned, few students were enrolling in religion courses in universities for preministerial training. Professional connections that had once obtained between theological study and the study of religion had been broken.

Some teachers of religion celebrated the severing of the connections. In the estimate of Edmund Perry, chair of the Department of History and Literature of Religions at Northwestern University, in 1966 the "Protestant tyranny" over departments of religion was coming to an end, creating a moment of freedom that held important consequences for the study of religion in the university: "1) The content of the undergraduate curriculum in religion will not be determined by considerations of the service it can render to Protestant seminaries; and 2) this content will be inclusive of convictional traditions, faithfully represented, other than the Judeo-Christian tradition. It is not just indiscriminate prediction to say that religion departments have come of age."[77]

If Perry exaggerated the coming of age of the study of religion in 1966, he did not exaggerate by much. In 1964 the name of the professional association for teachers of religion had been changed from the National Association of Biblical Instructors (NABI) to the American Academy of Religion (AAR), and two years later the organization's journal, formerly *The Journal of Bible and Religion*, became *The Journal of the American Academy of Religion*. Although the changes in nomenclature were not designed to exclude theological school professors—many of those professors would join the organization and write for the journal—the changes were born of the desire of teachers of undergraduates to lay claim to their own academic territory. Those faculty responsible for forming the AAR out of the NABI believed that the professional association should support research and scholarship as well as teaching among liberal arts professors, and that it should represent a broader task than the perpetuation of biblical studies and other seminary-inspired courses.[78] The founding of the AAR and its journal called attention to, and in some ways even created, the academic field of "religious studies,"* a field that defined itself in large measure as an alternative to the study of religion dominated by the aims of the Protestant divinity school.

Signs of the growing independence of religious studies emerged over the course of a decade. Prompted by the interests of undergraduate students, religious studies faculty added courses in non-Western religions on a scale unparalleled in the divinity schools. Sensitive to the religiously and culturally pluralistic setting of the university classroom, faculty in religious studies called for reflection on what it means to study religion in that setting.[79] Articles published in scholarly journals also signaled a field that was plotting its own course. In the 1970s, there was a marked increase in the number of articles on Asian religions, religion and the arts, and religion and the social sciences published in the *Journal of the American Academy of Religion*.[80] Publications of religious studies fac-

---

*Departments and programs in the liberal arts would continue to use diverse designations such as "religion," "history and literature of religion," and "religion studies," as well as "religious studies." After the mid-1960s, however, most of the literature devoted to the nature of the study of religion in universities used the designation "religious studies," and I use the term to denote a field that took on a quite different appearance from the postwar study of religion that was shaped within the mold of theological studies in the divinity schools.

ulty in other scholarly journals also began to eclipse those of faculty in the divinity schools. By 1980, their contributions to such journals as *Church History,* the *Journal of Biblical Literature,* and the *Journal of Religion* had outstripped by a wide margin the contributions of faculty in all American divinity schools and seminaries combined.[81]

A clear sign that faculty in religious studies were embarked on a venture to establish their autonomy appeared in their continuing engrossment with issues of theory and method. They believed that the *way* they studied their subject matter, quite as much as the subject matter itself, would set them apart from their backgrounds in theological education and situate them in their current university environment. Much of their concern with theory and method centered on the question of whether religious studies should be conceived strictly as a branch of the humanities, and on the related question of how humanistic and social scientific approaches to religion might be integrally related.[82] Frequently bound up with those questions were debates about the propriety of including theology in religious studies.

Some participants in the debates insisted that a postseminary model for the study of religion need not exclude forms of theologizing—those nonproselytizing, nondogmatic, nonapologetic forms that encourage students to reflect upon common human problems with religious categories, or that lead them to ponder critically the truth claims of religion, or that even lead them to develop creatively their own postures toward the religious dimensions of culture.[83] Others within the field, especially those who adopted the theories and methods of the social sciences, found these arguments for theology to be little more than thinly veiled attempts to retain partisan Christian perspectives in the study of religion and proof of a failure of nerve on the part of religious studies programs to establish an objective, detached study appropriate to the demands of a pluralistic university.[84]

Still others called for a candidly "reductionist approach" to the field, so long as that term meant explaining religion with causes other than those of "sacred transcendence" or with theories obtained from perspectives outside the views of religion itself. Reductionist explanations might be inappropriate to theological schools, one historian of Western religion argued, but they were altogether appropriate to a university where the study of religion should refuse to stake out its own "privileged universe of discourse" and where it should attend to methods and arguments generally operative in the liberal arts.[85] A recent study of faculty attitudes found that younger religious studies scholars were especially antipathetic to theology and were prone to model the study of religion on the descriptive, explanatory model of the social sciences.[86]

It is significant that in the midst of these sometimes heated quarrels about the nature of the field, after the mid-1960s the arguments no longer focused on how the study of religion could serve as an organizing force within the university, or on the manner in which it could operate as a principal carrier of the values of Western civilization. And gone was the pleading for the construction of the undergraduate curriculum according to the theological motifs of Christianity or the "Judeo-Christian tradition." Judged in the light of the disappearance of those earlier concerns, religious studies had abandoned the model of education nourished by the Protestant divinity school in the postwar period. Those occupying the field now would measure their task neither by the religious trends in the larger American culture nor by the programs of study in the divinity schools. They would gauge their work, instead, by how well it conformed to the canons of the disciplinary specialties in the contemporary American university.

Eager to differentiate their enterprise from the old theologically informed humanistic approach, some religious studies faculty were especially attracted to the subspecialties within the social sciences. In addition to making increased use of the social and cultural theories of the history of religions, they applied to religion the theories and methods of sociologists, anthropologists, cultural and social historians, and social psychologists, as well as those of phenomenologists, philosophers, and literary critics with a bent toward the tangible worlds of discrete cultures. Expansion of subject matter accompanied augmentation of approach as religious studies faculty took up the study of such areas as popular religion, Native American religions, newly emergent religions, civil or political religions, and religion and the arts.[87] Scholars trained in divinity school graduate programs in "church history" became "historians of Christianity," teachers with a background in "Christian ethics" became "comparative religious ethicists," and those educated as "Old Testament scholars" became "scholars of the Hebrew Bible."[88]

Concerned to avoid even the suspicion that the academic study of religion was itself a form of religion, religious studies faculty deliberately dissociated their tasks as scholars from those of practitioners of religion. The hope held out by some of the founders of separate departments of religion that their role as academics in the classroom, though clearly differentiated from the functions of chaplains and campus ministers, could somehow draw upon the context of the religious practice of students and their religious communities was a hope largely abandoned. One ethicist who argued in the mid-1980s that problem-centered theological reflection was still an acceptable undertaking in religious studies had to admit that the drift of such reflection was away from firsthand knowledge of the experiences of people in religious communities.[89]

By the 1980s, many scholars of religion in the university had steered back toward the model of "scientific objectivity" characteristic of the early twentieth century. It was a return with some differences, but it was a return nonetheless. In the terms of the Supreme Court decision that had given the field such a rhetorical boost in public institutions during the growth period of the 1960s, religious studies was devoted largely to teaching *about* religion, instead of instructing *in* religion. Faculty in the field could now argue an officially sanctioned position that they were engaged in an objective, disinterested study of religion, one that entailed no advocacy of a given religious outlook or set of religious values.

Many religious studies scholars acknowledged that this position oversimplified their task. Their self-description usually possessed little of the epistemological naiveté apparent in the old objectivist argument. They knew that to ask a question of a religious tradition is implicitly to frame an answer, that to describe any religious phenomenon is already to have made a judgment that some materials appropriate to that phenomenon are more valuable than a welter of others, that to interpret another religious perspective is to impose the presence of interpreter upon interpreted, that an intelligent reading of any text requires empathetic participation as well as critical distance.[90]

But as with their early twentieth-century predecessors, the appeals of the new scholars to objectivity were informed less by operative theory or method and more by an overarching worldview comprised of a system of academic values. They described their academic posture as that of "disinterested objectivity," "personal detachment," "disinterested irreverence," "the perspective of the outsider," and (shades of the late nineteenth century) as "nonsectarian" as a way of calling attention to their abandonment of a past and the adoption of a future. The past they repudiated—sometimes the past of their own divinity school educations—assumed that the study of religion in the university should in some fashion be bound up with the perpetuation of the Christian faith and should be modeled on the theological disciplines current in the divinity schools.[91] They replaced that assumption with the supposition that the scholar, as scholar, could take a position as an outsider to any specific religious commitment. Unlike their counterparts in the early twentieth century, however, they framed their objective worldview not out of admiration for the astonishing cultural achievements or the heady promises of certainty in natural science, but out of their perception of what constituted the scholarly requirements and disciplinary expectations of specialized competence in the university.

By the early 1990s, departments of religious studies had by no means won an utterly secure place in the American university. Some were still being singled out by university administrators as candidates for dissolution.[92] Yet in comparison with its status during those difficult years of the first half of the twentieth century, religious studies had won a respectably secure home in the university. In fact, in the view of some members of the field, religious studies faculty had grown too comfortable in their academic home. Ray L. Hart, when reflecting in 1979 upon the shape of the field at the conclusion of his ten-year term as editor of the *Journal of the American Academy of Religion*, found much to celebrate in the developments of a decade. Religious studies scholars had demonstrated to deans and faculty committees that they could study their subject "according to the rules of the house" and that, like other disciplines in the university, theirs had "organized itself for research and its publication across a broad spectrum of subdisciplines." But there was some danger, in the view of Hart and others, that scholars in the field had become too much at home, too bound to subdisciplinary specialization, too lacking in the sense of homelessness that sustains a critical and creative perspective on one's own academic environment.[93]

Any discomfort about too much comfort, however, could arise only from those who had seen a field of study cross many of the barriers to occupancy of the university. Not only had they convinced some key administrators and colleagues of the legitimacy of their enterprise; they had managed to win the approval of larger publics. By the mid-1970s, the National Endowment for the Humanities had added "ethics and comparative religion" to its representative fields in the humanities, and by the end of the decade the American Academy of Religion had joined the ranks of the constituent societies in the American Council of Learned Societies. In 1988, the *Chronicle of Higher Education*, which ten years earlier had judged religious studies to be in the throes of an identity crisis and in a state of overexpansion, devoted an article to the field's overall health and to the proliferating interest in the study of religion across a wide spectrum of academic disciplines.[94] Annual meetings of the American Academy of Religion included lectures by eminent scholars from cognate disciplines and by public figures like Jesse Jackson and William Bennett.

The professional meetings also displayed the increased specialization of religious studies. In over two hundred sessions filled with more than eight hundred formal papers, the annual meeting of the American Academy of Religion had become an assemblage of subspecialties as diverse as Japanese religions, women's studies in religion, North American religions, African American religions, Zoroastrianism, and scores of others. The lack of an apparent center to all this diverse learning prompted the leadership of the AAR in the late 1980s to appoint a plenary speaker each year to try to draw some connections among the assorted approaches and subject matters of the annual program. One of those speakers had to admit that an examination of the topics of the programs since the late 1960s led to the distinct impression that "we have become more and more like the Democratic party—a collection of interest groups strung together on a slender thread."[95]

More to the point, perhaps, the multiplicity of scholarly interests had come to resemble that of the Modern Language Association, the American Historical Association, and other professional societies in the humanities and social sciences. Like those academic societies, in gathering together representatives of diverse subdisciplines—themselves internally subdivided—the AAR had replicated the "plural organized world" of the academy.[96] By the 1980s, religious studies had come of age in a way Edmund Perry probably had not intended in his mid-1960s avowal: it had become as fragmented as every other mature academic discipline.

## DIVERGENT PATHS OF SPECIALIZATION

In the late twentieth century, religious studies and theological studies had taken separate paths that led, if not in opposite, certainly in different directions. Faculty both in the divinity schools and in departments of religious studies had adopted the strategy of specialization as a way of securing for the study of religion a legitimate place in the modern American university. That common aim, however, developed from distinctive values and led to different consequences in the 1970s and 1980s.

Prompted by ecumenical Christianity's shift to concern for globalization, by a changed international situation that had undercut Western Christianity's unilateral social influence, and by the undeniable presence of religious others in their midst, faculty in Protestant divinity schools continued their long heritage of specialization out of a sense of responsibility for the church's role in a radically pluralistic world. The divinity schools justified their place in a specialized university environment by appealing to the church's need to understand others in all of their particularity. In the same period, faculty in religious studies were motivated neither by a sense of responsibility to the church nor by a perception of Protestantism's changed position in the world. Although they may have been stimulated in part to specialize by the pressing religious and cultural pluralism in the university and around the globe, they were much more directly moved to adopt the strategies of specialization from their desire to establish a bona fide university discipline.[97] Determined to demonstrate to their university colleagues that the study of religion could operate as a discipline within the liberal arts and that such study need not be confined to the churchly realm of the divinity school, religious studies faculty sought to carve out their niche in the university with an approach that was detached, objective, and altogether nonapologetic. Responsive to the academic pluralism in their academic home, they also branched into areas of teaching and research and employed theories and methods that had been largely neglected by the divinity schools.

Claude Welch had detected most of the consequences of these disparate paths of specialization. Few graduate students aspiring to teach religion were passing through the requirements of the professional ministerial degree, and fewer still would conceive of their roles in the university as a form of the "teaching ministry."[98] A large majority of undergraduates were majoring in religion or taking courses in religion not because of professional plans but out of personal or intellectual interest or to fulfill a requirement. And university faculty were beginning to redefine their divinity school graduate specialties to match their actual performance as teachers and scholars in the university. Welch also foresaw, if only by way of urging, that religious studies faculty would move beyond the approaches and areas dictated by a theological framework into a wide assortment of methods, theories, and objects of study. And he detected a trend in graduate education that would only increase over the next twenty years: the study of religion was understood as a branch of the arts and sciences rather than as a component of the theological curriculum. During the 1980s, 40 percent of the entry-level faculty hired in public universities in the United States were products of graduate programs unaffiliated with divinity schools. When graduates of the University of Chicago are added in, the figure reaches 54 percent.[99] By the 1980s, the Chicago Divinity School was enrolling the highest percentage of its students in graduate degree programs other than in its professional ministry program, and the graduate curriculum had taken a decisive turn toward religious studies.[100]

The emphases at Chicago indicate the manner in which the distinctive directions of religious studies departments and divinity schools could nonetheless cross paths. The changing opportunities of the academic job market led divinity schools to reconsider the aims of their graduate programs. By the 1960s, all the Protestant university divinity schools had made the Ph.D. a degree granted by the graduate division of the arts and sciences, but before that time most of their doctoral students were in training to teach in seminaries, other divinity schools, and denominational colleges. With the rapid growth of undergraduate religious studies departments and programs, the market needs for their Ph.D. recipients shifted. In their planning for the 1970s, many of the divinity schools determined that in a tight job market for their graduates, more attention on the part of faculty should be paid to preparation of teachers in the newly emergent religious studies departments in public and large private universities.[101]

Courses for Ph.D. candidates were sometimes added in the areas of introduction to religion, Asian religions, theories of religion, and other subjects appropriate to the instruction of undergraduates. Faculty in undergraduate departments of religion occupying the same campuses as divinity schools—faculty previously excluded from graduate teaching—were brought into the graduate programs.[102] In 1963, Yale established a separate graduate department in religious studies devoted to scholarship in religion as distinct from professional education in the ministry. Some Yale Divinity School faculty were denied positions on the graduate faculty, and graduate students no longer were required to register in the Divinity School. These actions not only created strong tensions among some of the Divinity School faculty but also reversed the relative positions of status between religious studies and theological studies.[103]

During the 1970s, doctoral work at the Divinity School of the University of Chicago turned increasingly toward the examination of the nature of religion and a study of diverse religious traditions. Between 1969 and 1975, the stated purpose of the school shifted from study of the nature, content, and consequences of religion on the part of an institution "whose basic commitment is to the great traditions of Christian thought," to study of the various Christian traditions and other major world religions on the part of a school "mindful of its Christian origins." As Chicago theologian Langdon Gilkey said in 1974, at one time the Divinity School was centered on Christian theology "as the intellectual expression of the Christian faith," but that clearly was no longer the case. "At best this school as a whole finds its unity in the common enterprise of the study of *religion*; its history, its varieties, its ethical consequences, its manifestations in literature and the arts, its relations to psychology, sociology and the sciences." He understood his own role as a Christian theologian to be reflection upon the meaning and truth of the symbols of one religious tradition among many.[104] Religious studies had definitely exercised an influence upon divinity school education.

That influence had resulted in no radical reconstruction of graduate education in religion at the divinity schools, however, and neither the distinctive purposes of religious studies nor those of theological studies were served by the divinity schools that tried to mix the two. Despite the inclusion of faculty from departments of religious studies in graduate teaching, the addition of courses appropriate to undergraduate teaching, and the expansion of educational aims to meet the market opportunities in religious studies, most divinity-school-based graduate programs continued to bear the telltale signs of their Protestant theological heritage. Most still organized their graduate curricula according to the traditional fields of theology, church history, Bible, and ethics. They drew most heavily upon the large pool of divinity school faculty, rather than upon the much smaller pool of faculty in departments of religious studies, to educate graduate students. Most continued to enroll graduate students and upper-level ministerial candidates in the same seminars. And they found it difficult to secure divinity school faculty to teach graduate students how to handle those staples of the undergraduate curriculum, introduction to religion and approaches to religion.[105]

Theological schools, on the other hand, found that their own requirements for teachers were not being met by divinity schools that had tried to accommodate the demands of religious studies. Seminary deans complained about the difficulty of locating beginning-level professors who were equally committed to research and scholarship in religion and to the education of Protestant ministers. Some theological school leaders even claimed that because of the controlling interests of religious studies in divinity school graduate programs, it might be impossible in the future to staff seminaries with graduates of those programs. And some graduates of the programs who chose teaching careers in the seminaries felt caught between what they were taught and what they were expected to do—between their education in diverse theories and traditions of religion and the expectation that they educate future ministers into the practice of the Christian ministry.[106] By the end of the 1980s, it would appear that the alterations worked upon the divinity schools by religious studies had created a compromise graduate education that fully met the requirements of neither religious studies nor theological studies.

The attempted compromise between two distinctive purposes for the study of religion in American universities underscores a series of transformations that had occurred in the uses of specialization. For William Rainey Harper, Charles Foster Kent, and other early visionaries, the specialized study of religion in divinity schools was to be a major strategy for expanding the influence of Protestantism into broad reaches of American culture. Originally conceived as a way of drawing upon the power and resources of the modern American university to elevate the prestige, learning, and authority of the clergy, specialization was also defended as an effective instrument for spreading the influence of learned Protestantism among church laity, undergraduates, university teachers, and religious workers of all kinds. The force that would drive this influential specialization was "science," an approach to religion modeled on the methods of the natural sciences and governed by a worldview that valued progress, certitude, and objectivity.

As events of the twentieth century exploded that view of the world and as the theological sciences ran up against unyielding barriers in the churches and the universities, leaders in the divinity schools sought to infuse the specialties with theological interpretations of the issues weighing upon an anxious postwar America. They extended that same Christian theological perspective into university programs for the study of religion. The theological sciences thus became disciplines in an all-encompassing endeavor to humanize the university and the larger American society. From that endeavor, however, there emerged a new field, religious studies, that would take its bearings from multiple subdisciplines and from the pluralism of the university, rather than from the Christian theological perspective or the old humanizing intentions in the study of religion. The divinity schools themselves would find their own pluralism of orientation in a globalization movement marked by concern for Christian particularity and sympathy for the distinctive differences of other Christians and other religions and cultures. In the divinity schools and in departments of religious studies, for different reasons and with different aims in view, specialization was transformed from a strategy of Protestant influence into a means of preserving religious, educational, and cultural diversity.

# PART II

■

# PROFESSIONALIZATION

# CHAPTER IV

## *Theory and Practice*

When William Rainey Harper and other educational leaders urged upon the divinity schools the dual—to them, the complementary—functions of education in the academic specialties and professional training in the skills of the ministry, they propounded a view of the modern American university that would hold sway throughout the twentieth century. In that view, the university should offer to upper-level students preparation in the technical functions suitable to the practice of a profession and induction into the theoretical disciplines appropriate to advanced learning. An American society formed by the modern forces of specialization and technical competence mandated both tasks.

Throughout the century, university educators would note continuing conflicts between the theoretical and the practical demands of professional education, and students, faculty, and professionals themselves would continually disagree about the goals of professional education in the university.[1] Few American educators, however, would be willing to suggest that universities should surrender the task of professional education. To them and to many practicing professionals, as well, the American university has seemed the appropriate place to prepare physicians, attorneys, engineers, educators, artists, scientists—and ministers. It also has seemed the best place to correlate advanced theoretical knowledge with the practical skills of the professional. In the university divinity schools, the attempt to couple theory and practice became an ambitious effort to define and enhance the profession of the Protestant ministry.

### THE MINISTER AS PROFESSIONAL

Considerable ambiguity surrounds the words "professional" and "professionalism" for contemporary Americans. On the one hand, we remark favorably upon someone for behaving as a "true professional." On the other, we admit our need, often reluctantly, for the services of the professional. The one meaning of "professional" connotes dedication to values transcendent of self-interest and monetary reward; the other suggests measurement of worth by pay and advanced individual skills. The ambiguity of language points to the double standing of the professional in a democratic society. As Nathan O. Hatch has remarked, professionals "have furnished the kind of expertise that has made American efficiency the wonder of the world and at the same time served to entrench elites unresponsive to popular control. In the most vivid example of contradictory extremes, Americans admire professionals for their dedication to public service and revile them for the extent to which such claims serve as masks for financial greed."[2]

Despite the extreme responses, since the middle of the nineteenth century professionalism as the development of expert skills has carried with it for Americans the endorsement of upward career mobility. And it has embodied a fiercely democratic worldview, offering, in theory at least, the ladder of upward mobility to every social group in America.[3] Only after the Second World War would careers deemed "professional" proliferate beyond count and result in such title inflation as "sanitation engineer" and "tree surgeon." But the tendency to identify diverse career tracks as "professional" had already been set in motion by the late nineteenth century as national surveys added to the traditional professions of theology, law, and medicine such vocations as teaching, military service, engineering, dentistry, pharmacy, veterinary medicine, and accountancy.[4] During the same period, many of the professions became internally specialized, a convention evident in the formation of numerous professional societies devoted to subspecialties.[5]

The multiplying and subdividing of the professions in America have seemed to some analysts to result in a conflation of "profession" and "occupation." Sociologist Bernard Barber has suggested that for most Americans there is "no absolute difference between professional and other kinds of occupational behavior, but only relative differences with respect to certain attributes common to all occupational behavior."[6] And historian Laurence Veysey has proposed that the "professions" be defined "as nothing more than a series of rather random occupations that have historically been called that in our culture."[7]

Most attempts at definition, however, have differentiated between professions and other occupations by assigning the following characteristics to the professional: 1) acquaintance with an organized body of knowledge derived from specialized training; 2) commitment to public service that moves beyond the desire for personal profit; 3) adherence to occupational standards regulated by voluntary professional organizations; and 4) measurement of success by an explicit system of rewards that may be monetary or honorary, or both.[8] All of these characteristics add up to the professional's *authority* in the social order. Specialized knowledge for either public or private ends and the autonomy springing from self-regulation yield an effective power for shaping at least one dimension of a person's environment. In offering professional education to American citizens, therefore, the modern university extended to them the possibilities of power. Many professionals would secure their authoritative knowledge outside the walls of the university, but as Burton Bledstein has said, in large measure "the American university came into existence to serve and promote professional authority in society."[9]

Neither the idea of professionalism nor the authority associated with the professional's special knowledge sprang directly from the modern capitalist order, and institutions of higher education in America were not the first to offer training in the professions. The status of the professional originated in early Christianity as members of religious orders "professed vows" that set them apart as special agents of the faith. By the Middle Ages the "professions" had come to connote offices defined by the act of professing authoritative knowledge and belief. And in the thirteenth century, training in the professions of law, medicine, and theology were offered in many European universities.

Two critical changes were brought to this long tradition by nineteenth-century democratic capitalism and the modern university. First of all, professionalism was radically democratized. The rapid growth in the number of occupations deemed "professional" in nineteenth- and twentieth-century America signified a determination to unhitch the authority of occupation from class privilege and to dignify a wide range of expertise. As a consequence, the rapid growth of professions in America was unmatched on the Continent and in Great Britain. Second, American universities surpassed their European counterparts in providing education for the burgeoning professions and thus enlarged the opportunities for acquiring authoritative, professional knowledge. The college or university degree came to serve as an emblem of social standing in a nation that had repudiated a gentry.[10]

Both the democratization of the professions and the expansion of the American university into professional education carried important consequences for the Protestant ministry. For one thing, there was a significant decline in the percentage of the college- and university-educated entering the ministry. Estimates compiled in the 1930s indicated that between the colonial period and 1928 the percentage of highly educated persons choosing the ministry declined from 66 percent to 2 percent, with the most precipitous declines occurring after the Civil War.[11] The college-educated exercised the choices that came with increased availability of professional careers. Furthermore, most colonial colleges that had sent the majority of their graduates into the ministry became universities with diverse professional programs.[12] Leadership within the university also declined as an option for ministers. Prior to the Civil War, 90 percent of the college presidents were ordained clergy. A hundred years later, the office of the college or university president had been filled with other professionals, and rarely did a minister hold the presidency of a large public or private university. Similar changes had occurred on boards of trustees. Formerly dominated by ministers, by the 1930s none of the boards of thirty leading institutions of higher education surveyed at the time was made up of a ministerial majority.[13]

In the late nineteenth and early twentieth centuries, ministers intensified their laments about their low social status, laments that would continue throughout the present century. Twentieth-century social scientists have claimed that ministers' opinions of their status cannot be verified by empirical data respecting American attitudes toward ministers.[14] Despite the apparent high respect that Americans have bestowed on their clergy, however, ministers have often *perceived themselves* as occupying a profession judged by the society to be inferior to other professions. And, indeed, some typical measures of status have sustained the ministerial self-perception. Over the course of the twentieth century, salaries of ministers have not only dropped far below those of the highly esteemed white-collar professions of medicine, law, and engineering, they have also fallen below those of such trades as plumbers and masons. And since the middle of the nineteenth century, the large majority of Protestant ministers have received their higher education in denominational colleges and seminaries rather than in the more academically prestigious colleges, universities, and university divinity schools.[15]

Quite apart from the social and economic trappings of status, the American Protestant ministry has undergone a series of transformations since the colonial period that has deeply affected the authority of the profession. In Puritan New England, the clergyman derived his authority as much from the structure of the social order as from his specialized expertise in the Bible or his ordination by the church. His profession was a public office. Sustained by public funds and designated by the state as the watchman over the religion and morals of the community, the colonial New England minister shared with the government responsibility for maintenance of the commonweal. His chief functions were authoritative preaching and teaching and the regulation of community morality. With the disestablishment of the church in the American Republic and the spread of evangelical churches across the nation, the Protestant minister did not cease to effect a public posture. He continued to speak authoritatively for the religion and morals of the nation. The social basis for his authority had changed, however. Now he was increasingly responsible to the local congregation, and his authority was not guaranteed—it had to be won from a voluntary membership. Nineteenth-century clergyman Lyman Beecher put the change succinctly: "No minister can be forced upon his people, without their suffrage and voluntary support. Each pastor stands upon his character and deeds, without anything to break the force of his responsibility to his people."[16]

The publicly supported church into which one was born became the "denomination," a society voluntarily joined—and abandoned—by members of the congregation and built up in large measure by the persuasive talents of the minister. The minister's task was defined more by his functions as a leader of a voluntary organization than by his specialized professional knowledge, and his success was measured more by his ability to satisfy a lay clientele than by his authority to proclaim the word of God or his power to supervise the public morality. And as Protestant churches throughout the nineteenth century became more diverse in their needs and expectations, the minister's tasks increased in number, further changing the relatively simple duties of the colonial minister.[17]

The profession of the Protestant ministry for which the founders of university divinity schools sought to provide an advanced education was thus diffuse in its specialization, unsupported by a broad, incontestable social authority, and plagued by a lack of self-confidence. The solution to that state of affairs, according to the founders and their successors, was to provide Protestant ministers with education in advanced knowledge and in functional skills second in quality to no other profession.

## PROFESSIONAL STANDARDS

In 1915, Wilbur F. Tillett, dean of the Vanderbilt School of Religion, looked back on his early years as a faculty member of what was then the Vanderbilt Biblical Department:

When I came to the University in the fall of 1882, I found about seventy-five students enrolled in the Biblical Department with only two or three college graduates in the entire list, and many of the seventy-five were fearfully lacking in such education and culture as was expected in a body of theological students. In those days, however, the University did preparatory work as well as collegiate work and theological work, and a large number of the students for the ministry were either partially or wholly enrolled in sub-freshman classes.[18]

Tillett went on to claim that, with only a few exceptions, under his deanship completion of the sophomore year of college was required of ministerial students entering the Vanderbilt Biblical Department. Not until the 1930s, however, did Vanderbilt make ministerial education an unquestionably post-bachelor, graduate program of study.[19]

The situation at Vanderbilt was an extreme case, but not an exception in its essentials, during the early years of the university divinity schools. At most of the schools, special programs offering "diplomas," "certificates," or "combined degrees" allowed ministerial candidates with little or no college education to pursue a course of study in divinity, a system that sometimes permitted students to work simultaneously toward a college and a professional degree. At some of the Methodist divinity schools during those years, such students outnumbered the "graduate" or post-college Bachelor of Divinity candidates. At Harvard, Yale, and Union, where generally higher admission standards were maintained, a large minority of the post-college students left divinity school to enter their profession before completing the three years of study required for the ministerial degree.[20] At all of the schools, courses listed often went untaught, connections among the curricular components were seldom made, faculty found it impossible to assume similar educational levels on the part of their students, and few faculty or students felt caught up in the intellectual atmosphere of university life.

Part of the problem of divinity education at the time was the quality of students. As one Harvard Divinity School professor put it tersely in 1924, "neither schools, colleges nor seminaries can put a keen edge on soft metal."[21] Others recognized, however, that easy admissions policies rested on larger problems. As Robert L. Kelly complained in his 1920s survey of North American seminaries, there was no clear definition of what constituted a theological school and no standards by which to measure the professional education of ministers.[22] Despite their labored origins, the university divinity schools would assume the leadership in defining theological education and in setting its professional standards.

The setting of standards was desperately needed for more than the profession of the ministry. During the last quarter of the nineteenth century, standardized measurements of competence were nonexistent for most professions, and educational expectations were minimal. Medical education was weaker in its requirements than the ministerial education described by Dean Tillett at Vanderbilt. As one historian of medical schools has remarked, "A century ago, being a medical student in America was easy. No one worried about admission, for entrance requirements were lower than they were for a good high school. Instruction was superficial and brief. The terms lasted only sixteen weeks, and after the second term the M.D. degree was automatically given, regardless of a student's academic performance."[23]

A similar situation characterized the legal profession. Training for the bar at the turn of the twentieth century consisted of the options of the apprenticeship system, night school, and university law school, and these different programs of study lacked uniform professional and educational standards. Mr. Justice Hugo Black recalled that in 1904, although he was unable to gain admission to the College of Arts and Sciences at the University of Alabama, he was accepted without question into the University's Law School.[24] During the first quarter of the twentieth century, however, standards for medicine and law were established, and shortly thereafter Americans bestowed their highest respect upon those two professions. Theological educators thus looked to medicine and law for a professionalism worthy of emulation.

One critical development put the creation of standards by law and medicine beyond imitation by the ministry. In both cases, reform was heavily dependent upon regulations imposed by state laws. Stimulated by Abraham Flexner's famous exposé of conditions in medical schools— the Carnegie Foundation–funded *Medical Education in the United States and Canada* (1910)—the American Medical Association collaborated with state licensing boards to establish examinations for qualifying physicians, required a college education and scientific and clinical training of medical school students, and effectively closed down inferior schools by means of accreditation procedures. Similar developments occurred in the legal profession following a national study in 1913. States began to insist upon law school as the sole method for preparing for the bar, Harvard's case-study approach was made the measure of legal education, and (after World War II) state legislatures required that qualifying attorneys attend schools accredited by the American Bar Association and the Association of American Law Schools.[25]

If, because of the principle of the separation of church and state, theological school reformers could not rely upon government regulations to give force to their pleas for the elevation of professional standards for the ministry, they were not deterred from pointing to medicine and law as the models for the reforms they had in mind. One of the most pressing needs for theological education in 1914, declared the Reverend Anson Phelps Stokes, secretary of Yale University, was a "Flexner Report" for seminaries. Such a report would offer a critical review of the quality of theological schools, prompt the closing of at least a third of the schools, and make university-based divinity schools the "Harvard Law Schools" and the "Johns Hopkins Medical Schools"—that is, the standard-bearers—for the professional training of ministers.[26]

William Adams Brown of Union envisioned his massive 1934 evaluation of theological education, funded by John D. Rockefeller's Institute of Social and Religious Research, as just such a "Flexner Report" on ministerial training. Brown was persuaded that ministerial education could be prodded toward the same kinds of reforms and elevation of standards as those undertaken by law and medicine. In Brown's words, "It takes longer preparation and requires harder work to graduate from a first-class law or medical school than it did twenty or even ten years ago. If the ministry is to hold its own with the leaders of the other professions, it is essential that the graduates of the best theological schools should be subjected to a discipline not less rigorous."[27]

References to other professions as models for ministerial training continued long after the release of Brown's report. In 1964, the dean of Harvard Divinity School, Samuel Miller, argued that most theological education was too oriented to the past, too preoccupied with academic ideas, too neglectful of the practical needs of the people in the pews. A breakthrough in theological education of the kind effected by medical education a half century earlier was essential for establishing the practical relevance of ministerial education:

> One ponders the remarkable breakthrough in revolutionizing medical education in the United States, following the Flexner Report in 1910, by bringing the hospital into the school, by checking theory with actuality, by the forthright use of the autopsy as part of medical knowledge. Today theological education faces the same problem. How can the world be brought into the school? How can the actual concerns of the church and the real experience of human life be brought into closer and more critical juxtaposition with the intellectual activities of the school?[28]

The continuous appeal by theological educators to the progress made in the professional education of physicians and attorneys displayed a set of interrelated ideals that guided the university divinity schools in their efforts to train an educated Protestant ministry. In large part, the efforts were motivated by concerns for professional status. As Brown put it, if the ministry were to "hold its own" with other professions in American society, it must spring from an education as rigorous as that required of doctors and lawyers. In part, the efforts were also driven by the desire to find the right formula for combining theory and practice, a formula seemingly procured by law in its case-study approach and by medicine in its laboratory and clinical training. In Brown's words, for the minister to be as skillful in his profession as the lawyer or doctor in his, he must approach his subject with an understanding of its "general principles" and "with a knowledge that comes with practice."[29] It also struck theological educators as extremely important that both the raising of educational standards and the fusing of theory with practice in law and medicine had been accomplished through the leadership of university professional schools that were allied with professional accrediting associations. It seemed reasonable to conclude that the education of ministers should seek a similar alliance.

In the concluding section of his 1934 evaluation of theological education, William Adams Brown called for the formation of an association of theological schools. He argued that such an association should serve to inform church laypeople, colleges and universities, and prospective ministerial students of the need for the higher education of the Protestant minister. He also proposed that the association should be vested with the authority to establish and maintain the standards of that education. Wielding only "moral power"—that is, power devoid of the sanctions of the laws of the state—the accrediting agency could, through the cooperation and initiative of the theological schools themselves, elevate the profession of the ministry.[30]

In that same year, 1934, Brown and numerous other theological educators who shared his ideas assigned an accrediting function to the Conference of Theological Seminaries and Colleges, the society that had sponsored Brown's study, and in 1936 the Conference became the American Association of Theological Schools (later simply the Association of Theological Schools) in the United States and Canada, with an executive director and full powers of accreditation. In 1938, the AATS published its first list of accredited theological schools.

The movement for the creation of standards for ministerial education was dominated by the ideals of university graduate education. The Conference of Theological Seminaries and Colleges grew out of a meeting organized by the Harvard Divinity School and was formally convened by the president of Harvard University. The most vocal theological school leaders calling for professional ministerial standards and accreditation of seminaries were faculty based at university-related divinity schools—notably William Adams Brown of Union, Shailer Mathews of Chicago, Robert L. Calhoun and Luther Weigel of Yale, and Edwin Lewis of Drew.[31]

In the first AATS accreditation report, the forty-six approved schools out of sixty-one applicants included all of the university divinity schools except Harvard and Chicago, and those two institutions failed to make the first list only because of delays in processing their applications.[32] Standards used in the accrediting process were those that measured the institutions as graduate-level professional schools. To be approved without the "notation" of areas needing improvement, the schools were required to admit only students with B.A.'s from accredited colleges and universities, to award a professional degree only at the conclusion of at least three years of post-B.A. study, to provide balanced instruction in biblical, historical, theological, and practical studies, to maintain an adequate financial base and library, and to employ faculty who were proven scholars in their areas of expertise.[33]

The membership and functions of the AATS would enlarge over the years.[34] The accrediting of Protestant seminaries has remained the single constant in the history of the organization, however, and the view of professional education for the ministry as graduate-level training has endured through a history of the organization's periodic refinement of its accrediting standards. When the theological schools are measured by those standards, the AATS proved to be an effective accrediting agency for assuring the professional education of Protestant ministers. Admissions requirements for students were elevated, the scholarly competence of faculty was increased, a balanced curriculum was attained, and libraries were improved. In the academic year 1931–1932, the student bodies of forty-three of the schools that would later be accredited were composed of 75 percent college graduates. By 1936, college graduates at those schools had increased to 82 percent. By 1962, 89 percent of the students in over one hundred AATS schools were college graduates, and those same schools were enrolling 95 percent of the Protestant theological students in North America.[35]

If the AATS made a noticeable difference in elevating the standards of professional ministerial education, however, it did not resolve a stubborn tension between theory and practice. In the mid-1960s, an AATS-sponsored assessment of the state of professional ministerial education complained that practical training for ministers in theological schools functioned as a minor add-on to the theoretical disciplines of Bible, church history, and theology rather than forming an integral part of a comprehensive educational program.[36] In the 1970s, the ATS executive director was unable to convince the association to build into accrediting standards measurements of "readiness for ministry" on the part of theological students (although individual schools did institute their own measurements). And in his own efforts to stimulate reform of the theological curriculum so that it would have a more direct bearing on the preparation of ministers for their practical tasks, the director found himself "disappointed personally that some of the schools with respected names did not see this as an emphasis in which they needed help or that ATS was in a position to help."[37]

The old conflict that William Rainey Harper had noted at the beginning of the twentieth century between "scientific divinity" and "practical divinity" persisted. It was easier to measure professional education for the ministry with standards appropriate to advanced university specialization than with criteria pertinent to training in the skills of the practice of ministry. And it proved to be simpler to detect the need for the integration of theory and practice than to effect the integration.

The inability of the accrediting organization to institute standards for practical training in the ministry, however, had not prevented the divinity schools themselves from exploring the role of practical training in their programs of study. Like other professional schools in the university, they sought appropriate ways to combine advanced graduate specialization with preparation for a professional career. Over the course of a century, the divinity schools attempted to combine theory and practice through three distinctive approaches: the functional, the theological, and the contextual. Although specific schools could be found pursuing any one of the approaches at a given time over the last one hundred years, the functional method prevailed until the 1930s, the theological in the two decades after the Second World War, and the contextual after the mid-1960s.

## CHANGING SCHEMES FOR RELATING THEORY AND PRACTICE

In his acceptance address as the newly elected president of the Conference of Theological Seminaries and Colleges in 1932, Dean Shailer Mathews of the Divinity School at the University of Chicago elucidated a view of the professional education of ministers that characterized divinity school programs during the first four decades of the twentieth century:

> A divinity school is a professional school. That is to say, its general purpose is preparing its students for vocations in the field of religious leadership. Its task is not unlike that of the graduate schools of arts and science, the graduates of which are teachers and members of some profession such as physicians, commercial chemists, and commercial geologists. A divinity school must carry on research with the same freedom and reliance upon scientific method as prevail in any other graduate school. . . . A divinity school has an opportunity, not only to train men in methods of religious education and missionaries, but also to develop the spirit and techniques of research in the entire field of religion.[38]

Mathews's vision embraced the critical components in what he and others of the day called the "theological sciences." Ministers could be trained by the university to be as scientific in outlook and approach as any other professional, and the cultivation of religion and the development of scientific expertise were necessary, even complementary, tasks. Or, as Mathews had insisted twenty years before his presidential address, the profession of the ministry requires university-level education in the "technical efficiencies" of the academic and practical sciences.[39] Education of the minister was a matter of training in functions, practical and theoretical.

Mathews's prescriptions for a scientific, functional ministerial education emanated from his modernist Protestant conviction that the minister, once the purveyor of an infallible biblical revelation, now functioned as a leader of a social group dedicated to common social and psychological goals.[40] The university, in its devotion to research specialization and professional competence in the natural and human sciences, was the appropriate setting for the training of the minister as functionary. Yet Mathews's directives also sprang from his perception of the needs of churches and the changed position of the churches' ministers in society. He was convinced that the American Protestant churches now required of their ministers expertise in diverse functions—those of the generalist parish clergyman who needed such skills as biblical interpretation, sermon preparation, and psychology, as well as those of the specialist minister bound for the mission field, the Sunday school, or the college classroom. Under Mathews's deanship, the Divinity School at Chicago combined in its Bachelor of Divinity program prescribed courses suitable for the parish minister and elective courses aimed at more specialized ministries.[41]

Mathews proposed no structural means of holding together training in the functions of the ministry with education in advanced academic specialties. The combination of prescribed and elected courses allowed the graduate and the professional specialties to lie side by side. And merely urging Chicago students to gain "laboratory practice" as assistants in churches or as social workers in the city provided no assurances that graduate-level work in the classroom and practical experience outside the walls of the academy would find a correlation.

Mathews hoped that finally faculty and students would assume individual responsibility for making graduate education and professional training complementary functions. The faculty should direct their teaching of church history, Bible, or theology to the vocational responsibilities the students would assume as leaders of a religious community. And since such leadership was contingent upon an understanding of persons and institutions, the psychological and sociological implications of the various disciplines should be laid bare: "all the teachers in a seminary should have such sympathy with the tasks confronting a leader of a church that their teaching, both in substance and spirit is in sympathy with the general point of view which the social and psychological courses develop on the part of a student."[42] For their part, ministerial students should expect to derive more than simply information from their different courses. They should cultivate through research an independent way of thinking, they should develop in all their studies a sense of the laws of psyche and society that account for the forces of human relationships, and they should learn in a university setting the meaning of self-direction and the mastery of diverse situations.[43]

Although few educators at other university divinity schools of the time shared Mathews's thoroughly modernist dismissal of biblical authority or his desire to make the entire divinity curriculum hinge on the social sciences, most of them did assume with him that the chief purpose of theological education was the cultivation of scholarly and practical functions. And like him they proposed no structural means for integrating the functions.

At the Yale Divinity School between 1910 and 1926, the education of ministers was so functionally determined that multiple, distinctive tracks for separate forms of the ministry were offered on an elective basis without any hint that the tracks formed an educational whole. The centennial issue of the Divinity School's catalogue in 1922 was candid about the lack of unity in Yale's track system: "The School bears the single name of Divinity School, but the training provided is in reality that of five Schools"—one for training pastors, one for educating missionaries, another for developing the skills of the religion teacher, another for instructing future social workers, and still another for cultivating research competence in the history and philosophy of religion.[44] By the early 1930s, Yale Divinity was offering six "vocational groups" along with supervised fieldwork in a form of the ministry, but students in all groups were required to elect courses in the fields of Bible, church history, and theology.[45] Dean Luther Weigle justified the vocational orientation of the Yale program by insisting that it focused on present-day problems facing ministers, afforded future ministers the opportunity to specialize for a particular type of the Protestant ministry, and encouraged students to integrate curricular offerings into a practical package for themselves.[46]

Similar vocational tracking, justified with comparably high hopes for the student's ability to integrate learning for practical ends, appeared at the divinity schools at Union, Boston, Drew, Vanderbilt, Emory, Duke, and SMU.[47] Harvard Divinity School, which had been slow to adopt a practical course of study suitable for the various forms of the ministry, found faculty resources for expansion into the practical disciplines when Harvard entered into an alliance with neighboring Andover Seminary between 1908 and 1926.[48] At all of the divinity schools, "fieldwork" allowed divinity students to work in churches and other religious organizations—both as a means of earning income and as a way of gaining practical experience in the work of the ministry. In the first quarter of the twentieth century, fieldwork usually had little connection with the academic programs at the divinity schools, but increasingly the schools required that work in the field be supervised by faculty or by ministers who reported to the schools on the practical development of the students. Before the Second World War, however, the schools continued to struggle with the question of how best to relate the students' fieldwork to their advanced theological study, two features of their academic lives that tended to lie side by side.[49]

A largely detached parallelism characterized the entire functional approach to the relation between theory and practice. The absence of an effective institutional arrangement for correlating theory and practice, or even of relating the various forms of practical training, had laid a heavy burden upon individual faculty and students to find the right correlation on their own. Even those divinity school educators in the 1930s who had argued for training in diverse skills appropriate to ministerial functions had to admit that ways had not been found for effectively integrating professional education and graduate theological study. William Adams Brown of Union did not retreat from his position that every course in the theological school curriculum should be developed for its practical significance. Nevertheless, he admitted that divinity schools and seminaries had been too "course-minded and credit-minded" by pinning their hopes for a unified education on the principle of curricular expansion into diverse functions. Furthermore, Brown believed that many of the new practical courses directed to diverse ministries were quickly outdated. Schools for the professional education of ministers should concentrate on providing students "with a working philosophy of life." Then the practical and the theoretical dimensions of the ministry would coalesce on a perspective rather than on an individualistic integration of several functions. Dean Willard L. Sperry of the Harvard Divinity School offered similar criticism and counsel.[50]

The judgments about the limitations of the functional approach to ministerial education and the pleas for a unifying perspective pointed toward an alternative view of the relation between theory and practice represented by most divinity school curricular strategies from the late 1930s to the mid-1960s. During that period, the functional approach to ministerial education, preoccupied with skills needed by the Protestant minister for diverse functions, did not completely disappear. But function was subordinated to perspective. Reigning supreme in the divinity schools of the time was the conviction that the chief purpose of ministerial education was the development of a theological perspective that could guide the performance of all practical tasks. The conviction conformed to the dominance of theological themes in the years during and following the Second World War.[51]

The prevailing purpose of ministerial education now became the cultivation of a theological perspective that gathered into complementarity the theoretical and practical requirements of the Protestant ministry. And the statement of that purpose could manifest considerable impatience with the definition of ministerial education as the development of vocational functions.

"Theological education is never really to be calculated solely by reference to the functions, even the essential functions of the ministerial task," theologian and Duke Divinity School dean Robert Cushman insisted in 1961. Instead, the principal aim of theological education—"perhaps of all education properly conceived—*is not function but an integral being who can function appropriately.*" The formation of integral students, the basis of their proper functioning as ministers, should come from their thorough immersion "in the literature of the historic Christian faith so that the prophets, the apostles, the saints, and the Christian thinkers of all ages will be their familiar companions, and above all, [will] encourage in them the mind of Christ."[52] According to biblical theologian and Drew dean Bernhard Anderson, by 1962 the educational policy at his school had "increasingly emphasized that theological education is primarily 'education' in the basic disciplines, rather than 'training' in techniques and skills for the ministry." For Anderson, an emphasis on the disciplines of theology, church history, ethics, and biblical studies had its own practical meaning for the church: "The [theological] school is the Church at the point of doing the theological homework of the Church."[53]

For Merrimon Cuninggim, dean of the Perkins School of Theology at SMU in the 1950s, centering theological education on a core of basic disciplines, properly sequenced for the progress of the student, was a lesson to be learned from the turn to general education in universities immediately following the war. Although Cuninggim believed that the more theoretical disciplines should be applied to the tasks of the minister in the contemporary world, finally neither the core concept nor the intent of practical relevance constituted the overall aim of divinity education. Rather, the large, unifying aim was the construction and conveyance of Christian faith and experience. "In other words, training for the ministry is not the philosophy of the program [at Perkins]; rather, the undergirding purpose is communicating Christianity, and professional training then takes its place as a proper subsidiary aim."[54] Similar arguments for making the development of a theological perspective the dominant aim and unifying center of theological education were expounded at the other university divinity schools between 1945 and 1965.[55]

Efforts to cultivate that perspective among ministerial students led to experimentation with a variety of curricular arrangements. Diverse, widely separated departments were reorganized into a few major program divisions like "The Origin and Growth of Living Religions," "Religious Conceptions of Man and the World," and "Christianity at Work" at Yale or "The Life and Work of the Local Church," "Christianity and Culture," "The Christian Heritage," and "The Bible" at SMU.[56] Emphasis on disciplines that could cultivate a theological perspective ranged from a required set of courses for first-year students to a core curriculum staggered across three years of study. The incorporation of field experience into divinity education entailed an equally wide assortment of provisions. Fieldwork was sometimes overseen by a staff director, sometimes by all faculty, and sometimes by local ministers who were adjunct faculty. Practical experience was also provided by requiring students to assist in regional churches as part of their "lab work" in courses, by the use of local ministers to teach the practical dimensions of their tasks, and by the expansion of the curriculum into the areas of liturgy, religious art and architecture, and denominational polity. Amidst all of this experimentation, a pattern did predominate. In a reversal of the elective curriculum characteristic of the divinity schools until the 1930s, divinity schools adopted in the postwar years a prescribed curriculum in the "traditional," "basic," or "classical" theological disciplines.[57]

The aim of study in divinity was the development of a theological perspective from the traditions of Christianity, a perspective appropriate to the contemporary world and basic to the work of ministers in that world. The use of prescribed courses in the "classical" disciplines of theology, church history, and Bible to achieve that aim confirmed the avowal of Merrimon Cuninggim that practical vocational training should "take its place as a proper subsidiary aim." Practice should arise from a perspective formed from theory.

A seemingly more direct emphasis on practice emerged during the same period from teachers of "clinical pastoral education." Growing out of an early twentieth-century appropriation of therapeutic psychology and a liberal Protestant interpretation of the "minister as friend" rather than as an authoritative personality, ministerial counseling and clinical pastoral education constituted after the Second World War a widespread, highly institutionalized movement.

Borne along by a postwar anxiety that fostered popular advice about how the individual could handle the tensions of modern living, American middle-class culture came to represent what Philip Rieff called "the triumph of the therapeutic" or the preoccupation of Americans with finding individual contentment and fulfillment in a stressful world.[58] The themes of psychology and mental health pervaded films, advice about business management styles, and best-selling books of nonfiction. In 1957, *Life* magazine declared the times to be "the age of psychology."[59] Often sought out for guidance by anguished and unfulfilled parishioners, ministers discovered in clinical pastoral training and counseling skills ways to meet a very specific set of demands.

Education into counseling and pastoral care offered clergy ways of dealing with persons in desperate situations as well as supervised encounters with people in institutional settings, especially mental institutions and general hospitals. In 1950, the periodical *Pastoral Psychology* boasted sixteen thousand subscribers, of whom approximately fourteen thousand were pastors. By the middle of the decade, the National Council of Churches had established a Department of Pastoral Services, and a group of religious leaders and psychiatrists had created the National Academy of Religion and Mental Health. At the end of the 1950s, leaders in the movement had formed one hundred seventeen centers for clinical pastoral education, were offering clinical work at over forty theological schools, and had formed alliances with major medical centers. In the 1930s, few theological schools had offered courses in pastoral counseling; by the 1950s, virtually all of them did.[60]

Observers of the expansion of the area of pastoral care have noted several attractions that the field held for the theological schools. Especially in their promotion of the (often modified) methods of Carl Rogers's "nondirective" counseling—a method in which the pastoral counselor assumes a nonjudgmental attitude and helps clients arrive at solutions to their own personal problems—theological schools could beget pastoral counselors through limited training in an overcrowded curriculum.[61] Training in pastoral counseling also seemed to provide a nice blend of theory and practice. As one analyst of the movement has said, "If 'profession' implies the demonstrated capacity to perform a designated task, pastoral psychology was the one area of ministerial education where professionalism was more than a vague slogan."[62] Through courses in pastoral theology and fieldwork in supervised clinical settings, students could unite academic theory with professional practice in ways similar to the "case study" method in law and hospital training in medicine. In the judgment of Seward Hiltner, professor of pastoral theology at the University of Chicago Divinity School (later of Princeton Theological Seminary), the theoretical constructs of theology could be amplified—and even created—in the practical work of the minister as a helping professional.[63]

Pastoral psychology and clinical pastoral training would eventually provide a model for the "contextual" approach to ministerial education at some of the divinity schools. In 1970, for example, Candler appointed the president of the Association of Clinical Pastoral Education as a professor of clinical pastoral care and as the director of Candler's supervised ministry program.[64] Candler's development of contextual education for the ministry would thus be shaped in large measure by the model of clinical pastoral training. During its spectacular growth phase in the 1950s, however, clinical pastoral education did not govern the divinity school curriculum, and its chief representatives insisted that it participate in the larger theological task of assisting students to construct a basic Christian perspective.

At the Boston University School of Theology, where in the 1950s generous foundation grants established a pastoral counseling center with extensive training activities and endowed a chair of psychology and pastoral counseling, a basic core-course curriculum prevailed in which prescribed work in the "classical" disciplines outnumbered requirements in the practical.[65] Paul E. Johnson, director of the center and first occupant of the endowed chair, understood his task within the larger context of the personalist theology that had prevailed at the Boston School of Theology for decades. According to Johnson, the dynamic interpersonalism of pastoral counseling could yield theological insights and language appropriate to conceiving the personal relations between finite persons and ultimate reality.[66]

Other divinity school professors during the period insisted on the fundamental theological meaning of clinical pastoral training. David Roberts of Union proposed that psychotherapy could enhance the understanding of Christian doctrine. Albert Outler of Yale replied that the understanding of Christian doctrine could deepen psychological insights. Seward Hiltner argued that a Christian psychotherapy assumed, along with the process theologians at Chicago, the continued presence of God as a "healing and integrating power" in the universe.[67] The immensely practical implications of clinical pastoral training had not altered the purpose of education in divinity. Pastoral counseling had been incorporated into a course of study that sought to construct a perspective that was formed from the Christian and biblical traditions, that was based on the classical disciplines, and that was directed to a contemporary American culture seemingly yearning for religious answers to pressing human questions.

By the early 1960s, it was apparent that the construction of a theological perspective from the classical disciplines had not provided an altogether satisfactory formula for uniting the theoretical and the practical dimensions of divinity school education. Faculty responsible for homiletics, Christian education, and pastoral counseling were sometimes made to feel like second-class citizens in an environment dominated by theologians, church historians, and biblical scholars. That feeling was deepened by the confinement of diverse, loosely related practical specialties to one area of the curriculum while the classical specialties were assigned to three areas.[68] Faculty in the classical disciplines were inclined to teach their courses with little regard for the bearing that their specialties might have upon the vocational training of ministers. And faculty heavily involved in teaching doctoral students found that the supervision of the fieldwork of students made a distractive demand upon their time.[69] There was also some evidence that practical courses and fieldwork had not prepared divinity students for their later roles in the ministry. In a survey of its alumni/ae in the early 1960s, Yale Divinity School found that there had proved to be little relation between the way that students had been prepared practically for ministry and their actual ministries after graduation.[70]

By the middle of the 1960s, some divinity school educators were persuaded that the AATS-sponsored study of professional education for the ministry may have sharply stated a disquieting truth: *"Ministry today is generally discontinuous with the preparation provided for it."*[71] Robert Cushman of Duke, who had earlier insisted that theological education should form integral Christian beings through study of the classic Christian traditions, admitted that his own preference for the model of graduate work in the humanities may have contained serious limitations for professional education in the ministry: "I, for one, must concede that old-style theological education, as I have known it, has in truth not sufficiently and openly faced the fact and the nature of the discontinuity between itself and the actualities of ministerial practice."[72] Charles Ranson, who became dean of Drew Theological School in 1963, put the issue more bluntly. He found the Drew students to be "too enamored of academic theology" and unable to translate theology into plain speech or the practical needs of the churches.[73] Theory, it would appear, was still divorced from practice in the divinity schools that had replaced functionalism with the development of a theological perspective.

Recognition of the continuing divorce between theory and practice was prompted as much by a changed situation in church, culture, and student body, however, as by any perception of the limitations inherent in the theological approach. In the late 1960s, an anxious postwar American culture seemingly unified in its desire for Christian theological answers to pressing human questions was supplanted by a culture conspicuously fragmented by a pluralism of values, lifestyles, religious postures, and social expectations. The divinity schools found that they could not assume that the culture was fundamentally or even implicitly Christian, or that the Protestant churches would hold still while their future ministers were prepared for fixed tasks, or that the students would undertake their education knowing what practical training they needed. The situation that Yale theologian David Kelsey has described for the 1980s was already coming into focus in the late 1960s: "No longer can the theological school's curriculum assume that most students, having been socialized into the church at an early age, are familiar with the rudiments of the church and now need only to be introduced to a specialized role within the larger community of faith."[74]

The changed situation was eloquently described as early as 1970 by James T. Laney, newly appointed dean of the Candler School of Theology at Emory University. Even the culture of the South, previously so closely identified with Protestant Christianity, no longer provided a fixed context for ministerial education:

> ... the ethos that we have known and in which most of us took our shape is fast disappearing. That ethos consisted of sturdy and seemingly immutable institutions, of constellations of expectations that lay upon us and drew us out in certain patterns of life, of a clear understanding of what it meant to be Christian and moral. It was the ethos of Southern Christendom, a peculiar amalgam of Protestantism and Southern culture. Whatever its unique strengths and power as well as its tragic blind spots and weaknesses, the church of that ethos is no longer immutable.[75]

According to Laney, previously "everyone knew what a minister was and did," but that was no longer the case for a church constantly undergoing change. Formerly students went to seminary "with a kind of rough-hewn nugget of commitment" and "with some real literacy in the Bible," but those student attributes could no longer be presupposed even in the Bible Belt. Now the Protestant churches no longer exercised a decisive influence on the culture. Theological school students were motivated more by general moral passion than a faith commitment and were more literate in the vocabulary of social change than in the language of the Bible. Laney concluded that these changes in Southern culture—and indeed in American culture as a whole—were of great importance for theological education. Now the theological schools must understand the ministry as a process of contextual formation, as something that "takes shape," that is "plastic, fluid, creative, emerging."[76]

Divinity school students of the late 1960s and early 1970s were not only more socially concerned than biblically literate, and they were not only less shaped by a stable church than were previous generations. Like their undergraduate counterparts, they demanded more experimentation in education, they were less wedded to a traditional Christian definition of religion, and they were often engaged in a quest for careers that would make a significant difference in the shape that the larger social order would take. A strong antiauthoritarian sentiment sometimes held these strands together. As one student of the divinity school at Boston University exulted about a self-directed program in Church and Society, "Now I've found the important question is not what does some authority figure want me to learn, but what do *I* want to learn."[77]

With the ending of the war in Vietnam and the waning of the most volatile forms of the countercultural protest, the antiauthoritarianism and experimentalism of divinity students moderated considerably. Yet the increasing numbers of second-career, "nontraditional," and older students who comprised the divinity school student bodies following the days of the counterculture would still reflect a changed situation.[78] The student profile and the ministerial expectations that had prevailed in the schools for almost a century had ended. Divinity school programs designed to provide practical training in the ministry could no longer build upon students' long-term nurture in the churches in order to create a theological perspective appropriate to all forms of the ministry. Students now needed to be introduced to a contextual exploration of the constantly changing ministerial roles in a fluid culture and church.

During the 1970s and 1980s, divinity school educators differed in their ways of treating training for the ministry as a process of contextual education, but they shared the supposition that practical education in the ministry should amount to something quite different from training in the use of fixed professional skills. Unlike the proponents of the functional approach who had encouraged expansion into unrelated graduate and professional "efficiencies," the contextualists looked for opportunities in which students could attain an education that was simultaneously theoretical and practical. And although they continued to adhere to the conviction that graduate-level work in the traditional disciplines was indispensable to an educated Protestant ministry, the contextualists abandoned the argument of the previous generation that practical education is ancillary to the formation of persons by theological traditions. Theology itself should become contextual in that the reflective task should emerge in the actual practice of the ministry.

At the university divinity schools with Methodist affiliations and backgrounds, contextual education entailed replacing "fieldwork" with programs in "supervised ministry" or "field education" that required regular supervision and evaluation by faculty and academic analysis by students. The Candler School of Theology developed a program in supervised ministry that covered all three years of the students' work and required student exposure to diverse forms of the Christian ministry.

Employing a method of "reflection/action" in clinical educational settings, local churches, or community organizations, the Candler faculty, working alongside professional supervisors, encouraged students to join theological, historical, ethical, and biblical sophistication with practical experience as ministers. The program concluded with a professional assessment by faculty and fellow students.[79] The Perkins School of Theology at Southern Methodist University required an internship—amounting to a fourth year of study for most students—supervised by instructors, peers, and a lay committee.[80]

The divinity schools at Duke, Vanderbilt, Boston, Drew, and Claremont instituted similar supervised programs for contextual professional education.[81] The programs were clearly designed to serve the diverse and changing shapes of the contemporary Protestant ministry. They were also devised to allow students to fashion themselves experientially and analytically as ministerial professionals. As the Divinity School at Duke still informed its students in 1990, its program in ministerial formation aimed to assist them in "sharpening and clarifying their Christian vocations" and "integrating academic studies, personal faith experiences, and critical reflection into a personal spiritual foundation that produces a confident and faithful ministry."[82]

The nondenominational schools instituted a similar curriculum for ministerial training. Lacking ties to any specific denomination or denominational student body, however, Chicago, Union, Yale, and Harvard were more inclined to offer students opportunities to explore "experimental ministries" outside the boundaries of the institutional church. Especially during the student activist years of the late 1960s and early 1970s, those divinity schools established programs in which action and reflection could be combined through work in organizing urban neighborhoods, participation in protests against the war in Southeast Asia, or accompanying police officers on their night beats—as well as through involvement in the more traditional areas of pastoral counseling, religious education, or worship in a local church.

In 1965, the Divinity School of the University of Chicago replaced its Bachelor of Divinity degree with a Master of Theology–Doctor of Ministry program intended to prepare students for "new and emerging forms of ministry" as well as for "traditional and well-defined ministerial professions." Although the new program aimed eventually at "preparation for the profession of ordained ministry," the first stages of the program were designed to assist the student to confront "the question of meaning or significance in contemporary culture, including the churches, and questioning whether he should go into the Christian Ministry." In the last stages of the program, students had the option of participating in such "agencies of renewal" as the Urban Training Center in the city of Chicago.[83] At Yale, under the prompting of Dean Colin Williams in the early 1970s, the Divinity School emphasized the "field investigation of and critical reflection on" the major changes "occurring in religious institutions and (consequently) in the role of religious professionals." By affiliating with Berkeley (Episcopal) Divinity School, Yale also stressed clinical and experimental field-supervised ministerial training available through the Berkeley faculty.[84]

With the passing of the strident forms of student activism, much of the experimentation with extra-ecclesiastical ministries dissipated, but not arrangements devised to form ministers through contextual education. Because of scarce funding and the changing interests of students, by the mid-1970s Chicago had scaled back its Doctor of Ministry program to about one-sixth of the student body. It chose to address its professional program to "self-starter" students who could tap the resources of a predominantly research-oriented faculty and in a few courses could reflect critically on the practice of traditional forms of the ministry.[85] The other nondenominational schools, however, relied less on the self-direction of students, and by the 1980s their field education programs resembled those of their denominational counterparts. Yale required distribution credits in field education and highly recommended for its students an internship in a church-related ministry between their second and third years of residency. Union instituted requirements in a professional development program that entailed "supervised field placement." And there persisted through two major revisions of the curriculum at the Harvard Divinity School requirements in supervised field education for all ministerial students—requirements in what would eventually be called the Harvard "Arts of Ministry" program.[86] In each case, faculty and administration assumed that contemporary students needed to explore various forms of the Christian ministry. They assumed, as well, that academic work should include contextual learning carried out in the practice of the professions of the ministry.

By the 1980s, there were signs that hopes for a synthesis of theory and practice had not yet been realized through the pursuit of a contextual model of professional ministerial education. The attempted synthesis had been plagued by some of the same problems apparent in the earlier models. Some faculty in the traditional or classical disciplines, especially those heavily involved in teaching doctoral candidates, admitted to profound difficulties finding the time or the inclination to supervise learning in context.[87] In some cases, part-time and temporary faculty members handled practical courses and supervised field education, thus relieving faculty in the theoretical disciplines of the need to explicate the practical implications of their academic work.[88] One study of theological education concluded that the so-called "practical" fields themselves had turned very theoretical: "More often than not, the classes in Christian education, pastoral counseling, and church management focus on the 'theory' of the emerging discipline as much as they do on critical thinking about practice in the congregation."[89] A group of faculty evaluators of the contextual model at their own school conceded that the program of supervised ministry had been more successful at leading students to reflect upon their experiences with psychological rather than with Christian theological categories.[90] The dean of another divinity school concluded that the model had bred a "service-oriented and less verbal definition of ministry" than was appropriate to university education.[91] The troubling question of how to relate theory and practice continued.

## AN ENDURING LEGACY: THE TWOFOLD SCHEME

An influential set of assumptions has governed the divinity schools' different schemes for relating theory and practice. All of the approaches to professional ministerial education have adopted the postulate that theory and practice are two distinct spheres of human life that can be brought into relationship only through deliberate effort. Theory consists of the acquisition of knowledge, the attainment of perspective, and the critical reflection upon both knowledge and perspective. Practice is the bearing that one's life takes through concrete decisions and visible actions. It follows that if behavior is to avoid schizophrenia, practice must be informed by—indeed, it should be controlled by—theory. These assumptions about the meaning and relation of theory and practice derive from the Enlightenment's celebration of the autonomy of reason and the view of the relation between reason and will in classical Greek philosophy. But the assumptions have taken on a very modern form in a segmented, technological, bureaucratic social order. Theory as the mode of understanding and perspective has become a collection of mental techniques directed to a specific dimension of the world and appropriate to the production of particular results. Practice as the mode of behavior has come to mean a set of activities determined by specific contexts and aimed at particular, clearly defined effects. Theory should now inform practice by dictating both the means and the ends for the efficient performance of activities.

The suppositions about theory and practice have been concretely embodied in the structures of American society. Within the modern university they are evident in the proliferation of specialized and technical branches of learning, in the spectacular growth of professions and professional education programs defined by specific activities, and in the generation of countless methods designed to connect theory with practice. In university divinity schools they are apparent in the enduring presence of a "twofold scheme" for organizing the professional education of ministers.

Since the middle of the nineteenth century, most seminaries and theological schools have organized their curriculum according to a "fourfold scheme" (or some modification of it). Most course offerings, faculty appointments, and degree requirements have tumbled into the categories of theology, church history, Bible, and the practice of ministry. These categories for the organization of knowledge have helped to define, in the language of the late nineteenth and early twentieth centuries, the basic "sciences" in theological education.

With the appearance of divinity schools modeled on the modern American university, a more fundamental classification occurred: a twofold scheme that divided curriculum, faculty, and degree requirements into theory and practice.[92] The division has been conspicuous in all phases of the history of the divinity schools. The functionalists sought to develop among their students skills that were both theoretically sophisticated and professionally practical. The theologians aspired to produce persons highly educated in the Christian traditions who could then function as practical religious professionals. The contextualists sought concrete settings in which largely unformed ministerial candidates could explore vocational options and professional formation in a fluid church and culture. In every case, ways were pursued for the correlation of two separate spheres of learning that were appropriate to a university professional education. The functionalists urged students and faculty to strike alliances between graduate education and professional training. The theologians proposed that the functions or activities of the professional ministry be subordinated to work in the "classical" or "traditional" disciplines. And the contextualists looked for those field experiences of professional development where theory and practice could mutually illuminate and enliven each other.

A number of theological educators have recently brought the assumptions of the twofold scheme under severe criticism and have posed alternatives to an education premised on the theory/ practice polarity. Edward Farley has called for the abandonment of the "clerical paradigm" that views theological education as the provision of discrete disciplines to ministers. What is needed instead, in church and theological school alike, is the cultivation of *theologia*, a "habit of the human soul," an "actual, individual cognition of God" that arises from the Christian faith and gains specific shape in the church and in the concrete power structures of the world.[93] Joseph Hough and John Cobb have argued that the minister should be educated as a "practical Christian thinker" who provides leadership to the laity, who are also practical Christian thinkers. Theological education would then nourish the identity of the Christian as a participant in the life story of the faith and would promote awareness of the church's global tasks on behalf of the underprivileged and the survival of the biosphere.[94]

Craig Dykstra has proposed that the notion of practice should be reconceived as a "cooperatively formed pattern of activity that emerges out of a complex tradition of interactions among many people sustained over a long period of time." It follows that theological education should entail the study of the corporate practices of the church that shape the identities and life-orientations of Christians.[95] Don Browning has insisted that religious practices are heavily freighted with what Aristotle called *phronesis* or "practical wisdom." Theological education should thus embark upon a "fundamental practical theology" that analyzes descriptively, historically, and systematically the theory-laden practices of Christian congregations.[96]

Although some curricular experiments have been tried that have taken seriously such criticisms and proposals, at the end of the 1980s the old division between theory and practice still prevailed in the way divinity school faculty understood their responsibilities and in the way their courses were classified.[97] Noting the lack of any significant structural changes in the theological schools premised on the critique of the separation of theory and practice, Barbara Wheeler has pointed to the resistant power of vested faculty interests:

> The resistance to inspecting underlying structures and their values and assumptions is not only an individual matter. The existing pattern is more than a pedagogical arrangement; it is also a socioeconomic reality of departments whose fragile existence depends on an unstated

> comity agreement of mutual approval and support within the existing structure. Thus groups of faculty members, formed into departmental teams, adapt to criticism by adding courses, by making faculty appointments to departments, and by interdepartmental teaching, but they resist changes in the structure itself or even discussions that pose the possibility of such changes.[98]

As powerful as faculty interests and the internal dynamics of schools can be in creating resistance to structural change, larger cultural and social factors also account for the resistance. Divinity schools have adopted an approach to professional education prescribed by a culture that values specialized learning directed to specific domains of knowledge and that esteems skills developed for the achievement of measurable results. University professional education, including education in divinity, has thus promised its students an advanced, specialized learning and training in technical skills, as well as ways of correlating the two. There is no evidence that either the cultural values or the educational promises are abating on the contemporary scene. If anything, they are increasing. Over the last two decades, the United States has outstripped all other industrialized nations in the employment of scientists and engineers, has poured increasing percentages of the nation's wealth into technological research and development, and has placed a renewed emphasis on technical education, often at the expense of programs in the liberal arts. Surveys indicate that the American people validate this material expansion by putting great faith in technology and technical knowledge as the solutions to our most pressing problems. In the words of sociologist Robert Wuthnow, technology and technical knowledge provide late twentieth-century Americans with a potent "legitimating myth." That is, they furnish a view of the world and of history that combines "seemingly inevitable developments in the social infrastructure with belief in the unassailable sanctity of these developments."[99]

Practice understood as "practical wisdom" or the intelligent participation in the corporate practices of the church has emerged as a significant challenge to a century-old effort of divinity schools to correlate two separate spheres of theory and practice. Yet the challenge is made in defiance of a contemporary environment defined by technical knowledge and technological enthusiasms. It is also out of harmony with a modern American university that is overwhelmingly technical and pragmatic in its orientation. In fact, the division between theory and practice has proved to be wider in divinity education than in most other university professional programs. Unlike the specialized knowledge offered by schools of medicine, law, engineering, music, or business, that of the divinity schools has been tied to advanced work in liberal studies. Theoretical knowledge has been framed in divinity schools to nurture an understanding of self, world, text, and past. Except in some of the "practical" disciplines, knowledge has not been bent toward the technical solution of tangible problems.

The liberal orientation of advanced divinity education has created more than an academic problem of how to relate theory and practice. It has posed for the churches the question of how advanced study in biblical criticism, theological reflection, and historical interpretation could advance the work of the minister in a congregation. The alliance between the aims of the university and those of the church, an alliance necessary for the theoretical and practical education of professional ministers, would prove to be an awkward one.

# CHAPTER V

■

## *Two Yokes of Responsibility*

The founders of university divinity schools believed that as an institution destined to spread the principles of democracy and religion across the face of the nation, the university could become a natural ally of the churches. And as the institution occupying the frontiers of professional training and standards, the university could become the home for a brand of theological education that offered superior education for the clergy, elevated the profession of the ministry, and thereby best served the community of the church. Throughout their history, however, the divinity schools found it necessary to devise ways to bridge two communities that did not constitute a neat fit. Professional education of the clergy would have to deal with a gulf separating two communities of responsibility, the university and the church, quite as much as they would have to face a division separating theory and practice. In the Wesleyan terms of Dennis Campbell, most Protestant theological education has been pulled in two directions by two "yokes of obedience"—to the church and to the academy.[1]

Independent Protestant seminaries had contributed their share to the tension between church and academy prior to the development of divinity education in the university as those seminaries established graduate-level studies taught by specialist faculty, many of whom were immersed in advanced German scholarship. A special committee of the board at Andover Seminary reported in 1825 that German scholarship in the school's faculty dulled piety, led to skepticism, and served no useful purpose in preparing men for the ministry.[2] As theological education emerged within the walls of the modern American university, however, the tension between community of church and community of higher education intensified. The demands of the university environment created a professional culture that pulled even stronger against the demands of the churches.

Because of their close denominational ties with the churches, the Methodist university-related divinity schools have seldom revealed outright strife between university and church as two communities of responsibility.[3] Nevertheless, the history of all of the divinity schools is in large measure the story of a tension between two communities of professional responsibility. A significant attempt to bridge the two communities at the University of Chicago in the middle of the twentieth century provides a telling example of the abiding tension.

## A PROLONGED DIALOGUE, A CLASH OF IMPULSES

In a press release dated April 17, 1960, Lawrence A. Kimpton, chancellor of the University of Chicago, announced the termination of the University's seventeen-year-old Federated Theological Faculty. "It is with great reluctance," Kimpton said, "that the University of Chicago, along with the Disciples Divinity House and Meadville Theological School, now announce their withdrawal from the federation as of the earliest possible date and not later than May 1, 1963." The chancellor indicated that for more than a year efforts had been made to keep the federation intact, but an accord over the interpretation of the Articles of Agreement could not be reached with the fourth school in the federation, the Chicago Theological Seminary (CTS).[4] A grand experiment in theological education had come to an end.

In 1943, three denominational institutions had joined the Divinity School at the University of Chicago to form the Federated Theological Faculty (FTF). These small institutions had made their moves to the environs of the University much earlier—the Disciples House (Disciples of Christ) in 1894, CTS (Congregational) in 1915, and Meadville Seminary (Universalist/Unitarian) in 1926. They had in those early years struck informal alliances with the University that gave them access to university facilities but left them largely independent of University control. Such informal alliances conformed to President William Rainey Harper's vision for the University of Chicago. Especially as Harper grew skeptical of the ability of the Divinity School to embrace equally the demands of "scientific" and "practical" divinity, he thought it sensible to promote the coexistence in the same university setting of a nondenominational divinity school oriented toward graduate work and independent seminaries affiliated with the University but aimed principally at the specific needs of the churches.[5]

In the early 1940s, it seemed to leaders of the four theological schools that a significant step could be taken beyond mere informal affiliation. In a fervently ecumenical age, visions of closer denominational unity inspired the leaders of the schools to create an arrangement that would make economical use of financial resources, strengthen the ministerial degree among the affiliated schools, and promote faculty cooperation in teaching and research. Such a system of collaboration would be founded on the principle that all members of the faculty in the four schools would join together as *one university faculty*. Ernest C. Colwell, dean of the Divinity School at Chicago who in 1943 proposed and won endorsement for the FTF, believed that it was above all else the offer of university standing that swiftly persuaded the faculty of the seminaries to accept the idea of the federation.[6]

The resources brought to the Federated Theological Faculty were by no means equal, however. By virtue of a multi-million-dollar gift in 1925, CTS had ceased to be a small school. By the time the federation was underway, CTS had launched a building program, had increased the size of its faculty, and had expanded its enrollment of ministerial candidates. From the outset, then, CTS and the Divinity School, as the two largest of the institutions brought together, would play the principal roles in a consortium widely heralded as a model experiment in ecumenical theological education.

Five years after the disintegration of the Federated Faculty, Bernard M. Loomer, theologian and former dean at the Divinity School of the University of Chicago, sent an open letter to the president, faculty, and students of CTS prior to his departure for a faculty position in California. Loomer observed that the career of the FTF had been a mixture of commonality and conflict, of success and failure. The federation had created opportunities for "great and prolonged dialogue," high caliber teaching and writing on the part of a distinguished faculty, and a lively student body. The federation had also been marked by a "clash of impulses." Personality conflicts and a failure of "stature of spirit" among faculty, as well as honest but deep disagreements over the nature of theological education, had run through the life of the federation.[7]

Loomer did not overstate the huge successes of the federation. During its seventeen-year life, it had convened some of the most eminent scholars in the disciplines of theological education—including church historians Wilhelm Pauck, James H. Nichols, and Sidney E. Mead; theologians and philosophers of religion Bernard Meland, Charles Hartshorne, James Luther Adams, Daniel Day Williams, Nathan Scott, and Loomer himself; historians of religion Joachim Wach, Joseph Kitagawa, and Charles Long;

biblical scholars Amos Wilder, William A. Irwin, and J. Coert Rylaarsdam. These and other distinguished scholars were joined into one university faculty, and even those professors who faced off in heated debate
over the nature of their joint enterprise agreed that the union had created
an exciting intellectual milieu for students and teachers alike. As CTS
president Arthur Cushman McGiffert, Jr., put it, members of the Federated Faculty came "alive to each other's enthusiasms," and students "expressed surprise at the way in which ideas propounded in one classroom
overlapped and interlaced with those in another room."[8]

In Loomer's words, however, the FTF also had made for a powerful
"clash of impulses." Some of the most distasteful forms of academic
power politics and intrigue pervaded the scene. Reports circulated that
the Divinity School faculty expressed disdain for most CTS faculty and
students. Some professors accused faculty at other schools in the federation of trying to win over their colleagues on issues of educational philosophy and strategy. Administrators in the various segments of the federation squabbled over who should be in control. Strong personalities
among the faculty charged one another with creating all of the problems.
Toward the end, some CTS leaders plotted how to terminate the federation and make it appear that others were to blame for the failure of the
experiment.[9]

Issues of money, faculty appointments, and curricular development
also led to conflicts. In 1955, when the University of Chicago received a
grant from the Sealantic Fund that required the federated schools to
match every dollar of grant money with four dollars from other sources,
CTS hesitated to cooperate because it was planning its own financial
campaign. Later, after contributing to the match, CTS requested that the
University return income on the share of the CTS matching contribution
should defederation occur. The University denied the request. Disagreements between CTS and the University occurred over which institution
should set the requirements for the professional ministerial degree.[10]

Administrative design and philosophy were also constant causes of
friction. Under the federation's original Articles of Agreement, administration was lodged in a cabinet, consisting of the deans or presidents of
the four institutions, which controlled appointments and promotions,
but each school could operate with its own board and administrative
council to guide its distinctive policies. In 1955, after administration by
the cabinet and four institutional heads proved unwieldy, and after a long
and controversial search, a dean of the Federated Faculty was appointed
under revised Articles of Agreement. The CTS administration grew in-

creasingly uneasy over the fact that only the new dean of the federation reported directly to the University, an arrangement that heightened that administration's long-standing fears that a powerful university could easily gobble up the seminary. Differing interpretations of the meaning of "federation" permeated the arguments about structure. The administrators, board, and many faculty at CTS opted for the pluralistic implications of the idea and emphasized the need for the schools to retain their authority and integrity. Others within the federation insisted on the organic nature of the arrangement and accentuated the unity of the schools.[11]

The ultimate undoing of the FTF owed to no single cause, but running through the entire loosely woven fabric of the federation was the thread of a fundamental question. Which community—the university or the church—should provide the principal measure for the education of Protestant ministers? Disagreement over that question was most visible in arguments between the leaders of CTS and the Divinity School, but the dispute spread across the Federated Faculty.

Arthur Cushman McGiffert, Jr., cast the disagreement in terms of diversity of educational goals. He was convinced that some members of the Federated Faculty sought as their primary aim the cultivation of intellectual leaders who could detect the challenges presented to the churches by the modern world, who could establish a sense of connection with the past, and who could develop a passion for their studies "as ends in themselves as well as means." Other members of the Faculty, though scarcely repudiating the cultivation of intellectual leadership, were primarily "concerned to bring the student to self-consciousness as a religious leader, so that he would understand the way in which he affected others and how they regarded him and how he could act responsibly toward them as persons." In McGiffert's judgment, these different educational goals were represented by the Divinity School and CTS respectively, and they were entangled with the suspicions that each school harbored of the other. "The Divinity School felt that the Seminary might become subservient to the immediate needs of the churches; according to the Seminary, the Divinity School, enclosed within the University and lacking a vital connection with the churches, might wither into scholasticism."[12] As president of CTS, McGiffert himself worried that a scholasticism spreading among the Federated Faculty could result in the loss of close connections with the churches. That worry was closely bound up with his fears about the loss of CTS identity within a powerful university.[13]

Just a few months prior to the jettisoning of the Federated Theological Faculty, J. Coert Rylaarsdam, professor of Old Testament Theology within the Federated Faculty and a member of the Administrative Council of CTS, explicated a view similar to McGiffert's about the split dividing the Faculty and cleaving CTS from the Divinity School. Altogether unlike McGiffert, however, Rylaarsdam defended the intellectual cultivation of students of the Federation, castigated CTS leaders for a parochial preoccupation with the needs of denominational churches, and urged that CTS become a "house of study" that would stand responsible only for the collegiate and worship life of its students. In defending faculty freedom guaranteed by the University of Chicago, Rylaarsdam underscored McGiffert's observation about divided educational goals. He also doubtless confirmed McGiffert's deepest fears about university "scholasticism."

> First of all a university faculty is a free faculty. This does not mean that other faculty are not free, but that the freedom of a university faculty is defined in a distinctive way. Such a faculty is a self-perpetuating intellectual community which is expected to define and constantly to review its definition of its own task in teaching and scholarship and to provide such means as curricular programs and personnel to carry it out. The university administration, personified by the Chancellor, endows the faculty with these privileges and obligations; it both guarantees the freedom it bestows and retains the authority of judging the proficiency with which its assignment is carried out.[14]

In making the faculty a "self-perpetuating intellectual community" that defines its own tasks and develops its curriculum with a sense of responsibility to the university, Rylaarsdam insisted that he had by no means neglected the needs of the churches. The churches are best served when their future ministers are introduced to "theology as a special discipline, distinct from other sciences." Finally, however, the university, not the church, is the institution to which divinity school faculty are accountable. And since the Federated Faculty at Chicago, like other faculty at the University, have attained eminence for their work with graduate students, they should give chief attention to Master's and Ph.D. students rather than to Bachelor of Divinity students.[15] For Rylaarsdam and other Federated Faculty convinced of the primacy of the task of developing intellectual leaders in graduate programs, the expectations of the churches should take second place to—indeed, they should conform to—the mandates and opportunities of an advanced university education.[16]

CTS spokesmen felt that a sense of responsibility to the churches was overshadowed when theological education was measured so strictly by university guidelines. The CTS churchly sense of responsibility was not altogether denominational in its bearing, however. As Federated Faculty dean Jerald Brauer pointed out, CTS expanded its student recruitment beyond the Congregational denomination, an expansionist effort that in Brauer's judgment put CTS in direct competition with the nondenominational Divinity School.[17] Nor in looking to the needs of the churches did CTS entirely contradict the larger agenda of the Divinity School and other members of the Federated Theological Faculty. Throughout the life of the Federated Theological Faculty, the Divinity School continued to offer admission to students seeking the basic ministerial degree, and immediately following his appointment as FTF dean, Brauer launched a one-year Parish Training Program for ministerial candidates. Right down to the last days of the FTF, faculty who understood their roles chiefly as university professionals acknowledged the importance of including within their purview the traditions of the contemporary and historic churches.[18] The issue was one of emphasis, and from the point of view of the CTS leadership the FTF had tilted decisively toward the profession of the university scholar and away from the profession of the minister in the definition of its tasks.

CTS concerns over what McGiffert called "scholasticism" arose early in the life of the federation. In 1949, Fred Eastman, professor of religious drama, reported to the FTF that CTS alumni and other ministers were growing impatient with Chicago-educated clergy who were unsympathetic to the requirements of the parish ministry. Eastman also reported that numerous CTS-based students complained that they were expected to become academic specialists to the neglect of the cultivation of their "ministerial qualities" and "spiritual experiences."[19] In 1951, CTS president McGiffert pleaded with the Federated Faculty to make education for the profession of the parish minister the core mission of the federation. The community of the church, rather than a list of university requirements or the demands of individual "clients," should set the agenda for that professional education.[20] By implication, McGiffert also expressed disagreement with the Federated Faculty's recent designation of the Bachelor of Divinity degree as "minimal training necessary for leadership in the Church," with the Ph.D. degree held to be "more nearly adequate."[21]

CTS distress over the relative neglect of the Bachelor of Divinity as the basic professional degree developed on behalf of the churches continued to show up in curricular debates. In 1949, CTS reluctantly accepted as a provisional experiment two alternative patterns for the three-year B.D.: a "general" degree consisting of a basic sequence of courses almost wholly prescribed by the Federated Faculty; and a "specialized" degree that allowed the student to omit some basic courses in order to concentrate in an area of choice and that gave to the different schools in the federation control over one-third of the curriculum. CTS accepted the two-pattern degree as a compromise to a four-year B.D. originally proposed by a study committee, but in doing so it gave up the one-third control it had exercised over *all* of the B.D. curriculum under the original Articles of Agreement. CTS also sanctioned in principle the claim by a Federated Faculty chiefly interested in teaching graduate specialties that the Ph.D., not the "minimal" three-year degree, was the "more nearly adequate" preparation for the profession of the ministry.

Only a few weeks after assuming the presidency of CTS on May 14, 1959, Howard Schomer renewed the controversy over the B.D. degree by proposing to CTS and University of Chicago officials that each school in the federation should offer its own three-year B.D. alongside the four-year degree offered by the Federated Faculty. (The four-year degree had emerged to accommodate the year of field training instituted by Dean Jerald Brauer.) To Schomer's way of thinking, the parallel three-year B.D. would return the basic ministerial degree to a seminary of the church. To the thinking of other FTF members and University officials, Schomer's proposal would institute a Bachelor of Divinity program that directly competed with the program of the Federated Faculty.[22] Along with his insistence that the FTF resort to the old form of governance by a cabinet and his request that the University return income on the CTS contribution to the Sealantic campaign, Schomer's proposal for an independent B.D. degree struck the University of Chicago as altogether impossible. After a series of failed negotiations and compromise proposals, the Federated Theological Faculty was terminated.

Jerald Brauer, who now served as dean of the Divinity School rather than of a larger Federated Faculty, found himself "sitting in the same office with the same staff, but with a greatly reduced faculty and a 38% smaller academic budget."[23] Five faculty chose to join CTS, and within a year four senior professors took positions elsewhere, some of whom, according to Brauer, were "simply weary of the controversy."[24]

Over the next decade, however, Brauer and his colleagues at the Divinity School built again a distinguished faculty that included luminaries Paul Tillich, Mircea Eliade, and Paul Ricoeur. And although the experiment in federation was over, William Rainey Harper's less ambitious policy of seminaries responsible to the churches affiliating with the University and its Divinity School was aggressively pursued. By 1980, the Lutheran School of Theology, the Catholic Theological Union, the Jesuit School of Theology, and (Presbyterian) McCormick Theological Seminary had moved to the vicinity of the University of Chicago to share library resources and offer some opportunities for cross-registration of students. The Divinity School, which even during the days of the federation enrolled most of its students as master's and doctoral rather than as bachelor's candidates,[25] began to give even more of its attention to the graduate work suitable to the profession of teaching.[26] The Divinity School at the University of Chicago resolved many of the strains between university and church by accentuating the former and minimizing the latter.

## THE NECESSITY OF BRIDGE-BUILDING

Other university-related divinity schools did not opt so explicitly for the Chicago solution, nor were their attempts to reconcile churchly and university accountability ensnared in the same thicket of disagreements created by federations. Nevertheless, they did experience some of the same tension between university and church so apparent in that clash of impulses and prolonged dialogue known as the Federated Theological Faculty.

In part, the tension issued from a problem of image. The nondenominational divinity schools, in particular, earned the reputation among churches as training grounds for university scholars who had no intention of entering the parish ministry. Dean Willard Sperry of Harvard Divinity School obviously was miffed by this image when he observed in 1940:

> A group of recent Alumni have been visiting New England colleges with a view to recruits for the School. It is surprising and rather humiliating to discover how little Harvard Divinity School is known in these colleges as a place where men are trained for the ministry. So good a friend as Professor Pratt at Williams told me, even this year, that he had supposed that we trained only teachers and did little or nothing to fit men for the preaching and pastoral ministry.[27]

Sperry and his decanal successors periodically announced statistics to try to destroy the image: in 1939, 80 percent of Divinity School students were preparing for the ministry; in 1951, 86 percent of surveyed alumni were still in some form of the ministry; and in 1977, when special master's-level work for students uncommitted to the ministry was popular at Harvard and other schools, 43 percent of Harvard's divinity students were enrolled in the standard ministerial degree program.[28] Similar responses were triggered at other nondenominational divinity schools as rumors spread that those schools were dedicated to producing college and university teachers rather than ministers for the church.[29]

Because they have served principally as professional schools for a particular denomination, the Methodist divinity schools usually have eluded the suspicion that they have neglected the education of ministers. They have by no means escaped the allegation, however, that by virtue of their emphasis on university scholarship they have not taken the needs of the churches as seriously as they have taken the requirements of the university. In the 1920s, Dean Franklin Parker of Candler complained about older southern Methodist ministers warning Candler's recruits that professional, university-level education would mark an unfortunate departure from the tangible duties to the church.[30] In the 1930s, Dean Lynn Harold Hough of the theological school at Drew intimated that such warnings were not confined to southern folk. Hough told a conference of Methodist churches that he often heard ministers in the denomination "boasting of their ignorance of theology," and he cautioned his co-workers that Methodism has been "a happy hunting ground for intellectual obsessions" because "we have failed to understand the necessity of subjecting our deepest experience to the disciplines of the intelligence."[31] In the 1970s, a Methodist bishop in Texas had to assure the members of his ward that if they only knew the faculty at Perkins as well as he did they would recognize that those professors were altogether committed to the life of the church and the training of its future ministers.[32]

The image of the divinity schools as academic institutions disdainful of, if not downright hostile toward, the church and its ministry cannot be attributed solely to the churches' failure to know the facts about enrollments or to American Methodism's historic penchant for experiential religion. The image also has derived from the ready participation of divinity school faculty in university culture, sometimes with a corresponding detachment from the culture of the churches.

Willard Sperry, the dean disturbed by the public misperception of Harvard's role in the education of ministers, could say in 1954, "The Faculty [of Harvard Divinity School] does the best it can to prepare men for the ministry; the churches must then decide whether they wish to accept the graduates."[33] Sperry's comment was a technically accurate description of a nondenominational divinity school not associated with the official process of denominational ordination. Couched that way, however, his comment betokened more than a little aloofness from the specific needs of the churches. At Perkins in the 1950s, a professor drew considerable laughter from his class, but hardly from ministers and laypersons in the churches, when he reversed the slogan of a Texas Methodist evangelistic campaign from "Tell Texas About Christ" to "Tell Christ About Texas."[34] In 1960, the newly appointed dean at Perkins, Joseph Quillian, warned his faculty that "semi-knowledgeable criticism of the Church" comes too easily. "It would be helpful if any judgmental statements from us to students concerning the Church should be of the nature of considered, deliberate judgment" rather than "stereotyping, tangential judgmentalism which draws cheap and somewhat hollow laughter."[35]

Quillian acknowledged that careless judgmentalism did not characterize the Perkins faculty as a whole, and, indeed, such incidents do not add up to a total alienation between divinity schools and the churches. Rather, the incidents are emblems of an enduring tension, deeply structural in nature, between two climates of opinion, two communities of responsibility.

In one sense, the tension between the culture of the university and that of the church marked a defeat of the originating vision of William Rainey Harper and other founders of divinity schools. In that vision, academy and church would be locked together in the common causes of elevating the learning of the Protestant ministry and spreading the principles of Protestant religion across the globe. Contained within the vision was the hope that university and church would take their respective places within an extensive system of education in religion that would Protestantize the nation. But the grand system of religious education would not hold together, a pluralistic nation would not be won over to Pan-Protestantism, and academy and church, it turned out, would not so easily correlate for the mutual definition of the ministerial profession.

Part of the founding vision continued to inspire the divinity schools, however. The schools continuously sought to link the world of the university with the world of the churches, a goal implicit in late nineteenth and early twentieth century educational evangelism. That goal was the driving force behind the various schemes for relating theory and practice, the propounding of changing philosophies of theological education, and the development of courses to prepare men and women for the diverse ministries of the church.

The desire to couple church and academy also motivated the divinity schools to find means for keeping educated ministers educated, for educating the uneducated ministers already occupying the profession, and for directly educating the laity. Throughout the twentieth century, the divinity schools instituted "Ministers' Weeks" and lecture series for alumni, continuing education programs for ministers needing refresher courses, circulating libraries for clergy and laity in isolated rural areas, retreats for the spiritual and intellectual stimulation of both the laity and the ordained clergy, and programs of study for lay leaders in the churches.[36] To boost the social standing of ministers and to extend their education (and, in some cases, to increase income), in the 1970s some of the divinity schools joined other seminaries in instituting a Doctor of Ministry degree available either to ministers "in the field" or to those studying on campus.[37] Most of the divinity schools in all periods of their history have included faculty who could translate recondite theological knowledge into the language of the people in the churches, and they have boasted within their ranks great preachers whose sermons have joined theological learning with winsome public discourse.

But it has been necessary continuously to build bridges between university and church. Efforts at connection were necessitated by a division between two communities of responsibility that had been created by powerful historical forces. No force was more potent than the fundamentalist controversy in the 1920s. A deep division of worldview opened by that conflict, plus emerging expectations of the minister on the part of the churches and developing patterns in American higher education, meant that the divinity schools could presuppose no simple correlation of university and church in a definition of the ministerial profession.

## DIVISIVE FORCES

In a ringing address of 1922 that was widely distributed to American Protestants, Harry Emerson Fosdick, minister of the First Presbyterian Church in New York City, raised a critical and deliberately taunting question: "Shall the Fundamentalists Win?" Fosdick cut to what he considered the core of the matter. Fundamentalists were "illiberal and intolerant." They denied the name "Christian" to those who refused to accept the literal truth of the virgin birth, the inerrant truth of the Bible, and other doctrines judged to be fundamental to the Christian faith. In Fosdick's opinion, the fundamentalists thus further divided a Christian church that was already badly splintered. Furthermore, they repudiated new scientific knowledge respecting the physical universe and so would have believers disavow the very world that surrounds them. And they insisted on "quarreling over little matters when the world is dying of great needs" facing a postwar world.[38]

From his own modernist perspective, Fosdick certainly had discerned the implications of a potent movement that was shaking the foundations of American Protestantism. The higher criticism of the Bible, the Darwinian theory of evolution, toleration of diverse religious beliefs, concern for the unity of the Christian church and for the capacity of a unified church to heal the wounds of the world—all of these modernist Protestant advances decreed that the fundamentalists should not be allowed to win the minds and hearts of the people and thus turn American religion back toward an antediluvian dogmatism. The leaders of the divinity schools agreed. In the judgment of Shailer Mathews of the University of Chicago Divinity School, fundamentalism was little more than a throwback to the narrowly dogmatic confessionalism of seventeenth-century Europe.[39] In the opinion of Texas Methodist bishop E. D. Mouzon, who rose to the defense of the biblical criticism taught at SMU, fundamentalism was captive to a "dictation-dictatorial theory of the Bible" that utterly contradicted Methodism's emphasis on the spirit rather than the letter of Christianity.[40]

The forces released by the modernist/fundamentalist controversy were not easily stemmed, however, and Fosdick's question would continue to haunt American Protestantism throughout the twentieth century. Who, then, would win?

Following that widely publicized contest, the Scopes "monkey trial" in Tennessee in 1925, the fundamentalists were seemingly routed as a significant American cultural power. The press coverage of the spectacle portrayed the great Populist William Jennings Bryan as an ignorant opponent of evolution and a bumbling defender of the literal interpretation of the Bible, and his fundamentalist compatriots as backwoods hillbillies. As a consequence, in the words of George Marsden, "in the trial by public opinion and the press, it was clear that the twentieth century, the cities, and the universities had won a resounding victory, and that the country, the South, and the fundamentalists were guilty as charged."[41]

A series of heresy charges were brought against modernist professors and preachers, but the attacks were confined for the most part to Northern Baptists and Presbyterians, and the fundamentalists failed to gain control of any of the seminaries, colleges, or denominational boards of ecumenical Protestantism. The fundamentalists formed their own churches, schools, colleges, and agencies and thus separated themselves from the larger institutions of American religious and intellectual life. They also failed to lead out of the denominations most of those who continued to harbor grave reservations about evolution, biblical criticism, and other modernist postures—something that would turn out to be a Pyrrhic victory for the modernists. By mid-century the "evangelicals," who had arisen out of the same ideological and social backgrounds as the fundamentalists but who *were* able to command the attention of the American public on matters of faith and morals, had repudiated the sectarianism of the fundamentalists and had made clear that they would champion their religious and social conservatism *within* the mainline denominations.[42]

The university divinity schools played an active role in driving the fundamentalists to the institutional and intellectual margins of America. None of the schools escaped the suspicions—or the acerbic accusations— of fundamentalist preachers and laypersons that the professional education of ministers was in the control of infidel proponents of higher criticism and evolutionary theory. And none of the schools failed to meet their challengers with counterargument. Leaders of the divinity schools insisted that progress in Protestant piety and advances in scientific scholarship were altogether compatible developments.

The Divinity School at the University of Chicago, citadel of Protestant modernism, drew some of the heaviest fundamentalist fire. Chicago's Shailer Mathews, though more restrained in his response to the fundamentalists than some of his Chicago colleagues, was no less passionate than they in defending Christianity against those he took to be dogmatists who were out of touch with the modern world. He explained that his own modernist Protestantism was no "liberal dogmatism," no set of doctrines to be set against the beliefs of conservative Christians. Rather, it was an outlook that should inform the "evangelical convictions and attitudes which have been carried across the centuries by the succession of Christians." Modernism was, in essence, a human spirit, a frame of mind, defined by *"the methods of modern science to find, state, and use the permanent and central values of inherited orthodoxy in meeting the needs of a modern world."*[43]

As other divinity schools came under fundamentalist accusations, their leaders responded in a vein similar to Mathews. In the late nineteenth and early twentieth centuries, Boston University professor of Old Testament Hinckley G. Mitchell and philosopher of religion Bordon Parker Bowne were charged with departing from the fundamentals of the Christian faith (the former was so charged by a band of students). At Drew in the 1920s and 1930s, theologian Edwin Lewis was the object of repeated attacks by Drew graduate and fundamentalist minister Harold Paul Sloan. In the southern Methodist schools, faculty influenced by modern biblical scholarship were singled out for the accusation that they were heretics who were corrupting the minds of the nation's future ministers. Emory's Andrew Warren Sledd, Wyatt Aiken Smart, and William Arthur Shelton; SMU's John A. Rice; Vanderbilt's James H. Stevenson—all were under suspicion by Methodist clergy and laity. The nondenominational schools, by virtue of their freedom from church control, were often depicted by fundamentalists as hotbeds of a modernism oblivious to the historic fundamentals of the faith. Faculty and administrators of the divinity schools responded to the charges, often with the vocal support of denominational leaders, by claiming that the higher criticism of the Bible and new ways of theological reflection that harmonized with the theories of modern science were certain means of preserving the historic faith for educated, modern Americans.[44]

The equal mix of Protestant piety, social hopes, and Christian apologetics so typical of the divinity schools' response to fundamentalism was apparent in the words of John A. Rice, the SMU biblical critic charged with departing from the faith:

> ... the Bible must be judged in the light of its purpose, which is to bring God and men into such satisfying relations with each other as that they shall work together for the creation of a new social order characterized by righteousness, peace, and the joy of holy living over all the earth. Should errors in history, science, philosophy, or in any other field of inquiry be found, they need not disturb us. The infallibility of our inspired book depends not upon these, but rather upon the effective achieving of the end it sought and still seeks.[45]

Rice, who had done his graduate work at the University of Chicago, was the target of the notorious fundamentalist Texas Baptist in Fort Worth, J. Frank Norris. Norris's public onslaughts and the expressions of conservative concerns within the North Texas Methodist Conference Board of Education combined to force Rice to resign his faculty position at SMU.[46] The more common outcome of such controversies for divinity school professors, however, was victory of the accused against the accusers. The fundamentalists failed to capture the divinity schools, and most denominational leaders were persuaded by the argument that critical, scientific scholarship was an instrument for preserving the faith of thoughtful, educated people in the modern age.

During the years of the Cold War, fundamentalists again launched a series of attacks on the divinity schools. Closely intermingled with fears of the "communist menace" and "racial intermixing," mid-century fundamentalist accusations raised the specter of divinity schools and other institutions within ecumenical Protestantism actively contaminating the values of the "American Way of Life." The divinity school at Boston University, for example, was singled out as a prime source of Marxist social-gospel Methodism, and the dean of the Perkins School of Theology was branded by Texas fundamentalists as a "pinko" for his stand on racial integration at SMU.[47]

Such outbreaks of censure notwithstanding, the divinity schools remained invincible against the fundamentalist attacks. In fact, by mid-century the terms "fundamentalist" and "modernist" no longer defined either the intellectual context of the divinity schools or the religious climate of the country. The pervasive theological perspective of the schools had shifted from optimistic, progressivistic modernism to the sober realism of neoorthodoxy and existentialism. An ecumenically minded and denominationally oriented "new evangelicalism" had replaced separatist fundamentalism as the more commanding voice of Protestant conservatives. And both liberal and conservative Protestants were growing comfortable with those most modern features of the day: higher education and the technologies of the Western world. Shortly after the Second World War, the fundamentalist/modernist conflict in its old form had virtually disappeared from the American scene.

What had not disappeared was a heritage of deep division within American Protestantism. As one interpreter of the 1920s has remarked, "What had come of the conflict of the twenties was a deeply, permanently divided Protestantism. While Fundamentalists became for some decades less visible in many parts of the country, sent into exile at the margins of the culture, forced to rebuild institutions and shoot from distances, it became clear that original-stock Protestantism—from which both sides derived—no longer presented a single front."[48] The division would show up later *within* the denominations as theological and social liberals contended with conservatives who did not join the fundamentalist departure from the denominations.[49] And it would express itself repeatedly in tensions between divinity schools that had won their battles against the fundamentalists and churches that had not adopted the worldview defined by biblical criticism, modern science, and the speculations of modern theology.

At base the enduring split bequeathed by the fundamentalist/modernist controversy was one of worldview. It was a division between systems of meaning and value within which humans grasp the purpose of their existence and govern their behavior.[50] The pattern of meanings that eventually made up the world of the divinity schools comprised those beliefs and values defended so avidly by Harry Emerson Fosdick: toleration of diverse religious perspectives; a view of the Bible as a collection of human compositions subject to human error, even if somehow inspired by God; greater concern for the unity of Christianity than for the defense of the comparatively "little matters" of doctrine; openness to the latest scientific theories and a disposition to accommodate religious belief to science in all its forms. In about a half-century after Fosdick's defiant address, it was clear that few Americans, including those in the churches, occupied the world of religious meaning of the divinity schools.

Public opinion polls in the 1980s revealed that Americans inhabited a world of religious meaning that would strike Fosdick and his heirs as at best unenlightened and uninformed, and at worst as superstitious. Eighty percent of Americans believed that God works supernatural miracles and that humans will have to answer for their sins on a Judgment Day. About half of the Americans polled believed that God created the world in its present form within the last 10,000 years. Although belief in the literal, inerrant truth of the Bible declined in the 1960s and 1970s, in the 1980s 30 percent of all Americans and 37 percent of Protestants continued to adhere to biblical literalism. Eighty-four percent of all the Americans polled believed that Jesus was in some sense the Son of God, with only a fraction of Americans viewing Jesus as one of several of the world's major religious founders and leaders. Within the churches of ecumenical Protestantism, there was only a slight departure from the premodern worldview. Among Episcopalians and Presbyterians, denominations usually deemed "liberal," 20 percent of the members understood the Bible as reporting literal facts, and over half believed that the Bible should receive special treatment as the inspired word of God. Among white, adult members of all the mainline Protestant denominations, 80 percent believed in the certain coming of a Judgment Day, 78 percent believed that God performs supernatural miracles today, and 66 percent had "no doubt" that Christ will return to earth at some indefinite point in the future.[51]

Such statistics cannot support the conjecture that fundamentalism in its early twentieth-century separatist, institutional form endures as a powerful force in contemporary America. Nor do the statistics by themselves betoken a North American fundamentalism engaged in a new aggressive war against modernist convictions, although considerable evidence can be found elsewhere of just such a conflict, one that shares resemblances with a fundamentalist revolt around the world.[52] What *is* immediately apparent from the data is that some of the chief components in the fundamentalist worldview have not been replaced with those of the modern, critical, scientific perspective that have come to prevail in university divinity schools.

The inability of the divinity schools to shake the churches decisively out of their premodern worldview has resulted as much from the resolutely democratic character of the churches as from any innate failure of the critical scientific posture to win conviction among a pious people. The democratic temper of American religion was already apparent in the fundamentalist/modernist controversy. That conflict was in part a clash of elite and folk cultures, with William Jennings Bryan and other defenders of the fundamentals of the faith fueling their arguments with depictions of evolutionists and biblical critics as arrogant specialists who held the religion of ordinary people in contempt. "A religion that didn't appeal to any but college graduates," Bryan huffed, "would be over the head or under the feet of 99 percent of our people. The God I worship is the God of the ignorant as well as the God of the learned man."[53] Both the scientist and the biblical critic were portrayed as holding, in effect, that religious truth belonged to the domain of the highly educated expert.

"Ordinary citizens might be content to leave some fields to the experts," Ferenc Morton Szasz has remarked, "but others remained in the public realm, including social mores, public education, and the interpretation of the Bible, subjects on which ordinary people insisted they had a right to express an opinion."[54] Just as Protestant laypeople resisted the intrusion of the professional educator into their Sunday schools,[55] so they were inclined to defy any specialist who insisted that higher learning was a precondition to a proper understanding of the Bible, of God's creation, and of other things religious. Democratic folk have not been predisposed to turn their sacred worldview over to the educated elite.

The divinity schools, however, were not deterred from pursuing their goal of making the Christian faith palatable to the tastes of the thoughtful and educated, or of educating the uneducated into the perspective of the modern world. Such goals, however, were pursued by immersing ministers-in-training in the perspectives and values stemming from the Enlightenment and ensconced in the "liberal culture" manifest in parts of the university. Those perspectives and values did not align neatly with those of the churches. The divinity schools embraced a commitment to skeptical reason, an enthusiasm, in principle at least, for tolerance of lifestyles and social norms, and an affirmation of the freedom of the individual investigator.[56] These liberal values were joined with the university ideals of advanced specialization, disciplinary and subdisciplinary competence, and professional prestige. As the divinity schools assumed their roles as the academic pacesetters in the process of seminary accreditation, liberal educational ideals became the tests of Protestant theological education as such.[57]

With the exception of dropping Hebrew and Greek as required courses (an action that created no small amount of consternation among biblical scholars),[58] academic requirements for faculty and students were raised and an emphasis on specialization was increased during the course of the twentieth century. Individual scholars were encouraged to pursue their disciplines with singular intensity, to bring critical reason to bear on the most sacrosanct of subjects, and to measure their performance as professionals by the standards of the academic guilds. On occasion, divinity school deans were compelled to explain to other university administrators that theological faculty were not as productive in scholarly writing as were some other university professors because of obligations to church committees, boards, and publications.[59] And none of the schools was devoid of faculty who, in their preaching, lecturing, and writing, could speak the language of the laity as well as of the professional scholar. But the drift throughout the twentieth century was clear. The community of discourse in the divinity schools was that of the university scholar: specialized, derived from the research and reflection of the individual, and legitimated by scholars in the same discipline.

As a consequence, the world of the divinity school and that of the churches seemed to widen even beyond what had irritated William Jennings Bryan. In the words of Edwin S. Gaustad, "biblical criticism became increasingly an academic matter, ingrown, jargon-laden, esoteric, and aloof. Only occasionally, as with the translation and publication of the Revised Standard Version in the 1940s and 1950s, were sustained efforts made to keep lines of communication fully open between the ecclesiastical and the scholarly communities." Church history, challenged to find its place in a university environment filled with a host of diverse subspecialties and methods, "had to justify itself against new disciplines and demands, against the well-known if imperfectly understood information explosion."[60] By the 1980s, theology, ethics, and psychology of religion had become just as subspecialized and esoteric as other divinity school disciplines.[61] In the 1970s and 1980s, faculty committees were still fretting about how to link the community of the church with a divinity school community shaped by the university ethos of specialization and academic professionalization.[62]

The establishment of that linkage was rendered difficult by the churches' developing expectations of their ministers. On the one hand, since the nineteenth century, ministers in most Protestant denominations were expected to offer laypersons effective, authoritative participation in the life of their churches. On the other, as the conventions of professionalism spread across all sectors of society, laypeople demanded that their ministers possess special skills appropriate to the diverse tasks of an institutional leader. Early in their history, the divinity schools recognized the legitimacy of each set of expectations. Few theological educators would have disagreed with Henry Sloane Coffin's description of the goals of the ideal seminary at Union in 1926: the seminary should both develop particular professional skills and cultivate ministers who could inspire lay leadership in their congregations.[63] The divinity schools sought to embrace both the populism and the elitism regnant within churches influenced by a simultaneously democratic and professional culture.

The difficulty facing the divinity schools did not lie solely in the issue of how to reconcile two apparently contradictory sets of demands, however. It resided also in the nature of the demands themselves. The professional skills required of the congregational pastor (and to a certain extent of the missionary, the minister of education, and other specialist ministers) were an assortment of proficiencies that held together loosely at best and that the climate of ministerial training did little to bring into coherence.

As churches became "social congregations" with diverse goals and manifold activities,[64] laypeople wanted their ministers to possess talents appropriate to those goals and activities. In all but the largest churches that could afford the expense of multiple specialized ministries, the minister of a congregation had to take on the roles of preacher, teacher, worship planner and leader, financial manager, counselor, general administrator, community leader, and more. In the 1930s, William Adams Brown discovered in his study of the ministry that Protestant clergy felt pulled apart by the diversity of their tasks, believed that they were unprepared by seminary to handle those tasks, and, as a result, felt unprofessional in comparison with the likes of the psychiatrist, the social worker, and the educator.[65] Brown's collaborator in the study, Mark May, wrote that the functions of the minister were so disparate and the overall purpose of those functions so vague that entering the ministry was "like entering the army," where one never knows "what specific work he will be called upon to perform."[66] In the 1950s and 1960s, studies indicated that ministers who tried to rank their diverse duties found that their priorities departed from their congregations' expectations and that their rankings differed from the way they in fact spent most of their time. Administration, for example, an activity peripheral to what most pastors felt called or trained to do, consumed the greatest amount of their time and energy.[67]

For all of their suspicion of professional elitism and their championing of lay participation, members of Protestant congregations have continued to expect their ministers to perform discrete, and largely unrelated, professional tasks. In fact, a study in the 1970s revealed that clergy, much more than laity, were interested in creating an environment for active lay involvement in the churches. "Most laity, it seems, still perceive of the minister as the chief actor in the church, a professional who carries out certain functions."[68] And as a student of congregations concluded in 1985, the notion prevailed, especially "among churches peopled by the middle and upper-middle classes among which modern professionalism developed," that the minister was called to be a professional "for the delivery of expected human services."[69]

In the 1950s, H. Richard Niebuhr of the Yale Divinity School called for a new conception of the ministry, one that would draw upon the historic traditions of the Christian churches, the specialized education of ministers in the theological schools, and the current professional demands made by the churches. It was a conception that he labeled "the minister as pastoral director," probably a bad choice of terms since they seemed to connote the pastor as "manager," something that Niebuhr did not have in mind. Neither a pleaser of clients nor a "big operator," the pastoral director would bring all of the traditional functions of the ministry— preaching, teaching, administering the sacraments, caring for souls, presiding over a church—to focus on one primary role: "that of building or 'edifying' the church; he is concerned in everything that he does to bring into being a people of God who as a Church will serve the purpose of the Church in the local community and the world."[70] In this conception, the entire congregation engages in the service of ministry, and the ordained minister directs the congregation in its service. The diverse professional duties of the modern minister, including the time-consuming task of administration as well as the various disciplines in the minister's education, should now fall into place around a primary function: that of directing the church's service to God and the world.[71]

Although Niebuhr's theory of the ministry grew out of his understanding of the history and present shape of the Christian church and from his study of trends in theological education, he admitted that his notion of the minister as pastoral director was at best an emerging one. It had found full institutional embodiment neither in the churches nor in the theological schools. And although his view won hearty, if sometimes critical, approval from theological educators,[72] it did not accord nicely with the expectations of ministers on the part of American congregations.

Examinations of lay attitudes in the late twentieth century have shown that church members want their ministers to be professionals, to be sure, but professionals whose chief responsibility is representing, enlivening, and enhancing the religious piety of the individual. A study published in 1975 indicated that what establishes the authority and respect of clergy among laity is principally the minister's "religious authenticity," variously described as "having head and heart together," "living the gospel," and being "a man of God and a man of the world."[73] If not exactly expected to be the professional "nice person," the minister is expected to be the living embodiment of the religious piety of believers; that, more than anything else, earns respect from a congregation.

A study published in 1980 further disclosed that laypeople give far less weight than their clergy to ministries outside the congregation. They much prefer their ministers to be persons of "positive approach" and "flexibility of spirit" who will faithfully perform the tasks of "building congregational community," "relating faith to the modern world," and "competent preaching and worship." The study did find considerable variation among the Protestant denominations on the issue of whether the church's primary role is personal evangelism or social responsibility, but in all denominations a chasm divided the views of the clergy from those of the laity on the relative importance of the minister's service to the world. "Laity's idea of the clergy's task leads them to relegate extra-congregational ministries to the category 'OK—if there's time,' whereas clergy place them much higher on their totem pole of values." The "laity are less concerned about ministries to the outsider—the lonely and alienated." Laypersons also manifest much less concern than their ministers do about the clergy's continued theological learning. "Laity generally consider it of less importance that a beginning minister seek to be a theologian in life and thought. Their expectations fall well below those of their clergy in every denominational family."[74]

The authors of the 1980 study insisted that they did not want their findings to be used as a "market analysis" that would simply dictate what ministers should be doing. In their judgment, ministers' callings to their priestly and prophetic roles should transcend popular demand. Nevertheless, the authors did suggest that the contrasts between clerical and lay expectations of the ministry "signal the need for clergy who consider theirs a prophetic ministry to recognize the weight of opinion and tradition that surrounds many current evaluations by laity."[75] The contrasts also signify that H. Richard Niebuhr's concept of the minister as a leader who draws upon traditions and theological learning to direct the whole church toward service is still, at best, an emerging concept.

Another historical development has served to separate the community of the church from that of the university divinity school. Two types of higher education that have bred two very different kinds of thinking have come to characterize the two communities. This development goes a long way toward explaining the divergence both in worldview and in professional expectation in the communities.

Study for the ministry in the university always has represented the extension of a liberal education. Theological reflection upon the symbols and beliefs of Christianity, critical examinations of biblical texts, contemplation of ethical issues entailed in the application of Christian norms to the situations of daily living, study of historic religious traditions—all these features of theological education have involved the cultivation of the "liberal mind" that values skeptical inquiry, openness to diversity of perspective, and a sense of the importance of the past for illumination of the present. Despite the frequent complaints of divinity school faculty about the inadequacy of their students' background in liberal education and the recent influx of "second career" students who have minimal acquaintance with the liberal arts, the divinity school curricula have always built upon the liberal arts disciplines in the humanities and social sciences.

After the Civil War, Americans increasingly demanded courses of study appropriate to a corporate, industrialized, and technological society, and the large universities, especially the public institutions, emerged to meet those demands. Tax-supported universities eventually would dominate higher education and would train expanding numbers of undergraduates in technological, scientific, and business majors. By 1965, two-thirds of all American undergraduates were attending public, tax-supported universities, and the large majority of them were concentrating their studies in disciplines other than the liberal arts. In the late 1980s, 25 percent of all undergraduates (in both public and private schools) were receiving their bachelor's degrees in business and management, 9 percent in engineering, and 6 percent in the health sciences. In the aggregate, 55 percent were candidates for degrees in business, technology, the health sciences, and the natural sciences, while 10 percent were receiving degrees in all of the social sciences combined and 9 percent in the humanities combined.[76] And there was no evidence that the liberal arts within "general education" programs in large universities, which usually consisted of a wide assortment of introductory-level courses, had provided any coherent or extensive exposure of non–liberal arts majors to liberal learning.[77]

Sociologists have focused their attention on the correlation between *levels* of education and religious attitudes among the laity, noting, for example, that the higher the educational level the more liberal the social outlook and the less commitment to orthodox religious beliefs.[78] What has been overlooked by the sociological studies is the drift in the twentieth century toward the education of the laity in the scientific, technical, and preprofessional disciplines and the corresponding paucity of their exposure to the liberal arts. Furthermore, much of the sociological literature tends to encompass the clergy in the "new class" of service professionals—those professionals who, according to Peter Berger and others, derive their livelihood from the "knowledge industry" by producing, distributing, applying, and administering knowledge rather than goods.[79] What this categorization ignores is the difference between the *kinds* of knowledge that the clergy and most of their highly educated laypeople proffer. The engineer trained in differential calculus or the management consultant accustomed to thinking in the categories of market planning can be altogether mystified by a literary/symbolic analysis of the Bible or a historical inquiry into the changing traditions of Christian belief and practice. By the same token, of course, the minister is likely to stand bewildered before the knowledge specialties of the technically educated layperson.

In any case, the premodern worldview of religion can remain unaltered by the perspectives of liberal studies for the technically trained—and very modern—layperson. And the premodern worldview can even find embodiment in the taxonomies of technological discourse. In the words of a prominent professor of engineering (a person active in his Presbyterian church who spends long hours discussing religion with his students): "The Bible is like a handbook for building a bridge: it contains all the formulas for belief and the good Christian life."[80]

It would be hasty to conclude that such a formulaic construction of the Bible is "anti-intellectual." Rather, the construction springs from an intellect untutored in liberal studies. It would be equally foolhardy to understand the formulaic intellect as somehow more specialized than that of the literary critic, the philosopher, or the social historian. Rather, the layman's biblical perspective illustrates how a premodern religious worldview can be folded into the categories of a technical set of assumptions about how the world functions, assumptions unsullied by the technical education of liberal studies. In a society in which only four out of ten college graduates know that Jesus delivered the Sermon on the Mount and fewer than half of all adult Americans can name the gospels of the New Testament,[81] it is perhaps understandable how unexamined religion can be combined with the categories of technical reason. The division between community of church and community of university divinity school is, in great part, a product of the emergence of two very different kinds of education that nurture two distinctive types of thinking.

## ABIDING PROFESSIONAL TENSIONS

The Protestant ministry is not the only profession to have suffered tensions between its community of education and its community of service. Critics of American professional education as such have complained that the emphasis on specialized knowledge, research activities, and professional credentialing has led to a widespread neglect of the needs of the professional's clients. Legal education and medical training, viewed throughout the twentieth century by the clergy and members of the other so-called minor professions as the prototypes for connecting university education with client services, have not escaped the strictures. Such a broad criticism points to an abiding tension between communities of responsibility for many professions in America. In the words of a law professor at Yale, "Do the law schools exist primarily to train lawyers? Do they owe their allegiance to the universities, to the profession—or to the public interest? The question has not been answered satisfactorily in the hundred years it has been around, and its implications remain considerable."[82]

That unsatisfactorily answered question has led to calls for new paradigms of professional education that would more closely unite the specialized training and professional standards of the university with the interests of the public and the recipients of professional services. One proposal would model professional education on the feats of "artistry" rather than on "training the specialized intellect" or on the "practical applications of theory." According to this proposal, "university-based professional schools should learn from such deviant traditions of education for practice as studios of art and design, conservatories of music and dance, athletics coaching, and apprenticeship in the crafts, all of which emphasize coaching and learning by doing." No longer separated by technical scholarship on the one hand and specific professional functions and expectations on the other, the aims of the community of the university and those of the community receiving services would coalesce in a setting that blends thinking and action. University students would not be "taught things"; they would be "coached" how to handle specific situations in a constantly changing public which they serve.[83]

This proposed model for professional education has found its advocates among proponents of the reform of theological education.[84] Like the suggestions that would rethink the meaning of theory and practice, however, in the late 1980s the model of artistry had not led to a restructuring of the programs of study at the divinity schools. The so-called classical disciplines still constituted the core of a curriculum aimed at the production of students equipped with the latest technical scholarship within several areas of liberal education and governed by the standards of a profession of university educators. The communities of university and church were still divided—not by an impassable gulf, to be sure, but by a divide that required bridging on the part of both faculty and students.

The history of the strain between the two communities suggests that any radical reform of professional education in university divinity schools will not come easily or quickly, for the division has arisen from more than a mere contrast of academic procedures that can be adjusted in the light of changed educational goals. It has emanated, as well, from differences in worldviews and professional expectations. As the clashing impulses of the Federated Theological Faculty at the University of Chicago revealed so clearly, divinity school faculty are inclined to safeguard their freedoms and privileges as university citizens, and they are expected to live up to the scholarly demands of their home institutions and their professional societies. Divinity school students are similarly obligated. As professional learners, their performance is assessed with scholarly measures that have little to do directly with the professional expectations that will greet them in the parish or in other forms of the ministry.

Of perhaps greater importance, two incompatible worldviews have emerged in the schools and the churches. The alliance of the divinity schools with the university's critical, liberal perspective undermined assumptions about God, universe, and humankind constitutive of religious fundamentalism, but the alliance did not subvert the assumptions in the religious public. The modernist battle against fundamentalism was clearly won in the education of Protestant ministers. It was by no means so clearly won in the education of the laity. The increase in the technological, scientific, and business training of college-educated laity, largely at the expense of humanistic and social scientific education, rendered possible the blending of modern education with premodern beliefs among the laity. Short of a drastic reversal of educational trends in America, or a herculean effort on the part of the educated clergy and their professors, the deep division in religious worldview seems likely to endure. That division has been responsible for much of the tension between the yokes of responsibility in the professional conception of the Protestant ministry.

# PART III

■

# FORMATION AND REFORM

# CHAPTER VI

■

## Social Class and Social Gospel

On the same day, October 24, 1912, Drew University inaugurated Ezra Squire Tipple as its new president and celebrated the laying of the cornerstone for an imposing new refectory modeled after Christ Church Hall at Oxford University. During the ceremonies for the two events, Drew Old Testament professor Robert W. Rogers delivered some remarks about the significance of the new building. He expressed great pleasure that "Methodist preachers of tomorrow, who are here to study the various theological disciplines, are henceforth to dine amid surroundings of elegance, refinement and of historical suggestion." Rogers hoped that with the construction of the new dining facility Drew could seize an opportunity to cultivate gentlemen as well as learned and pious Methodist ministers. Rogers admitted that, to a large extent, gentlemen are "not made by their environment; there must be innate beauty of soul to make courtesy, gentleness and recognition of the rights of others spring to instant demand." Still, he thought that "these qualities are all helped to a finer, a more fitting expression by the silent influence of beautiful and comely material things."[1]

On May 13, 1924, Bishop Herbert Welch, one of Drew's most celebrated graduates, returned from the mission field in Korea to deliver the Drew commencement address. His observations about the Methodist ministry stood in stark contrast to those of Rogers a dozen years earlier. Welch warned of the "great danger of the development of a Protestant church of the middle class." He complained that ministers were too often "found in the homes of the rich or the middle class," were too preoccupied with the trappings of breeding and wealth, and were too engrossed in the building of middle-class church organizations—all of which indicated an unwillingness "to suffer degradation for the sake of social justice." Welch considered ministerial immersion in the culture of bourgeois manners and means the very abandonment of the Methodist heritage. "In the beginning of Methodism the poor had the gospel preached to them. Ours was not a church of the middle classes. The poor heard a message which they could understand. Methodism was a friend of the laboring class. When it ceases to be such—the little candle on the altar to God will be extinguished."[2]

The clash of attitude between Rogers and Welch sprang in part from differences in personal commitment. As a leading spokesman for an American Methodist social gospel, Bishop Welch was more concerned about the dislocations in American society outside the academy than was Professor Rogers, whose consuming interests continued to be archaeological research and the teaching of the Hebrew language. But the differences between the two Drew speeches grew also from changed times. The devastations of the Great War and the ensuing social and economic turmoil around the world made the cultivation of middle-class gentlemanly behavior seem like a pious sentimentality to Welch and many other Protestant leaders of the day. To be sure, those Protestant leaders would have had reservations about the appropriateness of Rogers's remarks in 1912, but in 1924 his encouragement of American ministers' delight in "comely material things" would seem an especially deplorable, self-indulgent disregard of the crises of the times.

According to the vision of William Rainey Harper and other divinity school founders, ministers should be taught to move comfortably within an environment of leisure, power, and wealth, since that setting constituted one part of their ministry and provided the resources for social change. But the clergy should also be trained to minister to the poor and desperate of the world, to those who were in need of religious and moral uplift and social relief. Many of the university divinity schools would never abandon completely the task of forming ministers in the high culture of the university, and all would continue to embrace the concerns and draw upon the resources of the American middle classes. Early in their histories, however, the schools turned to the task of forming ministers with the ideals and designs of a social gospel. Formation would then occur in the context of reform, and religious inspiration and cultural elevation in a climate of education for social change. The perspective of Herbert Welch, not that of Robert Rogers, came to characterize the divinity school outlook on the formation of ministers.

## FROM ETIQUETTE TO ETHICS

Rogers's suggestion in 1912 that the educational environment should provide ministers-in-training with good breeding expressed a goal long held by Protestant theological schools. Antebellum seminaries sought to take boys from farms and small towns and mold them into polite middle-class citizens. That aspiration, quite as much as the cultivation of piety or the instruction of the mind, often defined the task of early American theological education. Textbooks and lectures in pastoral theology instructed young ministers in dinner-table etiquette, warned them not to pick their teeth in public, and advised them how to develop other social graces that would admit them to the higher classes of Protestant congregations.[3] As Brooks Holifield has said, antebellum "pastoral theologians made no clear distinction between etiquette and ethics, between the manners acceptable to the elevated classes and the moral dispositions that embodied the central themes of the Christian tradition. All the maxims blended together."[4]

After the Civil War, pastoral theologians began to emphasize virility, toughness, and physical stamina rather than etiquette as the virtues appropriate to the grimy new world of city and industry. But the seminaries did not completely give up the aim of smoothing the ragged social edges off of ministerial candidates. In the early 1930s, the average seminary student still had been reared by parents with two years of high school and by fathers who were either farmers or manual laborers.[5] This typical family background led Union Seminary professor William Adams Brown to encourage seminary faculty in 1934 to counsel students "on those matters of personal decorum in which men with faulty social background are deficient."[6]

If seminaries continued to concern themselves with matters of personal decorum, however, by the turn to the twentieth century the schools were shifting their emphasis from social etiquette to social ethics. Formation of students now would be undertaken less through the cultivation of personal habits and more through the development of attitudes and skills appropriate to social change. The arguments justifying the new strategy of formation would be no less middle-class than the old, but the message respecting the nature of the formation was decidedly different. Social salvation, not personal breeding, would characterize the message.

Long before most of the university divinity schools developed their social gospel, Protestant Christians had responded to the social distresses created by the forces of industrialization, urbanization, and rural poverty in post–Civil War America. And in antebellum America, Protestant Christians had prepared the ground for the later gospel of social salvation with their home mission societies and reform movements. Never more than a minority view within the churches and the society as a whole, the social gospel in both its "conservative" and its "progressive" phases[7] nonetheless extended into all regions of the country, was lay as well as clerical in its leadership, was activist as well as reflective in its bearing, and was successful in winning a creedal position in the key denominations of ecumenical Christianity.[8] Although seminary and divinity school professors frequently were involved in the denominational formulations of the social message and were sometimes at the forefront of reform activities, the social gospel was by no means restricted to teachers of the clergy. In one way, however, the divinity schools formed an advance guard for the social gospel. They provided the training of ministers in the aims and strategies of social reform. And in drawing upon the disciplines and other resources of the university, the divinity schools became the leading educational institutions devoted to a philosophy of social reform.

Historians frequently have pointed out that the message of the mainstream social gospel movement, although directed to problems created by a bourgeois ethos, was essentially a middle-class creed. That is, the social gospel issued a call for social reform while professing the inherent worth and rights of the individual, affirming the fundamental integrity of American democratic capitalism, and holding to the conviction that upward social and economic mobility is the birthright of every American. The message also was relentlessly middle-class in its confidence in the powers of education. Education could lead people to choose the larger good over private interests, and it could train reformers who would lead others to correct the gross inequalities of class.[9] The divinity schools drew upon the programs and emerging social science disciplines of the university to promote just such an education.

Divinity education in the social gospel entailed, in part, acquainting students with those Americans who had suffered the heaviest blows from the forces of urban immigration, labor strife, and rural impoverishment. In the late nineteenth and early twentieth centuries, students at the Yale, Union, Boston, Drew, and Chicago divinity schools worked in inner-city settlement houses, joined home missionary agencies in relief work in the slums, preached to the unchurched in the cities, and received academic credit for their analysis of urban conditions and their philanthropic services.[10] Early in its history the theological school at SMU adopted the city of Dallas as its "theological clinic" for both sociological analysis and works of Christian charity.[11] A number of the schools also introduced their students to the plight of farm workers, especially in the South, through special rural ministries programs. Beginning in the 1920s, the

Duke Endowment supplied money for a rural church program in which ministerial students served as assistants to rural pastors under the supervision of the Divinity School. Similar programs were established at the Vanderbilt and Emory divinity schools in the 1920s and 1930s. During the Second World War and the years immediately following, Drew professor of rural sociology Ralph Felton, in collaboration with the predominantly black Gammon Seminary in Georgia, trained hundreds of black Protestant ministers for service in rural churches.[12]

Divinity school programs aimed at social relief and training usually were tethered to a curriculum that dealt with ethical issues at stake in America's urban and rural environments. University-related divinity schools, along with other Protestant seminaries, offered newly created courses variously entitled "Social Ethics," "Christian Sociology," "The Ethics of the Social Question," "Applied Christianity," "The Church and Industry," and "Social Pathology." Courses in the division of pastoral theology at some of the schools included segments on social ethics, and summer school programs and special guest lectures were established to deal with Christianity and social issues. The theological schools at Princeton, Andover, Chicago, and Harvard led the way in instituting clearly defined courses in social ethics, but by the early 1930s most Protestant theological schools were offering courses in the field.[13]

Because of the newness of the area of study, social ethics sometimes was greeted with skepticism on campus. Francis Peabody, the Parkman Professor of Theology at Harvard, at first found his course on social ethics in the 1880s criticized as bad economics from the right and as sentimentalism from the left, with students caricaturing it as Peabody's study of "Drainage, Drunkenness, and Divorce."[14] Eventually, however, Peabody's teaching won wide acceptance as his Divinity School courses on "practical ethics" attracted large numbers of students from several academic divisions at Harvard and as his book of social gospel theology, *Jesus Christ and the Social Question* (1900), attained a circulation of over 65,000 copies.[15]

Like many other social gospelers of the time, Peabody viewed Jesus not as a moral reformer but as a proponent of moral principles applicable to any social situation, and Peabody's ethical passions were driven by an optimistic, evolutionary view of the American social and economic orders. Like most of his colleagues in social ethics, Peabody also followed what he deemed an appropriately "inductive" method in his teaching: "I studied thus with my class the problems of Charity, Divorce, the Indians, the Labor Problem, Intemperance, with results of surprising interest. . . .

Each student made written reports of personal observation of some institution of charity or reform; and from these data thus collected I endeavored in each case to draw out the ethical principles involved." Such an approach, Peabody believed, was sufficient to call into question an uncritical endorsement of the theory of laissez-faire economics and could point to the need for economic reform according to Christian ethical principles.[16]

Peabody's method was hardly inductive in the sense of inferring general hypotheses from empirical data, but it was definitely an applied approach to ethics that sought to join social analysis with moral reflection. It was thus an approach that departed significantly from ethics as etiquette. It was an approach, as well, that combined theological ethics with the social sciences, which were emerging as distinctive, influential disciplines in American universities.

After the First World War, most scholars in the social sciences deliberately dissociated their methods of objective empiricism from theological presuppositions and from the causes of social reform, but in the years before the War they most commonly merged social gospel with social analysis. Many of the early social scientists were children of the Protestant manse who brought a moral earnestness to their social studies; others, lay and clerical alike, had been inspired by Protestant visions of an American society fashioned equally of democratic hopes and Protestant Christian teachings. Economist Richard Ely, an Episcopalian layman who had been reared in a strict Presbyterian home, defined his field as the study and promotion of the production and distribution of material goods in such a way that "the end and purpose of human existence for all members of society" harmonize "with the ethical ideal of Christianity."[17] The first course in sociology at Harvard, offered in 1891, was taught by Edward Cummings, social gospel minister of the South Congregational Church in Boston. G. Stanley Hall, a graduate of Union Theological Seminary who became an eminent psychologist at Johns Hopkins and then the president of Clark University, believed that psychology could illuminate the natural and social contexts of religious experiences without undermining the transcendent validity of those experiences.[18]

The merging of religious and ethical concerns with social analysis was most apparent in courses offered at the divinity schools under the rubric of "Christian Sociology." And the purpose of combining scientific and religious approaches under that rubric was most conspicuous at the University of Chicago's Divinity School.

President William Rainey Harper lured Albion Small to the University of Chicago in 1892 for the express purpose of establishing sociology as an empirical science second in importance to no other science. The scientific character of sociology did not mean for Small—or for Harper—however, an empiricism devoid of religious norms. During Small's three decades as chair of the sociology department, Chicago's sociologists shifted toward the national trend of a scientific method unencumbered by the concerns of social reform or social philosophy, and Small himself gave increasing attention to the specialized techniques of social analysis.[19] During most of his academic career, however, Small pursued sociology as a transparent combination of religious norms and empirical observation. Along with his colleagues Graham Taylor of the Chicago Theological Seminary, who lectured at the University, and Charles Henderson of the Divinity School, Small taught divinity students that they should infuse their social analyses with a social gospel.

According to Small's view of things, "the Christian revelation does not create antitheses between the individual and the social. It is the first and only synthesis of the individual and the social" and thus opens the way for the sociologist to embrace the central claim of the New Testament, "I am not ashamed of the gospel of Christ, for it is the power of God unto salvation."[20] The social twist that sociology gave to salvation could lead Small to say in 1910 that social science is the "holiest sacrament open to men." Since it embraces the whole life of the person, social science, much more than ritual, is the highest sacramental mode of existence. "The whole circumference of social science is the indicated field for those 'works' without which the apostle of 'salvation of faith' declared that faith is dead."[21]

Social gospel and social analysis were also fused by Charles Henderson, chair of practical sociology at the Divinity School. Henderson insisted that the laws of society detected by the social scientists must be made to serve social ethics. "It is only when a law, some common tendency to produce a definite social result, and promote a social end, is sought, that we have a truly scientific discovery." Although ultimate moral and religious laws like compassion and justice are not themselves produced by social analysis, laws governing social institutions like business organizations and politics can be produced by analysis. Henderson thus approached his students with the conviction that religious ethics are "impotent without the aid of a science of social politics" and that social science should develop "methods of organization and principles of social conduct which best promote social welfare."[22] Both Small and Henderson were confident that social science and social gospel were compatible forces for the achievement of social reform. Social science at the Divinity School of the University of Chicago was, in the words of Graham Taylor, sociology "with God left in it."[23]

Sociology as a form of social analysis blended with the hopes and precepts of a gospel of social regeneration characterized the discipline of ethics at the other divinity schools before the First World War. In a fashion similar to Harvard's Francis Peabody, Yale's William F. Blackman taught courses in Christian ethics that combined social gospel morality with an analysis of a wide range of issues in late nineteenth-century America—race, immigration, social class, the modern city, the wage system, and party government. Blackman complemented his classroom teaching by taking his students on field trips to settlement houses, relief bureaus, flophouses, and criminal courts in New York City. In the early twentieth century, Yale Divinity's Charles R. Brown and William B. Bailey propounded the views of the social gospel in courses in ethics and practical philanthropy respectively. Between 1918 and 1941, Harry F. Ward, a principal author of the Methodist Social Creed, served as professor of Christian ethics at Union Theological Seminary and there castigated the individualism, competitiveness, and economics of American capitalism as fundamentally incompatible with the ethics of Jesus. Less radical forms of the social gospel appeared earlier at Union in the instruction of professor of religious education George Coe and in the adoption throughout the school's curriculum of Baptist social gospeler Walter Rauschenbusch's *Christianity and the Social Crisis* (1907).[24]

Most of the Methodist divinity schools also bolstered their programs of social relief with a gospel of social reform. Harry F. Ward taught social ethics for four years at the School of Theology at Boston University before heading off to his long career at Union, but he was only one of a number of Boston faculty who bent their ethical reflections to such issues as prison reform, racial justice, rural poverty, and the capitalist economy. Boston graduate Francis J. McConnell, who became a Methodist bishop, president of the Federal Council of Churches, president of the American Association of Social Service, and a labor advocate during the Steel Strike of 1919, collaborated with the faculty of his alma mater to promote the combination of social-ethical analysis and social reform.[25]

The divinity school at Drew was relatively slow in offering courses in social ethics. Prominent Chicago church historian William Warren Sweet complained that although he and his Drew classmates in the early twentieth century were exposed to social conditions in New York City, they were not offered the opportunity to study Christian sociology. Ernest

Fremont Tittle, minister of First Methodist Church in Evanston, Illinois, and outspoken critic of racism, anti-Catholicism, and super-patriotism, issued a similar complaint about his experience with the Drew class of 1908. In 1909, however, Drew appointed Edwin Earp to a chair of Christian sociology, and Earp promptly linked city fieldwork with instruction in the principles of social redemption. In 1923, Drew brought William Marshall Gilbert to the faculty as a professor of home missions. Gilbert called the attention of his students to Americans usually neglected by middle-class Methodist ministers: immigrants, blacks, industrial workers, and farm hands. Gilbert also gave a meaning to the high culture of university education that had escaped Professor Rogers during the latter's remarks at Drew's building dedication. "I am looking for bilingual students," Gilbert said in his matriculation address, "Phi Beta Kappa men, if you will, who will study the language, folklore, customs, and history of some European group, like the Slavs, for instance. Then give their life to them, help them to find themselves, protect them from exploitation, and help them to blend the good of the old into the good of the new and become real Christian Americans."[26]

Lacking adequate financial resources, the divinity schools in the West and the South were unable to offer extensive work in social ethics, but they did manage, on a small scale, to combine social analysis with a theology of the social gospel.[27] Vanderbilt, in particular, relied upon the services of activist professor of ethics Alva Taylor to train ministers into the strategies and philosophy of social redemption. A lobbyist for labor legislation, a leader of the Commission on Interracial Cooperation, and an active campaigner for socialist presidential candidate Henry Wallace, Taylor with his social gospel inspired a large number of Vanderbilt students to make Nashville, Tennessee, a center for reform causes in the South.[28]

By the 1930s the social gospel no longer dominated the ethical outlook of the divinity schools, and by the 1940s it had been replaced by an ethics that insisted on a breach separating Christianity and culture. Global warfare, economic depression, and enduring racial injustice and conflict persuaded Protestant theologians that the aspirations of the social gospel were founded on naive expectations—expectations predicated on the hope that social reform could grow from the goodwill of well-intentioned reformers, on a confidence in the fundamental rectitude of American institutions, and on a conviction that society could be changed as the minds and wills of individuals were significantly altered by the power of education.

The dreams of the proponents of the social gospel included the old vision of a Protestant America, the very vision that inspired the founding of so many of the divinity schools. To be sure, the social gospelers gave a new emphasis to social salvation, they censured social Darwinism's heartless endorsement of the forces of the marketplace, and they called religion to an unmistakably *social* mission. Yet still they hoped to build a Protestant Zion in America. In the words of Drew's William M. Gilbert, they wanted to "blend the good of the old into the good of the new" so that citizens of the nation might "become real Christian Americans." As Robert Handy has pointed out, the social gospel reversed early nineteenth-century Protestant priorities when it made religion a means to the end of Christianizing American civilization, but in its own way the social gospel perpetuated an old Protestant triumphalism: "in its unreflective clinging to the idea of the triumph of Protestant civilization," the social gospel "exhibited real continuity with the earlier nineteenth century."[29]

Hopes for the triumph of a Protestant civilization were dashed for many mid-century theologians, and no theologian was more explicit about the misguided nature of those hopes than was Reinhold Niebuhr. Niebuhr revolted against the liberal optimism and moralistic preachments of the social gospel, and he faulted the social gospelers and many other liberal progressives for their lack of realism. He claimed, in short, that they had failed to incorporate within their ethics an adequate understanding of the ambiguous but necessary role of economic and political power for the achievement of social justice.[30] Niebuhr could still insist, however, that despite its glaring weaknesses, the social gospel was a most valuable heritage. It had liberated Christian ethics from an exaggerated concern for the morals and piety of the individual. "It delivered American Protestantism from meeting complex ethical problems of a technical civilization with an almost completely irrelevant individualistic pietism and moralism." And in comparison with so many Americans' continuing confusion of Christianity with the "spiritual values" of the free enterprise system, the social gospel appropriately "challenged the doctrine that laissez-faire would make for justice, citing the unjust consequences of the ever-growing concentration of power in industry."[31]

Niebuhr's critical appropriation of the social gospel tradition is testimony to the endurance of that tradition in the Protestant divinity schools. By the middle of the twentieth century the divinity schools clearly had given up the effort to immerse ministers in the Protestant triumphalism of the social gospel, but they had by no means abandoned the social gospel's moral earnestness, its commitment to social reform, or its dedication to educating ministers in applied ethics. The abiding legacy of the social gospel in the schools was apparent in their continuing attempts to deal with the practical-ethical implications of race in America.

## UNLEARNING THE LESSONS
## OF ABJECT SERVILITY

In 1902, Andrew Sledd, a Latin teacher at Emory College who would later become professor of Greek and New Testament at the Candler School of Theology, published an article in the *Atlantic Monthly* entitled "The Negro: Another View." Sledd was prompted to write the article by a sickening experience associated with the lynching of a black man outside Atlanta: he was shown a finger of the lynched man by a proud witness to the hanging. Sledd's resultant article led to a flurry of protests from his fellow white citizens in the Atlanta area.

Sledd argued that the "negro question is a national one." Northerners, with no experience or knowledge of actual conditions in the South, championed the cause of black people "with a bitter and undiscriminating zeal as earnest as it is misguided." Southerners, for their part, "remembering the negro as the slave, consider him and his rights from a position of proud and contemptuous superiority." Sledd did not conceal his own racist assumptions: "The negro is lower in the scale of development than the white man. His inferiority is radical and inherent, a physiological and racial inequality" that forbids all schemes for the "amalgamation of the races." But Sledd did contend that the black American has inalienable rights as a human being, rights denied in the practice of segregation in railway cars, restaurants, hotels, and churches. Lynching "is but a more inflamed and conspicuous expression of this same general sentiment" that would draw absolute distinctions between people based solely on color.[32] Sledd's most impassioned rhetoric was reserved for the southern sentiment apparent in the lynch mob:

> As for "teaching the niggers a lesson," that catch phrase of the lynching mob betrays its whole attitude and temper. It would teach the negro the lesson of abject and eternal servility, would burn into his quivering flesh the consciousness that he has not, and cannot have, the rights of a free citizen or even a fellow human creature. And so the lyncher seizes his opportunity at once to teach this lesson and to gratify the brute in his own soul, which the thin veneer of his elemental civilization has not been able effectually to conceal.[33]

Mrs. W. H. Felton, Georgia suffrage and temperance leader and patron of Emory College, joined the publisher of the Atlanta *Constitution* to attack Sledd as a traitor to the South. The ensuing public outcry and pressure from Emory's board of trustees forced the young Latin professor to resign his faculty position. Sledd's father-in-law, Methodist bishop Warren Candler, was incensed by the reactions to Sledd's article and in response turned out scores of his own essays against lynching. When he became the first president of Emory University, Candler gave the first faculty appointment in Emory's newly formed School of Theology to his son-in-law, who in the meantime had earned his doctorate in classics from Yale and had served as president of the University of Florida and of Southern University in Alabama.[34]

The "abject and eternal servility" foisted on black Americans by white Americans was often interpreted by social gospelers as an instance of economic class conflict, the lack of educational opportunity, or the problem of poverty.[35] Thus students of "Christian Sociology" and "Social Ethics" took up the matter of race as one item among many in their study of the social disruptions created by corporate capitalism and the growth of cities, and their field experiences exposed them to the conditions of blacks as well as whites in prisons, poor rural areas, and the industrial work environment.

By no means did all of the social gospelers view racial discrimination as a subordinate issue, however, and some even insisted on it as the defining crisis in the national experience. The stark reality of the bigotry of white Americans against black Americans, in particular, would not reduce simply for some religious reformers to problems of economics, literacy, poverty, or even class. Epidemics of lynchings in the early twentieth century (2,522 blacks were lynched between 1899 and 1918),[36] widespread insistence throughout the land on the inherent inferiority of the black race, and the systematic exclusion of blacks from schools, churches, and trade unions provoked black as well as white advocates of the social gospel to give the issue of race a special, central ethical emphasis.[37]

Some divinity school professors also attached special importance to the issue of race by linking instruction on the "Negro Problem" with public action and testimony. Chicago Christian sociologists Albion Small and Graham Taylor lifted up the significance of the issue by joining the NAACP's outcry against lynching. Union Seminary president and social gospel teacher Charles Cuthbert Hall brought Washington Gladden to New York in 1907 to lecture on "The Kingdom of God and the Race Problem." Candler dean and professor of church history Plato Durham, who preferred to draw out the contemporary moral implications rather than the historical details of the Christian past, courted the scorn of conservative business and religious leaders in Atlanta when he co-founded a regional committee on interracial cooperation. Alva Taylor of Vanderbilt made an entire career of educating students in the need for racial equality in the South, and he continuously arranged interracial meetings between white students from Vanderbilt and black students from Fisk.[38]

None of these early twentieth-century divinity school endeavors equaled the emphasis on the ethics of race that would appear during and following the civil rights movement. None, for example, focused as sharply on the theological and ethical foundations of racial integration as did the seminars offered in the 1950s and 1960s by Drew's George Kelsey on "Racism and the Christian Understanding of Man," by Boston's Paul Deats on "Christianity and Race Relations," or by Union's Roger Shinn on "Race and Christian Ethics." And none of the early ventures into Christian sociology undertook the same social studies of multiculturalism and multiracialism that would characterize the emphasis on "globalization" in the divinity schools in the 1980s. Albion Small's and Alva Taylor's courses in ethical and social analysis could not match in breadth of coverage the courses offered in the 1980s by Union's James Cone on "black theology, its dialogue with Third World theologies, the responses of Euro-American theologies, and the recent development of womanist theology." Nor could they match in sharpness of focus those of Harvard's Preston Williams and Constance Williams on the "historical, analytical, and moral-religious investigation of the black family in the United States."[39] If lacking a sense of the global importance of race for ethical reflection, however, and if deficient in the resources of the contemporary social sciences, the social gospelers in the early history of the divinity schools were the precursors of contemporary ethical and social analyses of race.

Some of the clearest lessons about race and racism, however, were not taught in divinity school ethics courses, nor even in the fieldwork designed to give those courses practical significance. They were taught, instead, in the schools' pursuit of policies and practices of racial integration within their own university communities.

Early in their histories, the nondenominational and Methodist divinity schools in the North led the way in the racial integration of institutions of higher education through their admission of black students, and many of those students went on to distinguished careers. John Bunyan Reeve, for example, a member of Union's class of 1861, served as the first dean of the School of Theology at Howard University, and Drew student William Robert Palmer became president of Central Alabama College in the early twentieth century. Martin Luther King, Jr., insisted that his doctoral work at the Boston University School of Theology exposed him to a personalist theology that undergirded his social philosophy throughout his career. During the years of the civil rights movement, faculty and students at the northern divinity schools joined the freedom rides to the South and participated in protest vigils and sit-ins in many racially segregated regions of the country. In the 1960s and 1970s, they agitated for the creation of black studies programs, defended the views of black power advocates, engaged in strikes on behalf of black student representation on university committees, and participated in university protests against a war in Southeast Asia that had led to the conscription of a disproportionate number of black Americans.[40]

The campus turbulence of the late 1960s and early 1970s, and even the instances of nonviolent protest of earlier years, surpassed the social gospel's cautious prescriptions for racial reform and repudiated that gospel's easy confidence in the merits of existing American institutions. In combining social action with ethical instruction, however, the divinity schools preserved an important strand of the social gospel heritage. That persistent part of the social gospel emerged most conspicuously in the 1950s in the South, where law and custom presented divinity schools with challenges more obdurate than those facing their educational counterparts in the North. In taking up the challenges through campaigns for racial integration, the southern divinity schools doggedly sought to overcome the social consequences of racism in their universities and in their surrounding communities.

In 1954, the U.S. Supreme Court simultaneously strengthened the civil rights cause and precipitated a bitter controversy across the South by declaring the segregation of public education unconstitutional. Two years prior to that court decision, however, Vanderbilt University chancellor Harvie Branscomb asked the dean of his School of Religion, John Benton, to report on the practices of southern theological schools respecting the "admission of negro students." The request was part of Branscomb's strategy of making the School of Religion a stalking horse for an open admissions policy at Vanderbilt. The School of Religion willingly adopted the role since, in the judgment of its faculty, such a policy "accorded with the Christian gospel." In 1953 the Divinity School quietly admitted Joseph A. Johnson, Jr., who later became the first black member of the

Vanderbilt board of trustees to be nominated through normal board procedures.[41]

In an informal poll of fourteen southern seminaries designed to answer the chancellor's question (with two schools failing to respond), Dean Benton discovered a wide variety of integration practices. Some schools admitted blacks as regular students; some did not. Most of the seminaries restricted enrollment to black students within their denominations, but by no means all of them imposed such a restriction. Half of the schools allowed black students to share dormitory facilities with white students, with the other half firmly opposing the practice. Of the southern Methodist university-related divinity schools, only Perkins at Southern Methodist University admitted blacks as regular students, and, Benton reported to Chancellor Branscomb, at Perkins "negroes are accorded full social privileges in the Seminary but not in the University as a whole."[42] Benton could not know at the time that the restriction at Perkins soon was to be lifted and that the policies of integration at Perkins in the 1950s were to form an important public test case for the desegregation of a southern university through the efforts of its divinity school.

In 1950, the board of trustees at SMU, with the urging of President Umphrey Lee, voted to admit blacks as regular students to one of its branches, the Perkins School of Theology. (Previously the School had recruited a few black ministers in the Dallas area to enroll in noncredit courses and to audit standard courses without credit.) Immediately following the board's decision, two blacks enrolled as regular students, but inadequate academic backgrounds resulted in their lasting only one semester. Plans for a more aggressive policy of integration emerged in 1951 when President Lee appointed Merrimon Cuninggim as dean of Perkins. Cuninggim, a native of Tennessee who had earned his doctorate at Yale, was joined in the move to Perkins by another son of the South, Yale theologian Albert C. Outler. In making the two appointments, Lee hoped to begin the elevation of the academic quality of the Perkins faculty. According to Cuninggim, the president also assured the two new appointees that they could resolutely recruit blacks as regular students at Perkins.[43]

The recruitment of full-time black students at Perkins was taken quietly and uneventfully. In the fall semester of 1952, five regularly enrolled black students, representing three different Protestant denominations, were admitted to the divinity school at SMU, and, despite some struggles owing to weakness of academic preparation, they were to receive their diplomas three years later as the first blacks to be awarded academic degrees by the University. Dean Cuninggim consulted frequently with the students, advised them to use their common sense about the extent of their involvement in campus activities, but encouraged them to make their own decisions. No publicity was released about the admissions, and the students decided to take a low profile by eating their meals in the Perkins cafeteria, rather than in the University student union, and to avoid playing contact intramural sports.[44]

A tempest did brew that first semester as one of the black students, finding the Perkins dining facility closed on a Sunday, joined a white friend for the evening meal in the University dining hall. The black student sat next to a white co-ed who later, in a burst of enthusiasm, wrote a letter to her mother which began "Dear Momma, The most wonderful thing happened to me tonight. . . . " As Cuninggim observed, "Momma did not think it was wonderful, nor did the rest of the mommas in the southern county-seat town from which she came."[45] Letters of complaint poured in to President Lee, who at first insisted that the black students eat only in the seminary dining hall but then decided to leave the decision to the students. The students agreed among themselves that the experiment in integration should not be compromised by insisting on access to the University facility. The incident passed, and throughout their academic careers the five students received wide support from SMU faculty and students.[46]

Serious opposition did eventually arise from a few clergy members of the SMU board, from some Dallas businessmen, and from the theological school's chief benefactor. The opposition was provoked by the revelation in 1953 that four of the black students were rooming with white students in the Perkins dormitory. Some members of the University board were incensed that they had not been consulted before allowing such a living arrangement, and a number of Dallas citizens were horrified at the "racial mixing" going on at their local university. There is some indication, also, that Merrimon Cuninggim's predecessor in the deanship, persuaded that integration was moving too fast at SMU and disgruntled by having been replaced as dean a year before his normal retirement, stirred up some of the opposition. In any case, the reluctant promise of the black students to cease rooming with whites did not satisfy those who had been offended by the whole episode. Wealthy Texas oilman and loyal Methodist layman J. J. Perkins, the patron for whom the School of Theology had been named, believed that allowing blacks to attend the University as regular students was rushing things, and he advised Dean Cuninggim to "get rid of the Negroes as soon as possible."[47]

The matter was finally resolved in early 1954 by the board's Committee on the School of Theology. Bishop Paul Martin, chairman of the committee, managed to pacify Mr. Perkins; Dean Cuninggim accepted responsibility for the dormitory arrangement; and the committee agreed that no extraordinary restrictions would be placed on black students. According to Cuninggim, Mrs. Perkins, who had been invited to attend the meeting of the committee, expressed disagreement with her husband on the matter of integration and indicated she believed that all the trouble had been stirred up by clandestine letter-writing. Shortly after the meeting, Mr. Perkins expressed his opinion to the former dean of the theological school that "within the next ten or fifteen years all the schools will admit negroes and I anticipate that the coming decisions of the Supreme Court will accentuate this development." He also had come to believe that "it would do much more harm to the University to put the negroes out now than it would to go on in a most conservative way on the present situation."[48]

For the most part, the university administration had been supportive of the integration experiment at Perkins, and the Law School and other units of SMU shortly followed the School of Theology in admitting full-time black students. Throughout the 1950s, however, it was the Perkins dean, Merrimon Cuninggim, who provided most of the public interpretation of the experiment.

Cuninggim contended that integration at the School of Theology proved the moral wisdom of what he called "ameliorative stubbornness" and "courageous prudence." Such a strategy called for patient education of the opponents of integration and alleviation of their fears of different races. It also entailed honestly facing the difficulties inevitably to be encountered in the integration of a racist society, as well as hoping for victory while greeting periodic setbacks with a kind of "divine carelessness."[49] Cuninggim was persuaded that in order to win over rather than alienate the opposition, the integrationist should move with prudent caution, "but each of us must be prepared to take the step just beyond the one that caution says is all we can do." Cuninggim was even willing to don the mantle of "gradualist": "I am a gradualist simply because I am a bad loser. And I say, in the effort to bring the Christian witness to bear upon the ordeal of the South, we can't afford to lose."[50]

Cuninggim insisted that finally the strength of his strategy rested on the Christian message and its ultimate success on the deeply religious character of the South:

> The vulnerable spot in the Southern armor is the widespread sensitivity to the Christian faith. The strongest sword in the hands of the church is its only appropriate weapon, the Gospel of Christ. Segregationists tend to make their argument on misunderstandings and falsehoods about many things, even sacred ones. . . . But they have not succeeded in identifying their position with the mind of Christ, for the spirit of Jesus is patently opposed to racial prejudice and discrimination. As Harry Ashmore says in his volume, *An Epitaph for Dixie*, " . . . not even the most determined bigot can make a segregationist out of . . . Jesus Christ."[51]

Something like Cuninggim's moral strategy of "ameliorative stubbornness" and his trust in the rudimentary Christian spirit of the South prompted faculty and students at other southern divinity schools to assume leadership on behalf of racial integration at their universities—but some with more success than others.

The Candler School of Theology was the first unit of Emory University to raise the issue of the admission of black students. Nothing in the Emory charter forbade such admission, but Georgia law and custom prohibited it, and the issue was not pressed until after the Supreme Court ruled in 1954 against the notion of "separate but equal" public educational facilities for blacks and whites. In the spring semester of 1956, the Candler faculty voted to send a message to the president and board members of the University indicating a "willingness to have Negroes in the student body." At that time the Candler faculty agreed not to discuss the matter publicly in order to avoid compromising the larger efforts of the University on behalf of integration. In January 1958, however, the University president excused the faculty from their vow of silence while counseling "discretion and judgment because of the delicate nature of the situation."[52]

Later in 1958, Candler dean William R. Cannon appointed an ad hoc faculty committee to deal with the matter of the admission of black students, and the committee issued a statement to the trustees urging the desegregation of the School of Theology. The authors of the statement grounded their plea on several arguments. They appealed first to the Christian Bible: "The Bible is a witness to God's love for man without regard to his national or racial identity," and the biblically informed Christian "must regard every man as a child of God. To treat him as though he were less is a betrayal of the character of God and a denial of the nature of man." The faculty also invoked the recent decision of the General Conference of the Methodist Church that there could be "no place in The Methodist Church for racial discrimination or enforced segregation." And, noting the recent desegregation of SMU through the initiative of the Perkins School of Theology, the authors of the Candler report endorsed Merrimon Cuninggim's strategy: "The gradualistic, educative, and cautious approach of Perkins is instructive."[53] Also in 1958, the students of Candler released the results of a poll they had conducted among themselves on the question, "Do you favor the admission of qualified Negroes as students in the School of Theology?" Of those responding, 262 answered "yes," 38 "no," and 37 "undecided."[54]

By early 1961, however, Emory still had not agreed to the integration of its student body, a situation that led to a rebuke from the accrediting team of the American Association of Theological Schools. The AATS evaluation of Candler noted that the sentiment among the school's faculty and students was decidedly in favor of desegregation but that integration was prevented by University policy. The AATS representatives could only conclude, "It is the judgment of this team that the exclusion of otherwise qualified students from the advantages of a Christian school of theology because of race compromises its own theological and moral position, resists unwarrantedly its educational mission, and creates an indefensible stumbling block for its graduates in their ministries at home and abroad."[55]

Desegregation was delayed because the Emory administration faced a legal and financial dilemma. On the one hand, the University would deny itself the opportunity to receive any federal funds and many foundation grants if it did not adhere to federal law forbidding "separate but equal" education. On the other, Georgia law required the racial segregation of educational facilities, and Emory would lose its state tax-exempt status if it did not abide by that law. In January 1961, the Georgia governor and General Assembly finally struck down the racial segregation regulation as applied to public education, but as a private school Emory still was governed by state segregation laws. In November 1961, the Emory board of trustees announced that the University would receive student applications "without regard to race, color, or creed." The following year the administration of the University fought the right of open admissions through the courts, and in September 1962, the Georgia Supreme Court ruled in favor of the University.

Emory promptly admitted two full-time black students to the School of Nursing. In 1964, the Division of Religion of the Graduate School at Emory admitted its first black candidate for the Ph.D., and in the fall quarter of 1965 the Candler School of Theology enrolled its first black student. Henry W. Bowden, chairman of the Emory board and general counsel to the University who had carried the fight through the Georgia courts, was awarded the Alexander Meiklejohn Award by the American Association of University Professors for the defense of academic freedom.[56] The faculty and students of a university divinity school had initiated a process of racial integration on religious, moral, and ecclesiastical grounds. University officials had seen the process through on humanitarian, legal, and economic grounds.

Unlike the state of Georgia, North Carolina had instituted no statutes enforcing segregation. Social custom and the racial climate in the state as a whole, however, as well as the practice of racial discrimination at Duke and other North Carolina schools, meant that the desegregation of Duke would come only after a period of prolonged efforts.

The first attempt to desegregate Duke was undertaken by students of the Divinity School. In a petition sent to the faculty and administration of the Divinity School in 1948, over one hundred ministerial students indicated that they would "welcome the fellowship, stimulation, and fuller Christian cooperation that we feel would exist here if Negro students were to join us in our common Christian study as ministers of the Gospel." The student petition was cautious and suggestive, rather than demanding, and it proposed no desegregation policies for the University as a whole: "We . . . hereby request that serious consideration be given, by the administration and faculty of the Divinity School of Duke University, to the admission of Negroes to the Divinity School as day students [i.e., devoid of dormitory privileges] without affecting the general University policy."[57]

The Divinity School faculty entered into discussions about the student petition, with some faculty expressing concern about the ability of Duke to accommodate black students when toilets, medical facilities, and even the chapel were segregated, and with others issuing pleas for further study of the issues. In 1949, the faculty voted to endorse the student petition and to forward it confidentially to the president of the University, A. Hollis Edens, for consideration.[58] Edens's response to Divinity School dean Harold Bosley was terse: "I appreciate your thoughtful and tactful approach to the question and I assure you that I understand your faculty's attitude in wanting to work toward 'a more equitable relationship between the races.' At the same time, I do not think that the interests either of the negro race or of Duke University will be served at this time by raising for discussion the question of admitting negroes to the Divinity School."[59]

That was only the first of a series of rebuffs that the faculty, administrators, and students of the Divinity School would receive from the University as they continued to press the issue of desegregation for more than a decade. When Harold Bosley, well-known liberal preacher and University of Chicago Ph.D., was appointed dean of the Divinity School in 1948, he immediately made plans to bring the Assembly of the World Council of Churches to the Duke campus in 1953. The World Council leadership expressed reservations about holding the meeting on a segregated campus; Bosley tried to embarrass the Duke board and president into a policy of integration on the basis of the reservations; President Edens would not be forced into policies by a dean who had already alienated him on other matters; and the World Council finally decided against Duke as a location for its meeting.[60]

Through the efforts of succeeding deans, the Divinity School continued to petition the University president and board for the racial integration of their institution, and the petitions began to take on a note of urgency as the civil rights movement gained momentum following the Supreme Court decision of 1954. In addition to calling attention to the "incompatibility of Christianity and racial exclusivism," the Divinity School students and the large majority of the faculty pointed to the integration of other seminaries in the South, invoked the mandate of the Methodist Church to remove all racial barriers from its theological schools, bemoaned the criticism being heaped upon Duke by the liberal religious press, and complained of the ability of the Divinity School to recruit and retain high-caliber faculty in a segregated institution.[61] A fundamental irony did not escape the faculty of the Divinity School. Under the pressure of federal law, public universities in North Carolina had desegregated, but Duke had not. In the words of a faculty petition in January 1961, "Secular institutions, by such contrast, are placing a school of theology in shameful contradiction with its Christian teaching."[62]

As shameful as the contradiction was, it did not disappear until September 1961, when the Duke board resolved to admit applicants to its graduate and professional schools without regard to race, creed, or national origin. The same resolution followed in June 1962 for the admission of Duke undergraduates. The racial integration of Duke had been delayed by a determined majority of Duke's board of trustees, a board chaired for several years by Willis Smith, who had won a seat in the U.S. Senate through a race-baiting campaign. President Edens, a gradualist who increasingly warned his board that racial integration would eventually govern all American institutions, was tentative in his recommendations to the board in the early years of his administration and was preoccupied with a power struggle over the university presidency in the later years.

With the death and retirement of several board members and the resignation of President Edens in the early 1960s, the way was opened for change. A group of administrators and faculty working with the University provost presented a number of desegregation resolutions to the board on chiefly economic grounds. "Reference to the moral and religious issues incident to this problem has not been included as these matters have been widely discussed and no doubt have been the focus of considerable self-examination by all concerned," the provost advised the board respecting the resolutions. "Throughout, particular attention is given to the probable effects of non-discrimination clauses on future governmental contracts and grants in which Duke is interested."[63]

During the fall semester of 1961, with the integration of Duke professional schools now permitted, the Duke Divinity School faculty developed plans for the recruitment of black ministerial students.[64] Although neither the faculty nor the students of that school could take credit for the arguments that would finally end racial discrimination at Duke, they had first challenged the practice and had kept the pressure on the University during a frustrating, lengthy struggle.

The divinity schools in the South functioned as a kind of conscience within their universities on the matter of race, raising issues on religious and moral grounds and volunteering to lead the way in the integration process. The performance of that moral function could meet rigid limits, however, as was so apparent in the "Lawson Case" at Vanderbilt in 1960. A complicated tangle of issues respecting race, law, academic politics, public perceptions, and faculty self-governance, the Lawson Case nonetheless provided a clear illustration of how the modern American university could be less than impressed by the claims of any one of its units to serve as its conscience. The case also graphically illustrated the difficulties of implementing integration when its proponents operated within a social climate created by powerful fears of disorder.

James Lawson, a black ordained Methodist minister and a native of

Ohio, transferred from the Oberlin (Ohio) School of Theology to the Vanderbilt Divinity School for the dual purpose of completing his ministerial degree and extending into the South his efforts on behalf of civil rights. An official of the pacifist Fellowship of Reconciliation, Lawson was an advocate of the nonviolent methods of Martin Luther King, Jr. In February 1960, Lawson helped to organize (but at that time did not participate in) a series of sit-ins at Nashville lunch counters that provoked violent reactions from a group of angry young white citizens. A local judge charged the nonviolent protestors with disorderly conduct, and city officials and the Nashville press portrayed the city as moving toward the very brink of social chaos. When Lawson refused to advise the protesters to desist from sit-ins to accommodate an arbitrary closing of the lunch counters when the protesters approached or to meet University handbook regulations against disorderly assemblies (written to ban panty raids in dormitories), University chancellor Branscomb found Lawson in defiance of the law and the executive committee of the Vanderbilt board gave Lawson a choice: withdrawal or expulsion from the University. Lawson chose expulsion.

The crisis following Lawson's dismissal consumed immense amounts of time and energy on the part of the Vanderbilt administration and faculty, attracted the wide attention of the nation, and threatened the very existence of the Vanderbilt Divinity School. The faculty of the Divinity School lodged a formal complaint through the University senate over the way in which "the rights, prerogatives and duties of this faculty in dealing with its own students were entirely disregarded and completely ignored."[65] After a series of debates, the senate requested the chancellor and the board to reconsider Lawson's dismissal, and deans and faculty entered into protracted discussions with the chancellor. At one time, twelve of the sixteen resident faculty of the Divinity School, including the dean, submitted their resignations in protest of the University administration's handling of the case, and shortly thereafter several professors from other units of the University threatened to resign. The spotlight of national publicity was turned on Vanderbilt as a center of racial and academic turmoil. The American Association of University Professors expressed concerns over the status of academic freedom at the University. Even after the resolution of the crisis, the visiting committee of the American Association of Theological Schools placed the Vanderbilt Divinity School on probation for one year because the committee members were troubled over the question of whether the Divinity School had "all possible freedom to pursue its calling responsibly within the University, Church, and society."[66]

After a series of abortive efforts to reconcile the interests of faculty, board, and administration, Chancellor Branscomb managed to resolve the crisis by winning University senate and board approval of a compromise plan. The plan accepted the Divinity School dean's resignation, allowed the other Divinity School faculty to withdraw their resignations, permitted Lawson to receive his ministerial degree by transfer of credit or by written examination but not by readmission, and pronounced the case closed. Lawson chose to complete his degree at Boston University rather than at Vanderbilt. Although all but one of the Divinity School faculty who had resigned withdrew their resignations, several would shortly leave for other teaching posts. The Divinity School recruited a new dean and a number of new faculty members, continued to admit black students, and was soon joined by all units of the University in the practice of admitting students without regard to race.[67]

J. Robert Nelson, dean of the Vanderbilt Divinity School, came under some criticism from his faculty for not keeping them informed of developments in the Lawson affair. Throughout the crisis, however, Nelson remained a trusted friend, confidant, and defender of Lawson. Shortly after his resignation as dean, Nelson pointed to some lessons to be learned respecting "the freedom and social responsibility of colleges and universities" and the need for "a more forceful witness to racial equality and Christian reconciliation." But he also attested to the way in which diverse, complicated factors were mingled in the events following Lawson's expulsion: "Administrative policy, disciplinary procedure, racial prejudice and the contention against it, legitimacy of the sit-in demonstrations, freedom to act on moral convictions, and inevitable misunderstandings of thought and intent were discernible factors."[68] Nelson had been deeply involved in bringing a university to terms with a gospel of social reform; he also had discerned the limits a divinity school could meet as it sought to serve as the conscience of a complex modern university.

From a late twentieth-century perspective, many of the actions of the divinity schools in the 1950s seem excessively cautious, and some of their concerns appear trivial. The gradualism at the schools, even when combined with "courageous prudence," was no ethic ignited by a consuming passion for social justice or by an ardent commitment to the values of racial difference. Worries over the consequences of integrated toilets and dormitories only barely included within their purview the economic, social, political, and psychological adversities and ignominies that had been heaped upon black Americans for centuries. It would require the greater efforts of the freedom rides and freedom marches, as well as the civil rights and voting acts of Congress, in the 1960s to expand both the power and the scope of an ethics of race. And it would require the insistent proclamation of pride in blackness to challenge the obscuration of distinctive difference implicit in many of the arguments for integration.

But as Martin Luther King, Jr., had seen, the early struggles to integrate lunch counters, buses, restrooms—and universities—were important battles against the black American's "sense of nobodiness" and were necessary first steps toward a fuller program of social, political, and economic equality.[69] In those early twentieth-century words of Emory's Andrew Sledd, the efforts to integrate the southern divinity schools were, for their times, bold attempts to unlearn "the lessons of abject and eternal servility." They also constituted for their times an education in the century-old tradition of a Christian social gospel.

## AN UNACKNOWLEDGED, CONTINUING HERITAGE

In 1958, Ernest Cadman Colwell, newly appointed first president of the Southern California School of Theology at Claremont, warned in his inaugural address that the neoorthodox censure of the social gospel could easily go too far: "To ridicule the Social Gospel is a popular theological pastime today, but without opportunity to know vitally the social and economic complex of this American culture the theological school is impoverished." Colwell urged his faculty to preserve the social gospel's concern for social justice and social reform: "The flame of social justice burns brightly in this dry Western air, and it is appropriate for a school here to strive for a constructive relationship to the society in which it lives and moves and has its being. This world today still needs the prophet's voice, however disquieting it may be."[70]

Neither Claremont nor the other divinity schools would neglect to fan the flames of social justice, nor would they fail to cultivate the voice of the social prophet. By the early 1980s, Claremont had developed a program that expanded the education of ministers well beyond Colwell's interest in the "social and economic complex of this American culture."

The Claremont faculty had developed a curriculum designed to train ministers in the "global context" of the church's ministry. The faculty were clear about the meaning they attached to that context: "By ministry in a global context we mean more than simply worldwide Christianity. We mean a perspective on ministry which sees each ministry in partnership with ministries around the world in the interest of justice for all the world's people."[71] In the 1970s and 1980s, other divinity schools developed their own programs aimed at creating ministries to eliminate injustices suffered by oppressed groups of people in this country and abroad.[72] President Colwell need not have worried back in 1958. Far from ridiculing the heritage of the social gospel, the divinity schools had enlarged the scope of that gospel. The spread of liberation theology in the divinity schools accounted for much of the expansion of education in the social gospel.

By the end of the 1980s, it was clear that the perspectives of liberation theology did not constitute a monolithic movement. That pervasive theology had developed three main branches—Latin American, African American, and feminist—and disagreements appeared within the several branches over theological interpretation, the nature of religious leadership, the strategies of social change, and the sources of theological reflection.[73] Most of the leading spokespersons for liberation theology had agreed on these critical matters, however: theological reflection should arise from particular social and political situations with the aim of transforming those situations; God wills that the poor, the oppressed, and the powerless of the world should be empowered to change their situations; and as champions of the interests of given groups of people, theologians should speak with impassioned voice rather than with academic detachment.[74] Despite the wide range of perspective among them, therefore, liberation theologians had preserved an essential strand of the social gospel heritage: formation of the church and its ministry should occur through social reform.

Although a heritage had been preserved, however, it had been preserved largely without acknowledgment. Liberation theologians typically have dated the emergence of their designation to the call for "salvation as liberation" by the Latin American Catholic bishops who met at Medellin, Colombia in 1968; the bishops' call was a socially activist interpretation of the Second Vatican Council's emphasis on the church as the "people of God."[75] And while they have looked to their own distinctive histories, proponents of the rights of women, African Americans, and other marginalized groups usually have not consciously appropriated the Protestant tradition of a social gospel. In at least one case a prominent liberation theologian has explicitly disavowed the social gospel of white American Protestantism. Black theologian and Union Seminary professor James Cone has insisted that "black theology's origin was not in the seminary or university," nor can it be found in the white churches. "Because black people received no support from white churches or their theologians, we had to search deeply into our own history in order to find theological bases for our prior political commitment to set black people free."[76]

Although largely unrecognized, the themes of the social gospel echo in the liberation theologians' protests against the injustices springing from the divisions of race, class, and gender. They are discernible, for example, in the language of feminist theologian Nelle Morton. A southerner and for decades a professor of Christian education at Drew, Morton was a relative latecomer to the cause of women's liberation. But, as she wrote shortly before her death, feminism radicalized her long-held social ethical positions and consolidated a wide range of issues that had marked her pursuit of diverse social causes:

> Feminism was not a new cause to me any more than the race issue and the peace issue had been new causes for me and the young people of the South. It merely set me at a new cutting edge to view myself, the universe, and other human beings on this globe in a more radical way, and to raise theological questions I had never dreamed of before. It was out of the radical feminist perspective that I began to see racism, war, poverty, anti-Semitism, class, economics, compulsory heterosexuality, and politics as connected and interconnected for all these are women's issues.[77]

No direct line can be drawn from the early social gospelers' concern for the disparate social and personal issues, on one end of the historical spectrum, to Nelle Morton's clustering of an assortment of those issues around the feminist revolution, on the other end. And the historical connections between the circumspect efforts at racial integration in the 1950s and Morton's bold moralism certainly do not follow an unbroken path. Still, as Morton recognized, new religious interpretations of the social order had a way of gathering up the old, and late twentieth-century responses to social problems could build upon the responses of mid-century. A social gospel tradition, though manifesting considerable change

over time, had continuously propelled the divinity schools from a preoccupation with social etiquette to engrossment with social reform. As a
consequence, the formation of ministers in divinity education had entailed preparing them for social reform. By the late 1960s, formation
through reform also would embrace patterns of social revolt.

# CHAPTER VII

■

## *Formation and the Heritage of Revolt*

Only a few of the programs of social reform inspired by the ideals of the social gospel were directed against the divinity schools themselves. Prior to the Second World War, protests against school practices and policies usually involved a handful of students and were focused on such isolated issues as a professor's unconventional point of view or specific requirements for graduation. When larger outbreaks of protest did occur, as in the pacifist demonstrations at Union Seminary in the 1930s and 1940s, they did not seriously disrupt the daily routines of the divinity schools.[1] Many students and faculty did upset those routines with their civil rights agitation during the 1950s and early 1960s, but it was the protests of the late 1960s that first made the disruption of institutions of higher education a decisive strategy of reform.

During the last few days of April 1968, almost one thousand students occupied several buildings at Columbia University and "liberated" the president's office. The protest was aimed at Columbia's sponsorship of weapons research, its plans to build a gymnasium on public land with a separate entrance for the residents of Harlem, and its disciplining of local leaders of the Students for a Democratic Society (SDS). Some one hundred students from Union Theological Seminary were involved in various phases of the Columbia protest, including second-year Union student Daniel E. Pellegrom, who served as president of the Columbia University Student Council. That same month, students and faculty at the Duke Divinity School joined other members of the University community in a vigil at the home of the University president. The Duke protesters simultaneously mourned the slain leader Martin Luther King, Jr., and demanded a better wage for nonacademic university employees (many of whom were black). In the spring of 1970, the dean and the leaders of the Student Association of the Yale Divinity School collaborated with Yale chaplain William Sloane Coffin, Jr., to launch a university-wide, nonviolent protest against what they claimed could only be an unfair trial in New Haven of nine Black Panthers accused of murder and kidnapping.[2]

As these cases illustrate, divinity school students across the nation, frequently joined by their teachers, were caught up in the university protests of the late 1960s and early 1970s, and the protests were numerous indeed. In the spring of 1969 alone, large-scale demonstrations occurred at three hundred colleges and universities, and the demonstrations at one-half of those schools entailed student strikes or some other form of the disruption of classes. Following the U.S. invasion of Cambodia and the National Guard's gunning down of student protesters at Kent State University in 1970, more than half of the nation's college and university students took part in demonstrations.[3] The student protests ranged in kind from the destruction of university property and occupation of university space with the force of arms, to the disruption of business as usual, to nonviolent marches and draft-card burnings, to "teach-ins," "special arrangements to replace regular classes," and "free university" courses on the issues of war, race, and American imperialism. As the 1960s passed into the 1970s, many of the issues under protest were rolled together. United States aggression in Southeast Asia, the exclusion of students from university decision making, the violent retaliation of authorities against youthful protesters, and the racism of American institutions could prompt the same sit-ins and set the agenda for the same teach-ins.

At some of the divinity schools, especially those in northern cities where student concerns more readily melded with black protests, the demonstrations were more explosive than at others. Student demonstrations at the southern schools tended to be relatively mild and decorous, and some administrators, while expressing moral sympathy with the demonstrators, were able to contain the dynamism of the student activist leaders.[4] None of the schools, however, was immune to some form of revolt aimed simultaneously at the university and the larger social context.

In neither the divinity schools nor the wider university environment did the revolts ever evolve into a mass movement of a student majority, and the protests often divided the faculty respecting procedures judged to be appropriate to institutions of higher education. Furthermore as extensive as they were on the nation's campuses, the protests never grew into a revolution among America youth as a whole, despite the campus efforts of young nonstudent radicals. As former SDS organizer Todd Gitlin has said, the youthful political leaders on campus never formed strong coalitions with other groups of America's youth, and the leadership became badly fragmented notwithstanding standardized appeals to

Marxist slogans: "The intellectual squalor and moral collapse of the SDS leadership followed, in fact, from their common and long-growing commitment to revolution on high. . . . As a whole the Left was outorganized. Genuflections toward History and Revolution could not make its social programs popular, its economics palatable, its mystique potent."[5]

As U.S. troops were pulled out of Vietnam in 1973, as the inflationary 1970s fixed student attention on the need for acquiring skills suitable for earning a living, and as the White House rhetoric of the 1980s insisted on a return to "old-fashioned" American values and institutions, the Sixties seemed to fade into an American dreamworld.* To some the age became a fantasy of countercultural, communal love-ins, be-ins, and gentle grooving on "grass," Zen, and folk songs. To others it was a nightmare of spoiled, affluent students throwing destructive temper tantrums against established authorities, and an age of gratuitous violence. Whether relived as utopian fantasy or recalled as demonic nightmare, the Sixties has seemed an age that America, thanks to some good fortune, got through. And for some educators, America's colleges and universities got through the age relatively unscathed.

One divinity school dean, while acknowledging that Vietnam and race were legitimate sources of unrest on campus during his administration, concluded in 1980 that "little of educational and institutional significance emerged from the student turmoil which remains constructively operative to the present day."[7] There is much to recommend his judgment. Many of the divinity schools had abolished letter grades in favor of a pass-fail system only to restore the traditional grading system after the student protests subsided. Most of the schools had made special arrangements to give students assignments on committees previously the province of faculty alone, only to witness the waning of student interest in the daily grind of committee work. According to one observer

---

*I mean by the period of the "Sixties" what now has become fairly commonplace in the dating of the decade: from the assassination of President John F. Kennedy in 1963 to the end of U.S. involvement in Vietnam in 1973. Although that period was laced with very diverse youth movements, by numerous rhetorics of hope and despair, and by myriad crosscurrents of political and cultural styles, it does frame a Zeitgeist that began with a major cause of national anxiety and ended with the elimination of another cause. The mood resident within the period for many American youth—and, indeed, for many of their teachers—is perhaps best summarized by Todd Gitlin: "Kennedy, King, Kennedy: they sometimes felt like stations in one protracted murder of hope. . . . What is assassination, after all, if not the ultimate reminder of the citizen's helplessness—or even repressed murderousness?"[6]

of trends in theological education, the student radicalism of the 1960s "lasted longer in many theological schools than in society as a whole," inspiring some of the schools to make social justice the central concern of admissions, study, and governance. Nevertheless, the changes in the schools were largely "cosmetic (the addition of new courses and instructors)," and they did not significantly affect the professional model that continued to prevail in theological education.[8]

The accuracy of these observations should not obscure some indelible marks made on the divinity schools by the radical Sixties. The student demands of the period led to increased numbers of women and minorities on faculties and in student bodies, and most courses in feminist and African American theology and history owe their origins to the period.[9] Changes growing out of the period also began to transmute the task of forming students for the Christian ministry. As the university became both the staging ground and the immediate object of protest against established American institutions, an altered set of educational values began to emerge for university divinity schools. At the end of the 1980s, those values were still in the process of finding clarification and institutional embodiment, but a pattern had surfaced. Formation for ministry now would be set within a tradition of deep reservations about established institutions and received traditions. The Sixties bequeathed to the university-related divinity schools a legacy of revolt as well as reform. The beginning stages of the legacy had already appeared in the 1950s.

## CRITICISMS OF CULTURAL CAPTIVITY

The popular portrait of the Fifties (a period which included the early 1960s) as an age of social quietism, idle economic affluence, political conservatism, and religious conformism proves, upon inspection, to be vastly overdrawn. If those were times of greater economic opportunity for increasing numbers of white Americans, they were also times when the moral and social consequences of American wealth were brought under harsh censure. If they marked a season of uncritical acceptance of Americanness, they were not devoid of severe criticisms of all things American. The Fifties may have posed a clear case, in the words of Arthur Schlesinger, Jr., of "the bland leading the bland,"[10] but they also produced numerous denunciations of the banality of the middle classes and their national leaders.

Discomfort with the comforts of the Fifties was especially apparent among the white, suburban, middle-class youth of the day. Some of those youth "howled" with the poet Allen Ginsberg against the child-devouring lifestyles of their parents, and many more of them were attracted to *MAD* magazine's cynical caricatures of the American Way of Life. The Fifties, in fact, spawned its own youth culture of alienation, made possible by an age of abundance that gave middle-class youth their own cars, phonograph records, books, and radios. They were thus enabled to celebrate in the face of their parents' middle-class decorum the sensuality of Elvis Presley, the rebelliousness of Jack Kerouac, the bold sexuality of Marlon Brando, the unconventional rhythms of black music, and the "hip" wisdom of the disk jockey.[11] Furthermore, for all of its alleged conformism, suburban life bred its own kind of independence among youth. "The suburban child of the 1950s was raised to be independent since status in the highly mobile suburbs came not from family connections, but from individual accomplishment and personality," one study of the times has concluded. "It did not matter what your parents did as much as whether you wore the right clothes, excelled in football and Little League, cheerleading and student government. . . . It was as though David Riesman had been understood partially, but only too well [on the matter of conformism], and the parents of the 1950s had rushed to produce individualistic children—just like their neighbors did."[12]

As some of these independent, vicariously rebellious middle-class young people entered the nation's divinity schools, they brought with them attitudes that were deeply critical of their society's values and institutions. Unlike their counterparts in previous generations, many divinity students were not socially disadvantaged youngsters just waiting to be molded by the high culture of the university into genteel citizens. Although not all of the divinity schools could claim with Yale Divinity in 1956 that one-third of their students were either Phi Beta Kappa or "Phi Beta Kappa quality," most could claim with Yale that they were admitting only students with grade averages of B or better from fully accredited colleges and universities and from families of solidly middle-class status.[13]

For the first time in their history, the divinity schools in the Fifties included numbers of students from America's affluent, well-educated classes, and many of those same students had been nurtured by a youth culture that repudiated middle-class conventions. Such students would find a congenial climate in the protests of the civil rights movement against the injustices engendered by the inequalities of class, and they would find appealing the divinity schools' demands for racial equality within the university. They also would be attracted to an intellectual ethos formed of the schools' penchant for excoriating institutional religion for its surrender to the values and social divisions of middle-class suburban life.

That ethos had begun its formation even before the Fifties. In 1929, two years before he joined the faculty of the Yale Divinity School, H. Richard Niebuhr sounded a note that would become a dominant theme among divinity school theologians three decades later. Niebuhr indicted the Protestant denominations for their division along the lines of caste and class:

> The division of the churches closely follows the division of men into the castes of national, racial, and economic groups. It draws the color line in the church of God; it fosters the misunderstandings, the self-exaltations, the hatreds of jingoistic nationalism by continuing in the body of Christ the spurious differences of provincial loyalties; it seats the rich and poor apart at the table of the Lord, where the fortunate may enjoy the bounty they have provided while the others feed upon the crusts their poverty affords.[14]

Niebuhr's indictment was a forerunner of a bevy of mid-century theological critiques that would castigate the churches for adopting and perpetuating the class divisions of American life, and the critiques would define much of the milieu of the divinity schools. By the 1950s and early 1960s, divinity school scholars had construed racial segregation as the most glaring instance of the narrow introversion of the white middle class, and segregation in the churches a clear sign of the cultural captivity of Protestant Christianity. In the judgment of Gibson Winter of the University of Chicago Divinity School, "white flight" to the suburbs simultaneously signaled mainline Protestantism's rejection of people of color, its neglect of the problems of the inner city, and its preoccupation with trivial middle-class concerns.[15] Winter and his fellow critics were persuaded that white Protestants were enthralled by class values that were decidedly non-Christian.

The sweeping theological condemnations of American religious life often built upon the writings of a fashionable company of social critics like David Riesman, William H. Whyte, Jr., and C. Wright Mills.[16] In *The Lonely Crowd* (1950), Yale social scientist Riesman developed the hypothesis that Americans were quintessentially "other-directed," rather than "tradition-directed" or "inner-directed" individuals. That is, Americans were uncertain of themselves and formed their identities by taking clues from their peers, from their power to consume goods, and from their attainment of social status. Translated into the terms of the popular psychology of the time, Americans were "conformists" whose chief goal in life was social and psychological "adjustment." In *The Organization Man* (1956), journalist William H. Whyte, Jr., reproved middle-class Americans for their abandonment of individuality as they pursued job security in large companies, aspired to a sense of "belonging" and "togetherness" in churches and other community organizations, sought to escape social conflict in a dreamworld of suburban living, took comfort in the safety of numbers, and generally worshiped at the feet of the god "organization." Throughout the 1950s, the popular writings of Columbia University renegade sociologist C. Wright Mills attributed the vapidity of middle-class life to its powerlessness. According to Mills, earlier middle-class people who owned their own shops, factories, or farms had been replaced by white-collar workers who were subject to the whims of a "power elite" constituted by the interconnected worlds of corporate, military, and government leaders. Although they had convinced themselves that they controlled the destiny of a democratic society, the new middle classes were, in fact, socially and politically powerless, and they compensated for their meaningless work and lack of social control with a life of instant gratification.[17]

The theological critics of the culture incorporated key features of these social commentaries into their own criticisms, but they insisted that the emptiness of middle-class life owed chiefly to its religion. In particular, they claimed that the religion which had experienced such a widespread revival in postwar America sanctified the morally complacent, socially conformist, and politically jingoistic lifestyles of white-collar, suburban America. Peter Berger of the Hartford Seminary proclaimed, in the language of biblical prophecy, that God was not pleased by America's "noise of solemn assemblies." Canadian journalist Pierre Berton complained of the "comfortable pew" occupied by the religious middle class in North America. Syracuse religion professor Gabriel Vahanian announced that "God is dead" in the sense that modern culture and the shallow religiosity of the 1950s had robbed the biblical deity of his transcendence. Martin E. Marty of the University of Chicago Divinity School concluded that America was on a "religious kick" stimulated by a generalized piety derived from the social mores of the nation.[18]

None of these theological criticisms attained quite the vogue or the influence, however, as did those contained in the book *Protestant-Catholic-Jew* by Will Herberg, who joined the faculty of Drew Theological Seminary shortly after the book's publication. Originally published in 1955, Herberg's volume went through multiple printings (and is still in print) and was widely adopted as a college textbook in the 1950s and 1960s. The book also won Herberg repeated invitations to lecture at colleges, universities, churches, and synagogues and made him arguably Drew's best-known professor of the time.[19]

In addition to providing a sociological and historical overview of American Protestantism, Catholicism, and Judaism, Herberg sought to determine what held those groups together. He judged the common link to be a religious posture which he called the "American Way of Life." By no means a lowest common denominator religion, this fourth American faith, this "civic religion," had its own distinctive creed and set of values. If defined in one word, the American Way would be "democracy," but democracy with a peculiarly American meaning: "On its political side it means the Constitution; on its economic side, 'free enterprise'; on its social side, an equalitarianism which is not only compatible with but indeed actually implies vigorous economic competition and high mobility." Herberg found the American creed to be optimistic in its commitment to progress and self-improvement. It was also idealistic to the point of a moralism that defined all ethical issues as either totally good or totally evil, and yet it was utterly pragmatic in judging the value of any undertaking simply by the achievement of success. Herberg claimed that the object of devotion of this religion was religion: Americans put their faith in the value of faith itself, regardless of its specific content, and their faith-in-faith served as a spiritual reinforcement for their feeling of Americanness.[20]

Herberg acknowledged that the religion of the American Way of Life had been shaped in part by traditional religion, especially by colonial Puritan hopes for the emergence of a unique people in the New World and by frontier Protestantism's pragmatism. The civic religion also drew upon and modified many of the symbols and rites of the traditional faiths. By the time of the great turn to religion in the 1950s, however, the distinctive perspectives of traditional religion had been smothered under the cloak of a generalized American religiosity. Protestantism, Catholicism, and Judaism had become alternative ways of being an American. Being religious was now a way of "belonging" and "adjusting." It was a way of "fitting in" with one's suburban neighbors inoffensively. And it was a way of affirming "America first" in a tense Cold War world.

For Herberg, a Jew whose thinking had been decisively shaped by the Protestant neoorthodoxy of Reinhold Niebuhr, the religious posture of the American Way of Life was idolatrous, chauvinistic, and vague. It was the worship of a human construct—religion—not devotion to a transcendent God. It required an ultimate commitment to the life of the nation, a commitment that replaced trust in a God who judges all nations. It dissolved crucial religious differences in an American sameness and thus blunted the unique claims of the religious traditions.[21] And in its other-directedness, the religion of the American Way bred a reprehensible moral and social complacency:

> The other-directed man, no matter how religious, simply cannot understand an Elijah or an Amos, a Jesus or an Isaiah; nor can he conceivably feel any warmth of admiration for these "zealots of the Lord." Zeal, nonconformity, uncompromising witness are so "unsociable," so terribly "unadjusted"! The very purpose of the other-directed man's built-in radar apparatus is to protect him against such perils; it protects him so well that it makes the prophetic faith of the Bible almost unintelligible to him.[22]

Despite such invective, neither Herberg nor the other theological prophets of the time totally despaired of the American religious situation. In a way so typical of earlier American Jeremiahs, divinity school theologians found reasons to hope for the revitalization of the religion of the nation, and they used the message of religious decline to try to provoke a recovery of the God of traditional religion.[23] Herberg drew special hope from the youth he encountered in colleges, and even in the suburbs, who seemed to be searching for a religion that provided a deeper spirituality than social belonging. And as the assertive social and political conservatism of his later years so clearly demonstrated, he never meant to suggest in *Protestant-Catholic-Jew* that the idealism and the pragmatism, or the free enterprise and democratic systems, were anything less than wholly admirable—only that they should not be apotheosized.[24]

Martin Marty, who shared Herberg's criticisms of religion-in-general, cautioned against juxtaposing Christianity and culture as a response to the cultural captivity of Protestantism, and he suggested that resources for the reform of American religion lay close at hand—in the theological schools' recovery of the biblical notion of servanthood, in the local congregation's ability to serve the larger community without adopting the values of that community, and in the "younger churches" of the world which were not subject to the presuppositions of American chauvinism.[25]

Marty's colleague at Chicago, Gibson Winter, also did not abandon hope for reform, but he was particularly relentless in his attack upon the class captivity of the American churches.

Winter believed that in their adoption of the cultural values and social patterns of white-collar, suburban, middle-class America, the Protestant churches had lost their very soul. Although they had prospered in finances and grown in social status during the postwar revival of American religiosity, the Protestant mainline churches also had experienced a kind of arrested development. They had turned in on themselves, offering their members the trappings of social standing in suburban neighborhoods, the friendliness of a warm handshake and a hot cup of coffee on a Sunday morning, a comforting sense of belonging to a community of the like-minded, and a wide variety of ways to stay busy in organizational activities. In the process, the suburban churches had abandoned significant ministries outside their boundaries, had shielded themselves from poverty and urban blight, and had perpetuated the social divisions that spring from associating only with one's "own kind." Winter claimed that suburban church life had become just another way of "getting along" and its ministers those who saw to it that middle-class people got along: "Healthy glands and an attractive smile have come to be the necessary, if not the sufficient conditions of a 'successful' ministry." The churches had become little more than social enclaves that supported the status and aspirations of middle-class neighborhoods.[26]

Winter was persuaded that the cultural captivity of the American churches entailed much more than the problem of introversion, much more than a selfish preoccupation with their own immediate middle-class needs. It meant, as well, the failure of the churches to provide their members with a satisfying answer to the religious quest: *"The churches can only embody or mediate a true identity to their members when the fellowship of members represents the interdependencies of human life. Inclusiveness is intrinsic and not accidental to the nature of the Church."*[27] In place of the church as a community of interrelatedness and reconciliation, the suburban church had become a spiritually impoverished "organization":

> The cultus of the Church has given way to the manipulations of the organization. In place of the sacraments, we have the committee meeting; in place of confession, the bazaar; in place of pilgrimage, the dull drive to hear the deadly speaker; in place of community, a collection of functions. This trivialization of religious life has made the middle-class search for religious meaning even more desperate. One begins to wonder after a time whether the search itself isn't pointless, since every

church activity seems to lead further into a maze of superficiality which is stultifying the middle-class community.[28]

For all of his tongue-lashing of the churches, Winter continued to believe that the churches could escape from their suburban captivity. He took some hope from the neoorthodox theological trend in the divinity schools that reclaimed the prophetic criticism of society's false gods and seemed to be infusing preaching and Christian education with a new vitality. But Winter drew his greatest confidence about the future from the strong emergence of lay responsibility, from new ministries directed to extra-ecclesiastical institutions such as hospitals, universities, and political organizations, and from instances of church planning which reached into different communities in the cities. Winter believed that these movements held the potential for converting the churches from their introverted ministries and trivialized middle-class preoccupations. And he was convinced that they could prompt the church once again to become a fellowship of reconciliation and a source of the religious experience of interrelatedness. As a professor of ethics and society at the University of Chicago Divinity School, Winter also was instrumental in shaping a curriculum in which ministers were trained to extend their horizons beyond the suburban enclave.[29] In calling for the renewal of the Protestant churches, Winter, like other theological critics of the day, hoped to summon American middle-class Protestantism out of its class captivity.

The pointed criticisms accompanying the summons, however, drove still another wedge between the divinity schools and the churches deemed so captive to the culture. Ministers-in-training were not only being liberally educated into worldviews incompatible with the perspectives of their parishes. They were not only pursuing professional expectations out of harmony with those of their parishioners. They were not only being measured more by the standards of the university than by those of the churches. They were also being told that most white, middle-class churches were introverted organizations dedicated to trivial activities and conformism. Considerable irony was entailed in that message. The suburban churches had prospered because postwar, suburban America had prospered, and for the first time in their history the divinity schools had flourished because their church support had flourished. Money flowed to the schools from the churches for the expansion of faculty and buildings, and a surplus of tuition-paying students from the suburbs applied for admission to the schools. The faculty at most divinity schools did not have to worry, for a change, about the academic background of future ministers, as students with good college educations entered well-funded and strongly staffed schools.[30]

Quite beyond the act of apparently biting the hand that fed them, the cultural critics in the divinity schools tended to attribute everything that was wrong with America to suburban religious life, and they offered few ways for reconciling the communities of church and academy which that attribution served to divide. As Benton Johnson has observed recently, the critics inverted the old idea that America was a virtuous nation especially favored by God, but the inverted notion could appear equally sanctimonious and alienating: "It consists of the notion that the United States in general and its bourgeoisie and their institutions in particular are a prime source, perhaps *the* prime source, of evil in the world today. . . . A milder version of this style of thinking is the vague sense that it is bad to be bourgeois and that whatever is wrong with the world must somehow be our fault."[31] When the theological critics singled out the suburban churches in their attacks on bourgeois life, they stripped the churches of all semblance of cultural relevance. "They tried to build a fire under the laity by depriving them of the remaining landmarks of church life. In the process, of course, they conveyed the impression that the churches are irrelevant to anything that matters in the world."[32]

That impression about the irrelevance—and triviality—of suburban church life was often conveyed to Protestant ministers-in-the-making. Divinity school students and young clergy in the late 1950s and in the 1960s were cast into a prototypical liminal situation. In the words of James Hudnut-Beumler, "They were caught between masses of individuals comfortably practicing an ecclesiastical religion influenced by popular piety and the denominational elites and theologians who counselled the perfection of obedience to biblical ideals even if faithfulness brought unhappiness."[33] Many students and clergy found their way out of the quandary by abandoning the ministry to the suburban parish. The 1960s and early 1970s marked a period when large numbers of young clergy pursued careers that were relatively independent of the local congregation: the campus ministry, hospital chaplaincies, various forms of urban ministries, and denominational staff work.[34]

The cultural criticism of the suburban captivity of the churches certainly was not the single, nor perhaps even the most salient, cause of the divinity schools' attempt to train clergy in alternative, flexible forms of the ministry; larger cultural and social factors were at work, as well.[35] The criticism, however, did create an atmosphere in the schools that was fundamentally unsympathetic to the suburban congregation and that encouraged the pursuit of ministerial options. Such an atmosphere was bred, for example, by the professor of Christian ethics who, even while challenging his divinity school students to perform the priestly as well as the prophetic tasks in the local congregation, described the typical middle-class congregation as a social club in which people did nice things for one another. He warned of the difficulties facing the professional minister within the congregation: "Since it is a club, it is not fitting for the club-manager to introduce anything offensive, anything controversial that would trouble the fellowship."[36] Many students would choose not to owe their allegiance to such an association.

## FROM CRITICISM TO REVOLT

The criticisms of American suburban life and religion during the Fifties were only the prelude to the revolts against American institutions in the Sixties. Neither the intellectual broadsides of the theologians nor the cultural rebellions of American youth manifested the same loss of confidence in established American authorities that would characterize the revolts of the Sixties. The theological critics of the American Way of Life remained persuaded of the fundamental integrity of American political, economic, and religious institutions. And Fifties divinity school students, even those who protested racial segregation, were a docile lot when compared with students a decade later. In the light of government lies about the course of the war in Vietnam, the collaboration of universities with the government in the prosecution of that war, the stubborn resistance of the cities to demands for racial justice, and the assassination of national leaders who for many young people represented the hope of the future, reasons for trust in authority often crumbled and motives for reliance upon established traditions often dissolved.

A widespread denigration of the sacred symbols of authority and tradition gave conspicuous expression to the mood of the times. America's youth burned Old Glory and about as often sewed the flag onto the seats of their blue jeans. Youthful protesters greeted university presidents by their first names. Black Power athletes raised their defiant fist-salutes on the victory stand at the Olympic Games. A religious commune created its logo by combining a cross with a yellow submarine (the latter borrowed from the movie about the Beatles).[37] The message apparent from those who extensively malign or mutate the potent symbols of a culture is clear: the sacrality of the authorities and traditions supportive of those symbols is subject to suspicion—and, indeed, to denial. That message contained definite implications for American Protestantism and its divinity schools. The Sixties struggle over the symbols of the culture divided Americans along lines of class as well as age—betokened by clashes between "long-hairs" and "hard-hats"—and it raised to a new pitch the centuries-old question of how churches that are thoroughly a part of a culture can maintain independence from the values and mission of the state.[38]

The struggle over symbols also pointed to a distinct radicalization of theology and ethics among the intellectual vanguard of ecumenical Protestantism. As Yale church historian Sydney Ahlstrom detected at the end of the 1960s, the "radical turn in theology and ethics" was a phenomenon of more lasting consequence and of greater social and cultural magnitude than the publicly shocking claims of the "death-of-God movement" or the titillating "new morality" of sexual permissiveness among youth. Both of those events were signs of more fundamental shifts caused by a cresting and coalescing of forces long in the making. Those forces included unregulated urban growth, with its attendant crises of management and morality; the expanding religious and ethnic pluralism of American life, which undercut Protestantism's claims to national hegemony; rapid technological and scientific developments (especially the trip to the moon), which elevated confidence in human technical capabilities and seemed to eclipse the relevance of divine reality; (paradoxically with the previous development) continued nuclear testing and the appearance of the Cuban missile crisis, which underscored the limitlessness of human destructiveness; and a war in Vietnam that in its inequalities of conscription and its direction of national attention away from domestic problems called into question the entire "American system."[39]

According to Ahlstrom, the convergence of these forces meant that the nation entered a period "when the old grounds of national confidence, patriotic idealism, moral traditionalism, and even of historic Judaeo-Christian theism, were awash. Presuppositions that had held firm for centuries—even millennia—were being widely questioned." And presuppositions about the Protestant churches were not immune: "the time-honored structures of American church life" seemed especially irrelevant to those who were radicalized by the times.[40]

Ahlstrom underestimated the forces of political, cultural, and religious conservatism that would resist the modern developments he had identified and that would lay claim to the authority of social conventions in reaction to the radicalism of the Sixties. One of his claims in 1970 seems almost droll today in the light of evangelical Christianity's galloping influence worldwide: "Traditional forms of evangelism, both at home and on 'foreign mission fields,' have been seriously questioned by all but the most culturally alienated religious groups."[41] Yet Ahlstrom had accurately detected a long-range consequence of the radicalism of the Sixties for many Protestant divinity school students and faculty: received authority, the authority of national and religious tradition, had been seriously undermined.

By the middle of the 1970s, the abiding antiauthoritarian and antiestablishment sentiments would compete in the divinity schools—especially in schools with denominational connections—with a renewed emphasis on the cultivation of professional skills appropriate to the demands of the churches. The national trend in higher education toward practical career preparation, brought on by an inflationary economy and job scarcity, affected the attitudes of many divinity school students. A number of divinity school faculty who had taught during the theologically dominated Fifties as well as during the socially oriented Sixties noted that the 1970s marked a return to a renewed professionalism among students. Beginning in the 1970s, students seemed to grow impatient with any form of learning not immediately relevant to their professional ministerial tasks, and they often appeared to be uncritical in their acceptance of the requirements of the institutional church.[42] Also by the mid-1970s, the "flexible curricula" and diverse committees of the Sixties, meant to appeal to students interested in social reform and self-directed study, began to seem out of joint with the needs of both the less radical students and the decidedly more conservative parish of the day.[43]

Sixties radicalism had not displaced the careerism and professionalism that would continue to characterize American higher education and so much American culture as a whole in the 1970s and 1980s. Neither the fondest radical hopes nor the deepest conservative fears materialized in the American universities and their divinity schools. Certainly the revolutionary New Left failed to create new political and educational structures. And Yale law professor Charles Reich's prediction of the emergence of a "new consciousness," initiated by America's youth who would shed their corporate apparel in favor of faded Levis and Army surplus boots and who would repudiate technical rationality in favor of self-knowledge and spiritual wisdom,[44] proved to be the most romantic of illusions.

Fears among conservatives that the educators of America's youth, having been nurtured in the radicalism of the Sixties, would convert their students to a rabid anti-Americanism also turned out to be unfounded. Few of the most radical students of the Sixties secured positions of significant social influence. Child-of-the-Sixties Camille Paglia only slightly exaggerates the situation when she claims that those youth who were determined to transform the world through psychedelia "blew their brains out on acid," and the political radicals "rarely went on to graduate school; if they did, they often dropped out. If they made it through, they had trouble getting a job and keeping it. They remain mavericks, isolated, off-center."[45] Todd Gitlin, another product of the times who *did* go on to graduate school and then became a professor in a major American university (the University of California, Berkeley), attests to his eccentricity when comparing himself to his students: "My generation numbers teachers more activist (for the moment) than their students, rock stars more anti-establishment than their audiences: this is mind-boggling for a generation who believed that youth had the privilege of vision."[46] Furthermore, those professors who proved to be more radical than their students had met the professional requirements for tenure, that most establishmentarian of American customs; they had become the university counterparts to the ambitious, upwardly mobile Young Urban Professionals in the corporate world.

If the fruits of the Sixties did not confirm either the wildest hopes of the radicals or the deepest fears of the conservatives, however, they did begin a process in the university that persisted in schools of liberal arts and in divinity schools. Alongside the renewed commitment to fixed institutional traditions and conventional professionalism there continued in those units of the university an ongoing challenge to received authority and skepticism about established traditions. A tradition of antitraditionalism had been set in motion, one that would provoke considerable public criticism of the modern university.

Much of that criticism was directed to the loss of intellectual unity, to the ideological fragmentation, to the militant politicization of the curriculum and faculty in the liberal arts. Such was the criticism of the director of the National Endowment for the Humanities Lynne Cheney, who claimed that faculty at colleges and universities in every part of the country had put teaching "into the service of politics, especially in the humanities."[47] In the words of journalist Roger Kimball, "The political dimension of [the] assault on the humanities shows itself nowhere more clearly than in the attempt to restructure the curriculum on the principle of equal time. More and more, one sees the traditional literary canon ignored as various interest groups demand that there be more women's literature for feminists, black literature for blacks, gay literature for homo-sexuals, and so on."[48]

The divinity schools did not escape the allegations. In the December 1990 issue of the *Atlantic Monthly*, writer and television producer Paul Wilkes charged America's Protestant, Catholic, and Jewish seminaries with "squandering a legacy" by allowing into their halls of learning "a flighty if implacable radicalism." Wilkes singled out the seminaries of ecumenical Protestantism as particularly prone to the mixing of theological instruction with the politics of race, class, and gender. "Radicalism threatens to become central to the curriculum in some schools, and faculty appointments are often made on the basis not only of scholarship but also of political outlook," Wilkes wrote.[49]

Representatives of both the humanities departments and the theological schools cried "Foul!" A group of scholars convened by the American Council of Learned Societies maintained that the conservative critics of America's colleges and universities attempted to impose a fixed, elitist literary canon upon a humanistic scholarship determined to accept the literary and historical legitimacy of the world's diverse, particularistic groups. They also averred that those critics ignored how every approach to a subject, including their own preferred study of male, Western culture, is inescapably political.[50] Similarly, defenders of the "radicalization" of some Protestant theological schools claimed that the critics either ignored or spurned the schools' positive response to social diversity, and they overlooked the way in which politicization is simply another way of empowering diverse peoples by integrating experience, learning, and social action.[51]

The debate over the politicization of theological education has been a component within the larger dispute in the university over canon and context and the nature of interpretation, and that dispute, in turn, has been part of a larger struggle over the proper relation between unity and diversity within a democratic society. Parties to the various debates usually have agreed on one crucial historical point, however: the Sixties formed a watershed for developments in higher education.

To educational conservative Allan Bloom, the Sixties marked the beginning of the end within the American university of any agreement on literary standards, political morality, or religious values. Thanks to the Sixties, the university world was engulfed in a sea of absolute relativism.[52] To educational progressive Todd Gitlin, the Sixties established a tradition, especially in the universities, of every authority having to prove itself worthy of allegiance, and the period opened the way for the assertion of the legitimacy of racial, sexual, national, and ethnic differences.[53] To a critic of theological education like Paul Wilkes, the present situation of the seminaries of ecumenical Protestantism signals a departure from the Fifties, when the seminaries attracted highly talented students, the mainline religion represented by those seminaries possessed considerable cultural clout, and the schools boasted a self-confident sense of purpose undisturbed by the political claims of minority-interest groups.[54] To defenders of today's theological schools, the Fifties should not be glorified as some Golden Age of theological education. New attitudes were created by the Sixties, attitudes that resulted in the theological schools' becoming more attuned to the real diversity in American society, more experimental in the search for educational models, and more inclusive than the education simply of the white, male suburbanite for the church's ministry.[55]

Defenders of diversity have been as capable of oversimplifying the past as the lamenters of a lost heritage have been of glorifying it. Those early twentieth-century educators like Dean Tillett of Vanderbilt, committed to changing the circumstances in which most seminarians were poor, lacking in social graces, and devoid of any higher education, would have been altogether perplexed by the strange attribution of power in a recent editorial in the *Christian Century*: "Seminaries once attracted the social elite—white males of European stock."[56] And compared to the current situation, the "good old days" for the seminaries in the 1950s seem statically homogeneous, devoid of the intellectual dynamism that can spring from cultural pluralism.

Whether romanticized or oversimplified, the years preceding the student revolts of the Sixties began to take on an air of antiquated history. And whether condemned as the source of social and conceptual chaos or condoned as the root of creative egalitarianism, the Sixties became the origins of the present. For both the universities and their divinity schools, the Sixties would establish the terms of the debate, and in many cases the items on the agenda, for the discussion of the purposes of higher education in America. For the divinity schools in particular, the radical decade would prompt new ways of conceiving, and new means of fostering, the formation of students for the Christian ministry. Alongside the turn to established authorities and adherence to vocational conventions there appeared the conviction that all authorities, religious or otherwise, are open in principle to challenge, and that all traditions, educational or otherwise, must prove their validity in arguments more practical and immediate than simple appeals to past warrants. At the heart of post-Sixties efforts to provide for the formation of ministers resided a continuing and partially institutionalized heritage of revolt.

The heritage was most apparent in the establishment of political organizations representing diverse student interests. To an extent unparalleled in the past, divinity school students formed interest groups, caucuses, special purpose clusters devoted to the empowerment of their members and the enhancement of their political influence within the schools. Special purpose groups for women students, black students, Hispanic students, evangelical students, lesbian and gay students, and others matched the formation of such groups within the larger university environment. The presence of the groups betokened a changed social orientation toward the formation of ministers for the churches. In the language of a Methodist divinity school, the student organizations served both as "support groups" and as "contexts for exploring issues" that would face students in the ministry.[57] In the words of a nondenominational school, the organizations were welcomed as products of a social and cultural diversity that "fosters a community whose members challenge and influence each other's views and ideas."[58]

However described, student groups which supported and vented social and theological difference constituted a significant presence on the divinity school campuses. To some faculty, that presence constituted an unfortunate politicization of the environment. One professor found that the students in his school were so divided into power caucuses that he sometimes felt "we're training people more for political careers or for political combat than for the Christian ministry."[59] To other faculty, the aggressive student assertion of difference was precisely what gave vitality and relevance to the divinity school scene. In the judgment of a feminist theologian, her divinity school's increasing student diversity represented the rich pluralism in the church and society as well as a "powerful catalyst for change in society."[60]

The celebrants and the critics agreed that the diverse political student organizations mirrored an intellectual as well as a social shift within Protestant theological education. In the vocabulary of "globalization" which gained such currency by the 1980s, the political presence of interest groups reflected the reordering of an education that now moved from "the particular to the general," from "ethnic and gender difference" to "solidarity with others."[61] After the Sixties, the postwar centering of divinity education on ecumenical theology disappeared as diverse groups in American society made their distinctive voices heard. Although the theological emphasis of the 1940s and 1950s had contained considerable

variety, it had generated a kind of intellectual consensus in its appropriation of the grand themes of the Christian past, in its confidence in the
power of Christians to unify sufficiently to meet the challenges of a postwar world, and in its optimism about its own cultural significance.[62] That
centering force of confidence and tradition was disrupted by the assertive
particularism of America's diverse groups.

Theology in the divinity schools found itself in a situation comparable
to that of the university divisions of the humanities and the social sciences. Claims of "universalism," or the assertion that truth is one and is
discernible as such, struck many of the proponents of particularism, at
worst, as a mask of the dominance of one group's truth over that of another and, at best, as an obscuration of the historicity and social incarna-
tion of all truth. In the field of history, for example, black historians
defined themselves not as " 'historians who happened to be Negroes,'
with a consensually acceptable integrationist viewpoint, but as *black* historians, committed to one or another form of cultural nationalism."
Women historians defined themselves not as " 'historians who happened
to be women,' seeking proportional representation in textbooks for members of their sex, but *feminist* historians with an overriding loyalty to their
sisters, and agendas which called for a thoroughgoing transformation
of historical consciousness."[63] Numerous liberal artists within the university were also persuaded that all claims to an objective, scientific, disinterested perception of truth ignored the intimate relation between
knowledge and power. They were convinced by the arguments of Michel
Foucault that the "disciplines" were instruments for exercising power
over the subjects studied, by the insistence of Edward Said that western-
ers had created the construct the "Orient" to control non-westerners, and
by observations of ethnographers about the manner in which the very
presence of a researcher deeply affects the object and the results of the
research.[64]

The aggressive particularism and insistent relativism of post-Sixties
university thought posed anew for Christian theologians questions that
had been pointedly raised by the German theologian Ernst Troeltsch
more than a half century earlier: How can Christianity's universal claims
be reconciled with Christianity's indisputable historicity and sociality?
And what constitutes Christianity's social unity in the light of its multiple and very different institutional forms?[65] At the end of the 1980s, divinity school theologians still were struggling with those questions, but
a trend to some answers was discernible. Social unity was a goal to

be sought, while diversity was the starting point. The unity of Christian truth was a social aspiration, not a metaphysical reality. Gone from the divinity school scene, certainly, were any Enlightenment professions of disinterested objectivity (professions already challenged by neoorthodoxy's repudiation of theology modeled on the natural sciences). Theological truth was now unquestionably something to be apprehended with passion and was bounded by the social reality of a group. Absent, also, was the defense of any social form of Christian unity into which human groups should attempt to integrate themselves. The sexual, ethnic, class, and racial particularities of religious peoples must be preserved and efforts at solidarity must safeguard difference.

The preference for particularity in the intellectual venture of the divinity schools was evident in two very different theological movements. It was apparent in the various forms of liberation theology, that late twentieth-century instance of social-gospel thinking which took its bearings from the particular circumstances of the oppressed peoples of the world. But it was apparent as well in assorted expressions of "narrative theology" among divinity school theologians. In their own very distinctive ways, thinkers such as George Lindbeck at Yale, Stanley Hauerwas at Duke, and Ronald Thiemann of Harvard called for a theology that was responsible to Christian communities. Reacting against theologies that took their clues from modern trends as well as against attempts to found theology on universal experiences, these theologians called for Christian thinkers to operate out of the distinctive stories, liturgies, and ethical principles that frame the Christian community.[66] In both the liberation theologies and the narrative theologies, particularism—the particularism of the racial, ethnic, or sexual group or of the greater religious community—was taken as the starting point and constant framework for theological reflection.

The models of reflection as well as the models of student life were "politicized" in that they were designed for people defined by the boundaries and empowered by ideals of specific social groups. And they shared with the spirit of the radical Sixties the suspicion of any authority or tradition that claimed universal social applicability. To be sure, efforts at consensus and conversation across social boundaries were not abandoned within the theological task. Shortly after becoming dean of Harvard Divinity School in 1986, for example, Ronald Thiemann argued that his university divinity school afforded excellent opportunities for promoting public discussion of issues vital to the public good in a manner that transcended special political interests.[67] And theological ethicist Joseph Hough, newly appointed dean of the Divinity School at Vanderbilt in 1990, claimed that Christian theology in the university could point "beyond the diversity and fragmentation of life toward a shared loyalty to the good of the whole."[68] Still, for such thinkers the integrity of social and religious difference should be preserved in any search for unity in public discourse.

In a way not seen in the past, therefore, the defense of unmeltable particularism formed the intellectual climate of the universities and their divinity schools in late twentieth-century America. And that climate included views of theology as an undertaking quite different from the abstract formulation of ideas or the disinterested pursuit of universal truths. According to Thiemann, theology should be a "formative activity"; theology should seek the "quite practical goal" of "the formation of religious identity and character" as it reflects upon the religious practices prevailing in religious congregations and other sectors of society.[69] In the terms of the widespread defiance of the old division between theory and practice, numerous divinity school theologians of the 1980s were calling for theology to become an eminently "practical" project by turning its attention to the practices and "practical wisdom" inherent within the formative traditions of religious communities.[70] The formation of divinity students was to occur in part, then, through the formative, practical thinking of theology.

In their insistence on the character- and identity-formation potential of theology, the divinity schools affirmed a brand of American pragmatism repeatedly demanded by students of the Sixties: learning should be "relevant"; knowledge should "work." As the 1970s and 1980s would demonstrate so clearly, the emphasis on relevant, practical knowledge could take a turn toward an unabashed preference for the acquisition of technical professional skills ("Valuable knowledge is what gets me a job"), or it could swing toward a preference for knowledge with personal or social consequence ("Valuable knowledge is what forms character or reforms society"). In the divinity schools, the former meaning was apparent in the ministerial vocationalism and professionalism that had reemerged by the mid-1970s; the latter was evident in the hopes for personal and social formation to be found in interest groups and in a theology of *praxis*.[71] The desire for a knowledge that would shape character also was manifest in the post-Sixties calls for experiments in "spiritual formation."

Beginning in the early 1970s, numerous theological educators became concerned over the lack of "character formation" or "spiritual formation" provided students in Protestant seminaries. A study sponsored by the American Association of Theological Schools concluded in 1972 that there was widespread complaint on the part of theological school students and recent graduates about their lack of development in religious piety. Grumbling such as the following was said to be typical: "I went through four years of divinity school, and no one ever asked me about the condition of my soul"; "Pastoral ministry made me frightfully aware of my own personal inadequacy in the spiritual life."[72] Such complaints were scarcely new. They were precisely those of Reinhold Niebuhr about his experience at the Yale Divinity School in the early twentieth century.[73] But in the 1970s the grievances began to prompt studies and seminars sponsored by the AATS and other organizations concerned with the future of theological education. And by the 1980s theological schools, including university-related divinity schools, were experimenting with ways to unite the training of the student mind with the development of the student soul.

Educators involved in the AATS study of 1972 found that the resurgent student demands for spiritual formation were in part the product of the Sixties counterculture: "the upsurge of interest in transcendental meditation, Zen, and psychedelic drugs in this student generation, whatever else might be said about it, must surely be seen as a deep yearning to deal with inner reality." That yearning for inner reality was being satisfied neither by the "establishment" of the local church nor that of the theological school. Of the latter, students asked for "involvement, not merely knowledge. They wish to see our faith credentials before listening to our theological expertise."[74]

Sixties-style student religiosity did not exhaust the pleas for spiritual formation; it opened the gates for later entreaties. Even as many students at Protestant divinity schools earnestly turned to the development of specific professional skills and as others chose to nurture their personal identities through interest and support groups, student commitment to spiritual formation at places of theological education seemed to intensify. Studies throughout the 1970s and 1980s found that students, especially those in the nondenominational divinity schools but also to a large extent those in the denominational schools, were demanding greater attention to personal religious development.[75] If the counterculture's interest in Zen and TM had largely disappeared from the student bodies of the schools, religious yearnings as such had not. Beginning in the late 1960s, increasing numbers of students entered divinity schools devoid of any lengthy nurture in the local churches, and those who had experienced such nurture were likely to have been exposed to a churchly devotional literature that emphasized the need for "self-fulfillment" and "spiritual self-help."[76] Divinity school students in the 1970s and 1980s continued to seek ways to build and augment their own spirituality.

For their part, the schools experimented with ways of enhancing spiritual formation. The Perkins School of Theology at SMU, for example, adopted the Wesleyan model of the "class meeting" and created small groups of students under staff or faculty direction that followed such disciplines as personal devotions and the keeping of a spiritual journal. Perkins also instituted small, multiple, student-led daily worship services.[77] The Yale Divinity School established an order for student worship which included the singing of morning prayer each Tuesday, liturgical drama and dance on Wednesdays, and the celebration of the eucharist on Fridays.[78] At the Harvard Divinity School, eminent New Testament scholar and former dean Krister Stendahl was appointed chaplain—the first in the Divinity School's history—to assist students with the integration of their spiritual and intellectual lives.[79]

By the end of the 1980s, experiments in spiritual formation were more a series of diverse trends than a massive movement sweeping over the theological terrain. There were instances of faculty indifference, and even resistance, to something that appeared to be inimical to the task of critical and analytical thinking, and endeavors in spiritual formation could be taken as still another demand upon limited faculty time.[80] Some students, especially those who commuted to divinity schools and those with family obligations, found it difficult to spare the time for the discipline required for intentional, conscientious spiritual formation.[81] And despite the frequent appeal by Protestant educators to the Roman Catholic model, there was lacking in American divinity school education—and in most recent American Protestantism—the same tradition of formal spiritual regimen of the kind entailed in the education of Catholic priests.[82]

Protestant proponents of spiritual formation also differed considerably on the meaning of "spiritual," a word that could connote meanings as sundry as the individual's inner life, the work of the Third Person of the Holy Trinity, a personal relationship with God, experiential or affective knowledge, and a disciplined life of prayer.[83] Furthermore, the process of "formation" posed for Protestant educators the issue of the degree to which the spiritual life could be cultivated by the individual and the extent to which community support was required. It also raised the question of whether the formalizing of spiritual formation might not crush the life out of a vital process by entrapping it in a segregated division of divinity education.[84]

Although lacking the power of a unified movement and troubled by crucial questions, the experiments in spiritual formation represented still another divinity school appeal to a practical, indeed to a pragmatic, form of knowledge that had made such a striking appearance among students of the Sixties. And the interest in spiritual formation harmonized with those theologies that would root the theological task in the practices of religious communities. According to George Lindbeck, Lutheran theologian at Yale Divinity, spiritual formation is the "internalization of a communal religious tradition" and is thus the prerequisite for theology which is, by definition, second-order reflection upon a communal religious tradition.[85] For David Tracy, Roman Catholic theologian at the Divinity School at Chicago, theological reflection requires a dialectical relation between community of thought and community of commitment: "the community of inquiry in the West lives through the power of the great Socratic ideal for true education—classically expressed in the saying 'The unreflective life is not worth living.' " By the same token, however, "communities of commitment and faith add to that classic Socratic ideal of the Western community of inquiry the equally important thought: 'And the unlived life is not worth reflecting upon.' "[86] Particularity and practicality had been joined in the still developing ideas and programs of spiritual formation.

## SCHOOLS, CHURCHES, AND THE HERITAGE OF REVOLT

In one respect, the heritage of the Sixties surpassed that of the Fifties in dividing the divinity schools from the churches of middle-class Protestantism. The decade of student revolt itself, although singling out the American university as the proximate representative of the moral bankruptcy of the American social system as a whole, did not exclude "establishment Protestantism" from its scathing assaults. Even with the return of the universities to relative normalcy after 1973, a definite measure of anti-institutionalism and antiauthoritarianism continued to characterize many divinity school faculty and students—indeed, it continued to characterize many Protestant leaders who were not directly responsible to local churches. As one historian of the period has pointed out, the Sixties

brought to a climax a long-standing tendency within liberal Protestantism to reject the constraints of religious institutions, and the aftermath
of the decade heightened within American Protestantism a persistent tension between the task of responding to present dilemmas and that of assuming responsibility for the faith of the generations.[87]

Certainly Sixties students' grave reservations about middle-class institutions and their traditions had made a lasting difference in the educational vision of the university divinity schools. Efforts at formation for
the ministry no longer could take for granted the values that had animated the schools for almost a hundred years. The insistent presence of
diverse interest groups, the tenacious particularism of the new theologies, and the earnest pragmatism of the proponents of spiritual development challenged the old conviction that the divinity school should form
the ministers of the future by baptizing them into the high culture of the
university and developing in them fixed skills appropriate to the leadership of middle-class churches. What the Fifties jeremiads against the cultural captivity of the churches had initiated, the Sixties revolts against
established authorities had completed: the renunciation of any generalized high culture in university or church in favor of the specific cultures
of particular groups, peoples, and spiritual expressions.

From the standpoint of white middle-class Protestants, the new movements within the schools against the old values of high culture could appear as repudiations of the churches themselves. One Methodist divinity
school dean, concerned about the loss of students to a neighboring conservative evangelical seminary, could complain in the 1980s that the commitment of his school to "specialized ministries," "unusual lifestyles,"
and "social ethics" was "more viable for a community organization or
for a national agency than for a parish and pastor."[88] In another respect,
however, the post-Sixties environment in the divinity schools marked a
time of renewed emphasis on the local congregation.

Even during the turbulent decade itself, few divinity school faculty understood their criticisms of church, culture, and traditional ministerial
tasks as an abandonment of education on behalf of the local churches.[89]
But by the 1980s many of those faculty were insisting that the local congregation could yield a new paradigm for theological education. Claremont professors Joseph Hough and John Cobb, for example, called for the
education of church leaders to take its rise from the shared internal history of the Christian community rather than from abstract disciplines
aimed at the production of unrelated professional skills.[90] Yale theologian
David Kelsey defined the theological school as "a community of persons

trying to understand God more truly by focusing its study of various subject matters within the horizon of questions about Christian congregations."[91]

Much of the new emphasis on the congregation arose from the pioneering work of the late James Hopewell of the Candler School of Theology, who challenged his fellow educators to treat the congregation simultaneously as paradigm, beneficiary, and object of study.[92] By the end of the 1980s, Hopewell's challenge had prompted considerable interest among the faculties in the divinity schools, but it was uncertain how it would find embodiment in the structures of the schools or in the scholarly agendas of the faculty. As Candler church historian Brooks Holifield said respecting his own discipline, "The congregation has been the primary social group within which religious commitments in America have found expression. Yet no one has tried to tell the story of religion in America from a perspective formed by the analysis of the congregation. . . . [W]e have no accumulated body of historical research on congregations and their typical activities."[93]

Despite the scarcity of scholarly resources for meeting the challenge, the awakened interest of divinity school faculty in the local congregation signaled a post-Sixties effort to find a viable alternative to both the anti-institutionalism and the resurgent professionalism of the period. The new interest in congregations was prompted in part by a changed student profile. Some faculty members' hope of finding a new educational paradigm *in* the congregation and *for* the congregation, as a replacement for the professional educational model that seeks to develop theoretical and practical skills for ordained clergy, seemed appropriate to the increasing numbers of students after the Sixties who entered divinity school without the goal of ordination clearly in mind. In the 1970s and 1980s, enrollments in the major professional degree aimed at those seeking ordination (the M.Div.) increased at a rate far less than that of the two-year master's degrees designed for the nonordained, and by the late 1980s only a little more than two-thirds of all theological enrollments were full-time students.[94] The nondenominational divinity schools, especially, had attracted numerous students who enrolled as religious seekers, as church lay leaders, as questers for alternatives to traditional career paths.[95] A theological education oriented to the training of lay as well as clerical church leaders and aimed at the communal experiences of religious people was an especially appropriate way of meeting the interests of a changing student body.

Yet something more was at stake than adjustment to opportunities at hand. Sixties-style dissatisfaction with conventional views of the ministerial profession and with traditional university expectations for professional education also played its role in the turn to the context of the congregation. The desire to transform theological education in the light of the local congregation, and to form divinity students within the horizons of the congregation, was an outgrowth of the Sixties revolts against the fixed professionalism and disciplines of the university.

The decade of revolt did not manage to abolish the professional paradigm or stem the tide of ministerial careerism within many of the divinity schools, but it did breed a deep dissatisfaction with traditional models of ministerial training, and it fostered the quest for new models. The insistence of the most radical students on an equal share in governance and the right to determine curriculum was not met, but their egalitarian demands prompted both faculty and students to question the neat divisions separating theory and practice, theological claim and social situation, academic study and spiritual formation. The age of revolt did not replace the age-old fourfold scheme for organizing theological learning, but it did directly challenge the objectivist assumptions about knowledge which had bolstered that pattern. Above all, the Sixties undermined reliance on fixed religious and social authority, even for those divinity schools that were not seriously disrupted by radical student protests. A tradition of lost confidence in tradition became an enduring heritage for American universities and their divinity schools.

The implications of the heritage of the Sixties are still emerging, but the effects of the decade's shaking of the fixed structures of authority and convention reverberated through the 1980s. One of the founding assumptions of the divinity schools had been overturned. Formation of people for the ministry no longer was assumed to be a simple matter of immersing students in the high culture and the higher learning of the university. The social backgrounds and the educational expectations of the students had changed, and the cultural and religious values of America and its universities had grown altogether diverse. The founders of Protestant divinity schools had not anticipated the degree to which the educational aims of specialization, professionalization, formation, and reform would have to be pursued within the conditions defined by an advancing pluralism in American universities and in American society as a whole.

# PART IV

■

# PLURALISM

# CHAPTER VIII

■

## *The Challenge of Social and Cultural Diversity*

The founders of university divinity schools believed that the world demanded more than reform and more than the formation of ministers devoted to reform. They were persuaded that the social world required, as well, a religious focus, one created in large measure by the instruments of education. America in the late nineteenth and early twentieth centuries already had manifested a social diversity that, to the eyes of many Protestant leaders, spelled social chaos. Successive waves of immigration and the agglomeration of folk of diverse ethnic and religious backgrounds in America's cities seemed to beget a nation that cried out for a unifying principle.

Early leaders of the divinity schools regarded Christianity in its Anglo-Saxon Protestant manifestations as particularly well-suited for preventing American social diversity from sliding into the anarchy of social discord. Chicago's William Rainey Harper gave the vision its most comprehensive expression. Harper believed that through an interconnected system of education, Protestant Christianity could act as a chief agent of democracy and simultaneously infuse American culture with a unifying spirit of respect for the integrity of the individual and prophetically call individuals and their social institutions to account before the God of all peoples. As a vital component of the university and a participant in the university's educational mission to the society at large, the divinity school was obligated to exert its unifying religious influence upon its university home and its national context.

As we have seen, the efforts to establish a unifying religious center in the nation often sprang from ardent hopes for the triumph of a Protestant civilization in America and around the globe. Missionaries who received their training at the divinity schools at the turn of the twentieth century carried with them into their service the aims of religious conversion as well as plans for social and educational aid. Early ecumenism among American Protestant educators contained a strong component of anti-

Catholicism, and the perceived perils of the "Other" played their part in stimulating the study of the religions of the world. The movements of social reform springing from the social gospel in America often were driven by hopes for an American Protestant Zion. Dreams of a Protestant establishment, fostered in part by fears of religious pluralism, were still apparent in the middle of the twentieth century when a number of liberal Protestants within the National Council of Churches and the divinity schools endorsed the efforts of the Billy Graham crusades to convert the nation to evangelical Protestant Christianity.[1]

Ecumenical Protestantism also had embraced a countervailing attitude, however, one that promoted the toleration of difference. For that reason, Martin Marty's comparative judgment respecting the devotees of this form of modern Christianity is altogether defensible: "I believe that those dominant Anglo-Saxon Protestant peoples, for all the evidences of racism and attachment to privilege they showed, yielded their hegemonic place in the culture more gracefully than one could have expected as they gradually learned to share space and power." Adaptability, toleration, and the (however grudging) yielding of power turned out to be stellar social virtues in a world torn by religious and ethnic conflict: "in most places in the world, in times of twentieth-century change, mixed populations did not have the good fortune to encounter such adaptable groups as these."[2]

Marty's judgment definitely applies to the Protestantism of the university divinity schools. For all of their early attempts to produce an educated clergy who could shape the core of the culture with a robust and authoritative Protestantism, the divinity schools also early had embraced the principle of respect for the diverse religions and cultures of humankind. The principle was apparent in the "nonsectarian" definitions of their educational aims. It was evident in the schools' shift in the comparative study of religions away from learning in order to convert to learning in order to understand and help those who were different. A respect for difference was also present in the social gospel's emerging concern for the welfare and rights of people of all races and classes, in ecumenical educators' eventual embrace of diverse Christians around the globe, and even in the theological jeremiads against the parochialism of suburban Christianity.

The tempering of the aim of social and cultural hegemony with a respect for diversity certainly did not mean that ecumenical Protestantism was eager to surrender its aim of providing a center for a diverse America. There is no evidence that divinity school leaders, for example, resolved without prompting to relinquish their vision of a "Christian"—that is, a Protestant—America. The persistent pluralism of the American situation forced them to abandon that vision. Already by 1920, so-called mainline Protestantism faced, in Robert Handy's apt phraseology, a "second disestablishment." To the constitutional principle of disestablishment had been added a numerical disestablishment brought about by the successive waves of immigration of non-Protestants and by the corresponding inability of mainline Protestantism to control government, family, school, and other American institutions.[3]

The changed situation did not result in the divinity schools' immediate cessation of attempts to educate ministers for the shaping of the national culture, but those attempts were gradually restricted in their scope, were considerably weakened in their evangelical zeal, and were eventually stripped of their messianic dreams. The moderating drifts were evident in the histories of the schools' attempts to influence the study of religion in higher education, in the changing nature of their participation in the ecumenical movement, and in the altered aims of the comparative study of religions. By the end of the Sixties, however, the divinity schools clearly had given up any attempt to create a religious center for a diversified America. A new pluralism, more radical in its assertiveness than any of its predecessors, had emerged in the nation, in the universities, and in the divinity schools themselves. What previously had been a challenge "out there" in the external social order had now become a challenge from within. And a different set of intellectual responses to the new challenge emerged, responses that struggled with how any universal religious and cultural meaning could be asserted that did not obscure the integrity of diverse centers of meaning and association.

## JUST WHOSE SCHOOL IS THIS, ANYWAY?

In 1959, Edward K. Graham, dean of the Graduate School at Boston University, posed a problem for his university colleagues: "Those who pay the tuition, as well as those who are paid by the tuition, have a natural tendency to ask just whose university this is, anyway. It is a perfectly fair question . . . not generally answered, except in terms so vague as to be meaningless or, as in the case of some critics, in terms so negative as to be querulous."[4] Graham had in mind the anomaly apparent at a university like Boston which had been founded as a Methodist institution but had become non-Methodist in the majority of its student body and faculty. But his way of raising the question of university ownership had wider applicability. In the years following Graham's remarks, the increasing diversity of tuition-paying students and the increasing diversity of their teachers would press with new intensity the question of institutional ownership. For divinity schools, as for other units of the American university, the role of higher education in a pluralistic nation was no longer a matter of launching missions to a social environment outside the walls of academe. The concern became the education of a diverse student body within the academy's own walls in such a way that the larger society was appropriately served. Prior to the Sixties, the divinity schools had not invited women and people of color to participate in answering the question "Just whose school is this, anyway?" Now, with or without invitation, they would participate, and as a result the divinity schools would begin to redefine their responses to diversity.

Before the civil rights movement and the integration of educational institutions, black Americans contributed in no significant way to the identities of university divinity schools. African Americans constituted a small, powerless presence in the schools, even in those northern schools that early in their histories had led the way in the eradication of racial barriers to university admissions. The northern schools could take considerable pride in their pre–World War II education of black ministers who later would assume leadership roles among their people, but the numbers of such students were small and their influence on the overall mission of the schools was nonexistent. In a study of black Protestantism in the early 1930s, Benjamin E. Mays and Joseph W. Nicholson found that in eleven northern Protestant seminaries (which included the divinity schools at Boston, Chicago, Drew, Union, and Yale), a mere sixty-nine black students were enrolled as regular students.[5] Mays and Nicholson observed that as a group black preachers were a woefully undereducated group of professionals: 80 percent of black urban pastors had no college education, and almost 90 percent of the few who enrolled in black seminaries had never graduated from college.[6] The authors sounded a warning that would be repeated by late twentieth-century scholars: a churchly tradition that had devalued clergy education in favor of a "divine call" and evangelical preaching meant that the ministerial profession was being left behind by a black laity who increasingly were graduating from college and were attaining conventional professional status.[7]

Policies of racial desegregation began to change the profile of the black clergy somewhat. Fifty years after the Mays/Nicholson study, the median level of education for urban black clergy was close to four years of college, more than a third of all black clergy had received some post-collegiate education, and somewhere between 10 and 20 percent of black clergy had completed work at an accredited theological school.[8] Although the situation in the 1990s was still characterized by an undereducated and underprofessionalized black clergy when their attainments were compared with those of professional black laity, some progress had been made in the professional education of black Protestant ministers. University divinity schools had contributed to the progress. Beginning in the late 1960s, the divinity schools had launched active programs to recruit black students and faculty, in some cases setting quotas for admissions and hiring.[9] Driven by the desire to represent the diversity within church and society, as well as by affirmative action mandates within the university, the divinity schools vigorously recruited African Americans as part of an overall effort to create communities inclusive of ethnic and racial differences.

Judged strictly in terms of the numbers of African Americans on campus at the end of the 1980s, the university divinity schools had surpassed the achievements of Protestant theological schools in the aggregate, although theological educators were less than satisfied with both sets of results. By the end of the decade, African American students accounted for 6 percent of the students in the Protestant schools affiliated with the Association of Theological Schools and 7.3 percent of students in all ATS schools.[10] Furthermore, a study published in 1988 indicated that many of the black and other minority students in Protestant theological schools were "in the older age groupings," a situation that did not bode well for the future: "it appears that a serious shortage of racial and ethnic minority, pastoral leadership in the predominantly white denominations of the United States will occur in the not so distant future."[11] Similar worries emerged respecting the paucity of African American faculty. In the late 1980s, those faculty constituted 4.2 percent of the teachers in ATS theological schools.[12]

Within the Protestant university divinity schools, African American faculty attained a higher representation—by 1991 they accounted for 7.9 percent of the schools' full-time teaching staff. That was still only a small fraction of the total faculty, however, and the sparse numbers of African American students seeking the Ph.D. in theological disciplines seemed to signal a future crisis in the availability of African American theological educators.[13] The statistics were somewhat better for African American students. By the dawn of the 1990s, divinity school recruitment had meant that 12 percent of all students enrolled in the basic ministerial degree program (the Master of Divinity) at all of the divinity schools were African Americans. Some of the divinity schools, such as Union (17 percent) and Drew (16 percent), had surpassed that average considerably and could claim even higher percentages when African American enrollments in programs other than the M.Div. were included.[14]

In terms of the numbers of African Americans on campus, therefore, the answer of the divinity schools to the question of ownership was ambiguous. The statistics, especially those for faculty, indicated that the schools still belonged largely to white Protestantism. The increase in the numbers of African American students, however, betokened at least the possibility of a new answer to the question, one reflected in curricular changes. In tandem with efforts in other parts of the university to include black studies within the curriculum, beginning in the late 1960s all of the divinity schools expanded course offerings in the history of the black churches in America, the ethics of race, black theology and black consciousness, and the African religious heritages. By the 1980s, the divinity schools also had expanded their stated educational missions to include racial diversity. Union Seminary in New York, for example, could with considerable justification describe its task as "fiercely dedicated to the ideal of creating a community from diversity," and Perkins at SMU announced that it was engaged in an effort to "image the inclusiveness of the church," to "resemble in microcosm the diversity of our society."[15] Although few Protestant divinity schools could boast of significant enrollments of Hispanics and other ethnic minorities,[16] all could point to the increases of African Americans in their student bodies as evidence of their dedication to the principle of racial and ethnic diversity.

Still, some faculty expressed grave concerns about the degree to which divinity education continued to be divided between two cultures, black and white. In 1986, while reminiscing about his forty years as a faculty member at the Duke Divinity School, Waldo Beach applauded the long way the school had come since those pre-Sixties days of racial segregation. Duke Divinity had managed to increase its black students to about 10 percent of the school's population. "But we still have a long way to go, with difficult problems, due to our inheritance of two cultural traditions—black and white—two styles of worship, preaching, and understanding of the gospel," Beach claimed. The long separation of black and white Protestant Christianity had resulted in black students feeling that "at Duke they are 'white-washed,' and graduate ill-equipped for the style of ministry expected of them."[17]

Black theologian Gayraud Wilmore has faulted the whole of theological education, Protestant and Roman Catholic alike, for the subordination of black to white religious culture. According to Wilmore, most Protestant and Catholic schools "determine their curricula and institutional priorities according to the needs of the churches that are composed primarily of the middle-aged, middle-class, white descendants of Western European people who live, for the most part, in predominantly white, nuclear family-centered, city-residential, suburban or small-town communities."[18] In the judgment of black ethicist and historian Peter Paris, what has arisen in theological education by virtue of the civil rights struggle is an insistence on the access of African Americans to white educational institutions. No serious thought has been given to the way in which those institutions might be significantly altered by the black presence. "Accordingly, few [schools] have thought about the necessity of reforming themselves in order to meet the needs of African Americans, and virtually none have thought seriously about reciprocal benefits that would be derived from interracial association."[19]

By the end of the 1980s, a strong claim to ownership, a definite sense of shaping the overall aims and programs of divinity education, did not seem to belong to African American faculty and students. It was a lack apparent in American society as a whole. In Paris's words, "Like many other institutions in our society, most theological schools continue to be in a state of transition from a racially exclusive to a racially inclusive future."[20]

The lack of a structurally transforming inclusivity also would trouble feminist theological educators. Born roughly during the same period as the struggle for black rights, contemporary feminism would insist on women's share of the ownership of American institutions of higher education. Like the advocates of African American religion, however, women theological educators would criticize the divinity schools for their failure to incorporate new perspectives into the overall aims and structures of divinity education.

Apart from the question of influence, women had won the right of mere presence in the divinity schools only after prolonged struggles against the resistance of both churches and seminaries. The Theological School in Oberlin, Ohio, was the first American seminary to admit a female student, Antoinette Brown. Although Brown would eventually be ordained in a Congregational church in South Butler, New York, her seminary denied her the right to sit before the Oberlin commencement audience in 1850 or be officially recommended for ordination.[21] In 1872, President William F. Warren informed the trustees of Boston University that the institution would welcome women and men on equal scholarly and professional conditions, and in 1873 the School of Theology at Boston admitted its first female student, Anna Oliver. Yet both Oliver and Anna Howard Shaw, the second woman to graduate from the Boston School of Theology, were denied full rights of ordination in the Methodist Church.[22] At the end of the nineteenth century, women who were allowed ordination in such denominations as the Congregational, Unitarian, Universalist, Baptist, and Disciples found little seminary encouragement and no faculty role models for their ministries, and they usually received less than enthusiastic endorsement from the churches they served.[23]

Nineteenth-century Protestant women created alternatives to the ordained ministry in their missionary societies, charitable organizations, and lay diaconates. Both inside and outside the denominations, women founded missionary organizations, often with funding provided from household budgets and always with programs under female control. Most of those independent missionary societies were folded into denominational, male-dominated bureaucracies in the early twentieth century, and women's missionary training schools which had supported the missions programs were either closed or absorbed into theological seminaries after the First World War. The deaconess movement, although it never flourished in the United States to the same degree as it did in Europe, did provide women in the American Protestant denominations, especially in Methodism, with nonordained ministries in such fields as nursing and social work during the nineteenth and early twentieth centuries.[24]

During the same period, Protestant women were active in extradenominational organizations like the Young Women's Christian Association and the Woman's Christian Temperance Union. Frances E. Willard, who served as president of the WCTU for twenty years, had aspired to the ministry but had been forced to seek an alternative in the WCTU as she found the path of ordination closed to her. Her words of criticism of the churches in 1887 were as impassioned as they were candid:

> When will blind eyes be opened to see the immeasurable losses that the church sustains by not claiming for her altars these loyal, earnest-hearted daughters, who, rather than stand in an equivocal relation to her polity, are going into other lines of work or taking their commission from the evangelistic department of the Woman's Christian Temperance Union?[25]

By the end of the first quarter of the twentieth century, university divinity schools had done little to persuade the churches to enlist the loyal daughters of Protestantism in the ordained ministry, but they had expanded courses of study in Christian social work and religious education, curricula thought to be suitable for women. (A few of the divinity schools were slow to admit female students at all. Harvard Divinity School, which had no division of religious education, resisted the admission of full-time women students until the middle of the twentieth century. Emory chancellor Warren Candler was a staunch opponent of co-education in any branch of his university—he shuddered at the thought of male and female students listening to anatomy lectures in the same classroom—but in 1922 he reluctantly permitted women students to enter the School of Theology. Another sixteen years elapsed before that school awarded a woman a Bachelor of Divinity degree.)[26]

By the 1920s, 14 percent of the students attending all Protestant theological schools were women, an increase from a mere 2 percent at the beginning of the century. The expansion was due largely to increased enrollments in programs in religious or Christian education.[27] Previously a domain of church work monopolized by male clergy, the field of religious education itself expanded during the early twentieth century because of the aggressive promotional activities of the Religious Education Association and because the age was so clearly infatuated with the acquisition of professional expertise.[28] Women began to dominate the profession since unordained women religious educators met less resistance from the local churches than did women who sought ordination and females were willing to work for low salaries.[29] By the late 1940s, two-thirds of all directors of religious education were women, but one survey of the time indicated that most of the male ministers for whom the women worked would have preferred male colleagues![30] Women directors of religious education were thus continuously subjected to the principle of "last hired, first fired" in the churches. Throughout much of the twentieth century conscientious divinity school leaders, although endorsing courses of study in subjects thought to be appropriate to women's roles in the churches, warned of the difficulties that were certain to confront their women students. In 1957, Professor Roland Bainton could observe that female students at his own Yale Divinity School were above-average scholars who nonetheless faced limited fieldwork opportunities, restricted job prospects, and low earning power.[31]

By mid-century increased opportunities for women in ecumenical Protestantism were being created by changes in the denominations and in society at large. The Sixties protests of the women's movement against fixed gender roles and the equal opportunity mandates of affirmative action awakened the churches and the theological schools to demands on the part of women students and professionals. The grounds for those developments, however, had been prepared in previous decades. The spectacular increase in college and university enrollments following the Second World War was not due simply to the return of veterans to college, courtesy of the G.I. Bill. It was due, as well, to a surge in the enrollment of female students. Between 1950 and 1960, women undergraduates attending all institutions of higher education increased 47 percent, and between 1960 and 1970 they increased another 168 percent. By 1987, women comprised 53 percent of the students enrolled in all programs in institutions of higher education in the United States.[32] The age of renewed emphasis on women's rights and consciousness-raising was thus the product, in part, of increased educational opportunities for women in postwar America. And the expanding numbers of postwar women who acquired an undergraduate education resulted in a corresponding increase in the numbers of women who would qualify for graduate training in divinity and the professional ministries in Protestant churches.

The war years themselves had been instrumental in breaking the boundaries of strictly prescribed gender roles. In the absence of men students, who had gone to war, colleges recruited students heavily among women, and American industry turned to the employment of women workers. The ferment of the war years also stimulated the churches to offer women new responsibilities in the ministry. In Europe university-trained women assumed pastoral duties as ordained ministers, and European Christian leaders revolted against the Nazi attempt to limit women's work to *Kinder*, *Kirche*, and *Küche*. At its first meeting in Amsterdam in 1948, the World Council of Churches included an international discussion of the "Life and Work of Women in the Church," and in 1952 women participants in the National Council of Churches, inspired in some measure by their European counterparts, entreated the American Protestant denominations to study the role of women in the churches. These developments, plus the shortage of ministers in a period of rapidly growing church membership, led to the admission of more women into the standard ministerial degree program at the seminaries and to the authorization of ordination of women in more of the Protestant denominations. In 1953 the Disciples of Christ called for the full participation of women in all leadership positions within the denomination; in 1956 the Presbyterian Church in the U.S.A. voted to ordain women and the Methodists granted full conference privileges to ordained women.[33] Eventually the American Lutheran and Episcopal denominations extended ordination to women. By the mid-1970s, all of the denominations in ecumenical or mainline Protestantism were ordaining women.

Changed social conditions, increased educational opportunities, the breaking of the gender barrier for ordination, and the active recruitment of women students by theological schools resulted in the rapid growth in the number of women seminarians beginning in the 1970s.[34] In 1972, 10.2 percent of all students attending ATS theological schools were women; by 1980 that figure had increased to 21.8 percent, and by 1989 to 29.4 percent. During the same time span, women enrolled in the Master of Divinity professional ministerial degree program within the ATS schools increased from 4.7 percent in 1972 to 14.7 percent in 1980 and to 25.9 percent in 1989.[35] By the end of the 1980s, women enrollments in the M.Div. programs of Protestant university divinity schools had outstripped even these ATS averages: nearly half, 48 percent, of the students in those divinity school programs were women, and at some of the schools (Harvard, Union, Yale, and Boston) women exceeded 50 percent of students pursuing the M.Div.[36] Women faculty had not attained the same representation in theological education at the end of the decade, but their increases had been impressive. In 1987, 18.5 percent of all full-time theological school faculty were women, compared to a 1971 figure of 3.1 percent for *all* women theological faculty (many of whom were part-time and adjunct).[37] By 1991, 24.3 percent of all full-time faculty at Protestant university divinity schools were women.[38]

Women theological educators warned that these statistical gains should not be confused with significant structural and curricular change—in fact, the gains seemed to point to the compelling need for such change. In 1980, the "Cornwall Collective," a group of nineteen female theological educators, fifteen from Protestant seminaries and four from Roman Catholic schools, registered their chagrin at the stubborn resistance of theological schools to the *influence* of their women students and faculty. Members of the Collective believed that despite the phenomenal increase in women students over the last few years, female faculty had remained marginal and powerless within the institutions of theological education.[39] "We are not only physically outside, excluded from positions of power such as [full-time] faculty appointments and top administrative positions," the Collective insisted, "we are psychically outside, because our history and experience are not taken seriously." The marginality was apparent, for example, in the theological school curricula: "In introductory courses the works of feminist or liberation theologians still appear at the end of the syllabus as optional choices for papers. However, the perceptions of these theologians have not modified the study or the interpretation of Paul or Aquinas, nor are they regarded as integral to the intellectual and spiritual formation of the minister."[40]

Five years later, the "Mud Flower Collective," composed of seven feminist theologians, complained of the same lack of curricular influence, but with an added sense of frustration. Determined to explore together the difference that their identities as women could make in theological reflection and other facets of theological education, the members of the Collective despaired of their ability to make much impact on the structures of the theological schools.[41] "We doubt that many theological educators with authority to effect significant institutional change will choose to do so, especially to enhance women's lives."[42] In 1991, Candler feminist and liberation theologian Rebecca Chopp echoed the basic outlook of the Mud Flower group. Chopp maintained that the irrefutable achievements of women in theological education over the last few years (the institution of inclusive language, the creation of new areas of research, the opening of new vistas for Christian spirituality) should not obscure the fact that the structures of theological education remained unaltered and that most calls for the reform of theological education ignored "an explicitly feminist agenda."[43]

To the eyes of feminist theological educators, therefore, as well as to those of African American theological faculty, the shape of divinity school education at the end of the 1980s was characterized by statistical gains in social diversity that had not yet significantly transformed the structures and processes of learning.

## PLURALISM: THE NATURE OF THE CHALLENGE

In their diversification of faculties, student bodies, and curricula, the divinity schools had not replicated the ethnic and religious diversity of either American or global Protestantism. Asians and Asian Americans combined, for example, constituted only 5.0 percent of the enrollments in the divinity schools' M.Div. degree program, and Hispanics only 1.7 percent.[44] And despite the increasing presence of evangelicals on many of the divinity school campuses, the schools were susceptible to a charge recently made against Presbyterian seminaries: "the embrace of pluralism" has been a "partial hug" in that the mainline churches and their seminaries have "demonstrated a distinct reluctance to deal with the powerful 'third force' in Christendom—the Pentecostal and charismatic movements transforming Christianity in the third world."[45]

Nevertheless, the presence of blacks and women at the divinity schools and the widespread demand for minority rights flowing from the Sixties raised the issue of pluralism for the schools in a most pointed way. Previously the domain almost exclusively of white males, university divinity schools now contained other groups that would insist on being heard. And the "politics of identity" that the diverse voices expounded throughout the American university produced a cacophony that made earlier attempts to articulate the social aims of education seem like the smoothest of harmonies. American universities and their divinity schools, and indeed American society as a whole, faced a new intellectual challenge to the principle of *e pluribus unum*. For the divinity schools, the challenge definitely had important theological implications.

The new challenge arose in part because of social changes that had occurred in the nation since the end of World War II, and most especially since the Sixties. Increased immigration from Asia, Latin America, and Africa, along with the racial integration of campuses and the spectacular increase in the number of women students, had transformed the student populations of most units of the universities into an assembly of ethnic, cultural, racial, and religious diversity by the end of the 1980s.[46] Yet the newness of the challenge facing divinity school and other university educators did not owe solely to these social changes. As important as the postwar trends were in creating a multicultural society and university, they alone could not account for the heated debates and the curricular alterations that would preoccupy American universities in the 1980s.

The telling shift was less the mere increase of Americans of diverse backgrounds and more the mingling of diverse groups of people with one another in the same space. As Peter Berger has observed, one significant consequence of the culmination of the "modernization process" has been the spread of "cognitive contamination" or the junction of diverse lifestyles, values, and beliefs. Whether through the shrinking of the world in mass communications or through the gathering of diverse peoples in one location (as in cities and universities), the worldview by which one lives becomes exposed to competing worldviews in modern societies. The result is not always an easygoing toleration: rubbing elbows with people of difference creates the potential for intellectual—and sometimes physical—conflict as the plausibility of a taken-for-granted worldview is threatened by that of others.[47]

Multiculturalism's presence in the universities has become a breeding ground for intellectual threat and conflict, and the defenses of the integrity of multicultural difference have involved cultural as well as social components. That is, worldviews, values, and boundary drawing—more than the mere fact of diversity—have been at stake in the university debates over multiculturalism. Divinity school faculty have been required to deal with a pluralism unlike that faced by their predecessors who set out to create a Protestant center for the social order. For all of their genuine animus toward sectarianism and their relative toleration of social diversity, the founders of the divinity schools were driven by a vision that was thoroughly suffused by hopes for the triumph of a Protestant Christian civilization in America and around the globe. The founders and their immediate successors did not, they could not, anticipate the degree to which defenses of diversity would characterize contemporary America. They did not anticipate the manner in which plural*ism*, as well as plural*ity*, would come to mark the society which they sought to shape with their educational strategies.

Pluralism, like all "isms," is an "ideology" in that it connotes an intellectual justification, a defense of a state of affairs. Unlike plurality, pluralism means the defense of the value, rather than simply the fact, of diversity. Richard Mouw and Sander Griffioen have differentiated three kinds of pluralism that emerge (and are sometimes confused) in contemporary discussions: "associational" pluralism, or the defense of the value of the diversity of groups; "contextual" pluralism, or the legitimation of diverse social and cultural contexts; and "directional" pluralism, or the advocacy of the diversity of visions of the good life.[48] The third meaning, because it implies intellectual and moral relativism, has constituted the most serious and the most difficult challenge to those who would take up the task of reflecting on the meaning of pluralism for theological education. All three meanings, however, illuminate the divinity schools' response to social diversity.

Beginning in the 1970s, divinity school leaders advanced convincing arguments for associational and contextual pluralism by offering intellectual justifications of the worth of the Protestant minister's knowledge of the world's diverse religious and ethnic groups and by defending the appropriateness of situating theological education in the contexts of race, class, and gender—contexts that have exerted shaping influences on religious perspectives. The schools created new courses to treat the role of women and minorities in Christianity, they expanded the study of the religions of the world, and they drew upon the social sciences to under-

score the importance of context. Despite the justifiable complaints of female and minority faculty about the failure of those changes to make a
distinct structural difference, divinity school administrators did reveal
a strong commitment to associational and contextual pluralism in their
recruitment of students and faculty.

A sign of the divinity schools' new emphasis on the pluralism of group
and context was apparent in the shift to a new understanding of "culture." Theologians of the previous generation were inclined to view culture in the most general terms: it was the total human construct, or "civilization" as such. In developing his theological system for the correlation
between Christianity and culture, Paul Tillich defined culture as "the totality of forms in which the basic concern of religion expresses itself,"
and Tillich was most concerned to detect the unitary religious drive of
"ultimate concern" in a myriad of cultural forms.[49] In his typology of the
relation between Christianity and culture, H. Richard Niebuhr understood culture as "human achievement," the "world of values," "the total
process of human activity." Niebuhr stated that the concept of culture
with which he worked "cannot be simply that of a particular society such
as the Graeco-Roman, the medieval, or the modern Western.... Hence
culture as we are concerned with it is not a particular phenomenon but
the general one, though the general thing appears only in particular
forms."[50]

It was precisely culture in its specific manifestations, however—the
values, activities, and achievements of particular groups of people—that
would preoccupy the new generation of divinity school scholars. And it
was the plurality of cultures, awakened by the increased diversity of students and faculty within the divinity schools as well as by the quickened
awareness of Christianity's global setting, that would define much of the
new theological task. That task would be viewed not as the correlation
of a generalized notion of Christianity with a generalized idea of culture, but as the situating of particular Christian perspectives within particular cultural contexts—for the sake of a black theology, a feminist theology, a liberation theology. In fact, the new theologians would hold that
the correlation of generalities masked a very specific theological agenda.
The theological reflections of previous generations had been "shaped by
the cultural agenda, both hidden and not so hidden, of a 'North Atlantic'
mind-set within which the concerns of people who are on the margins
of the white male elitist cultural consciousness are also marginalized
theologically."[51] The old theologies of culture, those that sought to correlate culture in general with the grand themes of the Christian tradition,

could only appear to the new generation of thinkers as theologies appropriate to an American culture—and to a faculty and a student body—dominated by white males.

Defenses of the diversity of association and context implicitly raised, but did not always explicitly confront, issues respecting the third meaning of pluralism. How is Christian theology to deal with pluralism as the "diversity of visions of the good life" that give direction to peoples' lives? Is it the task of the theologian to advocate, as well as describe, this diversity of vision? Is one set of values definitive of a superior life direction? How does one reach comparative judgments about the diverse values constitutive of distinctive worldviews? How, in short, does one take the measure of multiculturalism as a disparate set of values by which one understands and lives in the world?

Divinity schools have not been alone in facing such questions. Questions such as these have swirled through the schools' broader university environment since the 1970s. In schools of liberal arts, as well as in some of the professional schools, the defense of multicultural groups and contexts has raised the issue of how the principle of diversity itself should be defended. And that issue in turn has posed the question of whether the defense should entail the refusal to make comparative judgments respecting directional diversity. Most "postmodernism" and much feminism (the latter sometimes influenced by the former) have maintained that any educational pattern that does not honor the value of difference should be suspected of imperialism.* At the core of both postmodernism and feminism resides a resistance to all forms of "foundationalism"—that is, resistance to all appeals to metaphysical principle, all-inclusive context or group, or megatradition—from the conviction that such appeals obscure the distinctive differences springing from social and cultural origins. The safeguarding of difference also frequently has entailed

---

*There is considerable disagreement about the meaning of "postmodernism," even among postmodernists themselves, with much of the disagreement turning on such matters as when postmodernist thought arose, its relationship to modernity and modern thought (especially the Enlightenment), and the degree to which it sprang from changed social and cultural circumstances or from new artistic and literary impulses. As loose as the designation tends to be, it is probably no more vague and prompts no more disputes about links to historical antecedents than other epochal datings such as "modernism," the "medieval world," or the "classical period." In any case, for the purposes of this book "postmodernism" in the American university stands for the posture of those faculty who, influenced by such European intellectuals as Jacques Derrida and Michel Foucault, repudiate universal meanings in any text, historical event, cultural product, social or geographical context, or human subject.

attacks upon the Enlightenment assumption that knowledge can be obtained by a universalizing reason exercised by an objectivizing human
subject who tries to stand above all social and cultural contexts.

The curricular aim of avoiding all objective universalizing is apparent
in the perspective of postmodernist scholar Henry A. Giroux, who has
said, "Critical pedagogy needs a language that allows for competing soli-
darities and political vocabularies that do not reduce the issues of power,
justice, struggle, and inequality to a single script, a master narrative that
suppresses the contingent, the historical, and the everyday as a serious
object of study." This lack of a master script means for Giroux that "curriculum knowledge not be treated as a sacred text but developed as part
of an ongoing engagement with a variety of narratives and traditions that
can be re-read and re-formulated in politically different terms."[52] For
postmodernist feminist scholars Nancy Fraser and Linda Nicholson,
feminist educational theory should be deliberately "non-universalist" in
cast. When focusing on cross-cultural or trans-epochal concerns, "its
mode of attention would be comparativist rather than universalizing, attuned to changes and contrasts instead of 'covering laws.' " In any case,
feminist theory should "replace unitary notions of 'woman' and 'femi-
nine gender identity' with plural and complexly constructed conceptions
of social identity, treating gender as one relevant strand among others,
attending also to class, race, ethnicity, age and sexual orientation."[53]

Committed to turning their non- or antifoundational theory into concrete policy, postmodern and feminist faculty have carried their philosophy of diversity into the classroom and curricular design. Defenses of the
fundamental differences of race, class, ethnic origin, and gender have
informed the creation of new courses of study and have provided the
benchmarks of student learning for these faculty.[54] They also have led to
assaults on the conviction that courses in Western civilization should be
taught from a fixed canon of texts, assaults that have deeply divided faculty at American universities.[55]

Some of the most drastic proposals of postmodern antifoundationalism have appeared among philosophers of religion. According to Williams College religion professor Mark C. Taylor, "theology," or the creative reflective task of religion, is now destined to become "a/theology,"
with Friedrich Nietzsche's announcement of the "death of God" symbolizing the loss of absolute principles in the culture, the absence of fixed
meaning in texts, and the dissolution of the individual self. A/theology
becomes the free-floating interpretation of religious texts and the tracing
of human life in the time of the death of God as a "serpentine wander-

ing" through a process of "mazing grace."[56] For Charles Winquist of Syracuse University, theology becomes a mode of rejoicing in the darkness of the religious imagination during the time of the death of God.[57] Winquist's Syracuse colleague David Miller believes that the loss of a single center holding all things together creates a new polytheism worthy of celebration. The very disparateness of the human self which worships "one God at a time," according to Miller, allows for a fluidity and survival power required for life in a "pluriverse" of diverse meanings characteristic of our fragmented culture.[58]

The radical a/theologies vividly express a philosophical relativism implicit in other forms of contemporary thought that aim to validate social and cultural diversity. The relativism is seldom of the sort sometimes apparent in a privatized American culture—one which holds that all lifestyles are of equal value, that ways of life are matters that one can "get into" as a matter of casual choice.[59] Contemporary justifications of diversity have been too critical of Enlightenment rationalism and universalism, too suspicious of the dominance of males in a culture allegedly committed to objective learning, too wary of an American middle-class mainstream that blurs distinctive heritage, too critical of the static absolutism of previous theological and philosophical systems—to stand accused of endorsing all visions of the good life as of equal value.

Yet how is one to decide among the alternative worldviews and values available in a highly diverse world? Granting that perspectives on the world are usually undeniably political (that is, shaped by the possession or the lack of power), how does one adjudicate among competing worldviews? Admitting that general metaphysical principles and meganarratives can obscure the distinctive particularities of race, class, and gender, how does one evaluate the contributions of distinct groups to a human community? Assuming that certain Enlightenment assumptions about the range of reason and the ability of the human subject to transcend social situations can be wildly fictional and can mask subjective judgments, what forms of discourse are available in the university for discussing phenomena across the boundaries of group identity and private circumstance?

Sometimes those questions are judged to be irrelevant in a culture and at a time in which standpoints transcendent of specific visions are impossible. Such "relativism by default" has produced its fair share of criticism, and the criticism has issued not only from those intellectual and educational conservatives who believe that Western culture's survival depends upon unchanging metaphysical absolutes or upon a fixed collection of literary texts. It has come, as well, from those who have repudiated the fixity of thought or text that has disadvantaged and marginalized large numbers of people in the American university. But the sympathetic critics have warned of the hazards of a relativism by default so frequently at work in postmodernist and feminist theory.

Feminist scholar Elizabeth Fox-Genovese has accused both the radicals in the feminist movement and their conservative antagonists of surrendering to a particularly virulent form of American individualism. The struggle over the canon of literary texts, for example, "consists in a war between those who would preserve the older model of individualism, which rested upon the exclusion of women, African-Americans, and other dispossessed people, and those who would extend the claims of individualism equally to all." In their individualistic designs, both those who defend a fixed, pristine canon and those who seek to demolish any literary canon have lost sight of the way in which liberal education "must, in some measure, be accountable to the collectivity of its constituents—to a 'national community,' however internally variegated and periodically rent." Fox-Genovese recommends holding to the idea of a constantly revised canon of texts that reflects a common if variegated culture.[60]

The desire to maintain an accountability to something larger—and more inclusive—than one's own social, cultural, political, or sexual identity has led other critics to fault the relativism entailed in some forms of academic pluralism. Sixties political radical Todd Gitlin has complained that the identity politics in a leftist faculty's defense of particular interest groups (women, gays, people of color, etc.) has "ceded much political high ground to the right." In the Sixties, the political—and moral—high ground was occupied by the Left's "commonality politics" that, whether on Marxist or liberal democratic grounds, engaged in the civil rights and antiwar movements out of a concern for the "universal values of equality, justice, and peace." Whatever its failures, the older radical politics correctly aspired "to address itself not to particular men and women but to all, in the name of their common standing" as citizens in a democracy.[61] English professor John McGowan, while showing deep sympathy for the nonfoundationalism widespread among the university disciplines, has drawn upon Jürgen Habermas's critique of postmodernism to issue a plea for a "holistic interpretation of contemporary social reality" that appeals to inclusive democratic norms applicable to diverse individual and communal identities.[62]

These and other university scholars, while showing a suspicion of metaphysical absolutes and undifferentiated historical universals that can obscure the principle of difference within multicultural diversity, have implored their colleagues and fellow citizens to discover forms of discourse, modes of learning, and norms of behavior that can be shared across the boundaries of race, class, gender, and ethnic origin.[63] Similar entreaties have appeared on the part of divinity school faculty. In fact, the challenge of how to deal with pluralism of worldview has been particularly pressing for the divinity schools, for much is at stake theologically. The larger discussion of the meaning and value of pluralism has taken place within the university itself, but the discussion has assumed a particular cast for the divinity schools by virtue of their own intellectual tradition.

Christian theology traditionally has maintained that the truth of the Christian faith is a truth appropriate to all people in all manner of circumstances. The different perspectives that had prevailed in America's university divinity schools had never questioned that truth, however imperfectly beheld, is unitary and universal. The liberal theologies of the late nineteenth and early twentieth centuries assumed that the diverse religions of humankind approached one universal truth in distinctive ways. The pursuit of the "scientific method" in the several theological disciplines during the same period presupposed a unitary truth that could be objectively discerned and measured. The ecumenical theology that spread over most of the divinity schools at mid-century never questioned the absolute truth of the Christian faith, only that one Christian denomination's apprehension of that truth was absolute. And the American versions of neoorthodox theology, though they repudiated earlier claims to objective religious science and insisted on divine initiative for establishing human knowledge of the reality and revelation of God, never for a moment hesitated to appeal to a unitary divine truth that transcended the particularities of finite understanding.

In the 1970s and 1980s, divinity school theologians had by no means surrendered the tradition of universalism in the face of multicultural pluralism. Roman Catholic, foundational theologian David Tracy argued that the determination of the truth-status of religious claims in a pluralistic context requires "an explicitly transcendental or metaphysical mode of reflection."[64] Tracy's colleague at the University of Chicago Divinity School, Protestant theologian Langdon Gilkey, was persuaded that "anyone who demotes Christianity to a 'culture religion,' relevant only in its own cultural and historical situation, has already relinquished Christianity and adopted in its place some *other* universalist faith . . . possibly liberal democracy or Marxism." The task of the theologian, according to Gilkey, is to preserve the "sense of universal relevance and truth along

with that clear sense of our own relativity that alone can dissolve imperialism and generate charity."[65] Harvard theologian Gordon Kaufman
made much the same point: the universal "God" (which for Kaufman
is strictly a construct of the human imagination from the materials of
human culture) serves to relativize all finite experiences of and claims to
religious knowledge.[66] Claremont theologian John Cobb proposed that in
the Christ-image Christianity possesses a universal that preserves specific difference: "Christ, as the image of creative transformation [of human
existence], can provide a unity within which the many centers of meaning and existence can be appreciated and encouraged and through which
openness to the other great Ways of mankind can lead to a deepening of
Christian existence."[67]

Despite these theological attempts to reconcile universalism and particularism, Christian universalism as such has come under siege for its
*pretensions* to universal truth. The critics claim that theological universalism has promoted the cultural imperialism of Western, white male thought;
it has obscured distinctive social or ethnic context; and it has marginalized numerous groups of people. The women scholars in the Mud Flower
Collective, for example, express grave reservations about previous (white
male-dominated) theological systems that attempted

> to assess the nature and character of universals, to sweep with broad
> strokes the particularities of personal and specific events; to bypass the
> nitty-gritty pains and problems, whims and fantasies, of the common
> folk in an effort to direct us away from ourselves toward that which can-
> not be known in human experience.[68]

In the place of such abstract universalizing, the feminist scholars call for
theological reflection based on distinctive context and traditions—including the conflicting stories and experiences of women—so that theological education will promote genuinely open dialogue among open-
minded students and teachers.[69]

Criticism of "broad stroke universalizing" has shaped the way in which
the theological disciplines are being reconceived. Feminist biblical scholar
Elisabeth Schüssler Fiorenza, for example, has proposed that instead of
trying to secure some Archimedean point on the whole of the Bible
and its theological interpretations, feminist hermeneutics and theology
should listen "carefully to women's spiritual and religious experiences in
order to define new theoretical frameworks and approaches." Attention
to such experiences would allow women scholars to break into speech in
a patriarchal world and would "make our values, insights, and visions
integral to the theological discourse of the church."[70] According to black

theologian James Cone, the African American religious experience provides a basis for theological reflection that, unlike most Euro-American religious experience, is altogether concrete. "We have developed a spirituality that plants our feet firmly on this earth, because the God of our faith demands that we bear witness to the humanity of all by refusing to adapt ourselves to the exploitation that the few inflict on the many." The black theology springing from concrete black spirituality "has helped black churches to recover the authenticity of their faith so that they will not go woolgathering in a nebulous kingdom on high and forget their practical responsibility to live obediently in this world, liberating the poor from the misery of poverty."[71]

To the eyes of some divinity school educators, an overwhelming emphasis on the distinctiveness of association and context can result in a relativism that abandons concern for the public good. Harvard Divinity School dean Ronald Thiemann, a nonfoundational theologian who has repudiated any appeal to a fixed metaphysical or moral realm,[72] has nonetheless called for a public theology that transcends the limits of group and context in its appeal to civic values:

> We must find a way between the cultural and religious imperialism that would define the interests and values of one group as the common good, and the moral relativism that would assert that all values and ethical stances are nothing more than the opinions or personal preferences of those who hold them. The former position is a denial of pluralism, the latter a denial that we can share anything in common even as we acknowledge our differences.[73]

As manifestly uncomfortable as many contemporary divinity school faculty have been with nebulous universalizing, none has been willing explicitly to deem all life-shaping worldviews as being of equal value. To that extent they would seem to be open to the kind of public theology that Thiemann proposes. In any case, faculty demands for inclusion of particular narratives and experiences in theological education have involved criticisms of other particularities, and the criticisms have implied an appeal to categories more encompassing than those of race, class, gender, or ethnic origin. Feminist theological educators, for example, have faulted patriarchal assumptions prevalent in the history of theological education and have summoned faculty to transcend such assumptions.[74] And liberation theologians, eager to teach their students the theological significance of the world's disadvantaged classes, have implied that Christianity is a religion more closely connected with the suffering and defeated, rather than with the comfortable and successful, people of the globe.[75]

In addition, nonfoundational theologians have explicitly advocated certain universal values and virtues that can promote and preserve the distinctive voices springing from associational and contextual pluralism. Thus the members of the Mud Flower Collective have recommended engaging in a form of theological education "that is foundationally oriented toward justice and that is relational in character." Such an appeal to the universals of justice and relationship need not be abstract and general; they can be joined "with our experience of ourselves in relation" and can remain accountable to particular people—to "black and Hispanic women and those white women who are struggling against racial, sexual, and economic injustice."[76] Theologian Rebecca Chopp has suggested that the great variety of feminist perspectives can coalesce on the grand themes of justice, freedom, and humanity without obscuring the variety of perspective: "What the variety of discourses of feminist theologies share in common is the desire to speak of freedom, to envision new ways of being human, to speak of the desires of women, and to speak of what women have known, what have been women's burdens, and what woman has experienced as the 'other' of man."[77] James Cone has maintained that once black Christian theologians have appropriated their own African American heritage and appreciated their own sense of black integrity, they can identify with the struggles for freedom on the part of the oppressed people around the world and can defend the humanity of all people, including whites.[78]

Thus the widespread uneasiness with the type of universalism that breeds abstract generalities has not meant an epidemic abandonment of universalism as such among divinity school faculty. In addition to those thinkers like Gilkey, Kaufman, and Cobb who have appealed to the traditional Christian universal truths of God and Christ, others have invoked the social and moral ideals of justice, freedom, open human relationships, and common civic virtues. As one critic has noted, the intellectual grounds for the nonfoundationalists' turn to moral universals have not always been clearly justified.[79] Yet a quest has been undertaken for forms of universalizing that would honor the perspectives and experiences of peoples previously excluded from Protestant theological thinking. A new generation of divinity school thinkers has been seeking a mode of reflection upon the diversity of worldviews that would preserve the integrity of associational and contextual difference. That task has had little to build upon from the one hundred-year history of the divinity schools. The demography of the schools and their university homes—and of America as a whole—has changed dramatically since the founders expounded their educational evangel. Pluralism has become a powerful social and cultural force that requires new intellectual responses.

## THE PREPONDERANT REALITY OF PLURALISM

The preponderant cultural and social reality with which university divinity schools have had to contend in the late twentieth century is American pluralism, not American secularism. The assertive diversity of religious and cultural worldviews, not the marginalization or elimination of sacred worldviews, constitutes the heart of the challenge. In many parts of the world, especially in Northern Europe, there has been abundant proof that what the great social theorist Max Weber called the "disenchantment of the world" has followed from the modernization process. Reliance on detached scientific thought, rational planning, and technological control has resulted in the widespread disappearance of religious worldviews and the decline of traditional religious beliefs and practices among masses of people. In other areas of the globe, for example in Latin America, North America, and many parts of the Middle East, the secularization thesis simply does not apply. Religious people there show immense capacities both for adjusting their religious perspectives to modern developments and for re-enchanting their worlds as a countermovement to modern technological reason.[80]

The contemporary American scene is too shot through with religion, traditional and otherwise, and too many of the American people inhabit worlds defined by premodern religious beliefs, to support the thesis that the most pressing challenge facing the schools is the secularization of the national culture.[81] Furthermore, proponents of the identity politics of multiculturalism, despite their rejection of metaphysics and their suspicion of all universals, have been too passionate in their commitments, too earnest in their criticisms of the perspectives of others, and too eager to preserve worldviews within the boundaries of group and context to be treated as anything other than advocates of functional equivalents of traditional religious values and virtues. Pluralism—pluralism especially in the sense of justifications of a plurality of life's directions—characterizes the American scene and presents the greatest intellectual trial for university divinity schools.

Divinity school faculty and administrators have been induced to take up the challenge by the new diversity within American universities, and specifically by the increased numbers of African Americans and women within their own ranks. For the first time in their histories, university divinity schools have witnessed, and have been required to contemplate, the social diversity of American society represented within their own institutional boundaries. For the first time also they have encountered the clamor of diverse voices demanding to be heard in the university environment and in society at large. The reality of pluralism thus has presented an intellectual as well as a social summons. In responding, divinity school intellectuals have faced the difficult task of honoring the integrity of diverse worldviews and their contexts while probing their own religious traditions and the democratic culture for values, views, and social goals constitutive of the common good.

William Rainey Harper and other visionaries had set about to deal with America's increasing diversity by trying to create a Protestant Christian center for American society. The late twentieth-century heirs of Harper and the other founders of divinity schools were faced by multiple centers in a much more radically plural America. The heirs have had no hopes for, nor even any interest in, the construction of a unified religious empire. At best, they have hoped for participation in and preservation of a commonwealth of diversity. A similar hope would emerge in their views of the role of the divinity school within the contemporary university.

# CHAPTER IX

■

## *The Challenge of the Multiversity*

Those responsible for the founding of divinity schools had something grander in view than the perpetuation of the seminary heritage. They believed that, unlike stand-alone denominational seminaries which took their bearings strictly from the creeds and practices of the churches, the divinity schools should look also to the modern university for a definition of educational mission.

As the locus of a constantly expanding new learning, the university promised the creation of an educated ministry from the materials of specialized knowledge. As the place where practical skills could be honed on the toughest professional standards, the university promised a ministry that accorded with the values of a professionalized society. As a veritable city unto itself, the university could provide a breadth of perspective for ministers that comes from mingling with persons of diverse views and backgrounds. In the language of the nondenominational institutions, a university professional education in divinity avoided "narrow sectarianism" and thus prepared ministers to deal with a diversified modern world that required openness of mind, flexibility of spirit, and ecumenical collaboration. For the Methodist schools, a divinity education set within a university context of intellectual and social diversity was true to the Methodist legacy of tolerance of diverse views, and it promoted the movement of Methodism into an American middle-class, professional mainstream.

Yet the founders were persuaded that the divinity schools could do more than simply take their places alongside other professional schools in the university. They believed that the schools could assume a special role in American culture. In the words of the financial founder of Duke University in the 1920s, the ministry—along with law, education, and medicine—was "most in the public eye, and by precept and example can do most to uplift mankind."[1] Or as the chief benefactor of the Perkins School of Theology was to say twenty years later, he preferred to use his

*Photo courtesy of the Drew University Archives.*

millions to build up a theological school instead of a school of business because "the future will be determined by the ministry of the church."[2] Surely the task of uplifting and shaping human civilization as such applied also to one of civilization's chief institutions, the modern university. That more specific task fell, of course, to faculty and administrators rather than to millionaire patrons, and divinity school educators were not slow to articulate the terms of the challenge.

The university, quite as much as the social order, seemed to demand a unifying influence, and divinity school leaders were prepared to argue that their schools were particularly well-suited to provide an integrative center. Whether through the unification of learning in theological encyclopedia, the grounding of knowledge in the assumptions of faith, or the unveiling of religion's pervasive presence, the divinity school seemed poised to unify the modern multiversity. That high sense of calling would eventually be eroded by the adamantine realities of the university's structural and intellectual multiplicity, and it would be replaced by more cautious and realistic views of the role of the divinity school in its university home. But during most of their history, the divinity schools felt challenged to provide a center of learning within an internally divided university.

## SOME LESSONS IN A CRISIS

In 1890, Drew Theological Seminary received for installation in its new library a beautiful, round, stained glass window. The window was a gift of the widow of John B. Cornell, the generous patron for whom the Romanesque library building was named. The nine and one-half-foot rose window, manufactured in England from a design by Henry Holliday, portrayed Theology as the Queen of the Sciences surrounded by her attendants, the moral virtues of Faith, Hope, Charity, and Humility and the intellectual disciplines of Philosophy, Science, and Art.[3]

In 1890, Drew had not yet become a university in any sense; it was a school of theology only. (A college of liberal arts was added in 1928, and a graduate school in 1955.) Yet when they envisioned the seminary's purpose, the founders of Drew had placed the school in a special relation to the disciplines of the modern university. The charter for the school stated that the trustees could "organize faculties of arts, law, literature, and medicine, at such time as the said corporation may see fit."[4] Drew's first president, John McClintock, was the school's teacher of the course on theological encyclopedia and the author of a substantial text on that theological discipline which sought to unify all branches of human knowledge. McClintock also created a five-year course of study for those who had not attended college so that the seminary could connect theology with the "elementary branches of learning."[5] The rose window captured the aspirations of Drew and many other divinity schools during their early years: theological learning should lie at the center of—some would say it should exercise the reigning command within—the larger field of human learning. In the late 1960s, the Theological School at Drew became embroiled in a crisis which called into question the central role of theological education in the university, not to say the grand medieval view of theology as queen.

The event that triggered the crisis was the summary dismissal of the Theological School dean, Charles W. Ranson, on January 9, 1967, by University president Robert Fisher Oxnam with the (non-unanimous) authorization of the University's board of trustees. The firing of Ranson led to a series of protest marches, sit-ins, and boycotts of classes by Drew's divinity students. It also provoked public remonstrances by an outraged Theological School faculty and counter-charges by members of the board and by President Oxnam. It resulted in investigations by the Middle States Accrediting Association and by a special committee of the Division of Higher Education of the Methodist Church, extensive coverage by the secular and the religious press, and a heated dispute among University parties over matters financial and constitutional.[6]

The crisis took a heavy toll on the Theological School. In 1967, the School's faculty assured students and alumni that they would "see the issues through," but before the expiration of that year faculty resignations began to pour in to the president's office. By 1968, fourteen resignations included some of Drew's most distinguished professors: Karlfried Frölich and Howard Kee in New Testament and early church studies, Bernhard Anderson and Lawrence Toombs in Old Testament, Franz Hildebrandt and Gordon Harland in church history, and John Godsey in systematic theology. A solid core of eminent faculty remained, which included Will Herberg, Bard Thompson, George Kelsey, and Nelle Morton, but James Ault, who was appointed dean of the Theological School in 1968, was faced with the necessity of quickly recruiting and appointing a host of new faculty members if the School were to stay open for business. Enrollments suffered as prospective students hesitated to choose a school with such an uncertain future. For the academic year 1968–69, students seeking admission to the various ministerial professional programs combined had sunk to a total of twenty-one. During the following academic year, admissions were back up to a total of eighty-seven.[7] The Theological School at Drew University had not been floored by the crisis, but it had been sent reeling and staggering for two years. The blows had come from many directions.

Dean Ranson had been fired principally because he and his faculty had gone over the head of President Oxnam on an issue respecting finances and appointments. Ranson had demanded several faculty appointments, including the filling of a senior slot created by the death of prominent systematic theologian Carl Michalson in a plane crash in 1965. When Oxnam balked, claiming lack of money for the level of appointments requested and refusing to use an endowment originally intended for the Theological School but since assigned by the trustees to the general University endowment, twenty faculty members appealed directly to the board with Ranson's blessing. With authorization from the board's executive committee, Oxnam asked for Ranson's resignation, but Ranson insisted on receiving the request in writing. The faculty communicated to the board their lack of confidence in the president and asked to meet with the trustees in special session. When Ranson finally did receive the request for his resignation in writing, he insisted on clarification of the charges against him. The board then voted to dismiss the dean when he was not present. The ire of faculty and students was further provoked when President Oxnam appointed an acting dean without consultation with the faculty.[8]

The Drew University administration and the spokesmen for the board construed the direct appeal of the theological faculty to the board as a break with University protocol. They also judged the faculty to be arrogant and overbearing in the assessment of their own importance in the University, and they believed the dean's stubborn position of advocacy to be a refusal to acknowledge the larger needs of the Drew community.[9] The Theological School faculty, on the other hand, alleged that the summary dismissal of the dean was a serious breach of due process, and they found President Oxnam to be uncommunicative, unclear about financial policies, and fundamentally unsympathetic to the needs of theological education.[10] Outside investigators spread the blame for the Drew crisis as they noted such problems as the lack of participation of many trustees in board decisions, inadequate provisions for faculty governance, unclear cost assessments of units of the University, insufficient communication among faculty, trustees, and administrators, and the decision of theological students and faculty to make University problems public.[11] Quite apart from the question of blame, the crisis at Drew posed some large issues respecting the role of divinity in the life of a university. Those issues had begun simmering at Drew some ten years before the firing of Ranson.

In 1958, the faculty of the Theological School had voted unanimously to send to the trustees through University President Fred Holloway a statement of concern about the role of the School at Drew. The statement celebrated the advantages of the Theological School's existence within a university environment: direct engagement with faculty representing diverse fields of knowledge, the presence of the academic standards of a modern university, access to strong library resources, and participation in university-wide cultural programs. Yet the statement also pointed to some perceived perils. Above all, the faculty expressed worries about "the possible emergence of a university administration which either does not understand or is not in sympathy with the nature and goal of theological education." Operating from the perspective of Christian faith, standing responsible for the training of intellectuals and ministers for the church, and taking God as its chief subject matter, the School could not expect the University as a whole to share its mission. Therefore, the Theological School should be viewed as "relatively independent" of the University and should be assigned a "considerable degree of autonomy" in its recruitment, structure, and finances. Respecting the matter of capital, the faculty statement called for "clarification of the place of the Theological School within the financial structure of the university, and particularly for some dissipation of the cloud that hangs over the Wendell estate [the gift that was eventually assigned to the University endowment fund]." Moreover, the theological faculty requested regular reporting of income on the School's investments, lower overhead charges, and a "secure foundation of independent assets."[12]

Many of these same requests were renewed in 1962 to President Oxnam, Drew University's first non-ordained president.[13] There is no evidence that either set of requests was taken up formally by the trustees.[14] In any event, long before the crisis year of 1967, the faculty of Drew Theological School had grown anxious about their standing in the University. Previously an independent theological seminary with visions of university relations, the School now faced the prospects of loss of autonomy and even marginalization within a university of greater internal diversity. The actions of President Oxnam only confirmed the faculty's deep, long-festering fears.

Robert Fisher Oxnam, son of Methodist bishop and civil libertarian G. Bromley Oxnam, had been brought from Pratt Institute to Drew in 1960 with a charge from the trustees to shape a single university from the three schools of liberal arts, theology, and graduate studies. Oxnam entered a situation in which the Graduate School drew most of its faculty from the Theological School, an arrangement that led the theological faculty to complain about "add-on" teaching loads and to agitate constantly for a separate, well-financed budget for the graduate division. Recruitment efforts, begun in 1949 by Theological School dean Clarence Tucker Craig and continued in the 1950s by his successor Bernhard W. Anderson, resulted in a theological faculty of strong national, in some cases international, reputation. In the early 1960s, however, undergraduate enrollments at Drew rose steadily, whereas seminary enrollments leveled off. By 1965, the theological faculty were predicting that Graduate School enrollments might soon equal enrollments in the Theological School. Under President Oxnam the College of Liberal Arts flourished, as three new undergraduate dormitories and a host of new undergraduate programs were added.[15]

The president maintained, even during the height of the crisis, that he desired a first-rate Theological School at Drew, but he insisted that the School must pursue its mission of excellence within definite budgetary limits and with a recognition of the development needs of the University as a whole.[16] The demands of the Theological School for "relative independence," a "considerable degree of autonomy," and a greater share of the financial resources were viewed as unreasonable and parochial by the president and his advisors—and by spokesmen for the undergraduate college.

In its report on the Drew crisis, the special committee of the Methodist Church congratulated the College of Liberal Arts for acting with "commendable restraint."[17] Restraint certainly did characterize the public position of College representatives, but the Methodist committee should have known that back-room academic politics often prove to be an altogether different matter. In 1967, the dean of the College advised President Oxnam in a memorandum that "the Board must decide—and quickly—whether to put its emphasis on the College." Such an emphasis would entail siphoning off no more University funds for a Graduate School dominated by theological faculty. It would also involve turning over to the Methodist Church the future funding of the Theological School, directing University fund-raising efforts to the needs of the College of Liberal Arts, and focusing on the expansion of College facilities. The College dean showed no compassion for the Theological School: if the report of the Methodist committee were correct in declaring that the crisis had destroyed public and churchly confidence in Drew, "then the Theological School must largely stand convicted of aiding in its own ruin. It can only be hoped that the public relations tragedy we have witnessed has not wrecked the ability of other entities at Drew to garner funds."[18]

The vice president of Drew also showed little sympathy for what he took to be a petulant Theological School faculty. In 1958 he expressed to the president of the University dismay at the desire of "Dean Anderson and his Yale oriented faculty" to achieve autonomy at Drew. He believed then, as he would believe ten years later, that the Theological School was dominated by prima donnas who were more concerned about their national reputations than about the good of the University as a whole, and he insisted that Drew University in its entirety, not just the Theological School, should stake out a claim as a "liberal Protestant university with a distinctive emphasis upon values." As he said in a report to the Drew senate in 1968, he was convinced that there was financial support forthcoming for a university that adopted such a mission: "I am persuaded that there are men and women of wealth—both Methodist and non-Methodist—who would support an institution that tried to make its church affiliation mean something—that dared to be different."[19]

In an exceptionally fair-minded review of the Drew situation in the midst of the crisis, James M. Wall wrote in Methodism's *Christian Advocate* that some crucial educational issues had been raised that cut deeper than the power politics, personality conflicts, and battles over money so apparent in the fracas. Wall proposed that although Drew was an unusual university in that it consisted only of two basic units, a college and a divinity school, the debate raging on its campus embodied on a small scale questions by no means peculiar to Drew: "If the university becomes more 'secular'—focuses more on undergraduate education, and all the foundation and federal money *that* implies—what will happen to the church-oriented seminary? Can it maintain its graduate theological reputation as long as major money decisions are in the hands of the total university?" Wall believed that the largest issue at stake in the Drew crisis was this: "What is the place of a theological seminary on a university campus? The question belongs to every seminary and to the university of which it is a part."[20]

That series of questions had long plagued American universities and their divinity schools. Prior to the crisis at Drew, other divinity schools had approached the brink of extinction as their universities pursued financial and programmatic policies inimical to the schools' future existence.

During the first few years of the twentieth century, Vanderbilt University's chancellor James Kirkland pressed Vanderbilt's Biblical Department to become self-supporting in order to stop that division's drain on the University's endowment. When Vanderbilt eventually won independence from the Methodist Church through a court decision in 1914, the Biblical Department, which renamed itself the (interdenominational) School of Religion, was devastated for a long period in its finances and enrollments as the Methodist Church withdrew support.[21] In the late

1940s and early 1950s, Harvard Divinity School faced the prospect of eradication and of having its resources transferred to a department of religion in the Faculty of Arts and Sciences. James B. Conant, president of Harvard at the time, had little use for organized religion and even less use for a divinity school at Harvard. The Divinity School secured its future at Harvard only after a new president, Nathan M. Pusey, endorsed the importance of the school and raised a million dollars from John D. Rockefeller, Jr., for its revitalization.[22] In the mid-1950s, the University of Southern California, eager to demonstrate its nonsectarian status in order to finance its Medical School and obtain government monies for other units of the University, formally declared its independence from Methodist control and refused to recognize its School of Religion as a Methodist institution. Those decisions resulted in the Methodists' relocation of the school's faculty to Claremont in 1957.[23]

Such crises illustrate how divinity schools have been continuously required to prove their distinctive role in the university, and they demonstrate how that role has been closely entangled with matters of money, larger university aims, and the relative power of different schools on campus. Long before the emergence of these crises, however, visions of the overall purpose of the university divinity school had emerged, visions that assigned the school a unifying and integrative role within the academy. The rose window in the Drew library symbolized an enduring, widespread hope for divinity education in the university.

## VISIONS OF UNITY

In the nineteenth century, courses in theological encyclopedia offered at divinity schools aimed to unify human knowledge by "theologizing" it—that is, by interpreting all branches of human learning as aspects of the knowledge of God. By the time of the First World War, the formal "arrangement of the sciences and knowledges of men in order" through courses in theological encyclopedia had disappeared from the divinity schools' curriculum.[24] The goal of theologizing human knowledge, however, had by no means disappeared. Beginning in the 1930s, as divinity school leaders tended to conceive of theology as the unifying core of divinity education itself, theological reflection seemed to promise the unification of a university's fragmented intellectual scene. In some cases, theology was candidly recommended as a unifier while fully decked out as queen.

A sustained argument for a contemporary version of theology as queen of the university sciences was developed by William Adams Brown, professor of theology at Union Theological Seminary in New York, eminent leader in the ecumenical movement, member of the governing board of his alma mater, Yale University, and author of what is still the most extensive assessment of theological education in the United States. Brown's *The Case for Theology in the University*, published in 1938, was a response to Chicago president Robert Maynard Hutchins's Storrs Lectures at Yale. Brown agreed with Hutchins's indictment of the chaos of university education, a condition due to the absence of any unifying educational principle. But Brown faulted Hutchins for overlooking theology's capacity as educational unifier.

Hutchins had insisted that theology, once the proud queen of the medieval university, was now but a "feeble imitator" of the modern sciences shaped by vocationalism and empiricism and so was "degraded to the bottom of the educational hierarchy." Furthermore, as a science "based on revealed truth and articles of faith," theology represented an orthodoxy inappropriate to the "rational and practical order for the higher learning of today." Greek metaphysics, on the other hand, presented an appropriate unifying intellectual tradition for the present. As the consideration of first principles and causes, metaphysics could constitute the highest, unifying science that breeds wisdom, the proper aim of higher education as such.[25]

Brown responded that Hutchins had confused all theology with dogmatic theology. If theology were construed in its broader meaning as "the philosophy of the Christian religion," then theology could provide a unifying force within the fragmented American university—a point that Hutchins conceded in his preface to Brown's book.[26] In Brown's view, Christian philosophical theology brings a concreteness to the quest for first principles lacking in metaphysics. Like metaphysics, theology uncovers "the common assumptions which are necessary to any intelligible account of the universe."[27] Since Christian theology takes its orientation from a God represented in specific traditions and symbols that address the needs of humankind, however, it is superior to Greek metaphysics in the concreteness of its statement of first principles:

> The symbols of metaphysics are for the most part abstractions. They are general concepts, like being, substance, etc. The symbols of theology are concrete, drawn from the common life of man. Aristotle could talk about God, but he could not show man God. But when the writer of the Fourth Gospel would have men know what God is like he pointed them to Jesus. . . .
> This emphasis upon the concrete is a natural result of the fact that

theology approaches the study of the ultimate reality from the angle presented by religious experience.[28]

Brown believed that the theology of first principles, rooted in specific Christian symbols and nourished by tangible religious experience, was not to be confined to the domain of the divinity school. Professors of law, medicine, history, and literature, as well as the teachers of the nation's ministers, should promote in their instruction the philosophical insight springing from a recognition of the centrality of religion to human life and the potentially unifying force of the Christian philosophy within the life of the university.[29] And although the Christian philosophy could be much more directly promoted in the nation's Protestant and Catholic schools, it could also find a place within state universities as teachers in those universities sought to acquaint students "with the answers which have been given to these problems [of human existence] by the representatives of the different religions, and not least by the Christian."[30]

Clearly, however, it was a Christian theology of the kind taught by Brown himself at Union—a theological perspective sustained in the setting of Protestant divinity education—that he believed stood the best chance of unifying an intellectually fragmented university. And if it were objected that he thereby made university education turn on an axis of one religion, Brown was willing to defend the superiority of the Christian religion:

> If it be said that Christianity is not the only religion—there are others one might choose—it is enough to say that all organization involves choice. If choose we must, Christianity furnishes us with our most natural point of departure. Not only is it the religion which as a matter of fact lies at the heart of our Western culture; not only is it the religion which has in the past furnished democracy with its religious basis; it is the religion which through its missionary activity, bringing it into touch with all the faiths of mankind, furnishes the most convenient introduction to the study of those living issues with which every philosophy worthy of the name must deal.[31]

Brown mounted his defense of theology's role in the university as an explicit call for the restoration of theology's queenly status.[32] In the 1940s and 1950s, Henry P. Van Dusen, president of Union Seminary and like his colleague Brown an avid ecumenist, could still invoke the appropriateness of the queenly image of theology for the modern American university. As Van Dusen said in his presidential inaugural address in 1945, the whole of the human order "aches from inner stress and conflict" and cries out for a principle of coherence. Within institutions of higher education, theology is called to provide the unifying center as queen of the sciences:

> ... theology, a true knowledge of God, *is* the Queen of the Sciences—not because the Church says so or because superstition or tradition have so imposed it upon human credulity, or because it was so recognized in one great age of learning; but because of the nature of Reality, because, if there be a God at all, He must be the ultimate and controlling Reality through which all else derives its being; and the truth concerning him, as best man can apprehend it, must be the keystone of the ever-incomplete arch of human knowledge.[33]

Five years later, Van Dusen developed the same point in his Rockwell Lectures at Rice Institute, a preeminent scientific and technological university in Houston, Texas. Van Dusen told his Rice audience that a badly fragmented university curriculum would never attain coherence until truth is recognized as organic and every part of knowledge is seen in relation to God as the Unifier of organic truth. Although Van Dusen denied that his recommendation meant that "every lecture room should be transformed into a church and each teacher into a preacher," God as the unifying principle should be assumed in every class and pointed out in some, and each educational institution should publicly acknowledge the "Divine Mind without which its enterprise could not take place."[34]

By no means all mid-century pleas for theological learning as unifier installed theology as queen or even insisted on God as the organic center of all learning. Yet if other spokesmen for divinity education did not expect the moral virtues and the human sciences to gather submissively at theology's feet, they did believe that theology could offer the university some sage advice and some paradigmatic illustrations respecting the unity of human learning. The divinity school could thus become a model for the university as a whole.

That was a view developed in the early 1950s by theologian Bernard M. Loomer, dean of the Divinity School at the University of Chicago. Loomer shared with Chicago president Robert M. Hutchins an abhorrence of the fragmentation characteristic of American higher education. Loomer was persuaded that the American university had become a collection of independent departmental fiefdoms, with little communication across departmental lines, and university administrators had ceased to provide intellectual leadership as they had become managers of a corporation according to the principles of efficiency and compromise.[35]

Unlike Brown and Van Dusen, however, Loomer did not look to theology as restored monarchy for the unification of the university. He proposed, instead, that *religion* as the core of human life and the source of wisdom about everyday experience was *in fact* a pervasive fact of culture and if so treated by diverse disciplines could begin to bring some unity to the university. Rather than being installed as a reigning potentate, religion should be uncovered in the diverse intellectual domains of the university.

The unveiling would attest to the fact that all academic inquiries "covertly contain implicit religious outlooks operating in the form of assumptions, presuppositions, methodologies, and guiding principles." One could not expect all intellectuals within the university to recognize the religious worldviews and ultimate values implicit in their assumptions, however. That burden inevitably would fall upon religious intellectuals who "must not only know their own subject matter as competently as other faculty members know theirs; they must also know their subject matter in relation and as relevant to other disciplines." And it is the responsibility of the university divinity school—or the department of religion in some situations—to become "the university within the university," exemplifying the quest for operative religious assumptions within the disciplines and the search for substantial relations among the disciplines. Loomer did admit that no divinity school on the scene had picked up the task he described, but that fact itself accounted for the central problem in the university. "Divinity schools are admittedly weak intellectually, morally, and religiously. Universities are therefore correspondingly weak in these respects."[36]

Although stated in less ambitious—and less abrasive—terms than Loomer's, similar claims were made by other divinity school leaders for their schools after mid-century. Reflecting upon the possible role of theology in the life of Southern Methodist University, Perkins theologian and church historian Albert C. Outler eschewed in 1961 the notion that theology should try to institute any kind of imperialist reign in the university: "Theology never had a legitimate claim to be the *queen* of the sciences. Theologians deserve no preferred status amongst their colleagues—which is just as well since there is no disposition anywhere I know of to grant it." Nevertheless, the theological disciplines can pose across the life of the university questions that are germane to other fields of learning. "Among these are the questions about the unity of knowledge, the primacy of humane values, the issues of salvation and damnation—or, if you blanch at such terms, then the questions about authentic and inauthentic existence." While acknowledging that Perkins had not yet performed such a function at SMU, Outler believed that it could assume the task and, as the poser of fundamental, field-spanning questions, could contribute decisively to SMU's becoming a *uni*-versity.[37]

Similar hopes were expressed in 1969 by Walter Muelder, dean and professor of social ethics at the Boston University School of Theology, who maintained that theological reflection in the various disciplines of his school indicated "a commitment to integrated or wholistic thinking" that could serve as a "guardian of truth as a 'whole' from enemies both inside and outside the campus."[38] And in 1984, John Deschner, the Lehman Professor of Christian Doctrine at Perkins, proposed that "a good school of theology can be a conscience for the university." By "conscience" Deschner meant not an institutional moral magistrate but "*conscientia*—a knowledge-with, a knowing-alongside whatever else is known, a *con-scientia* of Gospel and human learning which generates dialogue" among the intellectual disciplines. Such knowledge promotes an intellectual *uni*-verse and liberates all humane thinking for the pursuit of the one truth in its various manifestations.[39]

By the 1960s, therefore, divinity school faculty who reflected upon the role of their schools within the larger university environment had not abandoned the hope that their educational enterprise could make important contributions to the unification of the university. But they had forsworn the language of theological imperialism in their articulation of that hope. Some divinity school leaders continued to insist that their schools, by virtue of the holistic thinking entailed in their intellectual tasks, were positioned to provide leadership for overcoming the fragmentation of knowledge. Yet they repudiated the attempt of the theological encyclopedists to connect all knowledge to the knowledge of God, and they forsook the effort of the philosophical theologians to demonstrate the first principles germane to all intellectual inquiry. By the 1960s, interpreters of the role of divinity studies within the university were more cautious in their recommendations, less grandiose in their views of what they could contribute to the life of the university, and more inclined to speak of collaborating with colleagues in other units of the university for the promotion of the unity of human knowledge and the enhancement of open inquiry.

That more cautious vision of divinity studies' contribution to the university already had been expounded by Yale's H. Richard Niebuhr in 1955. At that time, Niebuhr judged the notion of "theology as queen" to be an irresponsible, inaccurate historical reconstruction of theology's special place in the university. The belief that in the Middle Ages "academic lions and lambs lived in peace under the benign government of

Queen Theology; and all the faculties—of schools as well as of men—worked together for good" was a fabrication born of nostalgia for a mythical golden age. Truthfully, it was the church, not theology, that governed medieval universities, and theology was more servant than queen.[40]

Niebuhr also insisted that the "radical monotheism" of the Christian faith forbade the overlordship of any human institution for the sake of order quite as much as it proscribed a lazy toleration of proliferating, unconnected intellectual diversity. Niebuhr believed that radical monotheism or utter commitment to one God entails the rejection of all human claims (including theology's) to a special, absolute, domineering knowledge, but it also points to a transcendent truth approachable from different perspectives by those who love truth intellectually. Theology and the theological school thus were seen by Niebuhr as servants of truth along with other perspectives and divisions in the university: "In a university in which the radically monotheistic idea comes to expression, the various departments, schools, and methods are related to each other in mutual service, including the service of mutual limitation and creative conflict."[41]

Niebuhr's understanding of the theological school as servant, of theology as collaborator with other disciplines in a common quest for truth, and of the need for the mutual limitation of intellectual perspectives still offered the hope that divinity schools could help promote unity in the university. But Niebuhr offered no plea for a privileged status for the schools themselves in the pursuit of that unity. Niebuhr's views would echo in later proposals—in the recommendation of Albert Outler, for example, that theologians should press fundamental questions across the university, and in the proposal of John Deschner that schools of theology should promote "knowledge with" other forms of knowledge. Ideas similar to Niebuhr's would also appear in the suggestions of theological educators in the late 1980s and early 1990s. They were evident in Dean Ronald Thiemann's call for Harvard Divinity School faculty to join colleagues in other disciplines and professions for the "construction of a new vision for American public life" and in Joseph Hough's proposal of interdisciplinary university teaching and research devoted to the promotion of "discourse about the common good."[42]

Niebuhr's ideas about theology in the university marked a decisive shift in the visions of unity emerging from the divinity schools. Not only had the hope for theology's "return" as queen of the sciences been scuttled. Not only had the conviction that the knowledge of God could unify all knowledge been abandoned. There had disappeared, as well, the old vision of the divinity school as somehow occupying the center of American university life and from that position dispensing—if not as royalty, certainly as one potent force within a democracy—the unifying perspective of theological wisdom.

The replacement of that aspiration with the cautionary, limited view of the divinity school as a possible coconspirator with other units of the university for the attainment of common perspective and common purpose finds much of its explanation in the events of late twentieth-century America. The increasing student diversity within the university made claims about the complete coalescence of intellectual perspective appear altogether overblown. The insistence on specific ethnic and cultural identities emerging among university and divinity school students and faculty challenged all claims to complete theological unity. The Sixties protests, even the mild ones, against traditional institutions and conventions created a tradition of antiestablishmentarianism and rendered questionable any institution's claim to social and cultural centrality. But the increasing structural diversity of the modern university also contradicted the validity of the divinity school's affirmation of its centrality and unifying influence. Another form of "multiculturalism," one inherent within the life of the "multiversity" itself, annulled *any* school's claim to unifying centrality. It especially annulled any such claim by divinity schools.

## DIVERSITY OF STRUCTURE, DIVERSITY OF CULTURE

From the outset, the modern American university was launched in the direction of what Clark Kerr would call the "multiversity."[43] During the last half of the nineteenth century, the university already had begun to take on a plurality of social purpose, academic specialty, and bureaucratic function. And it became evident early in the history of the American university that no one person, whether broad-minded faculty member or expansive university president, could possibly encompass intellectually or programmatically the range of subject and function emerging within the academy. By the early twentieth century, however, definitions of the university tended to group themselves into one of three large educational purposes. The purposes of "practical public service," "pure research," and the "conservation of liberal culture" appeared as the goals of university education. None of those purposes, however, was able to unify the institution. And the lack of unifying purpose would render questionable the integrative, centering aspirations of the divinity schools.

The goal of practical public service proposed that the university should reach the various classes of society and meet the practical vocational demands of those classes. It was a goal embraced by many of the Ivy League schools and most of the public universities. "We must carefully survey the wants of the various classes of the community" and create courses of study which will meet the needs of all classes, including courses in the "useful arts," proclaimed Francis Wayland, president of Brown, in 1850.[44] "It is not by pouring over the dreamy and mystical pages of classical lore" that the student will find a place in the modern age, announced the members of a state senate committee on education in their report to the University of Wisconsin in 1858. The legislators contended that appropriately modern education will occur when nature is unlocked for her great practical secrets.[45]

Alongside the view of the university as a public service institution there appeared the notion of the university as a place of pure research. Proponents of this view were often explicit in their repudiation of any utilitarian ends of a university education. "Truth and right are above utility in all realms of thought and action," Harvard's Charles Eliot said in his inaugural address in 1869.[46] G. Stanley Hall, professor of psychology at Johns Hopkins and then president of Clark University during the last half of the nineteenth century, believed pure research to be the "native breath" of the university, "its vital air," and he found that air fouled by those who "prate of the duty of bringing the university to the people."[47]

The American university also was defined as the preserver and disseminator of liberal culture. Champions of this view saw the university as a place where the disciplined intellect could be cultivated, common human values could be inculcated, and the heart of the liberal democratic tradition could be conserved. That was the view of education lying behind Chicago president Robert Maynard Hutchins's prescription of a basic course in the "great books" of the world and a "general education" curriculum, both of which he believed would "draw out the elements of our common human nature" and teach students how to think for themselves.[48]

The aim of liberal culture, though on occasion the guiding ideal of strong university presidents, has been confined for the most part to the camp of the humanities and, even with the inclusion of the "liberal arts" in a general requirements curriculum, has not unified undergraduate education, much less graduate and professional study.[49] The ideal of the

university as an institution serving the practical needs of the social order and the diverse classes of society has likewise enjoyed no unifying
power. Despite the noblest of aims, the typical American university has
been slow to attract a truly representative diversity of social classes. During the last half of the nineteenth century, neither the state universities
nor the land grant colleges, with their explicit mandates to serve the diverse citizens of their states, lured the greatest number of students from
the farming and working-class sectors. Black colleges, teacher training
institutions, schools of nursing, and regional denominational colleges attracted many more. Not until after the Second World War did the state
universities begin to draw the largest increases in enrollment from the
various classes of society.[50] Furthermore, with the establishment of such
practical disciplines as sanitary science, domestic science, business administration, physical education, and many types of engineering, the
"useful arts" have borne no intrinsic relation to one another nor to the
other tasks of the university.[51] The ideal of "pure research," though frequently defended in many parts of the university, has always run up
against the requirements of the teaching task. And with increasing monetary support for research coming from outside the university after the
Second World War, the research ideal has merged readily into the notion
of utilitarian public service.[52]

By the early twentieth century, on any given American university campus, one could find enclaves of students, faculty, and administrators
defining the educational task as public service, or liberal culture, or research. And it became commonplace for university presidents to defend
all three ideals, their rhetoric gliding from one purpose to another without any apparent recognition of the incompatibility of the three.[53] Neither
the eclectic combination of the three views nor the ardent defense of any
one of them could provide a coherent center for the American university.
Much of the history of the American university has been the story of the
emergence in one place of three largely incompatible views of higher
education.

Following each world war, the purposes of the American university
were made even more multifarious by three closely related factors: great
surges in enrollment, the widespread expansion of the curriculum into
areas of practical relevance, and the external funding of faculty research.
During the decade of the 1920s, the student population doubled to over
a million, with the largest numbers of students turning to the career-ori-
ented disciplines of commerce, law, education, and home economics.[54]
During the inter-war years, major research universities allocated as much

as 40 percent of their annual revenues to research in science and technology, and they turned to private foundations to subsidize many of their research projects.[55]

After the Second World War, these developments increased exponentially. The G.I. Bill, the escalating enrollments of women students, and the rise of the "baby boom" generation sent enrollments in higher education rocketing to unprecedented heights. Between 1945 and 1960, enrollments increased by more than a million to almost 3,600,000. Between 1960 and 1990, they increased almost fourfold to more than 12,800,000, of which approximately 10,000,000 of the students attended public institutions that emphasized areas of study appropriate to careers in technology, business, law, and health care.[56] During the same postwar period, external funding became a crucial ingredient in many university programs, and by 1986 total government grants and subsidies accounted for over 40 percent of the income for all institutions of higher education.[57] In the late 1980s, 55 percent of all American undergraduates were candidates for degrees in business, the various technological sciences, the health sciences, and the natural sciences.[58]

Not even the three broad aims of research, public service, and liberal culture could comprehend the diverse purposes created by these twentieth-century developments. Research and public service were aligned and redefined by the infusion of extramural capital into the university. Liberal culture was proffered to students who turned increasingly to the practical disciplines for their degrees, and most of those students attended public institutions that specialized in the preparation of undergraduates for practical post-bachelor careers. The sheer swell in numbers of university students required the creation of numerous support systems with their own distinctive aims—systems for the provision of medical services, testing services, registration services, and a host of others. Extracurricular activities (including college athletics, which already had been expanded at most universities in the inter-war years),[59] frequently assumed a quasi-independent status and could even overshadow the academic aims of some universities after mid-century.

Some universities, of course, have become more structurally diverse than others. Degree of diversity has been dependent in part on the size of the school, in part on the extensiveness of extracurricular activities, and in part on the level of degrees awarded and the comprehensiveness of educational mission. (Different degree levels and missions have led the Carnegie Commission on Higher Education to use ten classification categories for institutions of higher education, ranging from "Research Universities I" to "Two-Year Colleges".) Divinity schools have found their homes in a variety of university settings, some with a more diverse set of values and purposes than others. The small university at Drew, with two basic academic programs, contrasts sharply with the high-level research atmosphere and multiple professional programs at Harvard, and the milieu at each of those schools is decidedly different from that of a university like Duke, which includes nationally prominent varsity sports along with distinguished research and professional programs. In none of the settings, however, has there appeared a compelling, comprehensive educational purpose or any sense of the unity of the whole.

When William Rainey Harper and other founders of the divinity schools commended the university city as an appropriate place for divinity students to acquire a breadth of social and intellectual perspective, they did not anticipate the degree to which the American university would become a megalopolis of disparate educational purposes, social processes, and academic and nonacademic values. And when they envisioned the divinity school as a possible intellectual center for a university already showing all the signs of powerful centrifugal forces, they did not foresee how those forces would advance to such a stage that the provision of unity by any unit of the university would be impossible.

The university would become by mid-century radically multicultural in the values that endorsed its own plurality of purpose, process, and structure. As Laurence Veysey has said, "The university may well be the most internally diverse institution there is. While a number of other institutions (a hospital, for instance) shelter a wide group of specialties, in none other that I can think of is their range so extremely diverse and numerous, indeed incongruous." On the typical university landscape, "there are not just 'two cultures,' as in the simplification of the late C. P. Snow, but at least several major subcultures and hundreds of specialties within them."[60] No unit on the academic landscape has been capable of unifying those major subcultures and their hundreds of specialties. Certainly the divinity school, as it has been surpassed in power and influence by other university programs on most campuses, has enjoyed no opportunity to serve as a unifying force within the multiversity.

## THE MATTER OF MONEY

Divinity schools have been particularly curtailed in their ability to provide an overarching purpose to the academy by their standing relative to other schools in most universities. That standing has been reflected in finances, a principal, if not the most effectual, source of power for working change in the corporate world of the modern university.

Few of the divinity schools were ever particularly well-heeled and most of them encountered serious financial problems during the years of the Great Depression, but in their early years their finances compared favorably with those of other professional schools. At Harvard in 1900, for example, the total endowment funds for the Divinity School (almost $6,500,000) exceeded those of the Law School, the University Library, and the College of Arts and Sciences and were outstripped by the endowment funds of the Medical School by only $1,500,000.[61] Between 1900 and 1926, Protestant seminaries as a group, including university-related divinity schools, nearly doubled their capital resources and equipment per enrolled student and thus managed to keep up with professional schools of comparable size in the growth of their financial and physical resources.[62]

Divinity schools also have been beneficiaries periodically of large grants beyond their founding gifts. Beginning in 1945, for example, the Perkins School of Theology received several million dollars from the J. J. Perkins family for the expansion of its plant and endowment. John D. Rockefeller, Jr., became a generous supporter of Protestant theological education on a broad front. In the 1920s Rockefeller's million-dollar challenge gift to Union Seminary stimulated a successful $4,000,000 campaign for that school, and in the 1950s his million-dollar gift rescued Harvard Divinity School from insolvency. In 1955, Rockefeller established the Sealantic Fund with a $20,000,000 gift to support Protestant theological education. He singled out university divinity schools as the institutions positioned to shape the future of education of Protestant ministers; the first round of grants, in the amount of $6,000,000, went to the theological schools at Chicago, Harvard, Yale, Union, Vanderbilt, and the Pacific School of Religion.[63] The Methodist divinity schools received a long-term financial boost from their denomination in 1968 when the Methodist General Conference adopted a plan for assessing local churches 2 percent of their budgets for the support of Methodist theological education.[64]

These and other substantial infusions of money, however, did not establish the divinity school as a presence capable of unifying an extremely diversified university. With the ascent in prestige and assets of law schools and medical schools following the First World War and with the growth in the professions in technology and business beginning in the 1960s, divinity schools did not possess the financial wherewithal, relative to other units of the university, to transform the academy. Harvard Divinity School, which in 1900 possessed endowment funds that compared very favorably with those of other programs at its university, in 1993 accounted for only 2 percent of the total market value of Harvard's endowment. Although Harvard Divinity today boasts one of the largest endowments among contemporary divinity schools, within its own university it has been far surpassed by the College of Arts and Sciences (which has twenty times more endowment money), the Medical School (six times more), the School of Business (three times more), and the Law School (two and one-half times more).[65] Many of the other divinity schools currently hold significant endowments when measured in terms of absolute dollars, but when those endowments are divided by expenditures the figures are much less impressive.[66]

By the 1990s, many of the divinity schools were relying heavily upon income generated from endowment funds to meet their annual expenses—an average of 26.25 percent of their annual income (as high as 65 percent for a few), compared with the national average of 5.30 percent for all independent institutions of higher education in the United States.[67] This heavy reliance on endowment was necessitated in part by relatively modest tuition charges levied by the divinity schools, charges considerably lower than those of most other professional schools. And unlike schools of medicine, law, and business, divinity schools have not been able to draw upon a pool of wealthy alumni/ae to bolster their endowments or operating revenues; on average only $110,000, or 7 percent of annual gifts, come from the schools' alumni.[68] Few government grants find their way directly to divinity schools—only a fraction of 1 percent on average—whereas such funding accounts for 59 percent of the annual revenues for public universities and 19 percent for independent colleges and universities.[69] Since the 1960s, the Methodist university-related divinity schools have continued to receive a sizable proportion of their gift revenues from their denomination—over 50 percent in some cases—but with the decline of mainline Protestant finances, denominational support has become stagnant.[70] When compared with many other professional schools and when measured against the current funding patterns in American higher education as a whole, divinity schools, it is clear, do not possess the financial resources that could give weight to any effort on their part to integrate a diverse university environment.

To be sure, universities have continued to support their divinity schools financially. Because the type of support has varied from university to university, however, and because sometimes indirect support has not shown up in divinity school budgets, it is impossible to generalize about the extent of university financing for such things as plant maintenance, development costs, and central administrative services.[71] Yet throughout the history of the divinity schools, the administrators of the schools have complained about unfair university assessments for crossover registrations between academic programs, high taxes for indirect costs, arbitrary calculation of overhead charges, inadequate provisions for student aid, and improper allocation of endowment earnings.[72] The faculty complaints at Drew in 1958 and again in 1967 were hardly unique. The expression of such grievances has become especially frequent within the last twenty years as universities have widely adopted some form of the budgetary philosophy variously labeled "Revenue Center Management," "Responsibility Center Budgeting," and "Every Tub On Its Own Bottom."

Taking their orientation from contemporary principles of business management, university presidents and their financial advisors have been seeking ways to make each school within the academy directly responsible for its income and expenses—and for its deficits. In the place of "general fund accounting," in which the university as a whole assumes responsibility for the costs of all of its units, responsibility center accounting makes each unit its own revenue and cost center. Every unit of the university is required to rest on its own financial foundation. Edward L. Whalen, who literally "wrote the book" on this system of budgeting for the university, has insisted that the system is a mere "tool, an instrument" that gives a true picture of each school's use of university resources, permits the dean of each school to set academic and fiscal priorities, and allows for the subordination of the budget process to educational goals.[73] Whalen also denies that the system is the same as that of the American for-profit business enterprise: "Businessmen readily associate responsibility center budgeting with 'full cost' accounting or with 'profit center' management. Responsibility center budgeting is neither of those. No responsibility center is a profit center. Every one of them is on the dole."[74]

Although every school may be on the dole, however, and although no unit of the university pursues profit in quite the same way as do divisions within a for-profit business corporation, the management model appropriate to the business world nonetheless prevails in responsibility center budgeting. The fundamental concepts governing the system are technical efficiency, cost containment, the production of income, and market sensitivity. Students are viewed as the university's market, enrollments are treated as a chief source of income generation, and the value of faculty research activities is measured by the recovery of indirect costs.[75] Under such a system, it is tempting for a university's central administration—and for a school dean—to subordinate educational to financial goals. And in periods of lean financial resources for institutions of higher education, the budget system rewards those schools that increase their enrollments, attract substantial monies for faculty research, and build impressive endowments.

Some tubs, such as divinity schools, do not rest quite as securely on their own bottoms as do other units of the university. Yet university administrations today are asking divinity schools to operate with at least some of the principles of responsibility center budgeting.[76] Although that situation by no means necessarily spells either the doom of the schools or even their impotence as participants in the larger life of the academy, it does curtail considerably any claims they might make about their status as unifying forces within the university. The matter of money makes their status much more ambiguous.

That ambiguity was illustrated at SMU in 1989 when A. Kenneth Pye, president of the University, combined high praise of the Perkins School of Theology with a criticism of the school's financial operations. Basing his remarks upon the reports of two task forces, Pye celebrated Perkins as "the gem in SMU's crown," "an essential component of the SMU of the future" which enjoys "a national reputation for academic achievement and strength" and provides a crucial link for the University with the United Methodist Church. Yet the president also remarked upon the potential decline of enrollments in the Perkins M.Div. program as the need for ministers dwindled, and he worried about the expense of maintaining Perkins' highly favorable faculty/student ratio. He also noted that although Perkins possessed a large endowment, the school was running a substantial deficit, was making no significant contribution to the overhead costs of the University, and was charging a tuition one-half the amount charged undergraduates at SMU.[77] It was clear that for President Pye the crown as a whole was more important than its most dazzling gem. The Perkins School of Theology "should be expected to pay its own costs and contribute equitably to the general expenses of the University. Failure to do so places unreasonable demands upon other schools in the University, limits their capacity to excel, and contributes to the University's deficit."[78]

SMU's presidential mandates to Perkins point to the continuing relevance of one of James Wall's questions in the midst of the Drew crisis: What becomes of the church-oriented seminary as a university focuses on diverse educational programs, courts federal funding, and makes money decisions appropriate to the total university community? One undeniable answer to the question is that the divinity school occupies no privileged place from which to mount a compelling campaign for university coherence.

## FROM FORCE FOR UNITY TO
## COLLABORATIVE CITIZENSHIP

When several seminary leaders recently were asked what, in their judgment, was the most important challenge facing theological schools, they did not identify finances—much to the surprise of their interviewer. Instead, they pointed to the alienation of theological education from other American institutions and claimed that their most formidable challenge was to make their schools more relevant to the broader culture.[79] The dominant concern of the seminary leaders accords with the history of the divinity schools and the challenges they have long faced within the American university. Finances often have presented troubling difficulties for the schools, and in the present era of shrinking resources and expanding costs for higher education the issue of funding for theological education in the university surely will intensify. Yet money is but one important part of the larger issue of influence. The divinity school continues to confront the question of its appropriate, effectual place within the diverse subcultures and subinstitutions which make up the American university. That has been one of the divinity school's crucial questions since it first sought to shape the larger American culture, including the American university itself, by adopting the university as its home.

Clearly the attempt on the part of divinity school leaders to unify the entire academy has proved to be an ineffectual way of defining the place of the divinity schools in the life of the American university. The founders of the schools sought to provide a social center for a modern America that was rapidly diversifying in religious worldview, ethnic identity, and institutional loyalty, but they underestimated the power of social and cultural diversity in the nation. Similarly, the founders and many of their successors sought to provide a structural and theoretical center for a modern American university that early in its life had embarked on a course of diversified institutional purpose, intellectual orientation, and social function, but they underestimated the power of the university's centrifugal forces. In its own internal diversity, the university revealed a stubborn resistance to all efforts to center its life and thought. The divinity schools, in the light of developments in professional education and changes in finances for higher education, were in no position to overcome the decentering forces.

Neither the theory of "secularization" nor that of "marginalization" quite explains the position that the divinity schools have assumed in their respective universities. It was not secular motives that led the Drew University vice-president to say, in the midst of the crisis afflicting Drew's Theological School, that the whole of Drew University should stake out its claim as a church-related institution devoted to a study of values. And it was not the marginalization of the Perkins School of Theology when the University's president called the "gem in SMU's crown" to strict financial accountability. To be sure, at times the divinity schools have suffered from the policies of university administrators who have been unsympathetic to organized religion, and there is no reason to think that the future will avoid all instances of such "secularism" among wielders of power within the university. Some schools have been more deeply involved in the life of their universities than others, and some have been closer to university decision makers than others. Neither secularization nor marginalization, however, precisely characterizes the history of the schools' relation to the American university. What does characterize that relation is the inability, despite the early dreams and the subsequent theorizing, of the divinity schools to center a severely decentered institution.

If the modern American university has consistently resisted all efforts at unification, however, it by no means has opposed all attempts to cross structural and intellectual boundaries. The coalescing of previously separate disciplines has been most conspicuous in the natural sciences—in biochemistry and biophysics, for example. A similar, if less widespread movement across rigid disciplinary lines has occurred within the humanities and the social sciences and has resulted in what Clifford Geertz has called some "blurred genres"—with scientific reports looking like belles lettres, philosophical speculations like literary criticism, anthropological treatises like travelogues.[80] Divinity schools have not lagged in their pursuit of interdisciplinary inquiry. Faculty at many of the divinity schools hold joint appointments in other units of the university. Institutes and centers devoted to cross-disciplinary and inter-school teaching and research have sprung up across the university scene, and a number of those centers of learning have been founded by university-related divinity schools.[81] Interdisciplinary cooperation has transformed neither the structure nor the mind of the modern American university, but it has betokened a university environment which tolerates, and can even promote, the formation of limited enclaves of collaboration that transcend the intellectual and structural fragmentation so endemic to the contemporary university.[82]

Given the possibilities of interdisciplinary and cross-disciplinary collaboration, the recommendations of H. Richard Niebuhr and his successors regarding the role of the theological disciplines within the university may be more attainable than those of his predecessors. When the divinity schools abandon the assumption that they and their perspectives can unify the university, they would seem to be in a better position to engage in what Niebuhr called "mutual service" with other schools, departments, and methods, including the "service of mutual limitation and creative conflict."

Efforts at mutual criticism and collaboration may not issue in significant instances of commonality of purpose and enterprise among units of the university. The fragmentation of the contemporary American university makes even such limited expectations of unity difficult to realize, and moments of collaboration do not assure a clear, distinctive purpose for the divinity schools within the university. Yet instances of collaborative unity are more likely to find realization than the grand hopes for unification which formed so much of the history of university-related divinity schools and which were aligned so intimately with the old triumphalist hopes of Pan-Protestantism. Both the historic developments of the university and the emergence of relentless social pluralism have defeated the divinity schools' early aspirations. The resulting present situation seems to call for the enhancement of efforts in collaborative university citizenship, not attempts to create a force for academic unity, as a step toward vital influence within the university.

# CONCLUSION

■

## *The Ambiguities of a Heritage*

Motivating visions by their very nature are largely devoid of ambiguity. Their power to inspire new social experiments depends upon the energies released by the certainty that dreams can be fulfilled. And though they may be predicated on present realities, visions anticipate a future not yet marred by the misgivings of hindsight.

The vision that animated the experiment in university-based education in divinity was no exception. William Rainey Harper, that bundle of energy, intelligence, and imagination who managed to comprehend in one person so many of the key elements of a projected educational scheme, did quickly perceive some ambiguity in the vision when he noted the difficulty of combining advanced graduate specialization with practical ministerial training. For the most part, however, Harper and other founders of divinity schools were confident that their dreams could be realized. They firmly believed that as components of a vast, interconnected system of religious education, university divinity schools could decisively shape American culture. Offering avenues to the latest specialized, advanced learning as well as access to fast-breaking developments in professional training, universities were the appropriate places for training ministers who would serve an increasingly specialized, professionalized America. As institutions where the social graces and the clash of ideas could be nourished and instruments for social change could be acquired, universities were the suitable training grounds for ministers to learn to move within the realm of wealth and power and yet also learn to tend a society suffering from the transformations wrought by urbanization and industrialization. And by finding a home in the intellectual centers of the nation, the divinity schools could absorb the exciting climate of diverse outlooks and still bring the unifying perspective of religion to the diversified city of the university.

The heritage that emerged from the aspirations of the founders was rendered ambiguous in part by the fact that the vision could not be fully realized. Changes that occurred in America over the course of a century, as well as consequences inherent within the vision itself, thwarted many of the strategies devised to implement the original dreams.

The changes, created by powerful social and cultural forces which washed over universities and other American institutions in the nineteenth and twentieth centuries, sank the hopes for a Protestant America, hopes that had been closely bound up with the founding idea of a university-related divinity school. America became more culturally and religiously diverse, and American diversity more antagonistic to the influences of Anglo-Saxon Protestantism, than the founders of divinity schools had foreseen. For that reason, the strategies instituted to unite higher with lower education, elite with popular religious knowledge, and the aims of the public university with those of the Protestant divinity schools never connected the critical parts into a single system, and each part had less impact on the culture than was hoped. The plurality and the pluralisms of the social order—and of the university, which would eventually reflect the social diversity and would add a stubborn structural "multiculturalism" of its own—also proved to be defiant of any centering, unifying efforts on the part of Protestant educational institutions. The folk religion of the American people—tenaciously prescientific in its worldview, thoroughly democratic in its rejection of professional elitism, and largely unconcerned with the intellectual development of ministers—was a force in the churches that survived the fundamentalist controversy and proved resistant to the ideas emerging from divinity education.

Then there were the strong currents building in the various technologies, in the professions, and in the patterns of funding for higher education. Emphasis on the development of technical skills and education in the universities overshadowed the acquisition of education in the liberal arts, a type of education fundamental to most of the disciplines in divinity education. The most prestigious and the most financially attractive professions were those which honed very technical, practical skills, so that the ministry began to look like one of the most impractical of professions. Funding for most higher education drew increasingly upon tax support, government and corporate grants, and strong endowments; the ability of the divinity schools to meet the spiraling costs of education was rendered correspondingly difficult and their financial status in the university comparatively weak. Given the impact of these forces, the language of some of the founders of divinity schools about the ability of educated ministers to shape the course of civilization began to have the ring of hollow rhetoric.

There were also factors internal to the founding vision itself that led to its compromise. In eagerly embracing the world of the modern university and its promotion of specialized learning, the divinity schools contributed to the fragmentation of the very knowledge they hoped to unify, and they divided education into discrete "sciences" for a ministry that sought an undivided presence in the culture. In seeking to create a ministerial profession second to no other profession and in trying to imitate the training appropriate to the prestigious professions, the schools constantly struggled to reconcile the theory and practice thought to be inherently compatible, and they found it difficult to prove ministerial training as practical as the professions most highly esteemed in American society. As the divinity schools followed the vision of thoroughly immersing future ministers in the life of the modern university, they inadvertently cut ministers off from the life of the churches. And as they took up the role of "prophetic criticism" of church and society behind the safe walls of the university, the schools further alienated themselves from the churches they sought to serve. The founding vision of the divinity schools overestimated the compatibility of university and church, specialized learning and ministerial task, theoretical sophistication and practical application.

Despite the patent flaws and the unintended effects of the founding vision, the experiment in university-based theological education deserves considerable respect. And although external social and cultural forces severely compromised the implementation of the full vision, the heritage bequeathed by the founding vision cannot be written off as a tradition of unequivocal failure.

The contribution of the divinity schools to university scholarship, though inspired originally by an unrealistic view of the schools' unifying influence, has been remarkable and many of its effects salutary. From the very beginning, as the schools built up their scholarly faculties (many of whom had taken their advanced degrees in Germany), scholars in divinity have continuously stood their schools in good stead within the research-oriented university.[1] In most years, divinity school deans in their annual reports could justifiably take pride in the contributions of their professors to the latest in graduate-level scholarship, and administrators in other parts of the universities often responded with equal pride.[2] In refusing to bend to the demands of a powerful folk religion that grants little or no honor to scholarship in religion, the divinity schools have demonstrated that piety and intellect need not occupy hermetically sealed compartments of life. And from the point of their early scholarly commitments to understanding the "Other," the schools have opened the way for treating what is religiously and culturally different with respect, empathy, and compassion. For all of its misguided triumphalism and imperialism, the Pan-Protestant vision of divinity education led to unbiased scholarship, the integrity of the life of the mind, and the scholarly exploration of the unusual.

In addition, by virtue of their scholarly principles as well as their confidence in the intellectual authority of the university, the Protestant divinity schools assumed the leadership for developing professional standards in ministerial education. Their role in the founding of the Association of Theological Schools as an accrediting agency, their adherence to university standards for graduate education, and their insistence on a college education for entering students made the schools the principal definers of what a theological education should be at a time when no uniform definition of such an education existed. It is unlikely that the emergence of standards for theological education in the United States would ever have occurred apart from the initiatives of university-related divinity schools.

One of the most venerable legacies of the divinity schools is a long, ardent commitment to social justice. In educational programs and in periodic outbreaks of social protest, the schools have conveyed the message to students and to the public that provision of succor to the needy and defiance of unjust laws and institutions are germane to Christian conviction. It is questionable that the divinity school can or should lay claim to being the moral conscience of the university. The claim is overwrought since it disregards the appearance of ethical reflection and moral sensitivity in other parts of the university. Yet from the early days of the social gospel to the present days of liberation theology, the divinity schools, unlike most units of the university, have built the study of the principles and strategies of social justice into their curriculum. And in their leadership in the racial integration of universities, their challenges to the smug conventions of middle-class life, and their defenses of the integrity of the sources of social diversity, the divinity schools have embodied in action what they have taught in principle. The schools eventually abandoned completely the old hope that through their social philosophies and social programs they would serve the triumph of Anglo-Saxon Protestantism, and for the most part they relinquished the old ambition of improving the etiquette of future ministers. Yet they never forsook the belief, a vital ingredient of those old aspirations, that they were supposed to train ministers fit to serve humankind in its disparate needs and diverse settings.

To the eyes of many people in the American public, the contemporary university must appear like a great stumbling, prehistoric beast which mindlessly consumes the nation's resources and continues to drag along its antiquated appendages, resists adaptation to a changing environment, and refuses to die. There is much to commend the image, but it does not capture the delicacy of the university and its constituent units. The more accurate image is that of a composite metal subjected to the shattering blows of history. The heritage of the divinity schools is a clear illustration of the fragility of higher education. However self-confident the divinity school founders may have been in the articulation of their vision, the heritage resulting from that vision is not unalloyed. It is a heritage comprised of successes and failures, false hopes and principled ideas, the effective realization of educational goals and the ironic reversal of the best of intentions. And it is a heritage constantly vulnerable to the shocks of external forces, such as changing cultural values, unsympathetic university administrations, and meager financial support.

This very mixed heritage stands as a ready resource for those who would re-envision the aims and structures of theological education. During the last fifteen years, the purposes of theological education in North America have come under careful scrutiny. Sponsored by the Association of Theological Schools and funded by the Lilly Endowment, a large number of critical studies of theological education have appeared. Most of those studies have been undertaken by educators in the divinity schools and include the names of scholars frequently cited in this book—Edward Farley of Vanderbilt, Don Browning of Chicago, David Kelsey of Yale, John Cobb of Claremont, Joseph Hough of Claremont and now of Vanderbilt, and the feminist scholars of the Mud Flower Collective. Although little consensus has emerged in these studies about steps appropriate to reform, all have attended to the basic questions of the goals, directions, and structures of theological education. And they have contested many of the hallowed assumptions which have prevailed in the history of divinity education—that practice should follow from theory, that the four-fold organization of the curriculum is the best scheme, that the chief purpose of theological education is training in clerical functions.[3]

Not since the 1930s, when the American Association of Theological Schools was formed as an accrediting agency and university divinity schools led others in the examination of the purposes and standards of theological education, has the future direction of the education of Protestant ministers been so thoroughly and critically reviewed. The creation of a new vision from these re-examinations might well avail itself of the ambiguous heritage of the university divinity schools. The history of the schools offers no blueprint for the future. Too many features of the founding vision are now obsolete, too many of the original strategies proved to be ineffectual, too many changes in higher education and in American culture as a whole have worked their effects during the last hundred years for the history to dictate the future. Yet there are strong segments of tradition from the heritage that may provide the building blocks for the future. And building on the past need not rule out learning from the mistakes that come from overreaching the possibilities of the present when hurrying toward Zion. The vision of William Rainey Harper and other founders needs to be examined for both its unrealistic expectations and its energizing power. Both the misgivings and the inspirations of hindsight can be pertinent to building for the future.

# NOTES

■

## Abbreviations

AB      Archives of the Boston School of Theology
ACT     Archives of the Claremont School of Theology
ACTS    Archives of the Chicago Theological Seminary
ACU     Archives of the University of Chicago, Regenstein Library
ADR     Archives of Drew University
ADU     Archives of Duke University
AEC     Archives of Candler School of Theology, Emory University, Pitts
        Library
AEU     Archives of Emory University, Robert W. Woodruff Library
AHD     Archives of Harvard Divinity School
AHU     Archives of Harvard University
ASC     Archives of the University of Southern California
ASMP    Archives of Perkins School of Theology, Southern Methodist Univer-
        sity, Bridwell Library
ASMU    Archives of Southern Methodist University, Fondren Library
AU      Archives of Union Theological Seminary, New York City
AV      Archives of Vanderbilt University
AYD     Special Collections of the Yale Divinity School Library, Record Group
        #53
AYU     Archives of Yale University

## Introduction: Visions and Strategies of Influence

1. Richard J. Storr, *Harper's University: The Beginnings* (Chicago: University of Chicago Press, 1966), 8–9, 31, 44–47, 357; Thomas Wakefield Goodspeed, *A History of the University of Chicago: The First Quarter Century* (Chicago: University of Chicago Press, 1916), 293.

2. William Rainey Harper, "The University and Democracy," in *The Trend in Higher Education* (Chicago: University of Chicago Press, 1905), 1–34.

3. Walt Whitman, "Passage to India," in *Leaves of Grass and Selected Prose*, ed. John Kouwenhoven (New York: Modern Library, 1950), 323.

4. William Rainey Harper, "America as a Missionary Field," in *Religion and the Higher Life* (Chicago: University of Chicago Press, 1904), 175.

5. William Rainey Harper, "Dependence of the West upon the East," in *Trend*, 135–36.

6. Harper, "America as a Missionary Field," 181.

7. Harper, "Bible Study and the Religious Life," in *Higher Life*, 141–72; idem, "Dependence of the West upon the East," 135–39; idem, "Higher Education in the West," in *Trend*, 140–50; James P. Wind, *The Bible and the University: The Messianic Vision of William Rainey Harper* (Atlanta: Scholars Press, 1987), 79–103, 110–12.

8. Goodspeed, *University of Chicago*, 134–37; Storr, *Harper's University*, 64; Wind, *Bible and University*, 138.

9. Leonard I. Sweet, "The University of Chicago Revisited: The Modernization of Theology, 1890–1940," *Foundations* 22 (October–December 1979): 328. Cf. Harper, "The University and Religious Education," in *Trend*, 76–77.

10. Goodspeed, *University of Chicago*, 121.

11. *Register of the University of Chicago, 1892–93*, ACU, 153.

12. *Register of the University of Chicago, 1892–93*, ACU, 2, 148; *1906–07*, 78. Harper was probably also motivated to make Old Testament studies a separate university department by his desire to protect himself from conservative Baptists. In any case, James Wind has observed that Harper's decision to place his own field outside the Divinity School may have had an unanticipated consequence: it may have "unwittingly doomed his passion, Old Testament studies, to a precarious institutional existence. In this plan critical study of the biblical texts was separated from the official ministerial curriculum, providing room for a wedge to be driven between criticism and reverence, the two essential components of his approach to the Scriptures." Wind, *Bible and University*, 117.

13. William Rainey Harper, "Shall the Theological Curriculum Be Modified, and How?" *American Journal of Theology* 3 (January 1899): 66.

14. *Register of the University of Chicago, 1892–93*, ACU, 138–47, 152, 154–55; *1893–94*, 220–21; *1912–13*, 305.

15. William Rainey Harper, "Why Are There Fewer Students for the Ministry?" in *Trend*, 198–203; idem, "The Theological Seminary in Its Civic Relationship," ibid., 227–31; idem, "Theological Curriculum Modified," 56–65.

16. Wind, *Bible and University*, 9.

17. Storr, *Harper's University*, 94–96; Harper, "Theological Curriculum Modified," 54–61; idem, "Seminary in Civic Relationship," 227–28, 231.

18. "The President's Report," *University of Chicago Decennial Publications*, 1 (1903), ACU, lxxiv–lxxv.

19. Shailer Mathews, *New Faith for Old: An Autobiography* (New York: Macmillan Co., 1936), 59.

20. Charles Harvey Arnold, *God Before You and Behind You. The Hyde Park Union Church, 1874–1974* (Chicago: Hyde Park Union Church, 1974); Wind, *Bible and University*, 40–46, 49–50, 96–102.

21. William Rainey Harper, "Some Present Tendencies of Popular Education," in *Trend*, 35.

22. Charles Harvey Arnold, *Near the Edge of Battle: A Short History of the Divinity School and the "Chicago School of Theology," 1866–1966* (Chicago: Divinity School Association of the University of Chicago, 1966), 116–17.

23. Robert W. Lynn, "A Historical Perspective on the Futures of American Religious Education," in *Foundations for Christian Education in an Era of Change*, ed. J. Marvin Taylor (Nashville, Tenn.: Abingdon Press, 1976), 8–11. For a lengthy discussion of "the development of an authentic American vernacular in education

that proffered a popular *paideia* compounded of evangelical pieties, democratic hopes, and utilitarian strivings" see Lawrence A. Cremin, *American Education: The National Experience, 1783–1876* (New York: Harper & Row, 1980).

24. Sweet, "Chicago Revisited," 340; Kenneth Sawyer, "The University of Chicago Divinity School: A Bibliographic and Archival Survey," typescript (1985), ACU, 35.

25. Harper, "Seminary in Civic Relationship," 216, 221–23, 226; idem, "Theological Curriculum Modified," 48–49; idem, "Religion and the Higher Life," in *Trend*, 5, 19.

26. *Register of the University of Chicago, 1892–93*, ACU, 154; *1912–13*, 305; *1915–16*, 270.

27. Henry F. May, *Protestant Churches and Industrial America* (New York: Harper & Row, 1967), 163–262.

28. Shailer Mathews, *The Social Teaching of Jesus: An Essay in Christian Sociology* (New York: Macmillan Company, 1897), 170–71.

29. Mathews, *New Faith for Old*, 136, 138–39.

30. The evidence is not clear that Bemis was dismissed by Harper solely or even fundamentally because of his statements on the strike since Bemis had been under criticism for some time respecting his teaching; clearly, however, Bemis's position on the faculty was weakened because of the controversy he provoked. See Storr, *Harper's University*, 83–85, 135–36.

31. Alan Trachtenberg, *The Incorporation of America: Culture and Society in the Gilded Age* (New York: Hill & Wang, 1982), 3–10, 140–81, 208–34.

32. Glenn T. Miller, *Piety and Intellect: The Aims and Purposes of Ante-Bellum Theological Education* (Atlanta: Scholars Press, 1990), 200–02; William Adams Brown, *Ministerial Education in America*, vol. 1 of *The Education of American Ministers* (New York: Institute of Social and Religious Research, 1934), 79–81.

33. This view of Harper's significance for his times is taken by Wind, *Bible and University*, 179.

34. Robert L. Kelly, *Theological Education in America. A Study of One Hundred Sixty-One Theological Schools in the United States and Canada* (New York: George H. Doran Co., 1924), 50.

35. Charles W. Eliot, "A New Definition of the Cultivated Man," in *Present College Questions* (New York: D. Appleton and Company, 1903), 4–7; idem, "Statement of President Eliot," in *An Appeal In Behalf of the Further Endowment of the Divinity School of Harvard University* (Cambridge: John Wilson and Son, 1879), 25–27; idem, "Theological Education at Harvard Between 1816 and 1910," in *Addresses Delivered at the Observance of the 100th Anniversary of the Establishment of the Harvard Divinity School* (Cambridge: Harvard University, 1917), 65–68.

36. George H. Williams, "The Three Recurrent Conflicts," in *The Harvard Divinity School: Its Place in Harvard University and in American Culture*, ed. George H. Williams (Boston: Beacon Press, 1954), 10; Levering Reynolds, Jr., "The Later Years (1880–1953)," ibid., 171–72.

37. *Harvard Divinity School Announcements, 1898–99*, AHD, 4–22; *Harvard Divinity School: Deans' Reports, 1884–85*, AHD, 108; Robert S. Morison, "The First Half Century of the Divinity School," in *Addresses at the 100th Anniversary of Harvard Divinity School*, 31; Reynolds, "The Later Years," 167–81.

38. Roland H. Bainton, *Yale and the Ministry: A History of Education for the Christian Ministry at Yale from the Founding in 1701* (New York: Harper & Brothers, 1957), 80–81, 165.

39. George Wilson Pierson, *Yale College: An Educational History, 1871–1921* (New Haven, Conn.: Yale University Press, 1952), 65, 95–128.

40. Bainton, *Yale and the Ministry*, 202–11.

41. Charles Reynolds Brown, "The Training of a Minister," in *Education for Christian Service*, by Members of the Divinity School of Yale University (New Haven, Conn.: Yale University Press, 1922), 4.

42. Henry P. Van Dusen, "Foreword" to Henry Sloane Coffin, *A Half Century of Union Theological Seminary, 1896–1945* (New York: Charles Scribner's Sons, 1954), 2.

43. Coffin, *Half Century of Union*, 58–59; Robert T. Handy, *A History of Union Theological Seminary in New York* (New York: Columbia University Press, 1987), 1–114.

44. Handy, *History of Union*, 124–26, 135, 150–53, 164, 168–70, 190–93; Richard Wightman Fox, *Reinhold Niebuhr: A Biography* (New York: Pantheon Books, 1985), 112–22.

45. Handy, *History of Union*, 130, 167–68, 238.

46. Charles Augustus Briggs, *The Authority of Holy Scripture: An Inaugural Address* (New York: Charles Scribner's Sons, 1891), 4; idem, *History of the Study of Theology* vol. 2 (New York: Charles Scribner's Sons, 1916), 211–12; Handy, *History of Union*, 121–24; Charles Cuthbert Hall, "The Expansion of the Seminary," *Union Theological Seminary Inaugural Addresses, 1898–1914*, AU, 17–36; Arthur Cushman McGiffert, "Presidential Address: 1918," *Union Theological Seminary Inaugural Addresses, 1915–1930*, AU, 16–37; Charles Augustus Briggs, "The Ideal of the Study of Theology," in *The Dedication of the New Buildings of the Union Theological Seminary in the City of New York, Nov. 27–29, 1910*, AU, 115–36.

47. George Marsden, *Reforming Fundamentalism: Fuller Seminary and the New Evangelicalism* (Grand Rapids, Mich.: William B. Eerdmans, 1987), 263–76.

48. Cited by Kenneth E. Rowe, "New Light on Early Methodist Theological Education," *Methodist History* 10 (October 1971): 59.

49. Rowe, "New Light," 59–60; Miller, *Piety and Intellect*, 408, 416–18; Paul N. Garber, "The Struggle for a Trained Ministry in the Methodist Episcopal Church, South," *Duke School of Religion Bulletin* 5 (May 1940): 40; Charles W. Ferguson, *Organizing to Beat the Devil: Methodists and the Making of America* (Garden City, N.Y.: Doubleday & Co., 1971).

50. James W. Fraser, *Schooling the Preachers: The Development of Protestant Theological Education in the United States, 1740–1875* (Lanham, Md.: University Press of America, 1988), 138, 140, 146; John T. Cunningham, *University in the Forest: The Story of Drew University* (Florham Park, N.J.: Afton Publishing Co., 1972), 21.

51. Hunter Dickinson Farish, *The Circuit Rider Dismounts: A Social History of Southern Methodism, 1865–1900* (Richmond, Va.: Dietz Press, 1938).

52. Cunningham, *University in the Forest*, 21.

53. L. C. Garland, "An Educated Ministry," *Nashville Christian Advocate* 29 (October 30, 1869): 1.

54. Earl W. Porter, *Trinity and Duke, 1892–1924: Foundations of Duke University* (Durham, N.C.: Duke University Press, 1964), 233.

55. These observations about Protestant hegemony are suggested by those of William Hutchison in his "Preface" and "Conclusion" to *Between the Times: The Travail of the Protestant Establishment in America, 1900–1960*, ed. William R. Hutchison (Cambridge: Cambridge University Press, 1989), vii–viii, 304–05.

## 1. Strategies for a System of Education

1. Reinhold Niebuhr, *Reminiscences*, transcript of a tape-recorded interview (Oral History Research Office, Columbia University, 1957), 12–14; *Colloquy: Conversations with the Faculty, Union Theological Seminary, 1976–1977*, ed. Malcolm L. Warford (Office of Educational Research, October 25, 1977), AU, 56.

2. Richard Wightman Fox, *Reinhold Niebuhr: A Biography* (New York: Pantheon Books, 1985), 26–27; *Bulletin of the Yale University School of Religion, 1915–16*, AY, 100–03; *The Union Theological Seminary in the City of New York: Alumni Directory, 1836–1970* (New York: Alumni Office of Union Theological Library, 1970), 399–414.

3. Robert L. Kelly, *Theological Education in America. A Study of One Hundred Sixty-One Theological Schools in the United States and Canada* (New York: George H. Doran Co., 1924), 152, 154–56; Mark A. May, *The Institutions that Train Ministers*, vol. 3 of *The Education of American Ministers* (New York: Institute of Social and Religious Research, 1934), 275–77, 281, 290, 295, 296–97; Mark A. May and Frank K. Shuttleworth, *Appendices*, vol. 4 of *Education of American Ministers*, 183; H. Richard Niebuhr, Daniel Day Williams, and James M. Gustafson, *The Advancement of Theological Education* (New York: Harper & Brothers, 1957), 145.

4. R. Niebuhr, *Reminiscences*, 16–18; Fox, *Niebuhr*, 28, 35; *Colloquy*, 56.

5. *American Higher Education: A Documentary History*, vol. 2, ed. Richard Hofstadter and Wilson Smith (Chicago: University of Chicago Press, 1961), 608, 636, 519, 493.

6. Revisionist historians of higher education have claimed that for decades treatments of nineteenth-century colleges in the United States were captive to the perspectives and special interests of university leaders, thus obscuring the diversity of the colleges and the manner in which many of them provided the foundations for the emergence of the modern university. See James McLachlan, "The American College in the Nineteenth Century: Toward a Reappraisal," *Teachers College Record* 80 (September 1978): 287–306; Douglas Sloan, "Harmony, Chaos, and Consensus: The American College Curriculum," *Teachers College Record* 73 (December 1971): 221–51; Frederick Rudolph, *Curriculum: A History of the American Undergraduate Course of Study Since 1636* (San Francisco: Jossey-Bass Publishers, 1977).

7. Fritz K. Ringer, *The Decline of the German Mandarins. The German Academic Community, 1890–1933* (Cambridge: Harvard University Press, 1969), 24–25, 103–06, 412–16; idem, "The German Academic Community," in *The Organization of Knowledge in Modern America, 1860–1920*, ed. Alexandra Oleson and John Voss (Baltimore, Md.: Johns Hopkins University Press, 1979), 411, 425.

8. John Higham, "The Matrix of Specialization," in *Organization of Knowledge,* 10–11.

9. Immanuel Kant, *On History,* ed. Lewis White Beck (Indianapolis, Ind.: Bobbs-Merrill, 1963), 3.

10. John Cole, "Storehouses and Workshops: American Libraries and the Uses of Knowledge," in *Organization of Knowledge,* 370–74, 367; Hugh Hawkins, "University Identity: The Teaching and Research Functions," ibid., 293–94; Dorothy Ross, "The Development of the Social Sciences," ibid., 107, 121; Laurence R. Veysey, *The Emergence of the American University* (Chicago: University of Chicago Press, 1965), 173–74.

11. Clark Kerr, *The Uses of the University* (Cambridge: Harvard University Press, 1963), 18–20.

12. Sloan, "Harmony, Chaos, and Consensus," 249.

13. Charles R. Gillett, "Detailed History of the Union Theological Seminary in the City of New York," vol. 2, typescript (n.d.), AU, 572–73; Robert T. Handy, *A History of Union Theological Seminary in New York* (New York: Columbia University Press, 1987), 288–89; *Drew Catalogue, 1888–89,* ADR, 39; *The Drew Gateway* 8 (April 1930), ADR, 4; Henry B. Wright, "Recent Epochs of Christian Life," in James B. Reynolds, Samuel H. Fisher, and Henry B. Wright, *Two Centuries of Christian Activity at Yale* (New York: G. P. Putnam's Sons, 1901), 107–08, 111–12; W. H. Sallmon, "The Young Men's Christian Association," ibid., 215–16, 242–50; Thomas H. English, *Emory University, 1915–1965* (Atlanta: Emory University, 1966), 104, 210–11, 214; *Harvard University Deans' Reports, 1936,* AHD, 63–64; Alan Seaburg, "A Learned Minister at Harvard: Willard Learoyd Sperry," *Harvard Theological Review* 80 (1987): 182–83; Charles Harvey Arnold, *God Before You and Behind You, The Hyde Park Union Church Through a Century, 1874–1974* (Chicago: Hyde Park Union Church, 1974), 38–41; Dorothy C. Bass, "Ministry on the Margin: Protestants and Education," in *Between the Times: The Travail of the Protestant Establishment in America, 1900–1960,* ed. William R. Hutchison (Cambridge: Cambridge University Press, 1989), 56–58; Merrimon Cuninggim, *The College Seeks Religion* (New Haven, Conn.: Yale University Press, 1947), 42–45.

14. Charles Augustus Briggs, *The Authority of Holy Scripture: An Inaugural Address* (New York: Charles Scribner's Sons, 1891), 30–31.

15. Douglas Clyde Macintosh, "Theology in a Scientific Age," in *Education for Christian Service,* by members of the faculty of the Divinity School of Yale University (New Haven, Conn.: Yale University Press, 1922), 141, 161.

16. Shirley Jackson Case, "The Historical Study of Religion," *Journal of Religion* 29 (January 1949): 5–14; Paul Schubert, "Shirley Jackson Case, Historian of Early Christianity: An Appraisal," ibid., 30–46.

17. Reinhold Niebuhr, "The Tyranny of Science," *Theology Today* 10 (January 1954): 471; Gordon Harland, *The Thought of Reinhold Niebuhr* (New York: Oxford University Press, 1960), 69–72.

18. *Harvard University Deans' Reports, 1939–40,* AHD, 1; Levering Reynolds, Jr., "The Later Years (1880–1953)," *The Harvard Divinity School: Its Place in Harvard University and in American Culture,* ed. George H. Williams (Boston: Beacon Press, 1954), 170–71, 214.

19. Boone M. Bowen, *The Candler School of Theology: Sixty Years of Service* (Atlanta: Emory University, 1974), 29, 189.

20. Walter G. Muelder and L. Harold DeWolfe, "Philosophy of the Curriculum," *Nexus* 1 (February 1958): 65.

21. Robert E. Cushman, "Fifty Years of Theology and Theological Education at Duke; Retrospect and Prospect," *Duke Divinity School Review* 42 (Winter 1977), ADU, 6–7, 12.

22. See, for example, *Harvard University Deans' Reports, 1955,* AHD, 105; "Minutes of the Senate, Perkins School of Theology," April 23, 1976, ASMP, 2; "Response to Faculty Discussion of STH Chapel," March 2, 1984, AB.

23. William Adams Brown, *Ministerial Education in America*, vol. 1 of *The Education of American Ministers,* 155, 158, 165.

24. H. Richard Niebuhr with Daniel Day Williams and James M. Gustafson, *The Purpose of the Church and Its Ministry: Reflections on the Aims of Theological Education* (New York: Harper & Row, 1956), 130; Niebuhr, Williams, and Gustafson, *Advancement,* 166–67.

25. Henry Ward Beecher, *Yale Lectures on Preaching*, vol. 2 (New York: J. B. Ford & Co., 1873), 160.

26. My paragraph summarizes a comprehensive overview of the changes in American congregational life by E. Brooks Holifield, "Toward a History of American Congregations," in *American Congregations,* vol. 2 of *New Perspectives in the Study of Congregations,* ed. James P. Wind and James W. Lewis (Chicago: University of Chicago Press, 1994), 23–53.

27. Bass, "Ministry on the Margin," 61–62.

28. *Proceedings of the First Annual Convention of the Religious Education Association, 1903* (Chicago: Religious Education Association, 1903), 237.

29. *Register of the University of Chicago, 1912–13,* ACU, 307; C. T. Holman, "Religious Education at the University of Chicago," *The Divinity Student* 4 (November 15, 1927), ACU, 81–92.

30. Kelly, *Theological Education,* 141.

31. Stephen A. Schmidt, *A History of the Religious Education Association* (Birmingham, Ala.: Religious Education Press, 1983); William Bean Kennedy, "The Church as Educator: Religious Education," in *Altered Landscapes: Christianity in America, 1935–1985,* ed. David W. Lotz with Donald W. Shriver, Jr., and John F. Wilson (Grand Rapids, Mich.: William B. Eerdmans, 1989), 280–95; Robert W. Lynn and Elliott Wright, *The Big Little School: Two Hundred Years of the Sunday School* (Birmingham, Ala.: Religious Education Press, 1980), 120–44; Sara Little, "Theology and Religious Education," in *Foundations for Christian Education in an Era of Change,* ed. Marvin J. Taylor (Nashville, Tenn.: Abingdon Press, 1976), 30–40.

32. Anne M. Boylan, *Sunday School: The Formation of an American Institution, 1790–1880* (New Haven, Conn.: Yale University Press, 1988); F. Michael Perko, "Religious Education," in *Encyclopedia of the American Religious Experience,* vol. 3, ed. Charles H. Lippy and Peter W. Williams (New York: Charles Scribner's Sons, 1988), 1605–06.

33. Boylan, *Sunday School,* 126.

34. Cited in Lynn and Wright, *Big Little School,* 131.

35. Ibid., 125. Some revisionist historians have found more continuities between the various phases of the Sunday school movement than Lynn and Wright have pointed out. See, for example, Jack L. Seymour, *From Sunday School to Church School: Continuities in Protestant Church Education in the United States, 1860–1929* (Washington, D.C.: University Press of America, 1982). Nevertheless, the effects of professionalization and specialization upon the Sunday school reform movement do appear to mark a significant and separate stage in the story.

36. Kennedy, "Church as Educator," 281. See also Seymour, *From Sunday School to Church School*, vii, for a type of optimism about the search for new directions in religious education emerging out of a recognition of the field's identity crisis.

37. *Harvard University Deans' Reports, 1941*, AHD, 2. For other examples of this recurrent justification of the divinity school–based Ph.D. see *Bulletin of Duke University* 24 (February 1959), ADU, 47; *Drew University Bulletin, 1953–54*, ADR, 9.

38. *Bulletin of Yale Divinity School, 1949–50*, AYD, 40–41; "Report of the Dean of the Divinity School to the President, 1952–54," AYD, 26–27. See also Roland H. Bainton, *Yale and the Ministry: A History of Education for the Christian Ministry at Yale from the Founding in 1701* (New York: Harper & Brothers, 1957), 265–66; Handy, *History of Union*, 249; Muelder and DeWolfe, "Philosophy of the Curriculum," 75–76; "Theological School Educational Policy Committee Proposals, April, 1956," ADR.

39. Charles Foster Kent, "Order and Content of Biblical Courses in College Curriculum," *Religious Education* 7 (April 1912): 43.

40. Ibid., 48.

41. Martha H. Biehle, "Fifty Years: 1923–1973. A Brief History of The National Council on Religion in Higher Education and The Society for Religion in Higher Education," typescript (New Haven, Conn., 1974), 1–4, 6–8, 12–18.

42. Charles Foster Kent, "The Undergraduate Courses in Religion at the Tax-Supported Colleges and Universities of America," *Bulletin of the National Council on Religion in Higher Education* 4 (1924): 29.

43. Biehle, "Fifty Years," 3–10, 19, 23–28.

44. Kent, "Undergraduate Courses in Religion," 30; Thorton W. Merriam, "Religion in Higher Education Through the Past Twenty-Five Years," in *Liberal Learning and Religion*, ed. Amos N. Wilder (New York: Harper & Brothers, 1951), 5.

45. Merriam, "Religion in Higher Education," 7–8; Patrick Murphy Malin, "The National Council on Religion in Higher Education," in *Liberal Learning*, 325–26; Biehle, "Fifty Years," 33–35.

46. Malin, "National Council," 332.

47. Clarence Prouty Shedd, "Religion in State Universities," *Journal of Higher Education* 12 (November 1941): 414. See also Shedd's *Religion in the State University*, Pamphlet 16 (New Haven, Conn.: The Edward W. Hazen Foundation, 1946).

48. Cuninggim, *College Seeks Religion*, 264–92.

49. Merriam, "Religion in Higher Education," 17.

50. This interpretation of the name change is based on my March 20, 1991 interview with Harry Smith, who was director of the Society from 1969 to 1978. It is based, as well, upon my own reading of events as a postdoctoral Fellow of the Society from 1970 to 1990.

## 2. Educating to Understand the Other

1. Martin E. Marty, *The Noise of Conflict: 1919–1941*, vol. 2 of *Modern American Religion* (Chicago: University of Chicago Press, 1991), 378.

2. Josiah Strong, *Our Country*, ed. Jurgen Herbst (1891; reprint, Cambridge: Belknap Press of Harvard University Press, 1963). This reprint of the revised edition of 1891 carries an introduction by the editor that surveys the emergence of Strong's ideas. For a history of the Evangelical Alliance and Strong's role in that organization see Philip D. Jordan, *The Evangelical Alliance for the United States of America, 1847–1900: Ecumenism, Identity and the Religion of the Republic* (New York: Edwin Mellen Press, 1982).

3. For an examination of the consequences of the negative treatment of "other religions" as "outsiders" to an alleged America "mainstream"—consequences for scholarship about religion as well as for religious identity—see R. Laurence Moore, *Religious Outsiders and the Making of Americans* (New York: Oxford University Press, 1986).

4. For a discussion of the issues dividing evangelicals in the 1870s see George M. Marsden, *Fundamentalism and American Culture: The Shaping of Twentieth-Century Evangelicalism: 1870–1925* (New York: Oxford University Press, 1980), 11–32.

5. Philip Schaff, "Introduction: Letter from the Old Catholic Congress" in *History, Essays, Orations, and Other Documents of the Sixth General Conference of the Evangelical Alliance, Held in New York, October 2–12, 1873*, ed. Philip Schaff and S. Irenaeus Prime (New York: Harper & Brothers, 1874), 485–87; Roswell D. Hitchcock, "Romanism in the Light of History," ibid., 436–37. See also Philip Schaff, *The History of the Creeds*, vol. 1 of *The Creeds of Christendom* (New York: Harper & Brothers, 1877), 146–47.

6. Strong, *Our Country*, 213–15.

7. *The World's Parliament of Religions*, vol. 1, ed. John Henry Barrows (Chicago: Parliament Publishing Co., 1893), 9.

8. David F. Burg, *Chicago's White City of 1893* (Lexington, Ky.: University Press of Kentucky, 1976), 263.

9. *World's Parliament*, 1:21–22.

10. Cited by Grant Wacker, "Second Thoughts on the Great Commission: Liberal Protestants and Foreign Missions, 1890–1940," in *Earthen Vessels: American Evangelicals and Foreign Missions, 1880–1980*, ed. Joel A. Carpenter and Wilbert R. Shenk (Grand Rapids, Mich.: William B. Eerdmans, 1990), 283–84.

11. *World's Parliament*, 1:62–64.

12. Ibid., 1:118–20, 114, 127–28, 138, 345–51, 554–64; 2:989–96, 1068–70, 1024–30, 1056–61, 1080–83, 832–41, 950–56.

13. Ibid., 1:66–151, 184, 18.

14. Cited in Burg, *White City*, 236.

15. Reid Badger, *The Great American Fair: The World's Columbian Exposition and American Culture* (Chicago: Nelson Hall, 1979), xvi.

16. Cited in Henry Warner Bowden, *Church History in the Age of Science: Historiographical Patterns in the United States, 1876–1918* (Chapel Hill: University of

North Carolina Press, 1971), 61. Cf. George H. Shriver, *Philip Schaff: Christian Scholar and Ecumenical Prophet* (Macon, Ga.: Mercer University Press, 1987), 96.

17. H. Richard Niebuhr with Daniel Day Williams and James M. Gustafson, *The Purpose of the Church and Its Ministry: Reflections on the Aims of Theological Education* (New York: Harper & Row, 1956), 17.

18. "Statement of President Eliot," in *An Appeal In Behalf of the Further Endowment of the Divinity School of Harvard University* (Cambridge: John Wilson and Son, 1879), 24.

19. Cited in Richard Morgan Cameron, *Boston University School of Theology, 1839-1968* (Boston: Boston University School of Theology, 1968), 19.

20. Walter G. Muelder and L. Harold DeWolfe, "Philosophy of the Curriculum," *Nexus* 1 (February 1958): 55.

21. *Drew University Bulletin, 1961-62,* ADR, 88-89; Letter from Dean Tillett to Chancellor Kirkland, July 2, 1915, AV; Boone M. Bowen, *The Candler School of Theology: Sixty Years of Service* (Atlanta: Emory University, 1974), 66, 136; Walter N. Vernon, *Methodism Moves Across North Texas* (Nashville, Tenn.: Pantheon Press, 1967), 288-89; Robert E. Cushman, "Fifty Years of Theology and Theological Education at Duke; Retrospect and Prospect," *Duke Divinity School Review* 42 (Winter 1977), ADU, 8-13; *Bulletin of the University of Southern California, 1948-50,* ASC, 12-13; Ernest Cadman Colwell, "Address to the Advisory Council Meeting of the Southern California School of Theology at Claremont, Sept. 19, 1958," typescript, ACT, 2.

22. Vernon, *Methodism Moves,* citing a Roman Catholic publication, 334. For a less superlative assessment of Outler's substantial contribution to ecumenicity on a wide front see John Deschner, "Albert Cook Outler: A Biographical Memoir," in *Our Common Heritage as Christians: Essays in Honor of Albert C. Outler,* ed. John Deschner, Leroy T. Howe, and Klaus Penzel (New York: Oxford University Press, 1975), xv-xviii.

23. Examples of these developments may be found in Robert T. Handy, *A History of Union Theological Seminary in New York* (New York: Columbia University Press, 1987), 240-41, 243-46, 262-64; Henry Sloane Coffin, *A Half Century of Union Theological Seminary, 1896-1945* (New York: Charles Scribner's Sons, 1954), 224-34; Roland H. Bainton, *Yale and the Ministry: A History of Education for the Christian Ministry at Yale from the Founding in 1701* (New York: Harper & Brothers, 1957), 263-64; *Yale Divinity News* (May 1957), AYD, 3; *Harvard Divinity School: Deans' Reports, 1955,* AHD, 111-12, *1968,* 9-10; Jerald C. Brauer, "Reminiscences," *Criterion* 19 (Winter 1980): 9-10; Earl Kent Brown, "The Ecumenical Orientation of the School of Theology," *Nexus* 10 (February 1967): 29-32; Bard Thompson, *Vanderbilt Divinity School: A History* (Nashville, Tenn.: Vanderbilt University, 1958), 18-22; Bowen, *Candler,* 100-03; "Report of the Dean of the School of Religion to the President of Duke University," *Bulletin of Duke University, 1940,* ADU, 90; "Agreement Between Claremont College and Southern California School of Theology, June 5, 1957," ACT; Merrimon Cuninggim, "Uneasy Partners: Higher Education and the Church," unpublished typescript, 35-56.

24. Robert A. Schneider, "Voice of Many Waters: Church Federation in the Twentieth Century," in *Between the Times: The Travail of the Protestant Establishment*

*in America, 1900–1960,* ed. William R. Hutchison (Cambridge: Cambridge University Press, 1989), 95, 103, 113.

25. See, for example, Arthur Cushman McGiffert, "Presidential Inaugural Address, 1918," *Union Theological Seminary, Inaugural Addresses, 1915–1930,* AU, 23, 27–28.

26. Henry Pitney Van Dusen, "The Role of the Theological Seminary," *The Inauguration of Henry Pitney Van Dusen* (November 15, 1945), AU, 31. Cf. *Harvard Divinity School: Deans' Reports, 1948,* HDS, 3–4.

27. Elias B. Sanford, *Origin and History of the Federal Council of the Churches of Christ in America* (Hartford, Conn.: S. S. Scranton Co., 1916), 466.

28. Robert McAfee Brown, "Personal Musings on the Changing Ecumenical Scene," *Journal of Ecumenical Studies* 6 (Spring 1969): 236.

29. For an analysis of these events and their bearing on movements for Christian unity see Jeffrey K. Hadden, *The Gathering Storm in the Churches* (Garden City, N.Y.: Doubleday & Company, 1969), 103–207; Wade Clark Roof and William McKinney, *American Mainline Religion: Its Changing Shape and Future* (New Brunswick, N.J.: Rutgers University Press, 1987), 13–22; H. George Anderson, "Ecumenical Movements," in *Altered Landscapes: Christianity in America, 1935–1985,* ed. David W. Lotz with Donald W. Shriver, Jr., and John F. Wilson (Grand Rapids, Mich.: William B. Eerdmans, 1989), 92–105; Marlin VanElderen, *Introducing the World Council of Churches* (Geneva: WCC Publications, 1990), 140–62.

30. Joseph C. Hough, Jr., and John B. Cobb, Jr., *Christian Identity and Theological Education* (Chico, Calif.: Scholars Press, 1985), 103.

31. Ibid.

32. Don S. Browning, "Globalization and the Task of Theological Education," *Theological Education* 23 (Autumn 1986): 43–44.

33. S. Mark Heim, "Mapping Globalization for Theological Education," *Theological Education* 26, Sup. 1 (Spring 1990): 12–16.

34. Joseph C. Hough, Jr., "School of Theology at Claremont: Project Burning Bush," *Theological Education* 22 (Spring 1986): 62–67; Jane I. Smith, "Globalization in the Curriculum of Harvard Divinity School," ibid., 85–91; Kosuke Koyama, "Ecumenical and World Christianity Center, Union Theological Seminary, NYC," ibid., 132–37.

35. "ATS Task Force on Globalization," *Bulletin of the Association of Theological Schools* 38 (1988): 105; 39 (1990): 104–05.

36. "ATS Task Force," (1988), 110, 112.

37. Ibid., 113.

38. Data on the institutional effects of these various movements are reported by David S. Schuller, "Globalization in Theological Education: Summary and Analysis of Survey Data," *Theological Education* 22 (Spring 1986): 19–56.

39. See Heim, "Mapping Globalization," 9–12.

40. *Breaking Barriers: Official Report of the World Council of Churches, Nairobi, 23 November–10 December, 1975,* ed. David M. Paton (London: SPCK, 1975), 100–19.

41. Ernest W. Lefever, *Amsterdam to Nairobi: The World Council of Churches and the Third World* (Washington, D.C.: Ethics and Public Policy Center of Georgetown University, 1979), 41. Lefever's book combines a summary of changes in the out-

look of the World Council of Churches with a sharp critique of the Council's alignment with "leftist" political causes.

42. Konrad Raiser, *Ecumenism in Transition: A Paradigm Shift in the Ecumenical Movement?* (Geneva: WCC Publications, 1991), 71–75.

43. Fumitaka Matsuoka, "Pluralism at Home: Globalization within North America," *Theological Education* 26, Sup. 1 (Spring 1990): 40, 42.

44. See Hough and Cobb, *Christian Identity*, 104–16, 129–30; "ATS Task Force," (1988), 114–15; (1990), 105.

45. James K. Mathews, "New Delhi, New Departure in Mission," *Nexus* 5 (March 1962): 2.

46. *The New Delhi Report* (London: SCM Press, 1962), 59.

47. William R. Hutchison, *Errand to the World: American Protestant Thought and Foreign Missions* (Chicago: University of Chicago Press, 1987), 1–2.

48. H. P. Beach, "Yale's Contribution to Foreign Missions," in *Two Centuries of Christian Activity at Yale*, ed. James B. Reynolds, Samuel H. Fisher, and Henry B. Wright (New York: G. P. Putnam's Sons, 1901), 296; Coffin, *Half Century of Union*, 207; Thompson, *Vanderbilt Divinity School*, 12.

49. Dana Robert, "Mission Study at the University-Related Seminary: The Boston University School of Theology as a Case Study," *Missiology* 17 (April 1989): 194–95; Russell E. Richey, "Drew Theological Seminary and American Methodism: Some Historical Reflections," in *Scholarship, Sacraments and Service: Historical Studies in Protestant Tradition*, ed. Daniel B. Clendenin and W. David Buschart (Lewiston, N.Y.: Edwin Mellen Press, 1990), 90–95; "Report of the Dean of the School of Religion to the President of Duke University," *Bulletin of Duke University, 1937*, ADU, 92.

50. *Bulletin of Southern Methodist University: School of Theology, 1954–55*, ASMP, 56.

51. Robert, "Mission Study," 196.

52. See, for example, Louis Henry Jordan, *Comparative Religion: Its Genesis and Growth* (1905; reprint, Atlanta: Scholars Press, 1986), x–xii.

53. My typology of the study of world religions largely parallels Grant Wacker's typology of views of mission in his "A Plural World: The Protestant Awakening to World Religions," in *Between the Times*, 257–68.

54. On Clarke see Wacker, "A Plural World," 270; George H. Williams, "The Attitude of Liberals in New England Toward Non-Christian Religions, 1784–1885," *Crane Review* 9 (Winter 1967): 79–80.

55. *Bulletin of Emory University: School of Theology, 1915*, AEC, 101.

56. *Bulletin of Vanderbilt University: School of Religion, 1923*, AV, 26–27.

57. See Bainton, *Yale and the Ministry*, 248.

58. Cameron, *Boston School of Theology*, 22–23; Charles D. Cashdollar, *The Transformation of Theology, 1830–1890: Positivism and Protestant Thought in Britain and America* (Princeton, N.J.: Princeton University Press, 1989), 422; William Fairfield Warren, *The Earliest Cosmologies* (New York: Eaton & Mains, 1909); *Catalogue of Boston University School of Theology, 1874*, AB, 57; *1896*, 122–23.

59. Jordan, *Comparative Religion*, 201.

60. John R. Mott, *The Evangelization of the World in This Generation* (New York: Student Volunteer Movement for Foreign Missions, 1900), 15–16.

61. Ibid., 10–19.

62. Hutchison, *Errand to the World*, 92.

63. *Re-Thinking Missions: A Laymen's Inquiry After One Hundred Years* (New York: Harper & Brothers, 1932), 15–17.

64. Ibid., 244.

65. Ibid., 108–09; see also 33–38, 46, 49, 61.

66. William Ernest Hocking, *Living Religions and a World Faith* (New York: Macmillan Co., 1940), 17, 21–22, 26, 31, 36, 249.

67. Hutchison, *Errand to the World*, 164–75; Robert E. Speer, *"Re-Thinking Missions" Examined* (New York: Fleming H. Revell Co., 1933), 11–13; Archibald G. Baker, "Reactions to the *Laymen's Report*," *Journal of Religion* 13 (October 1933): 379–98.

68. Hocking, *Living Religions*, 21.

69. Daniel Johnson Fleming, *Whither Bound in Missions* (New York: Association Press, 1925), 67, 122, 86, 80, 24–25, 205–06.

70. Hutchison, *Errand to the World*, 152.

71. Edmund Davison Soper, *The Philosophy of the Christian World Mission* (New York: Abingdon–Cokesbury Press, 1943), 228.

72. *Drew University Bulletin, 1914*, ADR, 17, 21.

73. Edmund Davison Soper, *The Religions of Mankind* (New York: Abingdon–Cokesbury Press, 1921), 17–19, 190–91, 284.

74. Handy, *History of Union*, 204–05; *Bulletin of the Graduate School of Yale University, 1964–65*, AYU, 113; Robert, "Mission Study," 197; *Drew University Bulletin, The Graduate School, 1956*, ADR, 139; *Bulletin of the Candler School of Theology, 1967*, AEC, 19–20; Thomas A. Langford, "Religion and the Department of Religion at Duke," *Duke Divinity School Review* 30 (Autumn 1965): 183–87; *Bulletin of Southern Methodist University: The Graduate School of Humanities and Sciences, 1967–68*, ASMU, 30.

75. Robert, "Mission Study," 196–97.

76. Williams, "Attitude of Liberals," 87.

77. George Foot Moore, *History of Religions*, vol. 1 (New York: Charles Scribner's Sons, 1914), vii. Cf. "Courses of Instruction, 1917–18," *Harvard University Deans' Reports, 1918*, AHD, 114.

78. Moore, *History of Religions*, vol. 2: x.

79. George Foot Moore, *The Birth and Growth of Religion* (New York: Charles Scribner's Sons, 1923).

80. See Arthur Darby Nock, *Conversion: The Old and the New in Religion from Alexander the Great to Augustine of Hippo* (1933; reprint, London: Oxford University Press, 1961).

81. *Harvard University Deans' Reports, 1931*, AHD, 195–96.

82. Ibid., *1960*, 9.

83. Ibid., *1965*, 6–7.

84. *Religious Diversity: Essays by Wilfred Cantwell Smith*, ed. Willard G. Oxtoby (New York: Harper & Row, 1976), 3–21.

85. Wilfred Cantwell Smith, "Comparative Religion: Whither—and Why?" in *The History of Religions: Essays in Methodology*, ed. Mircea Eliade and Joseph M. Kitagawa (Chicago: University of Chicago Press, 1959), 33–35.

86. Ibid., 55–56.

87. George Rupp, "Entering the Eighties," Convocation Address, 1979, typescript, AHD. Cf. *Harvard Divinity School Announcements, 1981–82*, AHD, 9.

88. Charles Long, who, along with many others, has so characterized the field at the Chicago Divinity School, has also suggested that the trait springs from the environment of the University of Chicago as a whole, one that is prone to concerns for "method and methodologies within the several disciplines of academic life." Charles H. Long, "A Look at the Chicago Tradition in the History of Religions: Retrospect and Future," in *The History of Religions: Retrospect and Prospect*, ed. Joseph M. Kitagawa (New York: Macmillan, 1985), 87.

89. A. Eustace Haydon, "Twenty-Five Years of History of Religions," *Journal of Religion* 6 (January 1926): 32.

90. Joseph M. Kitagawa, "The Nature and Program of the History of Religions Field," *The Divinity School News* 24 (November 1957), ACU, 13–16; idem, "The History of Religions in America," in *History of Religions: Methodology*, 3.

91. A. Eustace Haydon, "From Comparative Religion to History of Religions," *Journal of Religion* 2 (November 1922): 587.

92. Haydon, "Twenty-Five Years," 33.

93. Mircea Eliade, *The Quest: History and Meaning in Religion* (Chicago: University of Chicago Press, 1969), 1, 7.

94. Joachim Wach, *Sociology of Religion* (Chicago: University of Chicago Press, 1944), 1, 12–16.

95. For an overview of developments in history of religions methods at Chicago see Long, "A Look at the Chicago Tradition," 87–97. See also Kitagawa, "History of Religions" in *History of Religions: Methodology*, 14–30; Mircea Eliade, "Methodological Remarks on the Study of Religious Symbolism," ibid., 86–107.

96. Long, "A Look at the Chicago Tradition," 99–100, 102.

97. Joseph M. Kitagawa, "The History of Religions (*Religionswissenschaft*) Then and Now," in *History of Religions: Retrospect and Prospect*, 132–33.

98. Dinesh D'Souza, *Illiberal Education: The Politics of Race and Sex on Campus* (New York: Free Press, 1991), 14. D'Souza is convinced that, in contrast to the 1960s, revolutions going on in the contemporary university are occurring "from the top down." Much of my study of divinity schools attempts to show that leadership for change "from the top down" is hardly a new phenomenon in the American university.

## 3. Theological and Religious Sciences

1. "The Boom in Religious Studies," *Time*, October 18, 1971: 83–84; "Cut Doctorates in Religion, Report Urges," *Chronicle of Higher Education* 6 (October 26, 1971): 1, 3.

2. Robert Michaelsen, "The Perils of Legitimacy," *Christian Century* 89 (February 2, 1972): 117–19. For Littell see "Cut Doctorates in Religion," 3.

3. Martin E. Marty, "Rating Welch's Ratings," *Christian Century* 89 (February 2, 1972): 122–23.

4. The author recalls during his tenure as a professor of religious studies at the

Pennsylvania State University the defensive posture of his department created by two articles in the *Chronicle of Higher Education*—one dealing with the Welch Report, the other with a 1978 national conference on religious studies that, according to the reporter, indicated disciplinary confusion, overextension in the university, and uncertainty about future directions. (See "For Religious Studies, an 'Identity Crisis,' " *Chronicle of Higher Education* 16 [March 20, 1978]: 11.) The two articles framed the emergence and the deterioration of the graduate program in religious studies at Penn State, which was founded in 1971, declined by virtue of faculty attrition in the late 1970s, and was eliminated by the university administration in 1981. Although it would be foolish to suggest that the negative publicity was the only, or even the principal, cause of the death of that program in a university environment fraught with financial difficulties, intra- and interdepartmental politics, and declining enrollments in the liberal arts, the adverse publicity made it doubly difficult for those of us in the program to plead its case.

5. Marty, "Rating Welch's Ratings," 123.

6. Claude Welch, *Graduate Education in Religion: A Critical Appraisal* (Missoula, Mont.: University of Montana Press, 1971), 168, 173, 177–78, 175, 230, 234.

7. Ibid., 240, 30–31, 203, 209–10, 179, 189–90.

8. Ibid., 104, 66–88, 42–44, 3–5, 19.

9. Ibid., 13–23.

10. Thorton W. Merriam, "Religion in Higher Education Through the Past Twenty-Five Years," in *Liberal Learning in Religion*, ed. Amos N. Wilder (New York: Harper & Brothers, 1951), 7.

11. The consequences of the American adoption of the German model of the "theological sciences" are discussed by Edward Farley, *Theologia: The Fragmentation and Unity of Theological Education* (Philadelphia: Fortress Press, 1983).

12. The story of science in America before the founding of Hopkins is told by Robert V. Bruce, *The Launching of Modern American Science, 1846–1876* (Ithaca, N.Y.: Cornell University Press, 1987).

13. Ibid., 336.

14. William Rainey Harper, "Shall the Theological Curriculum Be Modified, and How?" *American Journal of Theology* 3 (January 1899): 53–54.

15. See the responses to Harper by George Harris of Andover Theological Seminary, Augustus H. Strong of Rochester Theological Seminary, and Charles Cuthbert Hall of Union Theological Seminary in "Modifications in the Theological Curriculum," *American Journal of Theology* 3 (January 1899): 324, 326–28, 338–39.

16. Although divinity school registration records in the late nineteenth and early twentieth centuries indicate that a few students took science courses in university departments, they more frequently took courses in philosophy, foreign languages, and literature, and in some years no divinity students elected science courses. See, for example, *Harvard Divinity School: Deans' Reports, 1893–94*, AHD, 117; *1903–04*, 169–70; *Union Theological Seminary Annual Catalogue, 1900–01*, AU, 36–41.

17. The efforts of theologians to define science and religion as separate spheres, as well as the scientific limitations of process theology, are discussed by Wayne Proudfoot, "Religion and Science," in *Altered Landscapes: Christianity in America,*

*1935-1985,* ed. David W. Lotz with Donald W. Shriver, Jr., and John F. Wilson (Grand Rapids: William B. Eerdmans, 1989), 268–79.

18. C. P. Snow, *The Two Cultures and the Scientific Revolution* (Cambridge: Cambridge University Press, 1961). I agree with Gary Wills that Snow's distinction has all the marks of scientific elitism and that it would be better to speak of different literary or scientific "prejudices" or ways of looking at culture. Furthermore, it would be more appropriate to speak of multiple prejudices or cultures in twentieth-century America, rather than simply two. Nevertheless, Snow has aptly called attention to a deep division of understanding created by the emergence of the scientific revolution. See Gary Wills, *Under God: Religion and American Politics* (New York: Simon and Schuster, 1990), 89, 93.

19. Glenn T. Miller, *Piety and Intellect: The Aims and Purposes of Ante-Bellum Theological Education* (Atlanta: Scholars Press, 1990), 166–69.

20. Glenn T. Miller, "Professionals and Pedagogues: A Survey of Theological Education," in *Altered Landscapes,* 205.

21. Peter Novick, *That Noble Dream: The "Objectivity Question" and the American Historical Profession* (Cambridge: Cambridge University Press, 1988), 134–35.

22. Ephraim Emerton, "The Study of Church History," *Unitarian Review and Religious Magazine* 19 (January 1883): 2.

23. Ibid., 18.

24. Ibid., 9.

25. Henry Warner Bowden, *Church History in the Age of Science: Historiographical Patterns in the United States, 1876–1918* (Chapel Hill: University of North Carolina Press, 1971); Paul Schubert, "Shirley Jackson Case, Historian of Early Christianity: An Appraisal," *Journal of Religion* 29 (January 1949): 41–43.

26. For an example of such assumptions respecting both testaments see Roy A. Harrisville, *Frank Chamberlain Porter: Pioneer in American Biblical Interpretation* (Missoula, Mont.: Scholars Press, 1976), 5–38; regarding the assumptions in pastoral care see E. Brooks Holifield, *A History of Pastoral Care in America: From Salvation to Self-Realization* (Nashville, Tenn.: Abingdon Press, 1983), 196–201.

27. Douglas Clyde Macintosh, "Theology in a Scientific Age," in *Education for Christian Service,* by members of the faculty of the Divinity School of Yale University (New Haven, Conn.: Yale University Press, 1922), 135–36, 154; Albert C. Knudson, *The Philosophy of Personalism: A Study in the Metaphysics of Religion* (New York: Abingdon Press, 1927), 253–54, 300–02, 418–19.

28. McClintock appealed to Schleiermacher's *Kurze Darstellung des Theologischen Studiums* as "perhaps the best" among the numerous German encyclopedias. John McClintock, *Lectures on Theological Encyclopaedia and Methodology* (Cincinnati, Ohio: Hitchcock and Walden, 1873), 14–17, 176.

29. "Report of the Commission Appointed in 1911 to Investigate the Preparation of Religious Leaders in Universities and Colleges," *Religious Education* 7 (October 1912): 329–32, 343.

30. Ibid., 332.

31. Ibid., 345. Italics in original.

32. Hugh Hartshorne, Helen R. Stearns, and Willard B. Uphaus, *Standards and Trends in Religious Education* (New Haven, Conn.: Yale University Press, 1933), 173.

33. *University of Illinois Installation of Edmund Janes James as President of the University*, ed. W. N. Stearns (Urbana, Ill.: University of Illinois, 1906), 27.

34. Herbert Leon Searles, *The Study of Religion in State Universities* (Iowa City: University of Iowa, 1928), 59, 11.

35. Merriam, "Religion in Higher Education," 15–16.

36. Cited in Searles, *Religion in State Universities*, 37. See also Robert Michaelsen, *The Study of Religion in American Universities: Ten Case Studies with Special Reference to State Universities* (New Haven, Conn.: Society for Religion in Higher Education, 1965), 2. Winton Solberg has illustrated how religious foundations and other institutions created a religious presence at state universities in his studies of the University of Illinois. See Winton U. Solberg, *The University of Illinois, 1867–1894: An Intellectual and Cultural History* (Urbana, Ill.: University of Illinois Press, 1968); idem, "The Catholic Presence at the University of Illinois," *Catholic Historical Review* 76 (October 1990): 765–812; idem, "The Early Years of the Jewish Presence at the University of Illinois," *Religion and American Culture: A Journal of Interpretation* 2 (Summer 1992): 215–45.

37. Robert Michaelsen, "The Iowa School of Religion," *Religious Education* 52 (April 1957): 130–32.

38. Charles Hawley, "The School of Religion at the State University of Iowa," *Religious Education* 24 (December 1929): 963; Marcus Bach, *Of Faith and Learning: The Story of the School of Religion at the State University of Iowa* (Iowa City, Iowa: School of Religion, 1952), 46.

39. David Blaine Cable, "The Development of the Accrediting Function of the American Association of Theological Schools, 1918–1938" (Ph.D. diss., University of Pittsburgh, 1970), 56.

40. William Adams Brown, *Ministerial Education in America*, vol. 1 of *The Education of American Ministers* (New York: Institute of Social and Religious Research, 1934), 68–69.

41. Hartshorne, *Standards and Trends*, 217; Charles S. Braden, "Enrollment Trends in Religion Courses," *Religious Education* 43 (December 1948): 338.

42. *College Reading and Religion: A Survey of College Reading Materials* (New Haven, Conn.: Yale University Press, 1948).

43. Hartshorne, *Standards and Trends*, 189–90.

44. Harold Remus, F. Stanley Lusby, and Linda M. Tober, "Religion as an Academic Discipline," in *Encyclopedia of the American Religious Experience*, vol. 3, ed. Charles H. Lippy and Peter W. Williams (New York: Charles Scribner's Sons, 1988), 1657.

45. John F. Wilson, "Introduction: The Background and Present Context of the Study of Religion in Colleges and Universities," in *The Study of Religion in Colleges and Universities*, ed. Paul Ramsey and John F. Wilson (Princeton, N.J.: Princeton University Press, 1970), 6–7.

46. Brown, *Ministerial Education*, 69; Edwards W. Blakeman, "A Realistic View of Religion in State Universities," *Religious Education* 43 (December 1948): 355.

47. Merrimon Cuninggim, *The College Seeks Religion* (New Haven, Conn.: Yale University Press, 1947), 148, 151. See also Hartshorne, *Standards and Trends*, 218; *College Reading*, ix.

48. Cuninggim, *College Seeks*, chaps. 16, 17.

49. Quoted in Robert Wuthnow, *The Restructuring of American Religion: Society and Faith Since World War II* (Princeton, N.J.: Princeton University Press, 1988), 39. Chapter 3 of Wuthnow's book summarizes the postwar years in terms of their sense of "promise and peril." See also Godfrey Hodgson, *America in Our Time* (Garden City, N.Y.: Doubleday & Company, 1976), chap. 3.

50. Winthrop S. Hudson, *Religion in America*, 2d ed. (New York: Charles Scribner's Sons, 1973), 382. See also Leonard I. Sweet, "The Modernization of Protestant Religion in America," in *Altered Landscapes*, 24; and Will Herberg, *Protestant-Catholic-Jew*, 2d ed. (Garden City, N.Y.: Doubleday & Company, 1960), 46–64.

51. For examples of the expansion and the admissions selectivity that were widespread among the divinity schools see *Harvard Divinity School: Deans' Reports, 1954–55*, AHD, 100–03; "The Dean's Page," *The Perkins Journal* 5 (Fall 1951): 4; "Report of Liston Pope, Dean, to the President and Fellows of Yale University for 1949–50," AYD, 3, 6–7; Jerald C. Brauer, "Reminiscences," *Criterion* 19 (Winter 1980): 4–6; Robert T. Handy, *A History of Union Theological Seminary in New York* (New York: Columbia University Press, 1987), 219–20, 222–23; Paul K. Conkin, *Gone with the Ivy: A Biography of Vanderbilt University* (Knoxville: University of Tennessee Press, 1985), 500–02.

52. Wilhelm Pauck and Marion Pauck, *Paul Tillich: His Life and Thought* (New York: Harper & Row, 1976), 219–20, 250–56; Richard Wightman Fox, *Reinhold Niebuhr: A Biography* (New York: Pantheon Books, 1985), 131–32, 229–38, 243–44.

53. See Paul Tillich, *The Shaking of the Foundations* (New York: Charles Scribner's Sons, 1948); idem, *The Courage to Be* (New Haven, Conn.: Yale University Press, 1952); idem, *Systematic Theology*, vol. 1 (Chicago: University Of Chicago Press, 1951); idem, *Dynamics of Faith* (New York: Harper, 1956).

54. See especially Reinhold Niebuhr's *The Nature and Destiny of Man: A Christian Interpretation* (New York: Charles Scribner's Sons, 1949); *Love and Justice: Selections from the Shorter Writings of Reinhold Niebuhr*, ed. D. B. Robertson (Philadelphia: Westminster Press, 1957).

55. This is a description of Drew Theological School by Will Herberg, "Some Comments on the Theological Scene at Drew," *Drew Gateway* 31 (Winter 1961): 81–86. For examples of theological diversity in other divinity schools see Richard Morgan Cameron, *Boston University School of Theology, 1839–1968* (Boston: Boston University School of Theology, 1968), 95–96, 115–16; Charles Harvey Arnold, *Near the Edge of Battle: A Short History of the Divinity School and "The Chicago School of Theology," 1866–1966* (Chicago: The Divinity School Association of the University of Chicago, 1966), 86–88; "Report of the Dean of the Divinity School to the President of Duke University," *Bulletin of Duke University, 1959*, ADU, 65–66; *Harvard Divinity School: Deans' Reports, 1956–1974*, AHD, 7.

56. This conviction is discussed by Sweet, "Modernization of Protestant Religion," 22, in his examination of the 1939 issue of *Christian Century* on "How My Mind Has Changed in This Decade." For an overview of the different postwar postures among American Protestant theologians, see Gabriel Fackre, "Theology: Ephemeral, Conjunctural and Perennial," in *Altered Landscapes*, 246–49. For examples of theological responses to the war and to the old confidence in science

see Edwin Lewis, "The War and Theology," *Drew Gateway* 14 (Winter 1943): 13–16; H. Richard Niebuhr, *Christ and Culture* (New York: Harper & Brothers, 1951); idem, *Radical Monotheism and Western Culture* (New York: Harper & Row, 1960); Bernard Meland, "A Long Look at the Divinity School and Its Present Crisis," *Criterion* 1 (Summer 1962): 22–25.

57. Brauer, "Reminiscences," 4–5.

58. Bernard M. Loomer, "The Aim of Divinity Education," *Announcements of the University Of Chicago: The Divinity School, 1950–51*, ACU, 2, 4.

59. Brauer, "Reminiscences," 5.

60. A number of divinity school faculty who taught in the 1950s and early 1960s, interviewed informally by the author, generally recalled the period as one marked by lively discussion of theological issues by both faculty and students. For other testimony see Brauer, ibid., 4; DeForest Wiksten, "The Seminary Experience: from Arrogance to Assurance," *Perkins Journal* 22 (Winter 1964): 22–23; Boone M. Bowen, *The Candler School of Theology: Sixty Years of Service* (Atlanta: Emory University, 1974), 127; Handy, *History of Union*, 216–20; John Oliver Nelson, "A Quarter Century's Difference, 1933–1958," *Yale Divinity News* 55 (May 1958): 4; Gordon Harland, " 'The Best Years of Our Lives,' " in *Drew Occasional Papers No. 1* (Madison, N.J.: Drew University Graduate School, 1980), 6–7.

61. James Barr, "Revelation Through History in the Old Testament and in Modern Theology," in *New Theology No. 1*, ed. Martin E. Marty and Dean G. Peerman (New York: Macmillan Co., 1964), 62; David W. Lotz, "A Changing Historiography: From Church History to Religious History," in *Altered Landscapes*, 322–28; Holifield, *History of Pastoral Care*, 324–42.

62. *General Education in a Free Society: Report of the Harvard Committee* (Cambridge, Mass.: Harvard University Press, 1952), 4–5, 44–51, 74; *Establishing the Goals*, vol. 1 of *Higher Education for American Democracy: A Report of The President's Commission on Higher Education* (New York: Harper & Brothers, 1948), 2, 5–17, 47–50, 61.

63. Cuninggim, *College Seeks*, 42, 118; Clarence Prouty Shedd, *Proposals for Religion in Postwar Higher Education* (Hadden, Conn.: Hazen Foundation, 1946), 10, 19; Will Herberg, "Toward a Biblical Theology of Education," *Religious Education* 48 (November/December 1953): 378. For other examples of calls for a theologically oriented study of religion as a unifying factor in higher education see D. G. Hart, "The Troubled Soul of the Academy: American Learning and the Problem of Religious Studies," *Religion and American Culture: A Journal of Interpretation* 2 (Winter 1992): 61–63.

64. Alexander Miller, *Faith and Learning: Christian Faith and Higher Education in Twentieth Century America* (New York: Association Press, 1960), 102–43.

65. Huston Smith, "The Interdepartmental Approach to Religious Studies," *Journal of Higher Education* 31 (February 1960): 61–65.

66. Clyde A. Holbrook, *Religion, a Humanistic Field* (Englewood Cliffs, N.J.: Prentice-Hall, 1963), 119–44; Luther Harshbarger, "On Developing a Program of Study in Religion," in *A Report on an Invitational Conference on the Study of Religion in the State University* (New Haven, Conn.: Society for Religion in Higher Education, 1965), 85–86, 88–91; Michaelsen, *Study of Religion*, 157–59.

67. Holbrook, *Religion*, 130.

68. George F. Thomas, *Religion in an Age of Secularism* (Princeton, N.J.: Princeton University Press, 1940), 27.

69. Ibid., 28.

70. For examples see Harshbarger, "On Developing a Program," 85, 91; Miller, *Faith and Learning*, 152–53; Holbrook, *Religion*, 41–43, 49–54; Wilfred Cantwell Smith, "Non-Western Studies: The Religious Approach," in *Report on Invitational Conference*, 51; Reinhold Niebuhr, "Religion and Education," *Religious Education* 48 (November/December 1953): 372–73; Theodore M. Green, "Religion and the Humanities," in *Religion and the State University*, ed. Erich A. Walter (Ann Arbor: University of Michigan Press, 1958), 129–34.

71. *Religion*, Paul Ramsey, ed. (Englewood Cliffs, N.J.: Prentice-Hall, 1965). For evidence of the dominance of the divinity school curriculum in university undergraduate and graduate programs in religion see Michaelsen, *Study of Religion*, 72–73, 127–30, 141–45, 152–53.

72. Paul Ramsey, "Princeton University's Graduate Program in Religion," *Journal of Bible and Religion* 30 (October 1962): 294.

73. Michaelsen, *Study of Religion*, 11.

74. Van A. Harvey, "Reflections on the Teaching of Religion in America," *Journal of the American Academy of Religion* 38 (March 1970): 25–26.

75. Robert Jay Lifton, "Protean Man," in *The Religious Situation: 1969*, ed. Donald R. Cutler (Boston: Beacon Press, 1969), 812–28; *Understanding the New Religions*, ed. Jacob Needleman and George Baker (New York: Seabury Press, 1978); Steven M. Tipton, *Getting Saved from the Sixties: Moral Meaning in Conversion and Cultural Change* (Berkeley: University of California Press, 1982), 1–30; Ronald B. Flowers, *Religion in Strange Times: The 1960s and 1970s* (Macon, Ga.: Mercer University Press, 1984), 1–27.

76. See, for example, *Harvard Divinity School: Deans' Reports, 1966–67*, AHD, 2–4; Martin E. Marty, "The Doctor of Ministry After Seven Years," *Criterion* 10 (Spring 1971): 19–21.

77. Edmund Perry, "The Lilly Study: An Unfulfilled Promise," *Journal of Bible and Religion* 34 (April 1966): 113–14. Perry's remarks were part of his commentary on a report sponsored by the Lilly Endowment on preprofessional education for the ministry. Perry and other college teachers of religion believed that the report was governed by the perspective of the American Association of Theological Schools, ignored developments in the study of religion within colleges and universities, and generally subordinated the worth of religious studies to what it could contribute to theological studies. See other articles in this issue of *Journal of Bible and Religion*, as well as Keith R. Bridston and Dwight W. Culver, *Pre-Seminary Education* (Minneapolis, Minn.: Augsburg Publishing House, 1965).

78. Dwight Beck, "Report of the NABI Self-Study Committee," *Journal of Bible and Religion* 32 (April 1964): 200; Clyde A. Holbrook, "Why an Academy of Religion?" ibid., 99.

79. Welch, *Graduate Education*, 192–94; Wilson, "Introduction," to *Religion in Colleges and Universities*, 14–21.

80. Ray L. Hart, "JAAR in the Seventies: Unconcluding Unscientific Postface," *Journal of the American Academy of Religion* 47 (December 1979): 513–14.

81. Robert F. Campany, "Trends in the Contributorship to Periodical Literature in Religion, 1950–1983: A Second Report," typescript prepared for the Council on Theological Research and Scholarship of the Association of Theological Schools in the United States and Canada (June 11, 1984), 1–2, 9, 11–12.

82. Many of the early discussions of the nature of the field as humanistic or social scientific were elicited by the thesis of Clyde Holbrook that it was essentially humanistic in that it should offer students an "ordered insight into life" and assist them in attaining self-understanding. Holbrook also held that theology as the "rational clarification of religious convictions" belonged in the college curriculum as a part of the free interchange of ideas. Through his work in the NABI and the AAR Holbrook was a leader in trying to secure for religious studies a scholarly independence from the theological schools, but his critics found his limiting of the field to the humanities, theologically interpreted, to be captive to a theological model of education, blind to the contributions of the social sciences, and productive of the suspicion on the part of the university that religious studies belongs to the domain of the theological school rather than to that of liberal studies. See Holbrook, *Religion*, 41–43, 167, 231–32; idem, "Why an Academy," 97–105; Harvey, "Reflections on Teaching," 25; John F. Wilson, "Mr. Holbrook and the Humanities, or Mr. Schlatter's Dilemma," *Journal of Bible and Religion* 32 (July 1964): 252–61. For later debates about religious studies as a program in the humanities see William A. Clebsch, "Religious Studies Now: Not Why Not? But Why Not Now?" *Religious Education* 70 (May/June 1975): 264–77; Jacob Neusner, "Religious Studies: The Next Vocation," *Bulletin of the Council on the Study of Religion* 8 (December 1977): 118–20; James M. Robinson, "Religious Studies as Humanizing Studies," *Soundings: An Interdisciplinary Journal* 71 (Summer/Fall 1988): 207–19.

83. See William F. May, "Why Theology and Religious Studies Need Each Other," *Journal of the American Academy of Religion* 70 (December 1984): 750–52; Mark C. Taylor, "The Cutting Edge of Reason," *Soundings* 71 (Summer/Fall 1988): 318–19; Jacob Neusner, "Understanding Seeking Faith: The Case of Judaism," ibid., 329–31. For a discussion of how these arguments led to openness to "a legitimate place for theology in religion studies" in one university department see James B. Wiggins, "The Department of Religion at Syracuse University," *Bulletin of the Council on the Study of Religion* 10 (October 1979): 110.

84. Donald Wiebe, "The Failure of Nerve in the Academic Study of Religion," *Sciences Religieuses/Studies in Religion* 13 (Fall 1984): 401–22; Ivan Strenski, "Our Very Own 'Contras': A Response to the 'St. Louis Project' Report," *Journal of the American Academy of Religion* 54 (Summer 1986): 323–35.

85. J. Samuel Preus, *Explaining Religion: Criticism and Theory from Bodin to Freud* (New Haven, Conn.: Yale University Press, 1987), ix–xxi, 209–11. Much the same view of the study of the Hebrew Bible has been taken by Robert A. Oden, Jr., *The Bible Without Theology: The Theological Tradition and Alternatives to It* (San Francisco: Harper & Row, 1987), vii–ix.

86. Ray L. Hart, "Religious and Theological Studies in American Higher Education: A Pilot Study," *Journal of the American Academy of Religion* 59 (Winter 1991): 732–33.

87. For surveys of some of these trends in the methods and areas of study

see Remus and others, "Religion as an Academic Discipline," 1663, 1666–68; Hart, "Troubled Soul," 66–70; Harvey, "Reflections on Teaching," 28–29.

88. See, for example, William A. Clebsch, "History and Salvation: An Essay in Distinctions," in *Religion in Colleges and Universities*, ed. Ramsey and Wilson, 40–72; David Little, "Comparative Religious Ethics," ibid., 216–45; Oden, *Bible Without Theology*.

89. May, "Why Theology and Religious Studies," 752.

90. For examples of awareness of such subtleties of interpretation among religious studies scholars who have construed the field in objectivist, nonadvocacy terms see Preus, *Explaining Religion*, xix–xx; William Scott Green, "Something Strange, Yet Nothing New: Religion in the Secular Curriculum," *Soundings* 71 (Summer/Fall 1988): 276–77; Stephen D. Crites and others, *Liberal Learning and the Religion Major*, The American Academy of Religion Task Force for the American Association of Colleges (Atlanta: Scholars Press, 1990), 13–18.

91. James M. Gustafson, "The Study of Religion in Colleges and Universities: A Practical Commentary," in *Religion in Colleges and Universities*, ed. Ramsey and Wilson, 330, 335; Crites and others, *Liberal Learning*, 3–4.

92. In 1993, deans at the University of Pennsylvania, Virginia Polytechnic Institute, and the University of Alberta at Edmonton indicated that they were recommending the closing of their religious studies departments and the assignment of religious studies faculty members to alternate academic units within the humanities and social sciences. Warren G. Frisina, "Three Departments of Religion Under Threat of Dissolution," *Religious Studies News* 8 (November 1993): 9.

93. Hart, "JAAR in the Seventies," 510–12. See also Robert Michaelsen, "Reflections on the Tie that Binds," *Soundings* 71 (Summer/Fall 1988): 349–53; Walter Capps, "Religious Studies and Creative Reflection," ibid., 373–79.

94. "After Years in Academic Limbo, the Study of Religion Undergoes a Revival of Interest Among Scholars," *Chronicle of Higher Education* 34 (February 3, 1988): A 5–7.

95. Robert S. Michaelsen, "Cutting Edges," *Journal of the American Academy of Religion* 59 (Spring 1991): 140.

96. See Laurence Veysey, "The Plural Organized Worlds of the Humanities," in *The Organization of Knowledge in Modern America, 1860–1920* (Baltimore, Md.: Johns Hopkins University Press, 1978), 68–69; Novick, *Noble Dream*, 579.

97. Confirmation of this difference appeared in Ray Hart's attitudinal survey. In seminaries and divinity schools, "globalization" and "internationalization" tended to connote the personal horizons of students and faculty, a meaning due in large part to the presence of international students and foreign faculty exchanges in the theological schools. On the other hand, religious studies faculty tended to equate questions about "globalization" and "internationalization" with "What scholarship in what countries do I read, and in what countries is my stuff read?" Hart, "Religious and Theological Studies," 777–78.

98. Hart's study found that although a sizable percentage of religious studies faculty hold an "intermediary seminary degree," that is probably a generational matter. "Thus if we look back at faculty under 40: in public universities, none (0%); in private colleges, 33.3%; in private universities, with departments only [no seminaries], 11.1%." Ibid., 789, n.119.

99. These statistics were developed from data provided by those schools examined, and from the catalogues of those schools listed, in the directories of the Council of Societies for the Study of Religion. See, e.g., *CSSR Directory of Departments and Programs of Religious Studies in North America*, ed. Watson E. Mills (Macon, Ga.: Mercer University Press, 1991). The highest numbers of entry-level professors at public universities who were trained at divinity schools hailed from the graduate programs at Chicago (13.68 percent), Harvard (9.40 percent), and Yale (6.84 percent). The highest numbers of appointments from graduate programs not based in divinity schools came from the University of California at Santa Barbara (7.26 percent), the University of Virginia (3.85 percent), Brown and Princeton (2.56 percent each).

100. Between 1978 and 1985, 9 percent of Chicago Divinity School students were enrolled in the professional ministerial program, the Doctor of Ministry, with the remainder enrolled in the masters and doctoral programs. Percentages were derived from enrollment figures provided by the Office of the Dean of Students of the Divinity School of the University of Chicago.

101. For examples see "Planning Profile of the Divinity School of Vanderbilt University, Period 1972-73—1978-79," typescript, AV, 7, 34; Martin E. Marty, "Coordinating Studies," *Criterion* 9 (Winter 1970): 11; "Priorities and Resources Committee Report, 1975," typescript, AHD, 16-19; "Report of the Committee on the Divinity School and the Department of Religious Studies," typescript (November 1967), AYD, 13-14.

102. *Bulletin of the Graduate School, Yale University, 1968-69*, AYU, 141, 148; *1969-70*, 147; *1971-72*, 144-54; Memorandum from Joseph Tyson to Herndon Wagers, April 21, 1972, ASMP; "Final Report of the Steering Committee of the Graduate Program in Religion, 1975-76," ASMP; *Faculty Bulletin of Duke Divinity School* 2 (February 9, 1960) ADU; "Religion in Boston University: Report of the Study Committee, 1970," AB, 32-34.

103. A description of the actions taken, and their educational purposes, is found in James M. Gustafson and Robert C. Johnson, "The Study of Religion at Yale," *Reflection* 63 (November 1965): 1-3. Faculty tensions over the founding of the Graduate Department in Religious Studies at Yale were created in part by the fact that Divinity School professors excluded from official status on the graduate faculty were expected to continue to teach graduate students, the establishment of the Department through administrative and board fiat after consultation with only a few Divinity School professors, and disagreements in the 1970s between faculty and Dean Colin Williams over governance and the relative importance of ministerial and graduate education. These strains and stresses are apparent in Memorandum of December 8, 1970 from James Gustafson to Colin Williams, AYD; "Annual Report of the Dean of the Divinity School of Yale University," 1963-64 and 1973-74, AYD; George Lindbeck, "Relations to the Department of Religious Studies," typescript (November 1972); Memorandum of January 20, 1978 from George Lindbeck to James Dittes, AYD; "University Council Committee Report," typescript (May 2, 1980), AYD, 4.

104. Langdon Gilkey, "Christian Theology," *Criterion* 13 (Winter 1974): 11. Other faculty attest to the prevalence of the study of religion at the Divinity School in this issue of *Criterion* devoted to "The Divinity School Fields and Pro-

grams at Mid-Decade." For statements of purpose at the Divinity School see *Announcements of the University of Chicago: Divinity School, 1969–70*, ACU, 1; *1974–75*, 6.

105. At Yale a seminar on college and university teaching and a course on approaches to the study of religion recommended for all first-year graduate students eventually disappeared because of unavailability of faculty interested in teaching the courses. Interview of the author with George Lindbeck, July 29, 1989; *Bulletin of the Graduate School, Yale University, 1968–69*, AYU, 148; *1971–72*, 144–54; *1972–73*, 152; *1973–74*, 158. The traditional theological school organization of the graduate curriculum, the heavy reliance on divinity school faculty, and the mixing of graduate and ministerial candidates in the same courses are apparent in the catalogues of the divinity schools for the 1970s and 1980s.

106. See George Lindbeck's report on his study of university divinity schools, sponsored by the Rockefeller Foundation, "Theological Education in North America Today," *Bulletin of the Council on the Study of Religion* 8 (October 1977): 87; Joseph C. Hough, Jr., "Ecumenical Seminaries and Constituencies: Theological Education and the Aims of the University," *Christianity and Crisis* 50 (April 9, 1990): 115; Rebecca S. Chopp, "Evaluation Report of Lilly Funded Projects on Theological Education: Younger Scholars Perspective" (n.p., 1991), 29, 34–35.

## 4. Theory and Practice

1. See Derek Bok, *Higher Learning* (Cambridge: Harvard University Press, 1986), 73–113.

2. Nathan O. Hatch, "Introduction: The Professions in a Democratic Culture," in *The Professions in American History*, ed. Nathan O. Hatch (Notre Dame, Ind.: University of Notre Dame Press, 1988), 2.

3. Burton J. Bledstein, *The Culture of Professionalism: The Middle Class and the Development of Higher Education in America* (New York: W. W. Norton, 1976), x, 38.

4. Bruce A. Kimball, Review of *Law School* by Robert Stevens and *Learning to Heal* by Kenneth Ludmerer, *Journal of Higher Education* 59 (July/August 1988): 458.

5. Bledstein, *Culture of Professionalism*, 86.

6. Bernard Barber, "Some Problems in the Sociology of the Professions," in *The Professions in America*, ed. Kenneth S. Lynn (Boston: Houghton Mifflin, 1965), 17.

7. Laurence Veysey, "Higher Education as a Profession: Changes and Continuities," in *Professions in American History*, 17–18.

8. Hatch, "Professions in a Democratic Culture," 1–2; Barber, "Problems in Sociology of Professions," 18.

9. Bledstein, *Culture of Professionalism*, x.

10. Hatch, "Professions in a Democratic Culture," 3. See also Bledstein, *Culture of Professionalism*, 33; Kimball, Review, 457–59; Everett C. Hughes, "Professions," in *Professions in America*, 2.

11. Mark A. May, *The Profession of the Ministry*, vol. 2 of *The Education of American Ministers* (New York: Institute of Social and Religious Research, 1934), 23–25.

12. Glenn T. Miller, *Piety and Intellect: The Aims and Purposes of Ante-Bellum Theological Education* (Atlanta: Scholars Press, 1990), 440.

13. Robert S. Michaelsen, "The Protestant Ministry in America: 1850–1950," in *The Ministry in Historical Perspectives*, ed. H. Richard Niebuhr and Daniel D. Williams (San Francisco: Harper & Row, 1956; rev. ed. 1983), 278; Dorothy C. Bass, "Ministry on the Margin: Protestants and Education," in *Between the Times: The Travail of the Protestant Establishment in America, 1900–1960*, ed. William R. Hutchison (Cambridge: Cambridge University Press, 1989), 56–57.

14. Robert L. Kelly, *Theological Education in America. A Study of One Hundred Sixty-One Theological Schools in the United States and Canada* (New York: George H. Doran Co., 1924), 154; Yoshio Fukuyama, *The Ministry in Transition: A Case Study of Theological Education* (University Park: Pennsylvania State University Press, 1972), 20–21.

15. Edwin S. Gaustad, "The Pulpit and the Pews," in *Between the Times*, 31–32; Michaelsen, "Protestant Ministry," 279–80; Donald M. Scott, *From Office to Profession: The New England Ministry, 1750–1850* (Philadelphia: University of Pennsylvania Press, 1978), 61–63.

16. Quoted in Sidney E. Mead, "The Rise of the Evangelical Conception of the Ministry in America (1607–1850)," in *Ministry in Historical Perspectives*, 218.

17. For a fuller story of the transformation of the Protestant ministry in America see Scott, *Office to Profession*; Mead, "Evangelical Conception of Ministry," 207–49; Martin E. Marty, "The Clergy," in *Professions in American History*, 73–90. For a discussion of the internal diversification of the churches, see chap. 1 of this book.

18. Letter from Wilbur Tillett to Collins Denny, May 31, 1915, box 3, Divinity School Records, AV.

19. Report of Dean Winton to Chancellor Kirkland for the year 1935–36, box 104, AV; *Bulletin of Vanderbilt University School of Religion, 1936*, AV, 10–12, 15.

20. *Bulletin of the University of Southern California, 1908–09*, ASC, 148–50; *1909–10*, 196; *1918–19*, 14; John T. Cunningham, *University in the Forest: The Story of Drew University* (Florham Park, N.J.: Afton Publishing Co., 1972), 58–60, 72, 91–92, 119; *Catalogue of Boston University School of Theology, 1874*, AB, 54; *Reports of the Dean of Candler School of Theology to the President of Emory University, 1917–18, 1926, 1928, 1929, 1932*, AEU; "Report of the Dean of the School of Religion to the President of Duke University," *Bulletin of Duke University, 1925–31*, ADU, 62, 64; *Bulletin of Southern Methodist University, 1919*, ASMU, 102, 156; Mary Martha Hosford Thomas, *Southern Methodist University: Founding and Early Years* (Dallas: Southern Methodist University Press, 1974), 45; Levering Reynolds, Jr., "The Later Years (1880–1953)," in *The Harvard Divinity School: Its Place in Harvard University and in American Culture*, ed. George H. Williams (Boston: Beacon Press, 1954), 187–88; Gerald Everett Knoff, "The Yale Divinity School, 1858–1899" (Ph.D. diss., Yale University, 1936), 421; Charles R. Gillett, "Detailed History of the Union Theological Seminary in the City of New York," vol. 1, typescript (n.d.), AU, 903–905.

21. From an address of Kirsopp Lake at a meeting in 1924 of the Conference of Theological Seminaries and Colleges, quoted in David Blaine Cable, "The Development of the Accrediting Function of the American Association of Theological Schools, 1918–1938" (Ph.D. diss., University of Pittsburgh, 1970), 47.

22. Kelly, *Theological Education*, 220.

23. Kenneth M. Ludmerer, *Learning to Heal: The Development of American Medical Education* (New York: Basic Books, 1985), 3.

24. From Black's "Reminiscences" as cited in Robert Stevens, *Law School: Legal Education in America from the 1850s to the 1980s* (Chapel Hill: University of North Carolina Press, 1983), 37.

25. Summaries of these developments in medicine and law are found in Ronald L. Numbers, "The Fall and Rise of the American Medical Profession," in *Professions in American History*, 63; Maxwell H. Bloomfield, "Law: The Development of a Profession," ibid., 43–44.

26. Anson Phelps Stokes, "University Schools of Religion," *Religious Education* 9 (April 1914): 323–35.

27. William Adams Brown, *Ministerial Education in America*, vol. 1 of *The Education of American Ministers*, 3–4.

28. *Harvard Divinity School: Deans' Reports, 1963–64*, AHD, 3–4.

29. Brown, *Ministerial Education*, 184–85, 190–91, 194, 223–26.

30. Ibid., 223–27.

31. Ibid., v–x.

32. Cable, "Development of the Accrediting Function," 108–12.

33. Ibid., 97–99.

34. Between 1960 and 1980, Roman Catholic, Eastern Orthodox, and a number of evangelical schools formed connections with the AATS, and the association expanded into such activities as the provision of faculty fellowships, the facilitation of change in theological school curriculum, and the promotion of the causes of women and minority students and faculty. See Jesse H. Ziegler, *ATS Through Two Decades: Reflections on Theological Education, 1960–1980* (Worcester, Mass.: Heffernan Press, 1984), 39–48, 82, 197–201.

35. Cable, "Development of the Accrediting Function," 113–14, 121.

36. Charles R. Fielding, *Education for Ministry* (Dayton, Ohio: American Association of Theological Schools, 1966), 15–18.

37. Ziegler, *ATS*, 76–79, 94–95.

38. Shailer Mathews, "The Function of the Divinity School," *Journal of Religion* 13 (July 1933): 258–59.

39. Shailer Mathews, "Vocational Efficiency and the Curriculum," *American Journal of Theology* 16 (April 1912): 171–72.

40. Mathews, "Function of the Divinity School," 253–54.

41. Edgar J. Goodspeed, "The Divinity School," *University of Chicago Magazine* 7 (March 1915), ACU, 138–39; Mathews, "Vocational Efficiency," 180.

42. Mathews, "Vocational Efficiency," 171.

43. Ibid., 175–76; Mathews, "Function of the Divinity School," 259–60.

44. *Bulletin of Yale Divinity School, 1822–1922*, AYD, 12.

45. Robert C. Johnson, "The Evolution of the YDS Curriculum," memorandum of November 1, 1979 to the Curriculum Committee of Yale Divinity School, AYD, 1–2; *Bulletin of Yale Divinity School, 1931–32*, AYD, 20–26.

46. *Reports of the Deans to the President of Yale University, 1930–31*, AYU, 9–11.

47. *Union Theological Seminary Annual Catalogue, 1910–11*, AU, 47–48, 52–73; *1919–20*, 51–55; *1930–31*, 48–49; *Catalogue of Boston University School of Theology,*

*1926*, AB, 331–34; *Drew Gateway* 8 (April 1930), ADR, 2–3; *Bulletin of Vanderbilt University School of Religion, 1915*, AV, 15–17; *Bulletin of the University of Southern California School of Religion, 1922–23*, ASC, 217–20; *1927–28*, 9–15; *Bulletin of Emory University School of Theology, 1915*, AEC, 83–85, 109; *Annual Catalogue of Duke University, 1926–27*, ADU, 275–76; *1930–31*, 61; *Bulletin of Southern Methodist University, 1919*, ASMU, 104; *1924*, 155–57.

48. Reynolds, "Later Years," 188–210; *Harvard Divinity School: Deans' Reports, 1907–08*, AHD, 156–57; *1914–15*, 138; *1915–16*, 130–31.

49. See, for example, *Harvard Divinity School: Deans' Reports, 1926–27*, AHD, 179; *1929–30*, 192; *1931–32*, 197; *Catalogue of Boston University School of Theology, 1932*, AB, 522; Richard Morgan Cameron, *Boston University School of Theology, 1839–1968* (Boston: Boston University School of Theology, 1968), 125–26; *Drew Gateway* 3 (January 1932): 8–9; Boone M. Bowen, *The Candler School of Theology: Sixty Years of Service* (Atlanta: Emory University, 1974), 51, 57; "Report of the Dean of the School of Religion to the President of Duke University," *Bulletin of Duke University, 1935*, ADU, 99.

50. Brown, *Ministerial Education*, 190–93; *Harvard Divinity School: Deans' Reports, 1933–34*, AHD, 233–34; Cable, "Development of the Accrediting Function," 77–78.

51. See chap. 3 of this book for a discussion of the dominance of theological themes in this period of history.

52. Robert E. Cushman, "Objectives of Theological Education—and Impediments," *Duke Divinity School Bulletin* 26 (February 1961): 16. Italics in original.

53. Bernhard W. Anderson, "Proposals for Administrative Organization," typescript (February 16, 1962), ADR, 2, 5.

54. Merrimon Cuninggim, "Changing Emphases in the Seminary Curriculum," *Journal of Bible and Religion* 23 (April 1955): 110–19.

55. Bernard Loomer, "The Aim of Divinity Education," *Announcements of the University of Chicago: The Divinity School, 1950–51*, ACU, 2, 4; Memorandum of James Gustafson to Robert Johnson regarding the purpose of the Yale Divinity School (1961), AYD; Robert T. Handy, *A History of Union Theological Seminary in New York* (New York: Columbia University Press, 1987), 228, 236; *Harvard Divinity School: Deans' Reports, 1958–59*, AHD, 1–8; Walter G. Muelder, "Some Issues Facing the Future of Theological Education," *Zion's Herald* 137 (June 1959): 3, 20; *Bulletin of Vanderbilt University Divinity School, 1958–59*, AV, 14; Eric L. Titus, "A History of the School of Theology at Claremont," typescript (1983), ACT, 15–20; "History of the Curriculum," *Report of the Long-Range Planning Committee, 1987*, AEC, 8.

56. *Bulletin of Yale Divinity School, 1949–50*, AYD, 20–21; *Bulletin of Southern Methodist University: Perkins School of Theology, 1954–55*, ASMU, 45–50.

57. The pattern was detected by H. Richard Niebuhr, Daniel Day Williams, and James M. Gustafson, *The Advancement of Theological Education* (New York: Harper & Brothers, 1957), 20–22.

58. Philip Rieff, *The Triumph of the Therapeutic: Uses of Faith After Freud* (New York: Harper & Row, 1966).

59. See E. Brooks Holifield, "Pastoral Care and Counseling," in vol. 3 of *Encyclopedia of the American Religious Experience*, ed. Charles H. Lippy and Peter W. Williams (New York: Charles Scribner's Sons, 1988), 1590.

60. These statistics furnished in ibid., 1591.

61. Ibid., 1592.

62. Glenn T. Miller, "Professionals and Pedagogues: A Survey of Theological Education," in *Altered Landscapes: Christianity in America, 1935–1985,* ed. David W. Lotz with Donald W. Shriver, Jr., and John F. Wilson (Grand Rapids, Mich.: William B. Eerdmans, 1989), 199.

63. Seward Hiltner, *Preface to Pastoral Theology* (New York: Abingdon Press, 1958), 50–51.

64. *Junction* 5 (April 1970), AEC, 9.

65. Cameron, *Boston School of Theology,* 118–21; Walter G. Muelder and L. Harold DeWolfe, "Philosophy of the Curriculum," *Nexus* 1 (February 1958): 59–60; Walter L. Holcomb, "Our Theology Curriculum Go-Round," *Nexus* 13 (Spring 1970): 15–16.

66. Paul E. Johnson, *Person and Counselor* (Nashville, Tenn.: Abingdon Press, 1967), 55–62.

67. For a review of the theological orientations of pastoral theologians see E. Brooks Holifield, *A History of Pastoral Care in America: From Salvation to Self-Realization* (Nashville, Tenn.: Abingdon Press, 1983), 324–42.

68. See, for example, Handy, *History of Union,* 236; "Documents, Reports, and Minutes of the Educational Policy Committee of Drew Theological School, 1959–1960," ADR.

69. See, for example, Howard Grimes, "A History of the Perkins School of Theology" (n.p., n.d.), ASMP, 26–28; *Reports of the Deans to the President of Yale University, 1967–68,* AYU, 1–2.

70. Johnson, "Evolution of Curriculum," AYD, 7.

71. Fielding, *Education for Ministry,* 15. Italics in original.

72. Robert E. Cushman, "Theological Education: A Reconsideration of Its Nature in Light of Its Objective," *Duke Divinity School Review* 33 (Winter 1968): 7.

73. Charles W. Ranson, *A Missionary Pilgrimage* (Grand Rapids, Mich.: William B. Eerdmans, 1988), 172–73.

74. David H. Kelsey, "A Theological Education About and Against the Church," in *Beyond Clericalism: The Congregation as a Focus for Theological Education,* ed. Joseph C. Hough, Jr., and Barbara G. Wheeler (Atlanta: Scholars Press, 1988), 40.

75. James T. Laney, "Formation of the Ministry," *Junction* 5 (April 1970), AEC, 1–2.

76. Ibid.

77. Barbara Rich in an interview with Robert Treese and Walter Holcomb, "Area D: Ministry in Church and Society," *Nexus* 19 (Winter 1976): 4.

78. See chap. 7 of this book.

79. *Bulletin of Emory University: The Candler School of Theology, 1971,* AEC, 9–10; *1973,* 7; "Self-Study Report of the Candler School of Theology, 1982," AEC, 33–41.

80. Claus H. Rohlfs, "A History of the Development of the Perkins Intern Program," *Perkins Journal* 31 (Winter 1978): 1–31; James M. Ward, "Dean Quillian as Dean of the Perkins Faculty," *Perkins Journal* 34 (Spring 1981): 9–10.

81. *Bulletin of Duke University: The Divinity School, 1977–78,* ADU, 23–24, 40–42; Planning Document: "Five Year Plan, Ten Year Vision," ADU, 3; *Bulletin of Vanderbilt University: The Divinity School, 1968–69,* AV, 258–59, 276–81; *1981–82,* 31, 35–38; Rich, "Area D," 2–7; *Drew University Catalogue, 1973–74,* ADR, 131–37, 150–61;

*1981–83*, 95–96; *Catalogue of the School of Theology at Claremont, 1973–75*, ACT, 17–21.

82. *Bulletin of Duke University: The Divinity School, 1990–91*, ADU, 55.

83. *Announcements of the University of Chicago: The Divinity School, 1965–66*, ACU, 25; Gibson Winter, "Theological Education for Ministry: Central Issues in Curriculum Construction," *Theological Education* 2 (Spring 1966): 189.

84. "Annual Reports of the Dean of the Divinity School of Yale University," 1969–70, 1971–72, 1973–74, AYD; Proposal of the Curriculum Committee of Yale Divinity School, 1971, AYD.

85. Martin E. Marty, "The Divinity School at Mid-Decade: An Essay and Guide," *Criterion* 13 (Autumn 1974): 20–21; Jay A. Wilcoxen, "The D.Min. Program Then and Now," *Criterion* 13 (Winter 1974): 8–9; William D. Obalil, "The Doctor of Ministry Program: A Student's View," ibid., 9–10.

86. *Bulletin of Yale University: The Divinity School, 1987–89*, AYD, 54–55; *Catalog of Union Theological Seminary in the City of New York, 1981–82*, AU, 47, 139–43; *1989–91*, 22–24; *Harvard Divinity School: Deans' Reports, 1971–72*, AHD, 1–3; *1980–81*, 1–5; *Harvard Divinity School Announcements, 1981–82*, AHD, 9–13; *1989–90*, 13–16.

87. See, for example, *Harvard Divinity School, Deans' Reports, 1976–77*, AHD, 7–8.

88. Discussion Document, Faculty Meeting, April 15, 1984, AB; "Annual Report of the Dean of the Divinity School of Yale University, 1969–79," AYD, 9; Marvin J. Taylor, "A Theological Faculties Profile: 1981 Data Compared with the 1971 Study," *Theological Education* 19 (Autumn 1982): 126–28.

89. Joseph C. Hough, Jr., and John B. Cobb, Jr., *Christian Identity and Theological Education* (Chico, Calif.: Scholars Press, 1985), 118.

90. "Self-Study Report of the Candler School of Theology, 1982," AEC, 42; "Revised M.Div. Curriculum: Summary of Changes, 1989," AEC, 4–5.

91. "Annual Report of the Dean of the Boston University School of Theology, 1988–89," AB.

92. The emergence of the twofold scheme as the more fundamental classification of the theological curriculum is the thrust of the article by Robert Wood Lynn, "Notes Toward a History: Theological Encyclopedia and the Evolution of Protestant Seminary Curriculum, 1808–1968," *Theological Education* 17 (Spring 1981): 118–41.

93. Edward Farley, *Theologia: The Fragmentation and Unity of Theological Education* (Philadelphia: Fortress Press, 1983); idem, *The Fragility of Knowledge: Theological Education in the Church and the University* (Philadelphia: Fortress Press, 1988).

94. Hough and Cobb, *Christian Identity*.

95. Craig Dykstra, "Reconceiving Practice," in *Shifting Boundaries: Contextual Approaches to the Structure of Theological Education*, ed. Barbara G. Wheeler and Edward Farley (Louisville, Ky.: Westminster/ John Knox Press, 1991), 35–66.

96. Don S. Browning, "Toward a Fundamental and Strategic Practical Theology," in *Shifting Boundaries*, 295–328; idem, *A Fundamental Practical Theology: Descriptive and Strategic Proposals* (Minneapolis: Fortress Press, 1991).

97. After several years of study, the faculty of the Divinity School at Vanderbilt defined the purpose of its ministerial education as the preparation of "the minister as theologian" and required students in the last semesters of their study to

elect courses with a "program focus" on some issue or problem in the practice of the ministry. Although areas of study were renamed, however, Area VI, "The Dimensions and Tasks of Christian Ministries (leadership, education, pastoral care, preaching and worship, denominational polities)," revealed the endurance of the division between theory and practice in the orientations of the faculty. See "Questioning an Axiom: The New Program for the Education of Ministers at Vanderbilt Divinity School" (Nashville, Tenn.: Office of University Publications, Vanderbilt University, 1982), 3–12.

98. Barbara G. Wheeler, "Introduction" to *Shifting Boundaries*, 14.

99. Robert Wuthnow, *The Restructuring of American Religion: Society and Faith Since World War II* (Princeton: Princeton University Press, 1988), 282.

## 5. Two Yokes of Responsibility

1. Dennis M. Campbell, "Theological Education and Moral Formation: What's Going On in Seminaries Today?" *Theological Education and Moral Formation*, ed. Richard John Neuhaus (Grand Rapids, Mich.: William B. Eerdmans, 1992), 1–21. For Campbell's own view of ordination as a "yoke" that binds one in obedience to the church see his *The Yoke of Obedience: The Meaning of Ordination in Methodism* (Nashville, Tenn.: Abingdon Press, 1988).

2. Glenn T. Miller, *Piety and Intellect: The Aims and Purposes of Ante-Bellum Theological Education* (Atlanta: Scholars Press, 1990), 71.

3. Nancy T. Ammerman and James Thobaben, "A Study of University Related Divinity Schools: Report on Data Analysis from Surveys of the Institutions, Faculties, and Deans," unpublished manuscript presented to the director of the University Divinity School Project (May 30, 1989), 28–29. In a brief note to me, a faculty member at one of the Methodist divinity schools made this calculation about the current state of his school: "If we divide faculty into 1) purely academic, 2) church interests, and 3) really trying to live in both worlds, I would locate only two faculty members purely in category # 1, seventeen in # 2, and thirty-nine in category # 3." The implication is that most faculty may feel a pull in two directions, but they nonetheless are about equally committed to the values of the university and those of the church. That dual pull probably characterizes faculty at the Methodist divinity schools during most of their history.

4. "News Release for Wednesday, April 27, 1960," University of Chicago Office of Public Relations, ACU.

5. "The President's Report," *University of Chicago Decennial Publications* 1 (1903), ACU, lxxv–lxxvi.

6. Ernest Cadman Colwell, *Adam and the Sun* (privately printed, 1976), 21.

7. Letter of April 23, 1965 from Bernard Loomer to Howard Schomer and others, ACTS.

8. Arthur Cushman McGiffert, Jr., *No Ivory Tower: The Story of The Chicago Theological Seminary* (Chicago: Chicago Theological Seminary, 1965), 262–63. See also Jerald C. Brauer, "Reminiscences," *Criterion* 19 (Winter 1980): 5–7.

9. These instances of academic power politics are found in "Summary of meeting between Loomer, Wallace, Keith and Gates and of a subsequent meeting be-

tween Loomer, Hawley and Keith held Wednesday, September 5, 1951, at University Club, Chicago" and letter from Arthur Cushman McGiffert, Jr. to Howard Schomer, December 21, 1959, ACTS; Minutes of the Federated Theological Faculty, February 10, 1949 and June 2, 1950, and Memorandum from Marcus Barth to Dr. Kimpton, March 25, 1960, ACU.

10. Issues of money, appointments, and curriculum are sketched in McGiffert, *No Ivory Tower*, 278–80, 285–87, and Aute L. Carr, "The Federated Theological Faculty of the University of Chicago: An Analysis of the Agreements, Structures, and Relationships, 1943–60," *Theological Education* 4 (Summer 1968): 73–75. Evidence of the enduring character of the issues is found in Fred Eastman, "A Memorandum to the Federated Theological Faculty," January 28, 1948, ACTS; letter from Arthur Cushman McGiffert to Ernest Cadman Colwell, May 25, 1949, and letter from Colwell to McGiffert, June 1, 1949, ACTS; correspondence between Howard Schomer and officials of the University of Chicago respecting the Sealantic grant, 1959–60, ACTS.

11. Details of the history of the administrative structure and differing philosophies of the federation are provided in Carr, "Federated Theological Faculty," 63–65, 69–73, and McGiffert, *No Ivory Tower*, 288–94. The persistent fears of CTS about the possible loss of its identity to the University of Chicago are evident in McGiffert, ibid., 250, 294, and Albert W. Palmer to alumni, "A Message from the President," June 22, 1943, and Howard Schomer, "Memo for Discussion," June 1959, ACTS. A sharply stated illustration of the different interpretations of the meaning of "federation" is apparent in the argument between Arthur Cushman McGiffert, Jr., and Sidney E. Mead in an open letter from Mead to McGiffert, July 27, 1951 and an open letter from McGiffert to Mead, August 30, 1951, ACTS; see also Bernard M. Loomer, "The Federated Theological Faculty Today," *The Chicago Theological School Register* 39 (September 1949): 6–12.

12. McGiffert, *No Ivory Tower*, 285–87.

13. Ibid., 253, 266, 273–74, 287.

14. J. Coert Rylaarsdam, "Faculty Responsibility for the CTS Heritage and Relationships," typescript (January 23, 1960), ACTS, 6.

15. Ibid., 2, 5.

16. For other representatives of this point of view see Carr, "Federated Theological Faculty," 68, and Loomer, "Federated Theological Faculty Today," 6–12.

17. Jerald C. Brauer, "Statement Prepared for the Provost of the University of Chicago, August 5, 1964," ACTS, 3.

18. Loomer, "Federated Theological Faculty Today," 6–12; McGiffert, *No Ivory Tower*, 292–93; Brauer, "Reminiscences," 6–7; Rylaarsdam, "Faculty Responsibility," 11; Bernard E. Meland, "A Long Look at the Divinity School and Its Present Crisis," *Criterion* 1 (Summer 1962): 29.

19. Fred Eastman, "Memorandum to the Federated Theological Faculty, January 26, 1949," ACU, 1–2.

20. Arthur Cushman McGiffert, Jr., "Professional Theological Education," typescript (December 3, 1951), ACU, 1–2.

21. *Announcements of the University of Chicago: The Divinity School, 1949–50*, ACU, 10.

22. Struggles over the meaning and control of the B.D. degree within the fed-

eration are described in Carr, "Federated Theological Faculty," 66, 72-74, and McGiffert, *No Ivory Tower*, 285, 292-93.

23. Brauer, "Reminiscences," 7.

24. Ibid.

25. "Statistical Report, Federation of Theological Schools, July 10, 1945," ACU; *Divinity School News* 20 (Autumn 1953), ACU, 7, and *Divinity School News* 23 (Autumn 1956), ACU, 7.

26. See chap. 3 of this book.

27. *Harvard Divinity School: Deans' Reports, 1922-55*, March 1940, AHD, 42.

28. Ibid., *1938-39*, 1; *1951-52*, 485-86; *1977-78*, Appendix.

29. *Yale Divinity News* 53 (January 1956), AYD, 9; Minutes of Faculty Retreat, September 16, 1972, box 3, Divinity School Records, AV.

30. Reports of the Dean of the Candler School of Theology to the President of Emory University, April 10, 1926, and April 23, 1929, AEC.

31. Lynn Harold Hough, "The Church and the Seminary," *Drew Gateway* 10 (July 1939): 58.

32. Kenneth Pope, *A Pope at Roam: The Confessions of a Bishop* (Nashville, Tenn.: Parthenon Press, 1976), 146.

33. Willard L. Sperry, "Preparation for the Ministry in a Nondenominational School," *The Harvard Divinity School: Its Place in Harvard University and in American Culture*, ed. by George H. Williams (Boston: Beacon Press, 1954), 274.

34. Merrimon Cuninggim, "Uneasy Partners: Higher Education and the Church," unpublished ms (1990), 44.

35. "Report of the Dean to the Faculty, Lakeview, September 23, 1960," ASMP, 13.

36. For examples of the countless instances of the extension of the educational programs of divinity schools to laypeople and ministers see Eugene Hawk, "Expanding Services of the Seminary," *Perkins Journal* 2 (Fall 1948): 3; George B. Ehlhardt, "The Extension Work of Duke Divinity School," *Duke University School Bulletin* 13 (May 1948), ADU, 28-29; *Harvard Divinity School: Deans' Reports, 1962-63*, AHD, 19; Robert T. Handy, *A History of Union Theological Seminary in New York* (New York: Columbia University Press, 1987), 168-70, 250-52; Boone M. Bowen, *The Candler School of Theology: Sixty Years of Service* (Atlanta: Emory University, 1974), 90-95.

37. See Jackson W. Carroll and Barbara G. Wheeler, "Doctor of Ministry Program: History, Summary of Findings and Recommendations," *Theological Education* 23 (Spring 1987): 7-51.

38. Harry Emerson Fosdick, "Shall the Fundamentalists Win?" *The Christian Work* 102 (June 10, 1922): 716-19, 722.

39. Letter of Mathews to Dr. G. Franklin Gehr, January 17, 1923, ACU.

40. Cited in Walter N. Vernon, *Methodism Moves Across North Texas* (Nashville, Tenn.: Parthenon Press, 1967), 285.

41. George Marsden, *Fundamentalism and American Culture* (Oxford: Oxford University Press, 1980), 186.

42. For analyses of the institutional careers of the fundamentalists and the evangelicals, as well as their relation to the larger culture, see Nancy T. Ammerman, "North American Protestant Fundamentalism," in *Fundamentalisms Ob-*

*served*, ed. Martin E. Marty and R. Scott Appleby (Chicago: University of Chicago Press, 1991), 1–56 and Robert Wuthnow, *The Restructuring of American Religion* (Princeton, N.J.: Princeton University Press, 1988), 135–37, 177–81. A case study that illustrates evangelicalism's emergence out of separatist fundamentalism is George Marsden, *Reforming Fundamentalism: Fuller Seminary and the New Evangelicalism* (Grand Rapids, Mich.: William B. Eerdmans, 1987).

43. Shailer Mathews, *The Faith of Modernism* (New York: Macmillan Company, 1924), 178, 23. Italics in original.

44. For instances of fundamentalist attacks on the divinity schools and responses by the leaders of the schools see Richard Morgan Cameron, *Boston University School of Theology, 1839–1968* (Boston: Boston University School of Theology, 1968), 40–42; "Statement of the Faculty," AB, 1–8; Russell E. Richey, "Drew Theological Seminary and American Methodism: Some Historical Reflections," in *Scholarship, Sacraments and Service: Historical Studies in Protestant Tradition: Essays in Honor of Bard Thompson*, ed. Daniel B. Clendenin and David Buschart (Lewistown, N.Y.: Edwin Mellen Press, 1990), 96–100; Bowen, *Candler*, 15–16, 35–37, 41–42; Mary Martha Hosford Thomas, *Southern Methodist University: Founding and Early Years* (Dallas: Southern Methodist University Press, 1974), 85–103; Paul L. Conkin, *Gone with the Ivy: A Biography of Vanderbilt University* (Knoxville: University of Tennessee Press, 1985), 117–19; Earl W. Porter, *Trinity and Duke, 1892–1924: Foundations of Duke University* (Durham, N.C.: Duke University Press, 1964), 218; Handy, *Union Theological Seminary*, 136–37.

45. John A. Rice, *The Old Testament in the Life of Today* (New York: Macmillan Company, 1920), xxxi. See also Rice's "Why I Believe in the Whole Bible as the Inspired Word of God," pamphlet reprint of an article from *The Methodist Quarterly Review* (April 1924): 9–12.

46. Vernon, *Methodism Moves*, 280–81. For an overview of the religion and politics of Norris see Barry Hankins, "The Strange Career of J. Frank Norris: Or, Can a Baptist Democrat Be a Fundamentalist Republican?" *Church History* 61 (September 1992): 373–92.

47. Cameron, *Boston University School of Theology*, 101; Robert Moats Miller, *Bishop G. Bromley Oxnam: Paladin of Liberal Protestantism* (Nashville, Tenn: Abingdon Press, 1990), 525–61; Folder of collected news articles labeled "Hysteria" by Dean Merrimon Cuninggim, ASMP.

48. Martin E. Marty, *The Noise of Conflict: 1919–1941*, vol. 2 of *Modern American Religion* (Chicago: University of Chicago Press, 1991), 213.

49. This is the basic thesis of Wuthnow's study of recent American religion in his *Restructuring*.

50. For the understanding of "worldview" as an inhabitable world of meaning formed of such dimensions as beliefs, symbols, and practices, I am dependent upon Ninian Smart, *Worldviews: Crosscultural Explorations of Human Beliefs* (New York: Charles Scribner's Sons, 1983). My understanding of worldview is also dependent upon the definition implicit in Clifford Geertz's view of "culture," or "the historically transmitted pattern of meanings embodied in symbols, a system of inherited conceptions expressed in symbolic forms by means of which [humans] communicate, perpetuate, and develop their knowledge about and attitudes toward life." Clifford Geertz, "Religion as a Cultural System," in *The Reli-*

*gious Situation: 1968*, ed. Donald R. Cutler (Boston: Beacon Press, 1968), 641. Students of the American scene who have made much of the legacy of the fundamentalist/modernist controversy as a divided worldview are Marty, *Noise of Conflict*, 161, and James Davison Hunter, *Culture Wars: The Struggle to Define America* (New York: Basic Books, 1991), 42.

51. George Gallup, Jr., and Jim Castelli, *The People's Religion: American Faith in the 90s* (New York: Macmillan Publishing Company, 1989), 4, 57–58, 61, 63, 66; *Religion in America. 50 Years: 1935–1985. The Gallup Report* 236 (May 1985): 5.

52. See, for example, Bruce B. Lawrence, *Defenders of God: The Fundamentalist Revolt Against the Modern Age* (San Francisco: Harper & Row, 1989) and Martin E. Marty and R. Scott Appleby, "Conclusion: An Interim Report on a Hypothetical Family," *Fundamentalisms Observed*, 814–42.

53. Quoted in Ferenc Morton Szasz, *The Divided Mind of Protestant America, 1880–1930* (University, Ala: University of Alabama Press, 1982), 133–34.

54. Ibid., 134.

55. See chap. 1 of this book.

56. This is Robert Booth Fowler's summary definition of "liberal culture" in his argument that religion has become a temporary refuge from the contemporary mind-set of many American institutions: *Unconventional Partners: Religion and Liberal Culture in the United States* (Grand Rapids, Mich.: William B. Eerdmans, 1989), 4–5.

57. See chap. 4 of this book.

58. When Hebrew was eliminated as a requirement at Drew Theological Seminary in 1921, Drew professor of Old Testament Robert William Rogers did not conceal his rage: "It is, at this moment, perfectly clear to my mind that the theological students of evangelical American Christianity intend to leave Hebrew to the Jews and the Jesuits. This is but another way of saying that they are stupid and unimaginative, that they are intellectually lazy and that they have no care for Old Testament scholarship." Quoted in John T. Cunningham, *University in the Forest: The Story of Drew University* (Florham Park, N.J.: Afton Publishing Company, 1972), 163.

59. For example, Memorandum from the Dean of the Boston School of Theology to the University Provost, January 17, 1989, AB.

60. Edwin Scott Gaustad, *"Did the Fundamentalists Win?"* in *Religion in America: Spiritual Life in a Secular Age*, ed. Mary Douglas and Steven M. Tipton (Boston: Beacon Press, 1983), 174.

61. The subdividing and narrowing of the divinity school disciplines is apparent in the registers of the courses of study at all of the schools. See also the discussions of specialization in Part I of this book.

62. For example, "Planning Profile, 1973–74: The Vanderbilt Divinity School," AV, 2–3; "Duke University Council Committee Report, May 2, 1980," AYD, 5; *Annual Reports of the Dean: Boston University School of Theology, 1985–86, 1987–88*, AB.

63. Henry Sloane Coffin, "The Ideals of the Seminary," *Union Theological Seminary Inaugural Addresses, 1915–1930*, AU, 53–54.

64. See chap. 1 of this book.

65. William Adams Brown, *Ministerial Education in America*, vol. 1 of *The Edu-*

*cation of American Ministers* (New York: Institute of Social and Religious Research, 1934), 58–59.

66. Mark A. May, *The Profession of the Ministry*, vol. 2 of *The Education of American Ministers*, 389.

67. James M. Gustafson, "The Clergy in the United States," in *The Professions in America*, ed. Kenneth S. Lynn (Boston: Houghton Mifflin Company, 1965), 74. See also Samuel W. Blizzard, "The Minister's Dilemma," *Christian Century* (April 25, 1956): 508–10.

68. *Readiness for Ministry: Criteria*, ed. David S. Schuller, Merton P. Strommen, and Milo L. Brekke (Vandalia, Oh.: Association of Theological Schools in the United States and Canada, 1975), 73.

69. Jackson W. Carroll, "The Professional Model of Ministry—Is It Worth Saving?" *Theological Education* 21 (Spring 1985): 27. Carroll also found that the professional model of the ministry is aspired to "by the increasing number of women entering the traditionally all-male sectors of the work force including the ordained ministry, and by those groups who are newly entering the middle and upper-middle classes—blacks and other ethnic minorities and members of rapidly growing evangelical denominations which have often had their initial appeal among the lower socioeconomic groups." Ibid., 27–28.

70. H. Richard Niebuhr with Daniel Day Williams and James M. Gustafson, *The Purpose of the Church and Its Ministry: Reflections on the Aims of Theological Education* (New York: Harper & Row, 1956), 82.

71. Ibid., 83–84, 95–116.

72. See, for example, Martin E. Marty, *The New Shape of American Religion* (New York: Harper & Row, 1958), 137–38; Robert E. Cushman, "Objectives of Theological Education—and Impediments," *Duke Divinity School Bulletin* 26 (February 1961): 3–5; Carroll, "Professional Model," 36–37.

73. John Fletcher, *Religious Authenticity in the Clergy* (Washington, D.C.: Alban Institute, 1975).

74. *Ministry in America: A Report and Analysis*, ed. David S. Schuller, Merton P. Strommen, and Milo L. Brekke (San Francisco: Harper & Row, 1980), 60–76, 79–83.

75. Ibid., 12, 88.

76. Manning M. Patillo and Donald M. Mackenzie, *Church Sponsored Higher Education in the United States: Report of the Danforth Commission* (Washington, D.C.: American Council of Education, 1966), 21; *Digest of Education Statistics, 1990* (Washington, D.C.: United States Government Printing Office, 1990), 247.

77. Thomas Deloughry, "The Study of Transcripts Finds Little Structure in the Liberal Arts," *Chronicle of Higher Education* 35 (January 18, 1989): A1, A32.

78. Among the legion of sociological studies of these correlations see Wuthnow, *Restructuring*, 171–72, and Wade Clark Roof and William McKinney, *American Mainline Religion: Its Changing Shape and Future* (New Brunswick, N.J.: Rutgers University Press, 1987), 65, 86, 110–11.

79. I have searched the sociological literature in vain for correlations between types of undergraduate degrees and social and religious attitudes among the laity. On the "new class" thesis see Peter L. Berger, "The Worldview of the New Class: Secularity and Its Discontents," in *The New Class?* ed. B. Bruce-Briggs (New

Brunswick, N.J.: Transaction Books, 1979), 49–56; James Davison Hunter, "The New Class and the Young Evangelicals," *Review of Religious Research* 22 (December 1980): 155–68; Roof and McKinney, *Mainline Religion*, 115–17.

80. Part of a conversation with the author during a long automobile ride in June 1988.

81. Gallup and Castelli, *People's Religion*, 60.

82. Robert Stevens, "Aging Mistress: The Law School in America," *Change* 2 (January–February 1970): 38. For similar questions respecting other cases of professional education see Edgar H. Schein with Diane W. Kommers, *Professional Education: Some New Directions* (New York: McGraw Hill, 1972), 59–60; Donald A. Schön, *Educating the Reflective Practitioner* (San Francisco: Jossey-Bass Publishers, 1987), 4–11, 327.

83. Schön, *Reflective Practitioner*, xii, 8–9, 17, 157.

84. For examples of proponents of the reform of theological education on the model of reflective artistry see Joseph C. Hough, Jr., and John B. Cobb, Jr., *Christian Identity and Theological Education* (Chico, Calif.: Scholars Press, 1985), 84–90, and Carroll, "Professional Model of Ministry," 30–33.

## 6. Social Class and Social Gospel

1. Cited in John T. Cunningham, *University in the Forest: The Story of Drew University* (Florham Park, N.J.: Afton Publishing Company, 1972), 148–49.

2. "Drew Celebrates Fifty-Seventh Commencement," *Drew Seminary Bulletin* 12 (June 1924), ADR, 1–2.

3. E. Brooks Holifield, "Class, Profession, and Morality: Moral Formation in American Protestant Seminaries, 1808–1934," in *Theological Education and Moral Formation*, ed. Richard John Neuhaus (Grand Rapids, Mich.: William B. Eerdmans, 1992), 61–62.

4. Ibid., 66–67.

5. William Adams Brown, *Ministerial Education in America*, vol. 1 of *The Education of American Ministers* (New York: Institute of Social and Religious Research, 1934), 110–11.

6. Ibid., 150.

7. I am following here the distinction made by Henry F. May between the "conservative" efforts at social and philanthropic relief and the "progressive" social gospel, with the latter balancing a concern for the salvation of the individual with a gospel of the redeemed society implemented by concrete measures of improvement and social change. Henry F. May, *Protestant Churches and Industrial America* (New York: Harper & Row, 1967), 170. I find May's differentiation among the three groups of Conservative Social Christianity, Progressive Social Christianity (Social Gospel), and Radical Social Christianity—distinctions that have become conventions since his book was first published in 1949—a helpful way of distinguishing among different religious social philosophies. Along with some recent historians of American Christianity's developing social conscience, however, I believe that representatives of the first two groups frequently spoke the same language and that May and especially some of his followers have underestimated

the way in which social gospelers actively participated in the shaping of the policies and actions of social reform.

8. Much recent scholarship has demonstrated the broad geographical, philosophical, and professional reaches of the social gospel. See especially John Lee Eighmy, *Churches in Cultural Captivity: A History of the Social Attitudes of Southern Baptists* (Knoxville: University of Tennessee Press, 1972); Ralph E. Luker, *The Social Gospel in Black and White: American Racial Reform, 1885–1912* (Chapel Hill: University of North Carolina Press, 1991); Norris Magnuson, *Salvation in the Slums: Evangelical Social Work, 1865–1920* (Grand Rapids, Mich.: Baker Book House, 1977); Ronald C. White, Jr., *Liberty and Justice for All: Racial Reform and the Social Gospel, 1877–1925* (San Francisco: Harper & Row, 1990). The story of the emergence of the social gospel among the denominations and in the Federal Council of Churches is told by May, *Protestant Churches*, 182–203, and by Charles Howard Hopkins, *The Rise of the Social Gospel in American Protestantism, 1865–1915* (New Haven, Conn.: Yale University Press, 1940), 290–91, 317.

9. Robert T. Handy, "Introduction" to *The Social Gospel in America, 1870–1920* (New York: Oxford University Press, 1966), 6, 10–11; May, *Protestant Churches*, 170–71; Ronald G. White and C. Howard Hopkins, *The Social Gospel: Religion and Reform in Changing America* (Philadelphia, Pa.: Temple University Press, 1976), xviii.

10. Roland H. Bainton, *Yale and the Ministry: A History of Education for the Christian Ministry at Yale from the Founding in 1701* (New York: Harper & Brothers, 1957), 191; Charles R. Gillett, "Detailed History of the Union Theological Seminary in the City of New York," vol. 2, typescript (n.d.), AU, 746; Robert T. Handy, *A History of Union Theological Seminary in New York* (New York: Columbia University Press, 1987), 100–01, 109–10, 252–53; Richard Morgan Cameron, *Boston University School of Theology, 1839–1968* (Boston: Boston University School of Theology, 1968), 46–49; *Catalogue of Boston University School of Theology, 1890*, AB, 111; *Boston University Bulletin, 1919–20*, AB, 455–56; Cunningham, *University in the Forest*, 137–39; *Register of the University of Chicago: The Divinity School, 1912–13*, ACU, 305–06.

11. *Bulletin of Southern Methodist University, 1919*, ASMU, 119–20.

12. Robert S. Michaelsen, "The Protestant Ministry in America: 1850–1950," in *The Ministry in Historical Perspectives*, ed. H. Richard Niebuhr and Daniel Day Williams (San Francisco: Harper & Row, 1956 & 1983), 264–65; Kenneth Willis Clark, "Four Decades of the Divinity School," *Duke Divinity School Review* 32 (Spring 1967): 164; *Bulletin of Vanderbilt University: School of Religion, 1930*, AV, 36–39; Boone M. Bowen, *The Candler School of Theology: Sixty Years of Service* (Atlanta: Emory University, 1974), 57, 82–85; Cunningham, *University in the Forest*, 230.

13. On the development of courses and topics in social ethics in Protestant seminaries, see James Dombrowski, *The Early Days of Christian Socialism in America* (New York: Columbia University Press, 1936), 60–73; Aaron Ignatius Abell, *The Urban Impact on American Protestantism, 1865–1900* (Cambridge, Mass.: Harvard University Press, 1943), 224–45; Brown, *Ministerial Education*, 126–27.

14. Dombrowski, *Christian Socialism*, 69.

15. Charles W. Eliot, "Theological Education at Harvard Between 1816 and 1916," in *Addresses Delivered at the Observance of the 100th Anniversary of the Establishment of the Harvard Divinity School* (Cambridge, Mass.: Harvard University, 1917), 47–49; Levering Reynolds, Jr., "The Later Years (1880–1953)," in *The Harvard*

*Divinity School: Its Place in Harvard University and in American Culture* (Boston: Beacon Press, 1954), 174, 180–82; Ralph Lazzaro, "Theological Scholarship at Harvard from 1880 to 1953," ibid., 258.

16. Dombrowski, *Christian Socialism,* 69–70.

17. Richard T. Ely, *Social Aspects of Christianity and Other Essays* (New York: Thomas Y. Crowell & Co., 1889) 124.

18. For sketches of the social gospel background of the social sciences, and the eventual abandonment of that background, see A. Laurence Moore, "Secularization: Religion and the Social Sciences," in *Between the Times,* 233–52; Dorothy Ross, "The Development of the Social Sciences," in *The Organization of Knowledge in Modern America, 1860–1920,* ed. Alexandra Oleson and John Voss (Baltimore, Md.: The Johns Hopkins University Press, 1979), 112, 116–17.

19. Robert C. Bannister, *Sociology and Scientism: The American Quest for Objectivity, 1880–1940* (Chapel Hill: University of North Carolina Press, 1987), 32–63.

20. Cited in Susan E. Henking, "Sociological Christianity and Christian Sociology: The Paradox of Early American Sociology," *Religion and American Culture: A Journal of Interpretation* 3 (Winter 1993): 53–54.

21. Albion W. Small, *The Meaning of Social Science* (Chicago: University of Chicago Press, 1910), 277.

22. Cited in Hopkins, *Rise of the Social Gospel,* 268–69.

23. Cited in Henking, "Sociological Christianity," 58–59.

24. Gerald Everett Knoff, "The Yale Divinity School, 1858–1899" (Ph.D. diss., Yale University, 1936), 306; Bainton, *Yale and the Ministry,* 190–91, 204–07; Handy, *History of Union,* 130, 190–91; Henry Sloane Coffin, *A Half Century of Union Theological Seminary, 1896–1945* (New York: Charles Scribner's Sons, 1954), 100–02.

25. *Catalogue of Boston University School of Theology, 1896,* AB, 124; Cameron, *Boston School of Theology,* 63–69; S. Paul Schilling, "The Drama of Social Ethics at the School of Theology," *Nexus* 23 (Summer 1980): 12–13; Paul Deats, "Bishop Francis J. McConnell and Social Justice," in *The Boston Personalist Tradition in Philosophy, Social Ethics, and Theology,* ed. Paul Deats and Carol Robb (Macon, Ga.: Mercer University Press, 1986), 147–49.

26. William Marshall Gilbert, "Specialized Training for Home Missionary Leadership," *Drew Seminary Bulletin* 11 (September 1923), ADR, 10. On developments of the social gospel at Drew, see William Warren Sweet, "Our Generation," *Drew Gateway* 2 (August 1931): 4; Robert Moats Miller, *How Shall They Hear Without a Preacher? The Life of Ernest Fremont Tittle* (Chapel Hill: University of North Carolina Press, 1971), 37–42; Cunningham, *University in the Forest,* 137–39, 164–66.

27. *Bulletin of the University of Southern California: Maclay College of Theology, 1919,* ASC, 15; *Bulletin of Southern Methodist University: School of Theology, 1919,* ASMP, 119; *Annual Catalogue of Duke University, 1925–26,* ADU, 249; Bowen, *Candler School of Theology,* 28.

28. Paul K. Conkin, *Gone with the Ivy: A Biography of Vanderbilt University* (Knoxville: University of Tennessee Press, 1985), 370–74.

29. Robert T. Handy, *A Christian America: Protestant Hopes and Historical Realities* (New York: Oxford University Press, 1971), 164, 170.

30. Reinhold Niebuhr, "The Protestant Clergy and U.S. Politics," in *Essays in Applied Christianity by Reinhold Niebuhr,* ed. D. B. Robertson (New York: Meridian Books, 1959), 106–17.

31. Ibid., 108; Reinhold Niebuhr, "Social Christianity," *Applied Christianity*, 103.

32. Andrew Sledd, "The Negro: Another View," *Atlantic Monthly* 90 (July 1902): 65–68.

33. Ibid., 70.

34. Mark K. Bauman, "A Famous Atlantan Speaks Out Against Lynching: Bishop Warren Akin Candler and Social Justice," *Atlanta Historical Bulletin* 20 (Spring 1976): 24–30; Bowen, *Candler School of Theology*, 174.

35. Hopkins, *Rise of the Social Gospel*, 319.

36. *Thirty Years of Lynching in the United States, 1889–1918*, originally published in 1919 by the National Association for the Advancement of Colored People (New York: Negro Universities Press, 1969), 29.

37. Luker, *Social Gospel in Black and White* makes this case for the social gospel. See also White, *Liberty and Justice*.

38. White, *Liberty and Justice*, 143, 182; Bowen, *Candler School of Theology*, 167, 169; Conkin, *Gone with the Ivy*, 371.

39. Russell E. Richey, "Drew Theological Seminary and American Methodism: Some Historical Reflections," in *Scholarship, Sacraments and Service: Historical Studies in Protestant Tradition: Essays in Honor of Bard Thompson*, ed. Daniel B. Clendenin and W. David Buschart (Lewiston, N.Y.: Edwin Mellen Press, 1990), 102–03; Cameron, *Boston School of Theology*, 102–03; Handy, *History of Union*, 234–35, 265; *Catalogue of Union Theological Seminary in the City of New York, 1989–91*, AU, 107; *Register of Harvard University: The Divinity School, 1989–90*, AHD, 89.

40. James F. Findlay, Jr., *Church People in the Struggle: The National Council of Churches and the Black Freedom Movement, 1950–1970* (New York: Oxford University Press, 1933); Handy, *History of Union*, 41, 178–79, 265–66, 280–82; Cunningham, *University in the Forest*, 118, 245–47; Martin Luther King, Jr., *Stride Toward Freedom* (New York: Harper & Brothers, 1958), 100; L. Harold DeWolf, "In Memoriam: Martin Luther King, Jr.," *Nexus* 12 (Fall 1968): 1–4; *Harvard Divinity School: Deans' Reports, 1966–67*, AHD, 20, *1968–69*, 3–6; Jerald C. Brauer, "Reminiscences," *Criterion* 19 (Winter 1980): 11; *Annual Report of the Dean of Yale Divinity School, 1973–74*, AYU, 2–4.

41. Conkin, *Gone with the Ivy*, 541–43.

42. Letter from John K. Benton to Harvie Branscomb, September 24, 1952, box 8, Divinity School Records, AV.

43. Merrimon Cuninggim, "Integration in Professional Education: The Story of Perkins, Southern Methodist University," *Annals of the American Academy of Political and Social Science* 304 (March 1956): 109; Letter of Eugene B. Hawk to Clifton N. Bonner, February 1, 1951, ASMP; Winifred Weiss and Charles S. Proctor, *Umphrey Lee: A Biography* (Nashville, Tenn.: Abingdon Press, 1971), 173–74; Robert W. Goodloe, "Welcome to Dean Merrimon Cuninggim and Dr. Albert C. Outler," *Perkins Journal* 5 (Fall 1951): 3; Letter from Merrimon Cuninggim to Charles Braden, August 7, 1964, ASMP, 1–2.

44. Cuninggim, "Integration in Professional Education," 109–10; idem, "Uneasy Partners: Higher Education and the Church," unpublished MS (1990), 13–19.

45. Cuninggim, "Integration in Professional Education," 110.

46. Ibid.; Cuninggim, "Uneasy Partners," 19–20.

47. Letter from J. J. Perkins to Bishop William C. Martin, August 17, 1953,

ASMP and letter from J. J. Perkins to Dean Cuninggim, August 27, 1953, ASMP. See also letter from Eugene B. Hawk to Bishop Paul E. Martin, April 3, 1953, ASMP and letter from Cuninggim to Braden, ASMP, 5–8.

48. Letter from J. J. Perkins to Dr. E. B. Hawk, February 13, 1954, ASMP; Cuninggim, "Uneasy Partners," 27–30.

49. Cuninggim, "Integration in Professional Education," 114.

50. Merrimon Cuninggim, " . . . To Fashion as We Feel," unpublished address delivered at the Conference on Christian Faith and Human Relations, Nashville, Tenn., April 25, 1957, ASMP, 9–10.

51. Merrimon Cuninggim, "The Southern Temper," *Perkins School of Theology Journal* 11 (Spring 1958): 29.

52. Minutes of Special Faculty Meeting of Candler School of Theology, December 13, 1957, AEC; Minutes of Regular Faculty Meeting of Candler School of Theology, January 9, 1958, AEC; Bowen, *Candler School of Theology*, 113.

53. Earl Brewer, Boone Bowen, and Paul Worley, "A Committee Document on Background Considerations Leading to the Statement of the Faculty on the School of Theology and Race," n.d., AEC, 2–7.

54. *Emory Alumnus* (February 1959), AEU, 25.

55. Cited in Bowen, *Candler School of Theology*, 114.

56. Thomas H. English, *Emory University, 1915–1965: A Semicentennial History* (Atlanta: Emory University, 1966), 100–02; Bowen, *Candler School of Theology*, 114–16.

57. Cited in Minutes of the Faculty of Duke Divinity School, June 1, 1949, ADU.

58. Minutes of Faculty Meeting of Duke Divinity School, September 16, 1948; March 23, 1949; June 1, 1949; June 2, 1949, ADU.

59. Letter from A. Hollis Edens to Harold A. Bosley, June 24, 1949, ADU.

60. Letter from G. Bromley Oxnam to Harold A. Bosley, November 2, 1948, ADU; letter from Harold A. Bosley to A. Hollis Edens, March 14, 1949, ADU; letter from A. Hollis Edens to Harold A. Bosley, March 22, 1949, ADU; letter from Benjamin E. Mays to G. Bromley Oxnam, March 25, 1949, ADU; letter from G. Bromley Oxnam to Harold A. Bosley, March 30, 1949, ADU; memorandum from Harold A. Bosley to the Board of Trustees of Duke University (n.d.), ADU; letter from G. Bromley Oxnam to Harold A. Bosley, July 5, 1949, ADU; letter from G. Bromley Oxnam to A. Hollis Edens, September 15, 1949, ADU; letter from A. Hollis Edens to Harold A. Bosley, June 23, 1951, ADU; Minutes of the Duke Divinity School Student Association, Wednesday, February 14, 1952, ADU. Peter Perretti has concluded, based on interviews with Divinity School faculty and an examination of correspondence, that early strains between Edens and Bosley—and between Bosley and many of his faculty—arose because of Bosley's insistence on new housing for himself and his family when he arrived at Duke as dean, his neglect of daily administrative duties, and his Northern liberal attitudes that conflicted with Southern ways. Peter Perretti, "The Divinity School and Desegregation: An Abortive Blow Against the Status-Quo, 1948–1952," student paper for History 196 c, April 2, 1976, ADU, 6–12.

61. "Petition of Faculty of Divinity School to President and Board of Duke University," December 14, 1955, ADU; "Report of the Dean of the Divinity School to

the President of the University," *Bulletin of Duke University, 1955–56,* ADU, 61; "Petition of Faculty to President and Board of Duke University," July 16, 1956, ADU; "Letter to President Edens and the Trustees of Duke University from the Editorial Board of *Response,*" *Response,* December 19, 1958, ADU, 1; "Report of the Dean of the Divinity School to the President of Duke University," *Bulletin of Duke University, 1958–59,* ADU, 69; "Petition of Faculty to President, Vice-President in the Division of Education, and Board of Trustees of Duke University," January 11, 1961, ADU.

62. "Petition of Faculty of Divinity School to President, Vice-President in the Division of Education, and Board of Trustees of Duke University," January 11, 1961, ADU.

63. Cited in Jorge Kotelanski, "Prolonged and Patient Efforts: The Desegregation of Duke University, 1948–1963," senior thesis, Department of History, Duke University, April, 1990, ADU, 127. The history of the responses of the Duke administration and board to appeals for desegregation are chronicled in ibid., 37–140.

64. "Announcements of the Dean," *Faculty Bulletin of Duke Divinity School,* September 26, 1961, ADU.

65. Minutes of Faculty of Vanderbilt Divinity School, March 4, 1960, box 38, Divinity School Records, AV.

66. Letter from James A. Jones to Chancellor Branscomb, December 2, 1960, with attached Accrediting Report, box 38, Divinity School Records, AV, 6.

67. The most impartial chronicle of the events surrounding the Lawson case, one on which the preceding paragraphs are heavily dependent, is that of Conkin, *Gone with the Ivy,* 547–80. For other accounts see Harvie Branscomb, "Racial Desegregation at Vanderbilt University," October 10, 1985, Records Group 100, AV; idem, "Some Corrections and Comments on Chapter XX, 'The Unwanted,' in Conkin's *Gone with the Ivy,*" Records Group 100, AV; J. Robert Nelson, "Vanderbilt's Time of Testing," *Christian Century* (August 10, 1960): 921–25.

68. Nelson, "Vanderbilt's Time of Testing," 921, 925.

69. Martin Luther King, Jr., *Why We Can't Wait* (New York: Signet Books, 1964), 81–82, 135–38, 148–50.

70. Ernest Cadman Colwell, "Theological Education—Isolation or Interaction?" *Bulletin of the Southern California School of Theology* 1 (February 1958), ACT, 6–7.

71. *Catalog of the School of Theology at Claremont, 1983–84,* ACT, 11. See also Joseph C. Hough, Jr., "Internationalizing Theological Education," *Theological Education* 15 (Autumn 1978): 58–61.

72. See, for example, Handy, *History of Union,* 314, 319–20; *Bulletin of Duke University, 1986–87,* ADU, 49–51; "Working Paper on the Mexican American and Other Programs Related to the Southwest and Latin America" (October 10, 1984), ASMP, 1–15.

73. For discussions of the branches and some of the divisions within the branches of liberation theology see Jane Redmont, "Theologies of Liberation," *Bulletin of Harvard Divinity School, 1981–82,* AHD, 8–9; Arthur F. McGovern, *Liberation Theology and Its Critics: Toward an Assessment* (Maryknoll, N.Y.: Orbis Books, 1989), xv–xviii; Susan Brooks Thistlethwaite, *Sex, Race, and God: Christian Feminism in Black and White* (New York: Crossroad Publishing Company, 1991).

74. Redmont, "Theologies of Liberation," 8–9; McGovern, *Liberation Theology,*

23–46; Rebecca Chopp, *The Praxis of Suffering: An Interpretation of Liberation and Political Theologies* (Maryknoll, N.Y.: Orbis Books, 1986); idem, *The Power to Speak: Feminism, Language, and God* (New York: Crossroad Publishing Company, 1989); Robert McAfee Brown, *Liberation Theology: An Introductory Guide* (Louisville, Ky.: Westminster/John Knox Press, 1993), 138–39.

75. See, for example, McGovern, *Liberation Theology*, 1–19; Linda Rennie Forcey, "Introduction" to *Yearning to Breathe Free: Liberation Theologies in the United States*, ed. Mar Peter-Raoul, Linda Rennie Forcey, and Robert Frederick Hunter, Jr. (Maryknoll, N.Y.: Orbis Books, 1990), 1–2.

76. James H. Cone, "Black Theology: Where We Have Been and a Vision for Where We Are Going," in *Yearning to Breathe Free*, 50. Although Cone claims the civil rights struggle and the thought of Martin Luther King, Jr., as his own heritage, he views that struggle as a decidedly black one and King as a black leader who, apparently, was not decisively influenced by the white theology of his divinity school education.

77. Nelle Morton, *The Journey Is Home* (Boston: Beacon Press, 1985), 191.

## 7. Formation and the Heritage of Revolt

1. For examples of student protests at the divinity schools see Richard Morgan Cameron, *Boston University School of Theology, 1839–1968* (Boston: Boston University School of Theology, 1968), 40–41; John T. Cunningham, *University in the Forest: The Story of Drew University* (Florham Park, N.J.: Afton Publishing Company, 1972), 139–42; Robert T. Handy, *A History of Union Theological Seminary in New York* (New York: Columbia University Press, 1987), 197–202.

2. David Langston and William McKeown, *The Student Movement at Union Theological Seminary, 1963–1969*, pamphlet written in cooperation with the Department of Ministry of the National Council of Churches (May 1971), AU, 9–14; H. James Lawrence, "The Duke Silent Vigil," *Duke Divinity School Review* 33 (Spring 1968): 89–108; *Yale Divinity News*, April 20, 1970, AYD, 1; *Coalition for the Defense of the Panthers*, January 30, 1971, AYD, 1.

3. Todd Gitlin, *The Sixties: Years of Hope, Days of Rage* (New York: Bantam Books, 1987), 342–43, 410.

4. See, for example, Boone M. Bowen, *The Candler School of Theology: Sixty Years of Service* (Atlanta: Emory University, 1974), 161–63.

5. Gitlin, *Sixties*, 389, 421.

6. Ibid., 311.

7. Jerald C. Brauer regarding the period at the Divinity School at the University of Chicago, in "Reminiscences," *Criterion* 19 (Winter 1980): 11.

8. Glenn T. Miller, "Professionals and Pedagogues: A Survey of Theological Education," in *Altered Landscapes: Christianity in America, 1935–1985*, ed. David W. Lotz, Donald W. Shriver, Jr., and John F. Wilson (Grand Rapids, Mich: William B. Eerdmans, 1989), 206.

9. Miller, ibid., recognizes these crucial changes, but he does not think they have yet made a significant structural difference.

10. Arthur Schlesinger's commentary comparing the 1950s with the 1980s, on the PBS television documentary "Robert Kennedy," Spring 1993.

11. For discussions of these forces of revolt already emerging in the Fifties see Theodore Roszak, *The Making of a Counter Culture: Reflections on the Technocratic Society and its Youthful Opposition* (Garden City, N.Y.: Doubleday & Company, 1969), 24; David Halberstam, *The Fifties* (New York: Villard Books, 1993), 254–56, 295–307, 456–86; Gitlin, *Sixties*, 12–13, 37–54, 104.

12. James Hudnut-Beumler, "Suburban Jeremiads: Religion and Social Criticism of the America Dream in the 1950s," unpublished MS, 309.

13. See, for example, *Yale Divinity News* (January 1956), AYD, 8; Handy, *History of Union*, 223; *Harvard University Divinity School: Deans' Reports, 1957–58*, AHD, 2–3; "Report of the Dean of the Divinity School to the President of Duke University," *Bulletin of Duke University, 1956*, ADU, 61–62; Wayne R. Jones and Walter L. Holcomb, "The School of Theology Student Body, 1955–1962," *Nexus* 6 (February 1963): 21–26.

14. H. Richard Niebuhr, *The Social Sources of Denominationalism* (New York: Meridian Books, 1929, 1957), 6.

15. Gibson Winter, *The Suburban Captivity of the Churches: An Analysis of Protestant Responsibility in the Expanding Metropolis* (New York: Macmillan Company, 1962), 34, 44–45, 51, 120.

16. The connections between the theological and the secular criticisms of mid-century American culture have been explored by Benton Johnson, "Is There Hope for Liberal Protestantism?" *Mainstream Protestantism in the Twentieth Century: Its Problems and Prospects* (Louisville, Ky.: Committee on Theological Education of the Presbyterian Church, 1986), 19–20, and James Hudnut-Beumler, *Looking for God in the Suburbs: The Religion of the American Dream and Its Critics, 1945–1965* (New Brunswick, N.J.: Rutgers University Press, 1994).

17. David Riesman, Reuel Denney, and Nathan Glazer, *The Lonely Crowd: A Study of the Changing American Character* (New Haven, Conn.: Yale University Press, 1950, 1960); William H. Whyte, Jr., *The Organization Man* (Garden City, N.Y.: Doubleday, 1956); C. Wright Mills, *White Collar: The American Middle Classes* (New York: Oxford University Press, 1951); idem, *The Power Elite* (New York: Oxford University Press, 1956).

18. Peter Berger, *The Noise of Solemn Assemblies: Christian Commitment and the Religious Establishment in America* (Garden City, N.Y.: Doubleday, 1961); Pierre Berton, *The Comfortable Pew* (Philadelphia, Pa.: Lippincott Publishers, 1965); Gabriel Vahanian, *The Death of God: The Culture of Our Post-Christian Era* (New York: George Braziller, 1961); Martin E. Marty, *The New Shape of American Religion* (New York: Harper & Row, 1958).

19. Harry J. Ausmus, *Will Herberg: A Bio-Bibliography* (Westport, Conn.: Greenwood Press, 1986), 27–28, 38–39; idem, *Will Herberg: From Right to Right* (Chapel Hill: University of North Carolina Press, 1987), 152, 173.

20. Will Herberg, *Protestant-Catholic-Jew: An Essay in American Religious Sociology* (Garden City, N.Y.: Doubleday, 1960), 78–79, 84, 263.

21. Ibid., 81–82, 87, 258, 263–64.

22. Ibid., 261.

23. See Sacvan Bercovitch, *The American Jeremiad* (Madison: University of Wisconsin Press, 1978).

24. Herberg, *Protestant-Catholic-Jew*, 79, 271-72; Ausmus, *Will Herberg, From Right*, 196-211.

25. Marty, *New Shape*, 114-17, 122-23, 161-69.

26. Winter, *Suburban Captivity*, 67-68, 99, 119-20, 158.

27. Ibid., 90. Italics in original.

28. Ibid., 92.

29. Ibid., 117, 198-201; Gibson Winter, "Theological Schools: Partners in the Conversation," in *The Making of Ministers: Essays on Clergy Training Today*, ed. Keith R. Bridston and Dwight W. Culver (Minneapolis, Minn.: Augsburg Publishing House, 1964), 164-65.

30. See chap. 3 of this book.

31. Johnson, "Is There Hope for Liberal Protestantism?" 23.

32. Ibid., 20.

33. Hudnut-Beumler, *God in the Suburbs*, 180.

34. Ibid., 181-82; Phillip E. Hammond, *The Campus Clergyman* (New York: Basic Books, 1966); Jeffrey K. Hadden, *The Gathering Storm in the Churches* (Garden City, N.Y.: Doubleday, 1969).

35. See chap. 4 of this book for a discussion of the changing churchly, cultural, and social features of American life that led to the contextual approach to the Protestant ministry.

36. Waldo Beach, "The Racial Crisis and the Prophet's Task," *Duke Divinity School Bulletin* 22 (February 1957): 7.

37. On "submarine churches" see William L. O'Neill, *Coming Apart: An Informal History of America in the 1960s* (New York: Times Books of Random House, 1971), 316-17.

38. I have dealt with some of the larger implications of this struggle over the sacred symbols of the culture in "Nation, Church, and Private Religion: The Emergence of an American Pattern" which first appeared in *Journal of Church and State* 14 (1972) and has been reprinted in *Readings on Church and State*, ed. James E. Wood, Jr. (Waco, Tex.: J. M. Dawson Institute of Church-State Studies, Baylor University, 1989), 99-108.

39. Sydney E. Ahlstrom, "The Radical Turn in Theology and Ethics: Why It Occurred in the 1960s," originally published in the 1970 volume of the *Annals of the American Academy of Political and Social Science* and reprinted in *Religion in American History: Interpretive Essays*, ed. John M. Mulder and John F. Wilson (Englewood Cliffs, N.J.: Prentice-Hall, Inc., 1978), 452-53.

40. Ibid., 446, 453-54.

41. Ibid., 447.

42. Numerous senior faculty whom I interviewed at several divinity schools remarked upon the uncritical vocationalism of a large segment of contemporary ministerial students in contrast to their counterparts in the Fifties and Sixties. See also Van A. Harvey, "Reflections on the Teaching of Religion in America," *Journal of the American Academy of Religion* 38 (March 1970): 21-22, and "Ogden Observes Softening in Perkins Community Mood," *SMU Now* 2 (October 28, 1974), ASMU, 1-2.

43. For example, *Yale Divinity School Self-Study, 1978-79*, AYD, 28, 31; *Catalogue*

NOTES TO PAGES 227-232 ■ 345

*of the Boston University School of Theology, 1973*, AB, 30–34, and *1980*, AB, 26; *Report of Self-Study: The Divinity School of Duke University, 1983*, ADU, 3–4.

44. Charles A. Reich, *The Greening of America* (New York: Random House, 1970).

45. Camille Paglia, *Sex, Art, and American Culture: Essays* (New York: Vintage Books, 1992), 210–11.

46. Gitlin, *Sixties*, 438.

47. Lynne V. Cheney, *Telling the Truth: A Report on the State of the Humanities in Higher Education* (Washington, D.C.: National Endowment for the Humanities, 1992), 6.

48. Roger Kimball, *Tenured Radicals: How Politics Has Corrupted Our Higher Education* (New York: Harper Collins Publishers, 1990), xv.

49. Paul Wilkes, "The Hands That Would Shape Our Souls," *Atlantic Monthly* 266 (December 1990): 59, 61, 71–75, 86.

50. George Levine and others, *Speaking for the Humanities*, American Council of Learned Societies Occasional Paper 7 (1989): 6–8.

51. Wilson Yates, "Seminaries: Back to the Future?" *Christianity and Crisis* 51 (April 8, 1991): 124–25.

52. Allan Bloom, *The Closing of the American Mind: How Higher Education Has Failed Democracy and Impoverished the Souls of Today's Students* (New York: Simon and Schuster, 1987), 51–61.

53. Gitlin, *Sixties*, xi, 436.

54. Wilkes, "Hands That Shape Our Souls," 59–61, 86.

55. Leon Howell, "Denominational Promise and Problems," *Christianity and Crisis* 51 (April 8, 1991): 99; Yates, "Seminaries," 124.

56. Mary Harris and Clinton Stockwell, "A Misguided Assessment of Seminary Education," *Christian Century* 108 (February 6–13, 1991): 133. On the status of students in the seminaries in the late nineteenth and early twentieth centuries, see chap. 4 of this book.

57. *Catalogue of the Candler School of Theology of Emory University, 1990–1991*, AEC, 46.

58. *Register of Harvard University: Harvard Divinity School, 1989/1990*, AHD, 49.

59. David Walter Lotz in *Colloquy: Conversations with the Faculty, Union Theological Seminary, 1976–1977*, ed. Malcolm L. Warford (Office of Educational Research, October 25, 1977), AU, 88.

60. Rebecca Chopp in an interview with Amy Greene, "Candler Seminary: Transforming Mission," *Christianity and Crisis* 51 (April 8, 1991): 114.

61. Fumitaka Matsuoka, "Pluralism at Home: Globalization within North America," *Theological Education* 26, Sup. 1 (Spring 1990): 38, 40. For an elaboration upon the meaning of "globalization" in theological education see chap. 2 of this book.

62. This is the assessment of the theology of the time in Presbyterian seminaries by John M. Mulder and Lee A. Wyatt, but it also applies to other seminaries. See John M. Mulder and Lee A. Wyatt, "The Predicament of Pluralism: The Study of Theology in Presbyterian Seminaries Since the 1920s," in *The Pluralistic Vision: Presbyterians and Mainstream Protestant Education and Leadership*, ed. Milton J. Coalter, John M. Mulder, and Lewis B. Weeks (Louisville, Ky.: Westminster/John Knox Press, 1992), 58. See also chap. 3 of this book.

63. Peter Novick, *That Noble Dream: The "Objectivity Question" and the American Historical Profession* (Cambridge: Cambridge University Press, 1988), 470.

64. Ibid., 471. See also Michel Foucault, *Discipline and Punish: The Birth of the Prison,* trans. Alan Sheridan (New York: Random House, 1979); idem, *Power/Knowledge: Selected Interviews and Other Writings, 1972–1977* (New York: Pantheon Books, 1980); Edward W. Said, *Orientalism* (New York: Pantheon Books, 1978); Mary Douglas, *Implicit Meanings: Essays in Anthropology* (London: Routledge & Kegan Paul, 1975).

65. See Ernst Troeltsch, *The Christian Faith* (Minneapolis, Minn.: Fortress Press, 1991); idem, *The Social Teachings of the Christian Churches* (Chicago: University of Chicago Press, 1976).

66. See George Lindbeck, *The Nature of Doctrine: Religion and Theology in a Postliberal Age* (Philadelphia: Westminster Press, 1984); Stanley Hauerwas, *Why Narrative? Readings in Narrative Theology* (Grand Rapids, Mich.: William B. Eerdmans, 1989); Ronald Thiemann, *Revelation and Theology: The Gospel as Narrated Promise* (Notre Dame, Ind.: University of Notre Dame Press, 1985). Many of the emphases of the narrative theologians can be traced to the theme of the "lived history" of Christianity in the thought of Yale theologian H. Richard Niebuhr. See Niebuhr's *The Meaning of Revelation* (New York: Macmillan Company, 1941).

67. Ronald F. Thiemann, "Toward a Critical Theological Education," *Harvard Theological Review* 80 (January 1987): 1–13; idem, "Toward an American Public Theology: Religion in a Pluralistic Democracy," Harvard Divinity School Alumni/ae Address, June 10, 1987, AHD, 6–12.

68. Joseph C. Hough, Jr., "The Marginalization of Theology in the University," in *Religious Studies, Theological Studies and the University-Divinity School,* ed. Joseph Mitsuo Kitagawa (Atlanta: Scholars Press, 1992), 66. This unifying contribution of theology, drawn from the work of H. Richard Niebuhr, is one of several which Hough thinks is possible within the university. Another contribution is one discussed by Hough's Vanderbilt colleague Edward Farley: the recognition of the corruptibility of all human understanding and a corresponding willingness to adopt new paradigms of knowledge. See H. Richard Niebuhr, *Radical Monotheism and Western Culture* (New York: Harper and Row, 1960), 93–99; Edward Farley, *The Fragility of Knowledge* (Philadelphia, Pa.: Fortress Press, 1988), 17–28.

69. Thiemann, "Critical Theological Education," 10–11.

70. See chap. 4 of this book.

71. Todd Gitlin, who as an SDS leader had little use for the religious expressions of the Sixties counterculture—for him they were little more than apolitical "spiritual trips" and "ultimate giggles"—does acknowledge that the political and the spiritual aspects of the times often intersected in the lives of protesting youth: in their drug culture, in their hatred of the war in Vietnam, in their distrust of standard cultural authorities, and, above all, in their music. Gitlin, *Sixties,* 134, 192, 202, 208–25.

72. "Report of the Task Force on Spiritual Development," *Theological Education* 8 (Spring 1972): 190.

73. See chap. 1 of this book.

74. "Task Force on Spiritual Development," 187, 166–67.

75. Tilden H. Edwards, Jr., "Spiritual Formation in Theological Schools: Fer-

ment and Challenge," *Theological Education* 17 (Autumn 1980): 7–52; Forster Freeman, "Spiritual Direction for Seminarians," *Theological Education* 24 (Autumn 1987): 44–56; Ronald E. Osborn, *The Education of Ministers for the Coming Age* (St. Louis: CBP Press, 1987), 179–84.

76. For a discussion of the dominance of devotional literature of the self-help variety in one denomination see Mark A. Noll and Darryl G. Hart, "The Language(s) of Zion: Presbyterian Devotional Literature in the Twentieth Century," in *The Confessional Mosaic: Presbyterians and Twentieth-Century Theology*, ed. Milton J. Coalter, John M. Mulder, and Louis B. Weeks (Louisville, Ky.: Westminster/John Knox Press, 1990), 198–206. For a discussion of the triumph of self-help therapeutics in the culture at large see chap. 4 of this book.

77. David Lowes Watson, "The Wesleyan Paradigm: Mutual Accountability," *Christian Century* 101 (February 6–13): 122–24; Marjorie Procter-Smith, "Daily Worship: An Instituted Means of Grace," ibid., 124–25.

78. *Bulletin of Yale University: Divinity School, 1987–89*, AYD, 35–36.

79. Wilkes, "Hands That Shape Our Souls," 84.

80. Edwards, "Spiritual Formation in Theological Schools," 25–26.

81. Procter-Smith, "Daily Worship," 125.

82. John W. O'Malley, "Spiritual Formation for Ministry: Some Roman Catholic Traditions—Their Past and Present," *Theological Education and Moral Formation*, ed. Richard John Neuhaus (Grand Rapids, Mich.: William B. Eerdmans, 1992), 79–80, 100.

83. See, for example, "Task Force on Spiritual Development," 162, 166, 168; Edwards, "Spiritual Formation in Theological Schools," 9–12; Freeman, "Spiritual Direction for Seminarians," 46–48.

84. See, for example, Steve Hancock, "Nurseries of Piety? Spiritual Formation at Four Presbyterian Seminaries," *Pluralistic Vision*, 97–98.

85. George Lindbeck, "Spiritual Formation and Theological Education," *Theological Education* 24, Supp. 1 (1988): 18–28.

86. David Tracy, "Can Virtue Be Taught? Education, Character, and the Soul," *Theological Education* 24, Supp. 1 (1988): 49.

87. Dorothy C. Bass, "Revolutions, Quiet and Otherwise: Protestants and Higher Education during the 1960s," in *Caring for the Commonwealth: Education for Religious and Public Life*, ed. Parker J. Palmer, Barbara G. Wheeler, and James W. Fowler (Macon, Ga.: Mercer University Press, 1990), 224–25.

88. Richard Nesmith of the Boston University School of Theology as quoted in Marjorie Heins, *Cutting the Mustard: Affirmative Action and the Nature of Excellence* (Boston: Faber and Faber, 1987), 75.

89. In the midst of overhauling its curriculum to accommodate a diversity of student types and different forms of the ministry, the faculty of the Duke Divinity School were clear about the focus of their educational aims: " . . . while the conventional and inherited styles of ministry are now certainly undergoing change, the Divinity School curriculum continues to prepare students for informed and discriminating discharge of the historic offices of church and congregation." *Bulletin of Duke University: Divinity School, 1969–1970*, ADU, 2; "The New Curriculum (as adopted January 22, 1969)," ADU, 1–2. For other examples see James Longsworth, "The Uncommitted Student," *Perkins Journal* 22 (Winter

1968–69): 18–19; Charles Love, "The B.D. as Propaedeutic to the Ph.D.," ibid., 30–31; "Report of the Dean of the Divinity School to the President and Fellows of Yale University, 1967–68," AYD, 2–4.

90. Joseph C. Hough, Jr., and John B. Cobb, Jr., *Christian Identity and Theological Education* (Chico, Calif.: Scholars Press, 1985), 4–5, 81–82.

91. David H. Kelsey, *To Understand God Truly: What's Theological About a Theological School* (Louisville, Ky.: Westminster/John Knox Press, 1992), 131.

92. See James F. Hopewell, "A Congregational Paradigm for Theological Education," in *Beyond Clericalism: The Congregation as a Focus for Theological Education*, ed. Joseph C. Hough, Jr., and Barbara G. Wheeler (Atlanta: Scholars Press, 1988), 1–9, and idem, *Congregation: Stories and Structures* (Philadelphia, Pa.: Fortress Press, 1987).

93. E. Brooks Holifield, "The Historian and the Congregation," *Beyond Clericalism*, 89.

94. Marvin J. Taylor, ed, *Fact Book on Theological Education, 1980–1981* (Vandalia, Ohio: Association of Theological Schools, 1981), 4–5; Jackson W. Carroll, "The State of the Art: Enrollment and Ethos in Seminaries Today," *Christianity and Crisis* 49 (April 3–17, 1989): 106; Kelsey, *To Understand God*, 20.

95. Ari L. Goldman, a *New York Times* writer who spent a year at Harvard Divinity School to deepen his awareness of his own Judaism and expand his knowledge of other religions, reports that only one among his friends at the Divinity School ended up an ordained minister. Ari L. Goldman, *The Search for God at Harvard* (New York: Random House, 1991), 276–82.

## 8. The Challenge of Social and Cultural Diversity

1. For the story of alliances struck after World War II between liberal and evangelical Protestants for the sake of a common Protestant establishment see Mark Silk, *Spiritual Politics: Religion and America Since World War II* (New York: Simon and Schuster, 1988), 61–64, 101–03, 120–25; idem, "The Rise of the 'New Evangelicalism': Shock and Adjustment," in *Between the Times: The Travail of the Protestant Establishment in America, 1900–1960*, ed. William R. Hutchison (Cambridge: Cambridge University Press, 1989), 278–97.

2. Martin E. Marty, *The Noise of Conflict: 1919–1941*, Vol. 2 of *Modern American Religion* (Chicago: University of Chicago Press, 1991), 12–13.

3. Robert T. Handy, *A Christian America: Protestant Hopes and Historical Realities* (New York: Oxford University Press, 1971), 184–225; idem, *Undermined Establishment: Church-State Relations in America, 1880–1920* (Princeton, N.J.: Princeton University Press, 1991), 126–91.

4. Edward K. Graham, "The Methodist Idea and the Relatively Independent University," *Nexus* 3 (November 1959): 36–37.

5. Benjamin Elijah Mays and Joseph William Nicholson, *The Negro's Church* (New York: Institute of Social and Religious Research, 1933), 52–53.

6. Ibid., 54–56.

7. Ibid., 49; Charles V. Hamilton, *The Black Preacher in America* (New York: William Morrow & Company, 1972), 17, 88–90; C. Eric Lincoln and Lawrence H.

Mamiya, *The Black Church in the African American Experience* (Durham, N.C.: Duke University Press, 1990), 129–30.

8. Lincoln and Mamiya, *Black Church*, 129.

9. See, for example, *Harvard University Divinity School: Deans' Reports, 1969–70*, AHD, 11–14, *1970–71*, 19–21; Robert T. Handy, *A History of Union Theological Seminary in New York* (New York: Columbia University Press, 1987), 266–67, 323; Boone M. Bowen, *The Candler School of Theology: Sixty Years of Service* (Atlanta: Emory University, 1974), 147–49.

10. Ellis L. Larsen and James M. Shopshire, "A Profile of Contemporary Seminarians," *Theological Education* 24 (Spring 1988): 26, 29; Gail Buchwalter King, ed., *Fact Book on Theological Education, 1988–89 & 1989–90* (Pittsburgh, Pa.: Association of Theological Schools, 1990), 36.

11. Larsen and Shopshire, "Profile of Seminarians," 28.

12. William L. Baumgaertner, ed., *Fact Book on Theological Education, 1986–87* (Vandalia, Ohio: Association of Theological Schools, 1987), 32.

13. The percentage is derived from the data base of the Auburn Center for the Study of Theological Education, with data provided by the divinity schools to the Association of Theological Schools. Concerns about the small number of black Ph.D. candidates—with a total of ninety-eight students in all ATS doctoral programs in 1990—are registered by Joseph C. Hough, Jr., "Future Faculty for University Divinity Schools: The University Divinity Schools Project, 1992," unpublished paper (n.d.), 14. Data recently obtained by the National Research Council indicates that between 1983 and 1994 a total of ninety-five African Americans earned U.S. research doctorates in religion and theology combined—a mere 1.93 percent of the doctorates awarded in theology, and 3.1 percent of those in religion. See Frank Crouch and Warren G. Frisina, "Government Figures Show Low Minority Representation Among Religion and Theology Doctorates," *Religious Studies News* 9 (February 1994): 1, 7.

14. These percentages are derived from statistics developed by Mary Lou Greenwood Boice and F. Stuart Gulley, "University-Related Divinity Schools Project: Admissions Report," unpublished paper of July 1993, Table H. Percentages do not include information from the Divinity School of the University of Chicago, which, as a matter of policy, did not supply figures.

15. *Union Theological Seminary in the City of New York* (Public Relations Pamphlet, 1989), AU, 3; *Perkins School of Theology, Southern Methodist University* (Public Relations Pamphlet, 1990), ASMP.

16. Boice and Gulley, "Admissions Report," Table H.

17. Waldo Beach, "Reflections and Anticipations After Forty Years at Duke," *News and Notes of the Duke Divinity School* 2 (1986), ADU, 12.

18. Gayraud S. Wilmore, "Theological Education in a World of Religious and Other Diversities," *Theological Education* 23, Supp. (1987): 150.

19. Peter J. Paris, "Overcoming Alienation in Theological Education," in *Shifting Boundaries: Contextual Approaches to the Structure of Theological Education*, ed. Barbara Wheeler and Edward Farley (Louisville, Ky.: Westminster/John Knox Press, 1991), 181.

20. Ibid.

21. Dorothy Bass Fraser, "Women With a Past: A New Look at the History of

Theological Education," *Theological Education* 8 (Summer 1972): 213–14; Rosemary Skinner Keller, "Women and Religion," in vol. 3 of *Encyclopedia of the American Religious Experience*, ed. Charles H. Lippy and Peter W. Williams (New York: Charles Scribner's Sons, 1988), 1555.

22. Graham, "The Methodist Idea," 38–39; Jannette E. Newhall, "There Were Giants in Those Days," *Nexus* 7 (November 1963), 18–22.

23. Fraser, "Women With a Past," 219–20.

24. Virginia Lieson Brereton and Christa Ressmeyer Klein, "American Women in Ministry: A History of Protestant Beginning Points," in *Women of Spirit: Female Leadership in the Jewish and Christian Traditions* (New York: Simon and Schuster, 1979), 304–14.

25. Quoted in Fraser, "Women With a Past," 216.

26. *Harvard University Divinity School: Deans' Reports, 1948–49*, AHD, 2–3; Thomas H. English, *Emory University, 1915–1965: A Semicentennial History* (Atlanta: Emory University, 1966), 72; Bowen, *Candler School of Theology*, 42–43.

27. Thomas Woody, vol. 1 of *A History of Women's Education in the United States* (New York: The Science Press, 1929), 369, 372; Robert L. Kelly, *Theological Education in America. A Study of One Hundred Sixty-One Theological Schools in the United States and Canada* (New York: George H. Doran Company, 1924), 181.

28. Fraser, "Women With a Past," 220; Brereton and Klein, "American Women in Ministry," 317.

29. Keller, "Women and Religion," 1558.

30. Kathleen Bliss, *The Service and Status of Women in the Churches* (London: SCM Press, 1952), 100.

31. Roland H. Bainton, *Yale and the Ministry: A History of Education for the Christian Ministry at Yale from the Founding in 1701* (New York: Harper & Brothers, 1957), 262–63.

32. *1988–89 Fact Book on Higher Education* (New York: Macmillan Publishing Company for the American Council on Education, 1989), 71–74.

33. My paragraph summarizes the work of Brereton and Klein, "American Women in Ministry," 318–20.

34. For examples of the active recruitment of women by the divinity schools see Handy, *History of Union*, 341; *Harvard University Divinity School: Deans' Reports, 1971–72*, AHD, 14–15; "The Report of the YDS Women's Center," February 29, 1980, AYD, 1; Jerald C. Brauer, "Reminiscences," *Criterion* 19 (Winter 1980): 12–13; "Perkins School of Theology Senate Meeting, April 23, 1976," ASMP, 2.

35. Marvin J. Taylor, ed., *Fact Book on Theological Education, 1980–81* (Vandalia, Ohio: Association of Theological Schools, 1981), 8; Gail Buchwalter King, ed., *Fact Book on Theological Education, 1988–89 & 1989–90* (Pittsburgh, Pa.: Association of Theological Schools, 1990), 36–37.

36. Boice and Gulley, "Admissions Report," Table F.

37. Marvin J. Taylor, "A Theological Faculties Profile: 1981 Data Compared with the 1971 Study," *Theological Education* 19 (Autumn 1982): 120–21; Baumgaertner, *Fact Book on Theological Education, 1986–87*, 31. Data divided according to full-time and part-time women faculty are not available for 1971.

38. Percentage derived from Auburn Center data base.

39. The Cornwall Collective, *Your Daughters Shall Prophesy: Feminist Alternatives in Theological Education* (New York: Pilgrim Press, 1980), xvi–xvii, 49–51.

40. Ibid., 4–5.

41. The Mud Flower Collective, *God's Fierce Whimsy: Christian Feminism and Theological Education* (New York: Pilgrim Press, 1985), 7, 196–205.

42. Ibid., 29.

43. Rebecca S. Chopp, "Situating the Structure: Prophetic Feminism and Theological Education," in *Shifting Boundaries*, 67–71.

44. Boice and Gulley, "Admissions Report," Table H.

45. John H. Mulder and Lee A. Wyatt, "The Predicament of Pluralism: The Study of Theology in Presbyterian Seminaries Since the 1920s," in *The Pluralistic Vision: Presbyterians and Mainstream Protestant Education and Leadership*, ed. Milton J. Coalter, John M. Mulder, and Louis B. Weeks (Louisville, Ky.: Westminster/John Knox Press, 1992), 67. A faculty member at one of the Methodist divinity schools observed that "African Americans and women helped to create a self-identical 'evangelical' voice in the schools—a voice that now complains about marginality. And to some extent the complaint has a measure of truth; theology faculties have been more open to the virtue of plurality when it means inclusion of Blacks, Hispanics, and women, than they have when it means inclusion of the new self-conscious evangelicalism." Confidential letter to the author, June 23, 1994.

46. *1988–89 Fact Book on Higher Education*, 67.

47. Peter Berger, *A Far Glory: The Quest for Faith in an Age of Credulity* (New York: Doubleday, 1992), 38–39.

48. Richard Mouw and Sander Griffioen, *Pluralisms and Horizons* (Grand Rapids, Mich.: William B. Eerdmans, 1993), 16–18.

49. Paul Tillich, *Theology of Culture*, ed. Robert C. Kimball (New York: Oxford University Press, 1959), 42.

50. H. Richard Niebuhr, *Christ and Culture* (New York: Harper & Brothers, 1951), 30–34.

51. Mouw and Griffioen, *Pluralisms and Horizons*, 136, summarizing the accusations of many liberation, black, and feminist theologians.

52. Henry A. Giroux, "Modernism, Postmodernism, and Feminism: Rethinking the Boundaries of Educational Discourse," in *Postmodernism, Feminism, and Cultural Politics: Redrawing Educational Boundaries*, ed. Henry A. Giroux (Albany: State University of New York Press, 1991), 49.

53. Nancy Fraser and Linda Nicholson, "Social Criticism without Philosophy: An Encounter between Feminism and Postmodernism," *Theory, Culture and Society: Explorations in Critical Social Science* 5 (June 1988): 390–91.

54. The literature dealing with these curricular developments is legion, but for illustrations see the essays contained in *Postmodernism, Feminism, and Cultural Politics* and in Ellen Carol DuBois and others, *Feminist Scholarship: Kindling in the Groves of Academe* (Urbana and Chicago: University of Illinois Press, 1985).

55. See Richard Bernstein, "In Dispute on Bias, Stanford is Likely to Alter Western Culture Program," *New York Times* (January 19, 1988), A-12; Carolyn Mooney, "Sweeping Curricular Change Is Under Way at Stanford," *Chronicle of Higher Education* (December 14, 1988), A-11; Dinesh D'Souza, *Illiberal Education: The Politics of Race and Sex on Campus* (New York: Free Press, 1991), 59–93.

56. Mark C. Taylor, *Erring: A Postmodern A/theology* (Chicago: University of Chicago Press, 1984), 15–16, 155–69. Taylor and other radical a/theologians claim to have drawn their inspiration from death-of-God theologian Thomas J. J. Altizer,

although Altizer's Hegelian absolutism renders questionable that he himself is an antifoundationalist. See Altizer's *The Descent into Hell: A Study of the Radical Reversal of the Christian Consciousness* (New York: Seabury Press, 1970); idem, *The Self-Embodiment of God* (New York: Harper & Row, 1977).

57. Charles E. Winquist, *Epiphanies of Darkness: Deconstruction in Theology* (Philadelphia, Pa.: Fortress Press, 1986).

58. David L. Miller, *The New Polytheism* (New York: Harper & Row, 1974), 3, 30, 76.

59. For discussions of this feature of American culture see Berger, *A Far Glory*, 39–40; Robert Bellah and others, *Habits of the Heart: Individualism and Commitment in American Life* (Berkeley: University of California Press, 1985), 217–27; Phillip E. Hammond, *Religion and Personal Autonomy: The Third Disestablishment in America* (Columbia: University of South Carolina Press, 1992), 167–77.

60. Elizabeth Fox-Genovese, *Feminism Without Illusions: A Critique of Individualism* (Chapel Hill: University of North Carolina Press, 1991), 187, 190.

61. Todd Gitlin, "The Left, Lost in the Politics of Identity," *Harper's Magazine* (September 1993), 16–20.

62. John McGowan, *Postmodernism and Its Critics* (Ithaca, N.Y.: Cornell University Press, 1991), 29–30.

63. Notable contemporary American scholars who have sought (very different) ways to encourage discourse across boundaries without invoking the principles of foundationalism include Richard Rorty in *Philosophy and the Mirror of Nature* (Princeton, N.J.: Princeton University Press, 1979), and idem, *Contingency, Irony, and Solidarity* (Cambridge: Cambridge University Press, 1989); Jeffrey Stout, *Ethics After Babel: The Languages of Morals and Their Discontents* (Boston: Beacon Press, 1988); Werner Sollors, *Beyond Ethnicity: Consent and Descent in American Culture* (New York: Oxford University Press, 1986).

64. David Tracy, *Blessed Rage for Order: The New Pluralism in Theology* (New York: Seabury Press, 1975), 52. By 1987 Tracy was showing much less confidence in the ability of transcendental metaphysical reflection to deal with the ambiguities of religious and cultural pluralism. See David Tracy, *Plurality and Ambiguity: Hermeneutics, Religion, and Hope* (San Francisco: Harper & Row, 1987).

65. Langdon Gilkey, *Society and the Sacred: Toward a Theology of Culture in Decline* (New York: Crossroad Publishing Company, 1981), 144.

66. Gordon D. Kaufman, *The Theological Imagination: Constructing the Concept of God* (Philadelphia, Pa.: Westminster Press, 1981), 11–16, 23, 87–88.

67. John B. Cobb, Jr., *Christ in a Pluralistic Age* (Philadelphia, Pa.: Westminster Press, 1975), 21.

68. *God's Fierce Whimsy*, 64.

69. Ibid., 152.

70. Elisabeth Schüssler Fiorenza, *Bread Not Stone: The Challenge of Feminist Biblical Interpretation* (Boston: Beacon Press, 1984), xx.

71. James H. Cone, *For My People: Black Theology and the Black Church* (Maryknoll, N.Y.: Orbis Books, 1984), 192.

72. Max Stackhouse of Andover Newton Theological Seminary has been perhaps the most outspoken critic of the alleged relativism of antifoundationalism, on the ground that without some appeal to "a metaphysical-moral realm that is

real [and] transcendent to the empirical world," there can be no knowledge that allows the public adjudication among competing claims and multiple worldviews springing from particular contexts. See Max L. Stackhouse, *Apologia: Contextualization, Globalization, and Mission in Theological Education* (Grand Rapids, Mich.: William B. Eerdmans, 1988), xii, 11, 143, 165.

73. Ronald F. Thiemann, *Constructing a Public Theology: The Church in a Pluralistic Culture* (Louisville, Ky.: Westminster/John Knox Press, 1991), 38. For Thiemann's nonfoundational theology see his *Revelation and Theology: The Gospel as Narrated Promise* (Notre Dame, Ind.: University of Notre Dame Press, 1985).

74. See, for example, Elisabeth Schüssler Fiorenza, "For Women in Men's Worlds: A Critical Feminist Theology of Liberation," in *Yearning to Breathe Free: Liberation Theologies in the U.S.*, ed. Mar Peter-Raoul, Linda Rennie Forcey, and Robert Fredrick Hunter, Jr. (Maryknoll, N.Y.: Orbis Books, 1990), 183.

75. Rebecca S. Chopp, *The Praxis of Suffering: An Interpretation of Liberation and Political Theologies* (Maryknoll, N.Y.: Orbis Books, 1986), 118, 131.

76. *God's Fierce Whimsy*, 141, 23–24.

77. Rebecca S. Chopp, *The Power to Speak: Feminism, Language, God* (New York: Crossroad Publishing Company, 1989), 11.

78. Cone, *For My People*, 193, 202–03.

79. David H. Kelsey, *Between Athens and Berlin: The Theological Education Debate* (Grand Rapids, Mich.: William B. Eerdmans, 1993), 147–50.

80. For this interpretation of the relative merits of the secularization and the pluralization theories see Berger, *Far Glory*, 29–38.

81. For a discussion of the extent of premodern religious perspectives among the American people see chap. 5 of this book.

## 9. The Challenge of the Multiversity

1. The quotation from James B. Duke is in Earl W. Porter, *Trinity and Duke: Foundations of Duke University* (Durham, N.C.: Duke University Press, 1964), 233.

2. The quotation from J. J. Perkins is in Bishop Paul E. Martin, "The Seminary for the Church," *Perkins Journal* 14 (Spring 1961): 20.

3. The rose window was crated and stored after the Cornell Library was razed in 1939; in 1981, it was placed over the entryway of Drew University's new Learning Center.

4. John T. Cunningham, *University in the Forest: The Story of Drew University* (Florham Park, N.J.: Afton Publishing Company, 1972), 68.

5. Ibid., 72–73.

6. These events are summarized in ibid., 252–59, and are reported in detail in the student newspaper for Drew Theological School, *The Circuit Rider*, issues 7 (January 13, 1967), 8 (January 19, 1967), and 15 (May 4, 1967), ADR.

7. Bernhard W. Anderson, "Why the Faculty Remains," *The Circuit Rider* 15 (May 4, 1967), ADR, 18; form letter from the secretary of the faculty to alumni of the Drew Theological School, January 18, 1967, ADR; Cunningham, *University in the Forest*, 262–63; "The Theological School," typescript (1970), ADR, 12–13.

8. "The Firing: A History," *The Circuit Rider* 7 (January 13, 1967), ADR, 5–13;

"History of the Crisis," *The Circuit Rider* 15 (May 4, 1967), ADR, 9–10; Cunningham, *University in the Forest*, 256–57.

9. Letter from Robert Fisher Oxnam to Frank P. Piskor, April 22, 1968, ADR; Minutes of a meeting between six students and Mr. Charles Parlin, February 10, 1967, ADR, 4; "Firing of Drew Dean Laid to Budget Dispute," *Newark Evening News* (February 13, 1967); "Drew Trustee Statement Avoids Heart of the Matter?" *Madison Eagle* (February 16, 1967); John L. Pepin, "The Supporting Role," typescript (1982), ADR, 85–87; Prince A. Taylor, Jr., *The Life of My Years* (Nashville, Tenn.: Abingdon Press, 1983), 142–43.

10. Will Herberg, "Crisis at Drew," *Christianity and Crisis* 27 (February 20, 1967): 25–26; Franz Hildebrandt, "An Open Letter to Dr. Charles C. Parlin," October 20, 1967, ADR, 1–4; Bernhard W. Anderson, "Issues Underlying the Present Crisis," *The Circuit Rider* 15 (May 4, 1967), ADR, 3–6; Charles W. Ranson, *A Missionary Pilgrimage* (Grand Rapids, Mich.: William B. Eerdmans, 1988), 174–80.

11. "Study of Control and Administration at Drew University," University Senate of The Methodist Church, July, 1967, ADR; "Report of the Middle States Association of Colleges and Secondary Schools: Evaluation Team for Drew University," February 18–21, 1968, ADR.

12. Minutes of the Meeting of the Faculty of Drew University Theological School, March 21, 1958, ADR, 1–5.

13. Bernhard W. Anderson, "Proposals for Administrative Organization," February 16, 1962, ADR.

14. The report of the special committee of the Methodist Church concluded that the requests never reached the board. "Study of Control and Administration," 18.

15. Cunningham, *University in the Forest*, 239–42; F. Taylor Jones, "An Effective Seminary in a Strong University," paper presented to the faculty meeting of Drew Theological Seminary, September 20, 1947, ADR; Gordon Harland, "The Best Years of Our Lives," *The Drew Graduate School Occasional Papers* 1 (1980): 5; "Report of a Faculty Conference," October 1–2, 1965, ADR.

16. "Minutes of an Advisory Committee to Consult with the President on the Selection of a Dean of the Theological School," September 29, 1967, ADR; Letter from Robert Fisher Oxnam to Frank P. Piskor, April 22, 1968, ADR.

17. "Study of Control and Administration," 42.

18. Letter from Richard J. Stonesifer to Robert F. Oxnam, August 3, 1967, ADR.

19. Memorandum from John L. Pepin to Fred Holloway, March 28, 1958, ADR; Memorandum from John L. Pepin to Robert F. Oxnam, February 3, 1967, ADR; Memorandum from John L. Pepin to Members of the Drew University Senate, July 17, 1968, ADR.

20. James M. Wall, "Drew's Dilemma: Who Calls the Seminary's Shots?" *Christian Advocate* (May 4, 1967): 24, 33.

21. Paul K. Conkin, *Gone with the Ivy: A Biography of Vanderbilt University* (Knoxville: University of Tennessee Press, 1985), 200–02; Bard Thompson, *Vanderbilt Divinity School: A History* (Nashville, Tenn.: Vanderbilt University, 1958), 13–14.

22. Richard Norton Smith, *The Harvard Century: The Making of a University to a Nation* (New York: Simon and Schuster, 1986), 185, 203; "Report of the Commission to Study and Make Recommendations with Respect to the Harvard Divinity

School," July 1947, AHD, 30; Nathan M. Pusey, "Harvard and Religious Faith," *Harvard Alumni Bulletin* (October 10, 1953): 71–80.

23. Eric L. Titus, "A History of the School of Theology at Claremont," typescript (n.d.), ACT, 47–50; K. Morgan Edwards, "The Historic Trek," Founders' Day Address, October 8, 1976, ACT, 3–6; Letter from Earl Cranston to Fred D. Fagg, Jr., November 7, 1952, ASC; Letter from Fred D. Fagg, Jr., to John O. Gross, January 16, 1953, ASC.

24. See chap. 3 of this book for a discussion of the disappearance of theological encyclopedia.

25. Robert Maynard Hutchins, *The Higher Learning in America* (New Haven, Conn.: Yale University Press, 1936), 101–02, 97–98.

26. Robert M. Hutchins, "Preface" to William Adams Brown, *The Case for Theology in the University* (Chicago: University of Chicago Press, 1938), vi–vii.

27. Brown, *Case for Theology*, 50.

28. Ibid., 64–65.

29. Ibid., 122–24.

30. Ibid., 88–89.

31. Ibid., 63.

32. Ibid., 1–2, 15, 41.

33. Henry Pitney Van Dusen, "The Role of the Theological Seminary," *The Inauguration of Henry Pitney Van Dusen* (November 15, 1945), AU, 22.

34. Henry Pitney Van Dusen, *God in Education: A Tract for the Times* (New York: Charles Scribner's Sons, 1951), 81–82.

35. Bernard M. Loomer, "Religion and the Mind of the University," in *Liberal Learning and Religion*, ed. Amos M. Wilder (New York: Harper and Brothers, 1951), 147–48, 150–51, 158–60.

36. Ibid., 149, 156, 164–67.

37. Albert C. Outler, "The Seminary for the University," *Perkins Journal* 14 (Spring 1961): 14–15.

38. Walter G. Muelder, "The Role of the School of Theology in Boston University," *Nexus* 12 (Winter 1969): 47.

39. John Deschner, "Where Honor Rests," *Perkins Journal* 37 (Summer 1984): 29.

40. H. Richard Niebuhr, *Radical Monotheism and Western Culture, with Supplementary Essays* (New York: Harper & Row, 1960), 93–94. The supplementary essay cited here, "Theology in the University," was originally published as "Theology—Not Queen but Servant" in the January 1955 issue of *Journal of Religion*.

41. Ibid., 97.

42. Ronald F. Thiemann, "Toward an American Public Theology: Religion in a Pluralistic Democracy," *Harvard Divinity School Alumni/ae Day Address* (June 10, 1987), AHD, 10–12; Joseph C. Hough, Jr., "The University and the Common Good," in *Theology and the University: Essays in Honor of John B. Cobb, Jr.*, ed. David Ray Griffin and Joseph C. Hough, Jr. (Albany: State University of New York Press, 1991), 117–21.

43. Clark Kerr, *The Uses of the University* (Cambridge: Harvard University Press, 1963), 18–20. See chap. 1 of this book for an elaboration of the influence of specialization on the development of the American multiversity.

44. "Francis Wayland's Report to the Brown Corporation, 1850," in *Ameri-*

*can Higher Education: A Documentary History,* vol. 2, ed. Richard Hofstadter and Wilson Smith (Chicago: University of Chicago Press), 478.

45. Richard Hofstadter and C. DeWitt Hardy, *The Development and Scope of Higher Education in the United States* (New York: Columbia University Press, 1952), 45–46.

46. "Charles William Eliot, Inaugural Address as President of Harvard, 1869," in Hofstadter and Smith, *American Higher Education,* vol. 2, 602.

47. Cited in Laurence R. Veysey, The *Emergence of the American University* (Chicago: University of Chicago Press, 1965) 123, 151.

48. Hutchins, *Higher Learning,* 66, 85.

49. Laurence Veysey's conclusions regarding the limited role of the liberal arts in shaping university education as a whole before 1910 are complemented by studies of the superficial treatment accorded the liberal arts in today's university general requirements. See Veysey, *Emergence of the University,* 215, 233, and Thomas J. DeLoughry, "Study of Transcripts Finds Little Structure in the Liberal Arts," *Chronicle of Higher Education,* 35 (January 18, 1989): A1, A32.

50. Lawrence A. Cremin, *American Education: The Metropolitan Experience 1876– 1980* (New York: Harper & Row, 1988), 556.

51. Veysey, *Emergence of the University,* 113–14.

52. Ibid., 142, 178.

53. Ibid., 58, 342.

54. *1988–89 Fact Book on Higher Education* (New York: Macmillan Publishing Company for the American Council on Education, 1989), 70; Roger L. Geiger, *To Advance Knowledge: The Growth of American Research Universities, 1900–1940* (New York: Oxford University Press, 1986), 109–11.

55. Geiger, *To Advance Knowledge,* 166, 232.

56. Francis Oakley, *Community of Learning: The American College and the Liberal Arts Tradition* (New York: Oxford University Press, 1992), 79–80.

57. *1988–89 Fact Book on Higher Education,* 145.

58. *Digest of Educational Statistics, 1990* (Washington, D.C.: United States Government Printing Office, 1990), 247.

59. Geiger, *To Advance Knowledge,* 116.

60. Laurence Veysey, "Higher Education as a Profession: Changes and Continuities," in *The Professions in American History,* ed. Nathan O. Hatch (Notre Dame, Ind.: University of Notre Dame Press, 1988), 20.

61. *Treasurer's Record, Harvard University, 1899–1900,* AHU, 47–53.

62. Mark A. May, *The Institutions That Train Ministers,* vol. 3 of *The Education of American Ministers* (New York: Institute of Social and Religious Research, 1934), 485–86.

63. These examples of large gifts from individuals and families are recorded in *Perkins School of Theology Bulletin, 1989–1990,* ASMP, 9; Robert T. Handy, *A History of Union Theological Seminary in New York* (New York: Columbia University Press, 1987), 154; Arthur Cushman McGiffert, Jr., *No Ivory Tower: The Story of The Chicago Theological Seminary* (Chicago: Chicago Theological Seminary, 1965), 278– 79.

64. The Candler School of Theology at Emory University paved the way for the General Conference decision when the Candler administration persuaded lo-

cal churches in the 1950s to contribute a 1 percent tax to the school for the support of ministerial training and then, with the collaboration of Duke Divinity School, made the policy jurisdiction-wide in 1960. The policy was made national and increased the assessment to 2 percent in 1968 and was further refined in 1972 by the General Conference of the Methodist Church. In his history of Candler, Boone Bowen documents the significant increase in funds made available to his school by both the 1 percent and the 2 percent plans. Boone M. Bowen, *The Candler School of Theology: Sixty Years of Service* (Atlanta: Emory University, 1974), 196–97. See also *The Book of Discipline of the United Methodist Church, 1992* (Nashville, Tenn.: United Methodist Publishing House, 1992), 467–68.

65. *Harvard University Fact Book, 1993–1994*, AHU, 42.

66. Anthony Ruger, "An Inquiry into Financial Resources," unpublished report prepared for the University Divinity Schools Project (1994), 12.

67. Percentages for divinity schools are derived from data developed by Anthony Ruger in "A Supplement to an Inquiry into Financial Resources," an unpublished report furnished to the author of this book. Data from the Divinity School of the University of Chicago are not included. The percentage for independent colleges and universities is in the *1988–89 Fact Book on Higher Education*, 151.

68. Ruger, "Supplement to the Inquiry."

69. Ruger, "Supplement to the Inquiry"; *1988–89 Fact Book on Higher Education*, 149, 151.

70. Ruger, "Inquiry into Financial Resources," 8.

71. Ibid., 4.

72. See, for example, *Harvard University Divinity School: Deans' Reports, 1923–24*, AHD, 176; Charles R. Gillett, "Detailed History of the Union Theological Seminary in the City of New York," vol. 2, typescript (n.d.), 809; "Report of the Dean of the Divinity School of Yale University, 1969–79," AYD, 11–12; "Report of the Dean of the Candler School of Theology, 1978–88," AEC, 1.

73. Edward L. Whalen, *Responsibility Center Budgeting: An Approach to Decentralized Management for Institutions of Higher Education* (Bloomington: Indiana University Press, 1991), 155, 6, 17, 14, 145.

74. Ibid., 156.

75. Ibid., 36–37, 149.

76. In 1991, Edward Whalen surmised that only the following universities had thoroughly adopted the principles of responsibility center budgeting: Cornell, Harvard, Johns Hopkins, Indiana, Miami (Florida), Pennsylvania, Southern California, and Washington. Ibid., 152. Furthermore, as indicated earlier in this chapter, the divinity schools' different ways of reporting income and expenses and the variety of financial relations with their universities render impossible accurate generalization about their university budget systems. Nevertheless, most of the divinity school deans indicated in their interviews with me that some of the basic principles of responsibility center budgeting were being applied to their institutions.

77. A. Kenneth Pye, "Toward the 21st Century: Excellence and Responsibility," an internal working document (September 1989), ASMP, 70–72, 75.

78. Ibid., 75.

79. "A Conversation with Barbara Wheeler," *Initiatives in Religion: A Newsletter of Lilly Endowment, Inc.*, 2 (Summer 1993): 4.

80. Clifford Geertz, *Local Knowledge: Further Essays in Interpretive Anthropology* (New York: Basic Books, 1983), 19–24.

81. A few examples of cross-disciplinary centers at divinity schools are the Institute for Antiquity and Christianity at Claremont, the Faculty Aquinas Seminar at Drew, the Center for the Study of World Religions at Harvard, and the Institute of Sacred Music at Yale. The faculty at the Divinity School of the University of Chicago have a particularly rich tradition of holding appointments in other departments and academic committees of the University, and faculty at many of the other schools have similar arrangements.

82. For a report on one failed attempt to reorganize a graduate program along lines other than departments within the humanities and social sciences, see Jonathan Z. Smith, " 'Religion' and 'Religious Studies': No Difference at All," *Soundings* 71 (Summer/Fall 1988): 241–42. For further discussion of interdisciplinary opportunities available to the study of religion within the contemporary university see Conrad Cherry, "Boundaries and Frontiers for the Study of Religion: The Heritage of the Age of the University," *Journal of the American Academy of Religion* 58 (Winter 1989): 822–24. For a discussion of opportunities for the formation of enclaves of intellectual cooperation see Mark R. Schwehn, *Exiles from Eden: Religion and the Academic Vocation in America* (New York: Oxford University Press, 1993), 76–79.

## Conclusion: The Ambiguities of a Heritage

1. As Glenn Miller has pointed out, study in Germany and familiarity with German scholarship among seminary faculty was common as early as the 1820s. Glenn T. Miller, *Piety and Intellect: The Aims and Purposes of Ante-Bellum Theological Education* (Atlanta: Scholars Press, 1990), 449–53. University divinity faculty continued that tradition and, like their colleagues in many other parts of the university, looked upon study in Germany as a mark of the highest level of scholarly sophistication. In the late nineteenth and early twentieth centuries, but also to some extent right down through the 1950s, catalogues of the divinity schools reveal a high number of faculty who obtained advanced degrees at German universities, especially in the areas of biblical studies and church history.

2. Most of the decanal annual reports over the entire lives of the schools consume considerable space describing faculty publications and other faculty achievements (e.g., lectures at colleges and universities and participation in scholarly professional societies). For a few examples of such achievements not going unnoticed in the larger university environment see Umphrey Lee, "The Perkins School of Theology and the University," *Perkins Journal* 1 (Fall 1947): 4–5; Paul K. Conkin, *Gone with the Ivy: A Biography of Vanderbilt University* (Knoxville: University of Tennessee Press, 1985), 561; "Report for the Steering Committee of the Consultation Task Force: Duke Divinity School, April 1, 1974," ADU, 1–2; Nathan M. Pusey, "Harvard and Religious Faith," *Harvard Alumni Bulletin* (October 10, 1953), 79–80.

3. My summary of the recent critical literature on the purposes of theological education draws upon the unpublished paper of Barbara Wheeler presented to the Council on Theological Scholarship and Research of the Association of Theological Schools in the United States and Canada on October 22, 1993, "The Legacy of Basic Issues," 1–18.

# INDEX

Strong, James, 21

Strong, Josiah, 55, 309n.2

Student activism, protests at divinity schools in 1960s and 1970s, 213–16, 225–37

Student organizations, establishment of political in 1960s, 231–32

Students, of divinity schools: activism of 1960s and 1970s, 213–16, 225–37; social diversity and cultural pluralism, 245–54. *See also* Race; Women

Students for a Democratic Society (SDS), 213, 214–15

Student Volunteers for Foreign Missions, 70, 73

Sunday schools: divinity schools and "lower" religious education, 42–45; revisionist histories of reform movement in, 307–308n.35

Supreme Court: 1963 decision on teaching of religion, 90, 117; and desegregation of public education, 198

Sweet, Leonard, 4

Sweet, William Warren, 192

Szasz, Ferenc Morton, 173

Tappan, Henry, 31–32

Taylor, Alva, 193, 197

Taylor, Graham, 191, 192, 196

Taylor, Mark C., 259–60, 351–52n.56

Technology: as "legitimating myth" of American society, 154; and premodern worldview of religion, 179–80; impact on visions of founders of divinity schools, 296

*Ten Great Religions* (Clarke, 1871), 71

Theological encyclopedia, courses in, 96–97, 276

Theological seminaries, proliferation of in nineteenth century, 12–13

Theological university, concept of divinity school as, 19

Theology: liberation theology, 67, 210–11; and radicalism of 1960s, 226–27; particularism and relativism of post-1960s, 232–34; and implications of pluralism for divinity schools, 255–66; and role of divinity school in university, 276–83; critical studies of education in, 299–300

Theory, and practice in ministerial education, 137–55

Thiemann, Ronald, 233–34, 264, 282

Thomas, George F., 110–11

Thompson, Bard, 70, 271

Tillett, Wilbur F., 131–32, 230

Tillich, Paul, 104–105, 257

Tipple, Ezra Squire, 185

Tittle, Ernest Fremont, 193

Toombs, Lawrence, 271

Trachtenberg, Alan, 12

Track system, professional education at Yale Divinity School, 140

Tracy, David, 237, 262, 352n.64

Transcendentalism, 78

Troeltsch, Ernst, 232

Union Seminary (New York): as model institution, 17–19; student body profile of, 29–30; religious life at, 34; mission study at, 77; and contextual education for ministry, 150; pacifist demonstrations in 1930s and 1940s, 213; racial diversity and educational mission of, 248. *See also* Columbia University

Unitarianism, Harvard Divinity School and, 14. *See also* Meadville Seminary

Universalism, and multicultural pluralism in theology, 262–66

University: role of in Harper's educational vision, 2–3; specialization and role of in society, 31–34; scientific study of religion in public, 99; contemporary status of departments of religious studies, 118; and growth of professions, 129; student protests of 1960s and 1970s, 214; impact of multiculturalism on, 256; role of divinity schools in, 270–83; cultural diversity and theological education in, 283–87; funding and theological education in, 287–92; collaborative citizenship as model for relations with divinity schools, 292–94; contribution of divinity schools to scholarship, 297–98; revisionist histories of, 305n.6; revolutions "from top down" in contemporary, 314n.98

University of Alberta at Edmonton, 322n.92

University of Chicago Divinity School: founding vision of Harper, 1–13; and religious education, 40–41; study of history of religions at, 81–84; and theology in 1950s, 106, 107; religious studies in 1970s and 1980s, 120–21, 121–22; professional education of ministers in early twentieth century, 138–39; Master of Theology–Doctor of Ministry program,

CONRAD CHERRY is Distinguished Professor of Religious Studies and Director of the Center for the Study of Religion and American Culture at Indiana University–Purdue University in Indianapolis. A widely published scholar in American religious history, his books include *The Theology of Jonathan Edwards, God's New Israel,* and *Nature and Religious Imagination.* He is also coeditor of *Religion and American Culture: A Journal of Interpretation.*